A Bibliographical Guide
to African-American
Women Writers

A Bibliographical Guide to African-American Women Writers_____

Compiled by
Casper LeRoy Jordan

Bibliographies and Indexes in Afro-American and African Studies,
Number 31

Greenwood Press_____
Westport, Connecticut • London

Library of Congress Cataloging-in-Publication Data

Jordan, Casper LeRoy.
   A bibliographical guide to African-American women writers /
compiled by Casper LeRoy Jordan.
     p. cm.—(Bibliographies and indexes in Afro-American and
African studies, ISSN 0742-6925 ; no. 31)
   Includes index.
   ISBN 0-313-27633-1 (alk. paper)
   1. American literature—Afro-American authors—Bibliography.
2. Women and literature—United States—Bibliography. 3. American
literature—Women authors—Bibliography. 4. Afro-American women in
literature—Bibliography. I. Title. II. Series.
Z1229.N39J67 1993
[PS153.N5]
016.8108'09287'08996—dc20   93-6561

British Library Cataloguing in Publication Data is available.

Library of Congress Catalog Card Number: 93-6561
ISBN: 0-313-27633-1
ISSN: 0742-6925

First published in 1993

Greenwood Press, 88 Post Road West, Westport, CT 06881
An imprint of Greenwood Publishing Group, Inc.

Printed in the United States of America

To the memory of
my parents
Leola Lloyd and John Jordan

To
four intrepid women
of the faculty at
Atlanta University School
of Library and Information Studies
Virginia Lacy Jones
Hallie Beacham Brooks
Annette Hoage Phinazee
Josephine Fawcett Thompson

To
the students
of AUSLIS
1967-1988

To
my siblings
Ida M. and John L. Jordan

and to
C.K.
P.B.

Contents

Preface

Whatever the condition of their lives, the black American woman has an ingenious and diverse history that has been only fragmentarily told. This bibliographical guide to African-American women writers is singular in contributing bibliographical documentation of black women writers from the first poet, Lucy Terry, in 1746 to the young black women of 1991. Some of the writers are easily recognizable, while others have either been veiled in anonymity or overlooked altogether. Genres represented include poetry, memoirs, biographies, criticisms, autobiographies, essays, short fiction, novels, diaries and journals. Book reviews, scientific and social science works have been omitted.

The 1980s and 1990s appear to have witnessed another renaissance of preoccupation with the literary progeny of African-American literature. Literary historians have recognized several periods in this century when there has been a resurgence or "renaissance" of black writing. These periods suggest a run of roughly thirty-year cycles. The New Negro Movement, more popularly known as the Harlem Renaissance, occurred in the 1920s and 1930s; the Black Aesthetic Movement marked the 1960s; and the present recurrence would seem to continue this sequence.

There appears to be a gender phenomenon in all this. Women writers in the Harlem Renaissance were relatively few in number, but included such brilliant and prominent figures as Zora Neale Hurston, Nella Larsen and Jessie Fauset. More black women were visible during the 1950s and 1960s, but male writers clearly dominated the field. The present period has discerned a reversal of gender dominance, with women writers far outstripping men. In 1992, an unheard of and historic situation transpired: three African-American women writers appeared concurrently among the top ten best seller listings: Alice Walker, Toni Morrison and Terry McMillan.

     The bibliographical control of African-American resources
has been considered over a number of years, and recently
considerable literature has been devoted to it. However, a
number of lacunae still exist. The literature addressing
women's studies, and especially black women, needs further
documentation.

     As a library educator interested in the control of and
access to the vast treasury of African-Americana for over
thirty years, I have observed that little or spotty study had
been paid to black women literary writers until recently. As
a teacher, I introduced the study of African-American library
resources to the curriculum of the library education program at
the Atlanta University School of Library and Information
Studies in the early 1970s at a time when few library schools
had such a course. As part of the class requirements, I asked
students to research and prepare either bio-bibliographies or
subject bibliographies in the field of black studies. The
output of the course staggered me and made me further aware of
the great need for additional research. The urge to delve
further into the area of women writers led to the present
guide.

     In an effort to promote research on the aspirations and
achievements of African-American women writers, I have sought
to expand and revise resources and to organize them in a
reference tool that would be useful in black studies as well as
women's studies and American studies. This resulting
bibliographical guide focuses on both the creative products of
black women (the primary sources) and the critical citations
about the writers (secondary sources). Considerable attention
is paid to self publications, subsidized publishers, and
products of the small literary presses.

     In the main body of the volume, the writers are arranged
in dictionary order, with primary sources entered
alphabetically by title followed by secondary sources entered
by author. All entries are numbered sequentially, with
secondary sources distinguished by (S) following the number.
Each writer is given a discrete number, and a decimal system is
used to enumerate the listings that follow. For instance,
Alice Walker is assigned number 644. Her "Your Soul Shines" is
entered as 644.119, and the first secondary source on Walker
(by Pam Abramson) follows as 644.120(S). Originally this work
was envisaged to have 1988 as a cut-off date; however, during
the final production of the manuscript, in 1991, my editor
suggested that the work would be improved if I extended the
coverage to include entries through 1991. To protect the
integrity of the indexing, which had been completed, we decided
to include the new entries for each author, both primary and
secondary, in an "Addendum: Supplement 1988-1991" section,
prefixing these items with the letter A. Thus, to use the
Walker example again, A644.201 to A644.204 are four primary
sources added for 1988-91, and A644.205(S) to A644.218(S) are
recent secondary sources on Walker.

Additional features of the volume include listings of Anthologies, which are enumerated and given the appended letters AN, and General Works enumerated with the appended letter G. Recent items that could not easily be entered within the main section on writers or the section on anthologies and general works are included in a "Supplement: Additional Writers and Sources, 1988-1991," which forms the final section of the volume preceding the index. The established numbering system is continued. The author index provides access to primary and secondary authors in all sections of the volume, utilizing the coded numbering system.

This bibliographical guide can be used profitably in small public libraries as well as large research libraries. It documents materials obtained from unindexed periodicals as well as bibliographies, books and indexes. It is my contention that at present there is no publication nearly as comprehensive in covering the vast panorama of the attainments of black women in the creative literature field. It is my hope that this guide will meet long neglected research needs and fill some fissures in the literature. However, the materials continue to proliferate, and research and documentation must continue apace.

I am grateful to my careful and empathetic editors at the Greenwood Publishing Group: Marilyn Brownstein, Senior Editor, Humanities, and Ann E. LeStrange, Assistant Manager of Editorial Administration. Their untiring counsel and advice assisted me in honing the manuscript to a more skillfully finished work. I am appreciative of the hundreds of students in my classes at Atlanta University, who grumbled at the assignments and produced noteworthy results -- I now know what they endured. I wish to acknowledge Ann Allen Shockley, Associate University Librarian at Fisk University. Shockley has been a good friend for many years, and her obsession with black women writers and her valuable and critically acclaimed Afro-American Women Writers, 1746-1933: An Anthology and Critical Guide (1988) spurred me on to compile my own guide. Incidentally, a perusal of the index to the present work will show that Shockley has written more about these writers than anyone else. Several special collections on African-Americana provided generous assistance in the completion of the manuscript, most notably the Samuel Williams Collection of the Atlanta-Fulton Public Library and its staff (Janice White Sikes, curator, Joyce E. Jelks, Gloria Mims, Sharon Robinson and Herman "Skip" Mason, Jr.) and the Atlanta University Center Robert W. Woodruff Library's Special Collection staff (Wilson Flemister, Dovie Patrick and Minnie Clayton). I was especially fortunate to have access to the private collection of one of the forerunners of the black aesthetic movement, Russell Atkins, who has an incomparable archive of materials dealing with publications during the 1950-1970 era. I am unremittingly grateful for all of this help.

Finally, I must recognize the stamina, forbearance and support of many friends, family and colleagues who plagued me with the enquiry, "When is the book coming out?" Carpe diem!

Codes Used for Collected Works

ADOFF. Adoff, Arnold, ed. Celebrations: A New Anthology of Black American Poetry. Chicago, IL: Follett, 1977.

AFRO. Afro-American Voices, 1770s-1970s. New York: Oxford Book Company, 1970.

AMERICAN. The American Negro Writer and His Roots. Selected papers from the first conference of American Negro Writers. Washington, DC: American Society of African Culture, 1960.

BARAKA & BARAKA. Baraka, Amiri and Baraka, Amina. Confirmation: An Anthology of African-American Women. New York: Quill, 1983.

BELL. Bell, Roseann P., Parker, Bettye J. and Guy-Sheftall, Beverly, eds. Sturdy Black Bridges: Visions of Black Women in Literature. New York: Doubleday, 1979

BIGSBY. Bigsby, C.W.E., ed. Black American Writers, 2 Vols. New York: Penguin Books, 1971.

BLACKSONGS. Blacksongs, Series I: Four Poetry Broadsides by Black Women.   Detroit, MI: Lotus Press, 1977.

BONTEMPS. Bontemps, Arna, ed. The Harlem Renaissance Remembered. New York: Dodd, Mead, 1972.

BRAITHWAITE. Braithwaite, William Stanley, ed. Anthology of Magazine Verse for 1927 and Yearbook of American Poetry. Boston, MA: Brimmer, 1927.

BRASMER. Brasmer, William and Consolo, Dominick, eds. Black Drama: An Anthology. Columbus, OH: Charles Merrill, 1970.

BROWN-GUILLORY. Brown Guillory, Elizabeth, ed. Wines in the Wilderness: Plays by African-American Women from the Harlem Renaissance to the Present. Westport, CT: Greenwood Press, 1990. African-American playwrights anthology.

BRUCK. Bruck, Peter and Karrer, Wolfgang, eds. <u>The Afro-American Novel Since 1960</u>. Amsterdam: B.R. Gruner, 1982.

BULLINS. Bullins, Ed, ed. <u>The New Lafayette Theatre Presents: Plays with   Aesthetic Comments by 6 Black Playwrights</u>. New York: Anchor/Doubleday, 1974.

BULLINS, 1969. Bullins, Ed, ed. <u>New Plays from the Black Theater</u>. New York: Bantam Books, 1969.

BURNETT & FOLEY. Burnett, Whit and Foley, Martha, eds. <u>Story in America</u>. New York: Vanguard Press, 1934.

BYERMAN. Byerman, Keith E. <u>Fingering the Jagged Grain: Tradition and Form in Recent Black Fiction</u>. Athens, GA: University of Georgia Press, 1985.

CHAPMAN. Chapman, Abraham, ed. <u>Black Voices: An Anthology of Afro-American Literature</u>. New York: New American Library, 1968.

CHILDRESS. Childress, Alice, ed. <u>Black Scenes</u>. New York: Doubleday, 1971.

CHRISTIAN. Christian, Barbara. <u>Black Women Novelists: The Development of a Tradition, 1892-1976</u>. Westport, CT: Greenwood Press, 1980.

CLARKE, 1966. Clarke, John H., ed. <u>American Negro Short Stories</u>. New York: Hill & Wang, 1966.

CLARKE. Clarke, John Henrik, ed. <u>Harlem, U.S.A.</u> Berlin: Seven Seas Publishers, 1964. Camden, ME: 1974.

COUCH. Couch, William Jr., ed. <u>New Black Playwrights</u>. Baton Rouge, LA: Louisiana State University Press, 1968.

CULLEN. Cullen, Countee, ed. <u>Caroling Dusk: An Anthology of Verse By Negro Poets</u>. New York: Harper, 1927.

CUNARD. Cunard, Nancy, ed. <u>Negro: Anthology Made by Nancy Cunard, 1931-1933</u>. London: The Author at Wishart & Co., 1934. Reprint. New York: Negro Universities Press, 1969 and New York: Ungar, 1970.

CURB. Curb, Rosemary, ed. <u>Twentieth-Century American Dramatists</u>. Detroit, MI: Gale Research, 1981.

DAVIS & GATES. Davis, Charles T. and Gates, Henry Louis, Jr., eds. <u>The Slave's Narrative</u>, New York: Oxford University Press, 1985.

DAVIS & HARRIS. Davis, Thadious M. and Harris, Trudier, eds. <u>Afro-American Fiction Writers After 1955</u>. Detroit, MI: Gale Research, 1984.

DAVIS & HARRIS, 1985. Davis, Thadious M. and Harris, Trudier, eds. Afro-American Writers After 1955: Dramatists and Prose Writers. Detroit, MI: Gale Research, 1985.

DREER. Dreer, Herman, ed. American Literature by Negro Authors. New York: Macmillan Publishing Company, 1950.

EVANS. Evans, Mari, ed. Black Women Writers (1950-1980): A Critical Evaluation. New York: Doubleday, 1984.

FIFTEEN. 15 Chicago Poets. Chicago, IL: Yellow Press, 1976.

FISHER. Fisher, Dexter, ed. The Third Woman: Minority Women Writers of the United States. Boston, MA: Houghton, 1980.

FOLEY. Foley, Martha, ed. The Best American Short Stories for 1946. Boston, MA: Houghton, 1946.

FOUR. Four Black Poets. Bk Mk Press, 1977.

FRANKLIN. Franklin, John Hope, ed. Black Leaders of the Twentieth Century. Urbana, IL: University of Illinois Press, 1982.

GAYLE. Gayle, Addison, ed. Black Expression, New York: Weybright Talley, 1969.

GILBERT. Gilbert, Mercedes. Selected Gems of Poetry, Comedy and Drama. Boston, MA: Christopher Publishing House, 1931.

GILBERT & GUBAR. Gilbert, Sandra M. and Gubar, Susan, eds. The Norton Anthology of Literature by Women: The Tradition in English. New York: W. W. Norton, 1985.

GREENE. Greene, J. Lee. Time's Unfading Garden: Anne Spencer's Life and Poetry. Baton Rouge, LA: Louisiana State University Press, 1977.

GREINER. Greiner, Donald J., ed. American Poets Since World War II. Detroit, MI: Gale Research, 1980.

HARLEY & TERBORG. Harley, Sharon and Terborg-Penn, Rosalyn, eds. The Afro-American Woman: Struggles and Images. Port Washington, NY: Kennikat Press, 1978.

HARPER & STEPTOE. Harper, Michael S. and Steptoe, Robert B., eds. Chant of Saints: A Gathering of Afro-American Literature, Art and Scholarship. Urbana, IL: University of Illinois Press, 1979.

HARRIS & DAVIS. Harris, Trudier and Davis, Thadious M., eds. Afro-American Poets Since 1955. Detroit, MI: Gale Research, 1985.

HARRIS & DAVIS, 1986. Harris, Trudier and Davis, Thadious M., eds. Afro-American Writers Before the Harlem Renaissance. Detroit, MI: Gale Research, 1986.

HARRIS & DAVIS, 1987. Harris, Trudier and Davis, Thadious,
eds. <u>Afro-American Writers from the Harlem Renaissance to
1940</u>. Detroit, MI: Gale Research, 1987.

HARRISON. Harrison, Paul C., ed. <u>Kuntu Drama: Plays of the
African Continuum</u>. New York: Grove Press, 1973.

HATCH. Hatch, James V., ed. <u>Black Theater, USA: Forty-Five
Plays by American Negroes, 1847-1974</u>. New York: Free Press,
1974.

HATCH & SHINE. Hatch, James and Shine, Ted, eds. <u>Black
Theater USA.</u> New York: Free Press, 1974.

HEMENWAY. Hemenway, Robert, ed. <u>The Black Novelist</u>.
Columbus, OH: Charles Merrill, 1970.

HERNTON. Hernton, Calvin. <u>The Sexual Mountain and Black
Women Writers: Adventures in Sex, Literature and Real Life</u>.
New York: Anchor/Doubleday, 1987.

HOFFMAN. Hoffman, William M., ed. <u>New American Plays</u>. New
York: Hill & Wang, 1968.

HOLLIS. Hollis, Burney, ed. <u>Swords Upon This Hill</u>.
Baltimore, MD: Morgan State University Press, 1984.

HUGHES & BONTEMPS. Hughes, Langston and Bontemps, Arna W.,
eds. <u>The Poetry of the Negro, 1746-1949</u>. New York:
Doubleday, 1949.

HUGHES & BONTEMPS, 1970. Hughes, Langston and Bontemps,
Arna, eds. <u>The Poetry of the Negro, 1746-1970</u>. Rev. ed. New
York: Anchor/Doubleday, 1970.

HULL. Hull, Helen, ed. <u>The Writers Book</u>. New York: Harper,
1950.

JOHNSON. Johnson, Charles Spurgeon, ed. <u>Ebony and Topaz: A
Collectanea</u>. New York: National Urban League, 1927.

JOHNSON, 1931. Johnson, James Weldon, ed. <u>The Book of
American Negro Poetry</u>. New York: Harcourt, 1922, rev ed.,
1931.

JONES & NEAL. Jones, LeRoi and Neal, Larry, eds. <u>Black
Fire</u>. New York: William Morrow, 1968.

JOSEY. Josey, E.J., ed. <u>The Black Librarian in America</u>.
Metuchen, NJ: Scarecrow Press, 1970.

KIBLER. Kibler, James E., Jr., ed. <u>American Novelists Since
World War II, Second Series</u>. Detroit, MI: Gale Research,
1980.

KING & MILNER. King, Woodie and Milner, Ron, eds. <u>Black
Drama Anthology</u>. New York: Columbia University Press,
Signet, New American Library, 1972.

LOCKE. Locke, Alain LeRoy, ed. The New Negro: An
Interpretation. New York: Boni, 1925.

LOCKE & MONTGOMERY. Locke, Alain LeRoy and Montgomery,
Gregory, eds. Plays of Negro Life: A Sourcebook of Native
American Drama. New York: Harper, 1927.

LOGAN & WINSTON. Logan, Rayford W. and Winston, Michael R.,
eds. Dictionary of American Negro Biography. New York: W.
W. Norton, 1982.

LONG & COLLIER. Long, Richard A. and Collier, Eugenia W.,
eds. Afro-American Writing: An Anthology of Prose and Poetry.
University Park, PA: Pennsylvania State University Press,
1985.

MAINIERO. Mainiero, Lina, ed. American Women Writers. Vol.
2. New York: Ungar, 1980.

MAINIERO, 1979. Mainiero, Lina, ed. American Women Writers:
A Critical Reference Guide from Colonial Times to the
Present. New York: Ungar, 1979.

MICKELSON. Mickelson, Anne Z. Reaching Out: Sensitivity and
Order in Recent American Fiction by Women. Metuchen, NJ:
Scarecrow Press, 1979.

MILLER. Miller, R. Baxter, ed. Black American Poets Between
Worlds, 1940-1960. Knoxville, TN: University of Tennessee
Press, 1986.

MILLER, 1971. Miller, Ruth. Backgrounds to Blackamerican
Literature. Scranton, PA: Chandler Publishing Co, 1971.

O'DANIEL. O'Daniel, Therman, ed. Langston Hughes: Black
Genius. New York: William Morrow, 1971.

PARONE. Parone, Edward, ed. Collision Course. New York:
Random House, 1968.

PERRY. Perry, Margaret. The Harlem Renaissance: An
Annotated Bibliography and Commentary. New York: Garland
Publishing, 1982.

PLAYS. Plays to Remember. Literary Heritage Series. New
York: Macmillan Publishing Company, 1968.

POOL. Pool, Rosey E., ed. Beyond the Blues. Detroit, MI:
Broadside Press, 1971.

PRYSE & SPILLERS. Pryse, Marjorie and Spillers, Hortense,
eds. Conjuring: Black Women, Fiction, and Literary
Tradition. Bloomington, IN: Indiana University Press, 1975.

QUARTERMAIN. Quartermain, Peter, ed. American Poets, 1880-
1945, Third Series. Detroit, MI: Gale Research. 1987.

RAINWATER. Rainwater, Catherine, ed. <u>Contemporary Women
Writers</u>. Lexington, KY: University Press of Kentucky, 1985.

RICHARDSON. Richardson, Willis, ed. <u>Plays and Pageants from
the Life of the Negro</u>. Washington, DC: Associated Publishers,
1930.

RICHARDSON & MILLER. Richardson, Willis and Miller, May,
eds. <u>Negro History in Thirteen Plays</u>. Washington, DC:
Associated Publishers, 1935.

RODGERS. Rodgers-Rose, LaFrances, ed. <u>The Black Woman</u>.
Beverly Hills, CA: Sage, 1980.

ROWE. Rowe, Kenneth, ed. <u>University of Michigan Plays</u>. Ann
Arbor, MI: University of Michigan Press, 1932.

SANCHEZ. Sanchez, Sonia, ed. <u>Three Hundred and Sixty
Degrees of Blackness Comin' at You</u>. New York: 5X Publishing
Company, 1971.

SEWELL. Sewell, May Wright, ed. <u>World's Congress of
Representative Women</u>. Chicago, IL: Rand McNally, 1894.

SHOCKLEY. Shockley, Ann Allen, ed. <u>Afro-American Women
Writers, 1746-1933: An Anthology and Critical Guide</u>. Boston,
MA: G.K. Hall, 1988.

SMITH. Smith, Barbara, ed. <u>Home Girls: A Black Feminist
Anthology</u>. New York: Kitchen Table: Women of Color Press,
1983.

STERNBURG. Sternburg, Janet, ed. <u>The Writer on Her Work</u>.
New York: W. W. Norton, 1980.

STETSON. Stetson, Erlene, ed. <u>Black Sister: Poetry by Black
American Women, 1746-1980</u>. Bloomington, IN: Indiana
University Press, 1981.

TATE. Tate, Claudia, ed. <u>Black Women Writers at Work</u>. New
York: Continuum, 1983. African-American women writers.

TURNER. Turner, Darwin T., ed. <u>Black American Literature:
Essays, Poetry, Fiction, Drama</u>. Columbus, OH: Charles
Merrill, 1970.

TURNER, 1969. Turner, Darwin T., <u>Black American Literature:
Poetry</u>. Columbus, OH: Charles E. Merrill, 1969.

TURNER, 1971. Turner, Darwin T. <u>A Minor Chord: Three Afro-
American Writers and Their Search For Identity</u>. Urbana, IL:
University of Illinois Press, 1971.

VINSON. Vinson, James, ed. <u>Contemporary Novelists</u>. New
York: St. Martin's, 1972.

WASHINGTON. Washington, Mary Helen, ed. <u>Invented Lives:</u>
<u>Narratives of Black Women 1860-1960</u>. New York: Doubleday,
1987.

WASHINGTON, 1980. Washington, Mary Helen, ed. <u>Midnight</u>
<u>Birds: Stories of Contemporary Black Women Writers</u>. New
York: Anchor/Doubleday, 1980.

WATKINS. Watkins, Mel, ed. <u>Black Review No. 2</u>. New York:
William Morrow, 1972.

WHITLOW. Whitlow, Roger. <u>Black American Literature: A</u>
<u>Critical History</u>. Chicago, IL: Nelson Hall, 1973.

WILLIS. Willis, Susan. <u>Specifying: Black Women Writing the</u>
<u>American Experience</u>. Madison, WI: University of Wisconsin
Press, 1987.

WORMLEY & FENDERSON. Wormley, Stanton L. and Fenderson,
W.H., eds. <u>Many Shades of Black</u>. New York: William Morrow,
1969.

YEARBOOK. <u>Yearbook of Short Plays, First Series</u>. Evanston,
IL: Row Peterson, 1931.

African-American Women Writers

001. ABRAM, THERESA WILLIAMS (1903-).

001.1 <u>Abram's Treasures</u>. New York: Vantage Press, 1967.
Poetry.

001.2. <u>Rhythm and Animals</u>. Oklahoma City: Best Way, 1971.
Poetry

002. ABRAMSON, DOLORES.

002.1 "The Light." In SANCHEZ, pp. 137-138. One act
drama.

003. ADA.

003.1 "Lines, On the Suppression, by a Portion of Our Public
Journals, of   the Intelligence of the Abolition of Slavery
in the British West Indies." In   STETSON, pp. 20-21.

003.2 "Lines Suggested on Reading 'An Appeal to Christian
Women of the South' by A.E. Grimke." In STETSON, pp. 17-19.

003.3 "To the Memory of J. Horace Kimball." In STETSON,
pp. 21-22.

003.4 "Untitled." In STETSON, pp. 19-20.

004. ADAMS, DAISIE HASSON.

004.1 <u>Merchant of Dreams</u>. New York: Exposition Press, 1947.

005. ADAMS, DORIS B.

005.1 _Longing and Other Poems_. Philadelphia: Dorrance &
Company, 1962.

006. ADAMS, JANUS.

006.1 _St. Stephen: A Passion Play_.   In BARAKA & BARAKA.
Excerpt.

007. ADAMS, JEANNETTE.

007.1 "Directions To My Lover." _Essence_ 10 (February 1980):
78.

007.2 _Love Lyrics_. Elmsford, NY: Author, 1982.

007.3 "Love Lyrics No. 2." _Essence_ 16 (February 1986): 133.

007.4 _Picture Me In a Poem_. Elmsford, NY: Author, 1980.

007.5 _Sukari_. Elmsford, NY: Author, 1979.

008. ADRINE-ROBINSON, KENYETTE.

008.1 _Be My Shoo-gar_. Cleveland Heights, OH: Kenyette
Productions, 1987.

008.2 "Let's Go." _Essence_ 18 (October 1987): 144.

                    1988-1991 Supplement
A008.3 "Haiku." _Essence_ 20 (November 1989): 107. Poem.

009. AFIF, FATIMAH.

009.1 "Tanka." In BARAKA & BARAKA.

010. AHMAD, DOROTHY.

010.1 "Papa's Daughter." _Drama Review_ 12 (1968): 139-145.
One act drama.

011. AI (1947-).

011.1 "Before You Leave." _Essence_ 16 (April 1986): 188.

011.2 _Cruelty_. Boston: Houghton, 1973.

011.3 "Blue Suede Shoes." _Iowa Review_ 11 (4): 87-91 (1981).
Callaloo 9 (1): 1-5 (Winter 1986).

011.4 _Conversation: for Robert Lowell_. St. Paul, MN:
Bookslinger, 1981.

011.5 "Guadalajara Hospital." _Virginia Quarterly Review_ 54
(4): 704 (Autumn 1978).

011.6 "Ice." _Chicago Review_ 29 (Spring 1978): 4.

011.7 "The Journalist." _Missouri Review_ 9 (1): 66-69 (1985-
1986).

011.8 _The Killing Floor: Poems_. Boston: Houghton, 1979.

011.9 "Kristallnacht." _Poetry_ 135 (March 1980): 340-341.

011.10 "On Being One Half Japanese, One Eighth Choctaw, One
Quarter Black and One Sixteenth Irish." _Ms_. 6 (May 1978):
58.

011.11 "The Psychiatrist." _Poetry_ 135 (March 1980): 338-339.

011.12 "The Ravine." _Ms_. 6 (May 1978): 59.

011.13 "Salome." _Ms_. 11 (December 1982): 74.

011.14 _Sin_. Boston: Houghton, 1986.

011.15 "Sleep Like a Hammer." _Chicago Review_ 29 (Spring
1978): 6.

011.16 "Talking To His Reflection in a Shallow Pond."
Michigan Quarterly Review 17 (4): 505-506 (1978).

011.17 "They Shall Not Pass." _Iowa Review_ 11 (Winter 1980):
103.

011.18 "Twenty-Nine (a Dream in Two Parts)." _Ms_. 6 (May
1978): 59.

011.19 "Winter in Another Country." _Poetry_ 135 (March
1980): 336-337.

011.20 "Yellow Crane Pavilion." _Paris Review_ 77 (Winter-
Spring 1980): 117.

Secondary Sources

011.21(S) Kearney, Lawrence and Cuddihy, Michael. "Ai: An Interview." Ironwood 6 (2): 27-34 (1978).

1988-1991 Supplement

A011.22 "Little America Confidential." Callaloo 12 (Spring 1989): 391. Poem excerpt.

012. ALBA, NANINA (1915-1968).

012.1 The Parchments I. n.p., Merchants Press, 1963. Poetry.

012.2 Parchments, II. n.p., 1967. Poetry.

Secondary Sources

012.3 (S) Bogle, Enid. "Nanina Alba." In HARRIS & DAVIS, pp.3-8.

013. ALEXANDER, ADELE LOGAN.

013.1 "Grandmother, Grandfather, W.E.B. DuBois and Booker T. Washington." Crisis 73 (February 1983): 8-11

013.2 "How I Discovered My Grandmother." Ms. (November 1983): 29-33.

014. ALEXANDER, ELIZABETH.

014.1 "The Dirt Eaters." Callaloo 9 (Winter 1986): 7-8.

014.2 "Ode." Black American Literature Forum 23 (Fall 1989): 495. Poem.

014.3 "Poems." Callaloo 12 (Spring 1989): 265.

014.4 The Venus Hottentot. Charlottesville, VA: University Press of Virginia, 1990.

Alexander, Margaret Walker. SEE 645. WALKER, MARGARET.

015. ALLEGRA, DONNA.

015.1 "A Prayer for My Soul." Essence 9 (September 1978):
24.

Allen, Sarah A. **SEE** 309. HOPKINS, PAULINE ELIZABETH.

016. ALLISON, MARGARET M.

016.1 The Sun Look Upon Me and I Am Black. Madison, WI:
Author, 1970. Poetry.

017. ALLMAN, REVA WHITE.

017.1 I've Known Love. New York: Vantage Press, 1975.

018. AMINI, JOHARI (1935-).

018.1 "Ceremony." In STETSON, pp. 191-194.

018.2 Folk Fable. Chicago: Third World Press, 197?.
Poetry.

018.3 "(For William) Poem." Black World 19 (Auguat 1970):
81.

018.4 A Hip Tale in Death Style. Detroit: Broadside Press,
1972. Poetry.

018.5 Let's Go Somewhere. Chicago: Third World Press,
1970. Poetry.

018.6 "The Promise." In STETSON, pp.195.

018.7 "Story for the Remainder." In BARAKA & BARAKA,
pp.51-53.

018.8 "There Is No Title: Only Echoes." Black World 19
(September 1970): 67. In BARAKA & BARAKA, pp. 50-51.

018.9 "To a Poet I Knew." Negro Digest 18 (September 1969):
24.

018.10 "Untitled." In ADOFF, pp.242-243.

018.11 "Wednesday." <u>Black World</u> 19 (June 1970): 54-56.

Secondary Sources

018.12(S) Brown, Fahamisha Patricia. "Johari M. Amini." In
HARRIS & DAVIS, pp.17-23.

SEE ALSO 400. LATIMORE, JEWELL.

019. AMIS, LOLA ELIZABETH JONES (1930-).

019.1 <u>Three Plays</u>. New York: Exposition Press, 1965.
Includes "Helen," two act drama; "The Other Side of the
Wall", three act drama and "Places of Wrath," three act
drama.

020. ANDERSON, ANITA TURPEAU.

020.1 <u>Penpoints: Group of Poems and Prose Writings</u>.
Fairmont Heights, MD: Campbell Press, 1943.

021. ANDERSON, EDNA L.

021.1 <u>Through the Ages: A Book of Poems</u>. Philadelphia:
Dorrance & Company, 1946.

022. ANDERSON, GLORIA EDWARDS.

022.1 <u>Pearls of Black</u>. Detroit: Harlo Press, 1975.

023. ANDERSON, KATHY ELAINE.

023.1 "Ahmos." <u>Obsidian</u> 5 (1-2): 106 (Spring-Summer 1979).

023.2 "Derrick." <u>Obsidian</u> 5 (1-2): 106 (Spring-Summer
1979).

023.3 "For Mulaaka." <u>Essence</u> 10 (October 1980): 25.

023.4 "The Grandpa." Obsisian 5 (1-2): 107 (Spring-Summer
1979).

023.5 "Louisiana Shade." Southern Review 21 (July 1985):
672-681.

023.6 "To Be Signed for the Deaf." Essence 10 (October
1980): 19.

024. ANDERSON, MIGNON HOLLAND.

024.1 Mostly Womenfolk and a Man or Two: A Collection.
Chicago: Third World Press, 1976.

025. ANGELOU, MAYA (1928-).

025.1 All God's Children Need Traveling Shoes. New York:
Random House, 1986.

025.2 And Still I Rise. New York: Random House, 1978.

025.3 "Black Scholar Interviews: Maya Angelou." Black
Scholar 8 (January-February 1977): 44-53.

025.4 "The Bridge." Essence 16 (March 1986): 66.

025.5 "Caged Bird." Ladies' Home Journal 100 (July 1983):
40.

025.6 Gather Together In My Name. New York: Random House,
1974. Autobiography.

025.7 "Glass Rain." Essence 1 (January 1971): 34-35.

025.8 "The Health-Food Diner." Ladies' Home Journal 100
(July 1983): 40.

025.9 The Heart of a Woman. New York: Random House, 1981.
Essence 12 (January 1982): 76. Excerpt.

025.10 I Know Why the Caged Bird Sings. New York: Random
House, 1969. Autobiography.

025.11 "Insomniac." Ladies' Home Journal 100 (October
1983): 192.

025.12 Just Give Me a Cool Drink of Water 'For I Die. New
York: Random House, 1971. Poetry.

025.13 "Maya's Journey Home." Reader's Digest 121
(September 1982): 89-94. Excerpt from I Know Why the Caged
Bird Sings.

025.14 <u>Mrs. Flowers: A Moment of Friendship</u>. Minneapolis:
Redpath Press, 1986.

025.15 "My Arkansas." In STETSON, p.266.

025.16 "Now Long Ago." <u>Essence</u> 6 (December 1975): 64.

025.17 <u>Now Sheba Sings the Song</u>. New York: Dutton, 1987.

025.18 <u>Oh Pray My Wings Are Gonna Fit Me Well</u>. New York:
Random House, 1975.

025.19 "On Diverse Deviations." In STETSON, p. 267.

025.20 "One Heartland Black Artist Speaks of Other Heartland
Black Artists." <u>International Review of African American Art</u>
7 (3): 4-5 (1987).

025.21 "The Peckerwood Dentist and Momma's Incredible
Powers." In GILBERT & GUBAR, pp. 2002-2007.

025.22 <u>Poems: Maya Angelou</u>. 4 vols. New York: Bantam Books,
1986.

025.23 "Recovery." <u>Ladies' Home Journal</u> 100 (October 1983):
192.

025.24 "Rehearsal for a Funeral." <u>Black Scholar</u> 6 (June
1975): 3-7.

025.25 "The Reunion." In STETSON, pp. 54-58.

025.26 "Save the Mothers." <u>Ebony</u> 41 (August 1986): 38.

025.27 "Sepia Fashion Show." In STETSON, p. 267.

025.28 "Shades and Slashes of Light." In EVANS, pp. 3-5.

025.29 <u>Shaker, Why Don't Sing?</u> New York: Random House,
1983.

025.30 <u>Singin' and Swingin' and Gettin' Merry Like
Christmas</u>. New York: Random House, 1976.

025.31 "Still I Rise." In STETSON, pp. 265-266.

025.32 "To a Man." <u>Ebony</u> 38 (February 1983): 50.

025.33 "Where We Belong, A Duet." <u>Ebony</u> 38 (February 1983):
46.

025.34 "Why I Moved Back To the South." <u>Ebony</u> 37 (February
1982): 130-134.

025.35   "Woman Me." In STETSON, p. 264.

025.36   "Author Maya Angelou Raps." <u>Sepia</u> 26 (October
1977): 22-27.

Secondary Sources

025.37(S) Arensberg, Liliane K. "Death as Metaphor of Self in I Know Why the Caged Bird Sings." CLA Journal 20 (December 1976): 273-291.

025.38(S) "The Black Scholar Interviews: Maya Angelou." Black Scholar 8 (4): 44-53 (January-February 1977).

025.39(S) Bloom, Lynn Z. "Maya Angelou." In DAVIS & HARRIS, 1985, pp. 3-12.

025.40(S) Cameron, Dee Birch. "A Maya Angelou Bibliography." Bulletin of Bibliography 36 (January-March 1979): 50-52.

025.41(S) Cudjoe, Selwyn R. "Maya Angelou and the Autobiographical Statement." In EVANS, pp.6-24.

025.42(S) Davis, Curt. "Maya Angelou: And Still She Rises." Encore 6 (12 September 1977): 28-32.

025.43(S) Eliot, Jeffrey. "Author Maya Angelou Raps." Sepia 26 (October 1977): 22-27.

025.44(S) Eliot, Jeffrey. "Maya Angelou: In Search of Self." Negro History Bulletin 40 (May-June 1977): 694-695.

025.45(S) Hiers, John T. "Fatalism in Maya Angelou's I Know Why the Caged Bird Sings." Notes on Contemporary Literature 6 (1): 5-7 (January 1976).

025.46(S) Kent, George E. "Maya Angelou's I Know Why the Caged Bird Sings and Black Autobiographical Tradition." Kansas Quarterly 7 (Summer 1975): 72-78.

025.47(S) McMurry, Myra K. "Role Playing As Art in Maya Angelou's Caged Bird." South Atlantic Bulletin 41 (May 1976): 106-111.

025.48(S) Neubauer, Carol E. "Displacement and Autobiographical Style in Maya Angelou's The Heart of a Woman." Black American Literature Forum 17 (Fall 1983): 123-129.

025.49(S) Neubauer, Carol E. "An Interview with Maya Angelou." Massachusetts Review 28 (2): 286-292 (Summer 1987).

025.50(S) Oliver, Stephanie Stokes. "Maya Angelou: The Heart of the Woman." Essence 14 (May 1983): 112-114.

025.51(S) O'Neale, Sondra. "Reconstruction of the Composite Self: New Images of Black Women in Maya Angelou's Continuing Autobiography." In EVANS, pp. 25-36.

025.52(S)   Paterson, Judith.   "Interview: Maya Angelou -- A
Passionate Writer Living Fiercely with Brains, Guts, and
Joy."   Vogue 172 (September 1982): 416.

025.53(S)   Smith, Sidonie A.   "The Song of a Caged Bird: Maya
Angelou's Quest After Self-Acceptance."   Southern Humanities
Review 7 (Fall 1973): 365-375.

                    1988-1991 Supplement

A025.54   "Black Family Pledge."   Shooting Star Review 3
(Winter 1989/Spring 1990): 39.

A025.55   I Shall Not Be Moved.   New York: Random House, 1990.

                      Secondary Sources

A025.56(S)   Eliott, Jeffrey M., ed.   Conversations with Maya
Angelou. Jackson, MS: University Press of Mississippi, 1989.

A025.57(S)   Fox-Genovese, Elizabeth.   "Myth and History:
Discourse of Origins in Zora Neale Hurston and Maya Angelou."
Black American Literature Forum 24 (Summer 1990): 221.

A025.58(S)   Jones, Marsha.   "Maya Angelou: On Mastering
Language."   about...time 17 (December 1989): 20.

A025.59(S)   Lupton, Mary Jane.   "Singing the Black Mother:
Maya Angelou and Autobiographical Continuity."   Black
American Literature Forum 24 (Summer 1990): 257.

A025.60(S)   McPherson, Dolly A.   Order Out of Chaos: The
Autobiographical Works of Maya Angelou.   NY: Peter Lang,
1990.

A025.61(S)   Redmond, Eugene B.   "Boldness of Language and
Breadth: An Interview with Maya Angelou."   Black American
Literature Forum 22 (Summer 1988): 156.

Anthony, Florence.   SEE   11.   AI.

026.   ARKHURST, JOYCE COOPER (1921-).

026.1   The Adventures of Spider.   Boston: Little, 1964.
Young people's literature.

027.   ARMSTRONG, DENISE CARREATHERS (1950-).

027.1 "A Black Man's Love Song." <u>Black Books Bulletin</u> 7
(2): 53 (1981).

027.2 "When a Black Man Smiles." <u>Black Books Bulletin</u> 7
(3): 61 (1981).

028. ARMSTRONG, NAOMI YOUNG.

028.1 <u>A Child's Easter</u>. Author, 1971.

029. ARNOLD, ETHEL NISHUA (1924-).

029.1 <u>She Knew No Evil</u>. New York: Vantage Press, 1952.

030. ARTHUR, BARBARA.

030.1 <u>Common Sense Poetry</u>. Berkeley: Respect International
Enterprises, 1969.

Asante, Kariamu Welsh. **SEE** 668. WELSH, KARIAMU.

031. ATHENS, IDA GERDING.

031.1 <u>Brethren</u>. Cincinnati: Talaria Publication Company,
1940.

032. AUNT SALLY.

032.1 <u>Aunt Sally, or the Cross the Way of Freedom; Narrative
of the Slave Life and Purchase of the Mother of Rev. Isaac
Williams of Detroit, Michigan</u>. American Reform Tract and
Book Society, 1858.

033. AUSTIN, DORIS JEAN.

033.1 <u>After the Garden</u>. New York: New American Library,
1987.

034.   AYERS, VIVIAN.

034.1 Hawk and Vivian Ayers. Houston: Hawk Press, 1957.
Poetry.

034.2 Spice of Dawns: A Book of Verse. New York: Exposition
Press, 1953.

035.   BACON, MARY ALBERTA.

035.1 Poems of Color. New York: Exposition Press, 1948.

036.   BAGBY, JEANNE S.

036.1 "Elegy for the World of J.F.K." Liberation 8 (January
1964): 13.

036.2 "Enigmas of East-West Dialogue." Liberation 9 (March
1964): 20.

036.3 "Hopi Bible." Liberation 9 (December 1964): 27.

036.4 "O What Farewells." Liberation 6(March 1961): 9.

036.5 "Whose Darkness?" Liberation 9 (August 1964): 26.

037.   BAGLEY, JOYCE M.

037.1 Jots of Thoughts. New York: Vantage Press, 1974.

038.   BAILEY, GERTRUDE BLACKWELL.

038.1 If Words Could Set Us Free. New York: Exposition
Press, 1974.

039.   BAKER, AUGUSTA (1911-).

039.1 Golden Lynx and Other Tales. Philadelphia:
Lippincott, 1960. Children's stories.

039.2 <u>Talking Trees and Other Stories</u>. Philadelphia:
Lippincott, 1955. Children's stories.

040. BALDWIN, JO ANN.

040.1 "Hole They Call a Grave." <u>Black World</u> 24 (June 1975):
70-73.

041. BALKUM, SYLVIA LOUISE.

041.1 "Alone." <u>about... time</u> 11 (June 1983): 24.

041.2 "He Looked At Me." <u>about... time</u> 11 (June 1983): 24.

041.3 "I Am." <u>about... time</u> 11 (June 1983): 24.

041.4 "I Like Me." <u>about... time</u> 11 (June 1983): 24.

041.5 "My Best Friend." <u>about... time</u> 11 (June 1983): 24.

041.6 "The Phone Call." <u>about... time</u> 11 (June 1983): 24.

041.7 "Some Days." <u>about... time</u> 11 (June 1983): 24.

041.8 "The Tryouts." <u>about... time</u> 11 (June 1983): 24.

042. BAMBARA, TONI CADE (1939-).

042.1 "Baby's Breath." <u>Essence</u> 10 (September 1980): 90-91.

042.2 "Black Theater." In GAYLE.

042.3 "Black Theater Of the 60s." In   MILLER, 1971.

042.4 <u>The Black Woman: An Anthology</u>. New York: New American
Library, 1970.

042.5 "Christmas Eve at Johnson's Drug N Goods." In LONG &
COLLIER, pp. 698-712.

042.6 "<u>For Colored Girls</u> -- And White Girls Too." <u>Ms.</u> 5
(September 1976): 36,38. Ntosake Shange

042.7 <u>Gorilla, My Love</u>. New York: Random House, 1972.
Short fiction.

042.8 "Hammer Man." <u>Negro Digest</u> 15 (February 1966): 54-60.

042.9 "Luther on Sweet Auburn." First World 2 (4): 54-55
(1980).

042.10 "Madame Bai and the Taking of Stone Mountain." In
BARAKA & BARAKA, pp. 59-69.

042.11 "Maggie of the Green Bottles." In FISHER, pp. 196-
201.

042.12 "Mama Hazel Takes To Her Bed." Black World 2
(October 1971): 62-67.

042.13 "The Mamma Load." Redbook 154 (November 1979): 33.

042.14 "Salvation Is the Issue." In EVANS, pp.41-47.

042.15 The Salt Eaters. New York: Random House, 1980.
Fiction.

042.16 The Sea Birds Are Still Alive. New York: Random
House, 1977.

042.17 Tales and Stories for Black Folks. New York:
Doubleday, 1971.

042.18 "Wall of Respect." Obsidian 7 (2-3): 108-114
(Summer-Winter 1981).

042.19 "What It Means To Be a Black Woman." Black Collegian
35 (1980): 34.

042.20 "Witchbird." Essence 7 (September 1976): 52-54.

Secondary Sources

042.21(S) Burks, Ruth Elizabeth. "From Baptism to
Resurrection: Toni Cade Bambara and the Incongruity of
Language." In EVANS, pp. 48-57.

042.22(S) Byerman, Keith E. "Women's Blues: The Fiction of
Toni Cade Bambara and Alice Walker." In BYERMAN, pp. 104-
170.

042.23(S) Deck, Alice A. "Toni Cade Bambara." In DAVIS &
HARRIS, 1985, pp. 12-22.

042.24(S) Guy-Sheftall, Beverly. "Commitment: Toni Cade
Bambara speaks." In BELL, pp. 230-250.

042.25(S) Jackson, Angela. "The War Chant of the Architect
(Toni Cade Bambara)." Black American Literature Forum 19
(3): 100 (Fall 1985).

042.26(S) Jackson, Deborah. "An Interview with Toni Cade
Bambara." Drum Magazine (Spring 1982).

042.27(S) Salaam, Kalamu ya. "Searching for the Mother
Tongue: An Interview." First World 2 (4): 48-52 (1980).

042.28(S) Tate, Claudia. "Toni Cade Bambara." In TATE,
pp. 12-38.

042.29(S) Traylor, Eleanor W. "Music As Theme: The Jazz
Mode In the Works of Toni Cade Bambara." In EVANS, pp. 58-
70.

1988-1991 Supplement

A042.30 "Gorilla, My Love." Shooting Star Review 3 (Winter
1989): 34. Short fiction.

Secondary Sources

A042.31(S) Butler-Evans, Elliott. Race, Gender, and Desire:
Narrative Strategies in the Fiction of Toni Cade Bambara,
Toni Morrison and Alice Walker. Philadelphia: Temple
University Press, 1989.

043. BANGHAM, MARY DICKERSON.

043.1 "Secret Storm." Negro Digest 11 (May 1962): 57-64.

044. BANKS, BARBARA (1948-).

044.1 Dragonseeds. New York: St. Martin's, 1977. Short
fiction.

045. BANKS, CAROL TILLERY.

045.1 "A Difference." Essence 15 (February 1985): 111.

045.2 "Even My Pain's Gonna Be Pretty." Essence 12
(September 1981): 19.

045.3 Hello To Me, with Love: Poems of Self-Discovery. New
York: William Morrow, 1980.

045.4 "Inside." Essence 17 (April 1987): 110.

045.5 "Point of View." Essence 15 (February 1985): 111.

045.6 "So." Essence 15 (February 1985): 147.

045.7 "Untitled." <u>Essence</u> 14 (October 1983): 88. 15 (March 1985): 137.

046. BARAKA, AMINA.

046.1 "For the Lady in Color." <u>Black Scholar</u> 12 (July-August 1981): 54-55.

046.2 "Haiti." In BARAKA & BARAKA, p. 71.

046.3 "Hip Songs (for Larry Neal)." <u>Black Scholar</u> 12 (July-August 1981): 55.

046.4 "I Wanna Make Freedom." In BARAKA & BARAKA, pp. 72-73.

046.5 "Looking for the Lyrics (for Jayne Cortez). <u>Black Scholar</u> 12 (July-August 1981): 54.

046.6 "Sometime Woman." <u>Black American Literature Forum</u> 16 (Fall 1982): 105.

046.7 <u>Songs for the Masses</u>. Author, 1979. [published under the name Sylvia Jones]

046.8 "Sortin-Out." <u>Black American Literature Forum</u> 16 (Fall 1982): 106.

046.9 "Soweto Song." In BARAKA & BARAKA, p. 70.

046.10 <u>What Was the Relationship of the Lone Ranger to the Means of Production? A Play in One Act</u>. New York: Anti-Imperialistic Cultural Union, 1978.

Secondary Sources

046.11(S) Buffalo, Audreen. "A Revolutionary Life Together: Amina and Amiri Baraka." <u>Essence</u> 16 (May 1985): 82.

1988-1991 Supplement

A046.12 "Poems." <u>Black Scholar</u> 19 (July/August - September/October 1988): 98.

A046.13 "Soweto Song." <u>Essence</u> 19 (February 1989): 129. Poem.

047. BARKER, MILDRED.

047.1 "Trees Past the Window." <u>Negro Digest</u> 12 (November 1962): 53-57.

Barnett, Ida B. Wells SEE 667. WELLS, IDA BELL.

048. BARON, LINDA MICHELLE.

048.1 "...And free." <u>Essence</u> 12 (March 1982): 25.

049. BATES, ARTHENIA JACKSON (1920-).

049.1 "Blame it on Adical." <u>Callaloo</u> 1 (December 1975): 45-57.

049.2 "The Creative Spirit." <u>The Baptist Advocate of Baton Rouge</u> (2 April 1983): 1-2.

049.3 <u>The Deity Nodded</u>. Detroit: Harlo Press, 1973. Fiction.

049.4 "Good Grazin." <u>Obsidian: Black Literature in Review</u> 1 (1): 67 (1975).

049.5 "The Higher Fatality in <u>Madame Bovary</u>." <u>Southern University Bulletin</u> 46 (September 1959): 109-114.

049.6 "Home and Me." <u>Negro Digest</u> 14 (September 1965): 43-47.

049.7 "Homesick." <u>Obsidan: Black Literature in Review</u> 1 (1): 68-70 (1975).

049.8 "Lost Note." <u>Delta</u> 19 (1965): 46-52.

049.9 "On Clean Cooking." <u>Mahagany of Baton Rouge</u> (June 1979): 9.

049.10 "The Second Stone." <u>Last Cookie</u> 1 (1): 37-42 (1972).

049.11 <u>Seeds Beneath the Snow: Vignettes From the South</u>. New York: Greenwich, 1968. Short fiction.

049.12 "Sound of the Lyre Off Main Street USA." <u>Negro American Literature Forum</u> 2 (Spring 1986): 11-14.

049.13 <u>Such Things from the Valley</u>. Norfolk. VA: H.C. Young Press, 1977.

049.14 "W.E.B. DuBois: The Editor's Role in Afro-American
History." The Baptist Advocate of Baton Rouge (2 February
1984): 1-2.

049.15 "Wake Me, Mama." Black World 20 (July 1971): 57-68.

                    Secondary Sources

049.16(S) Parker, Bettye J. "Reflections: Arthenia Bates
Millican." In BELL, pp. 201-208.

049.17(S) Smith, Virginia Whatley. "Arthenia J. Bates
Millican." In DAVIS & HARRIS, 1985, pp. 195-201.

049.18(S) Ward, Jerry. "Legitimate Resources of the Soul:
An Interview with Arthenia Bates Millican." Obsidian 3 (1):
14-34 (Spring 1977).

050. BATES, EVELINE.

050.1 "Tree of Knowledge." Liberation 9 (May 1964): 25.

051. BATSON, SUSAN.

051.1 "Hoodoo Talkin'." In SANCHEZ, pp. 145-178.

052. BATTLE, EFFIE T.

052.1 Gleanings from Dixie-Land in Ten Poems. Okolona, MS:
Okolona Messenger, 1914.

053. BEATY, DIANE.

053.1 "Flame Eternal, Light the Ages." Crisis 86 (May
1979): 175.

054. BELINDA.

054.1 "The Cruelty of Men, Whose Faces Were Like the Moon."
The American Museum or Repository of Ancient and Modern
Fugitive Pieces, &c. Prose and Poetical 1 (June 1787).

Petition of an African slave to the Legislature of
Massachusetts.

055. BELLINGER, CLAUDIA.

055.1 Wolf Kitty. New York: Vantage Press, 1959.

056. BENNETT, GWENDOLYN (1902-1981).

056.1 "Advice." "Fantasy." "Hatred." "Lines Written at the
Grave of Alexander Dumas." "Quatrains." "Secret." "Sonnet I."
"Sonnet II." "To a Dark Girl." "Your Songs." In CULLEN.

056.2 "The American Negro Paints." Southern Workman 57
(January 1928): 111-112.

056.3 "The Ebony Flute." column in Opportunity 4-6 (August
1926-May 1928).

056.4 "Epitaph." Opportunity 12 (March 1934): 76.

056.5 "The Future of the Negro in Art." Howard University
Record 19 (December 1924): 65-66.

056.6 "Hatred." Opportunity 4 (June 1926): 190.

056.7 "Heritage." Opportunity 1 (December 1923): 371.

056.8 "I Go To Camp." Opportunity 12 (August 1934): 241-
243.

056.9 "Lines Written at the Grave of Alexander Dumas."
Opportunity 4 (July 1926): 225.

056.10 "Moon Tonight." "Song." In BRAITHWAITE, pp. 31, 32.

056.11 "Negroes: Inherent Craftsmen." Howard University
Record 19 (February 1925): 172.

056.12 "Nocturne." In JOHNSON, 1931.

056.13 "On a Birthday." Opportunity 3 (September 1925):
276.

056.14 "Purgation." Opportunity 3 (February 1925): 56

056.15 "Rounding the Century: Story of the Colored Orphan
Asylum and Association for the Benefit of Colored Children in
New York City." Crisis 42 (June 1935): 180-181, 188.

056.16 "Song." "Dear things." "Dirge." Palms 4 (October
1926): 21-22.

056.17 "Street Lamps in Early Spring." Opportunity 4 (May 1926): 152.

056.18 "To Usward." Crisis 28 (May 1924): 335. Opportunity 1 (May 1924): 143-144.

056.19 "Tokens." In JOHNSON, pp. 149-150.

056.20 "Wedding Day." Fire!! (November 1926): 26-28.

056.21 "Wind." Opportunity 2 (November 1924): 335.

Secondary Sources

056.22(S) Daniel, Walter C. and Govan, Sandra Y. "Gwendolyn Bennett (1902-1981)." In HARRIS & DAVIS, 1987, pp. 3-10.

057. BERGES, RUTH.

057.1 "Jeanne Comes Home." Liberation 6 (September 1961): 27-30.

058. BEST, MARGARET S.

058.1 Serenity. Author, 1969.

059. BETTS, CHARLOTTE.

059.1 I See a Black Dawn. Fort Smith, AR: South & West, 1974.

Bibb, Eloise SEE 628. THOMPSON, ELOISE BIBB.

060. BINNS, KAREN GENEVIEVE.

060.1 "Bondage (South Africa)." Essence 17 (May 1986): 147.

061. BIRAM, BRENDA M.

061.1 "Fashion Note." Negro Digest 15 (November 1965): 70.

062. BIRD, JESSIE CALHOUN.

062.1 Airs from the Wood Winds. Philadelphia: Alpress,
1935.

062.2 "Proof." In STETSON.

063. BIRTHA, BECKY (1948-).

063.1 For Nights Like This One: Stories of Loving Women. E.
Palo, CA: Frog in the Well, 1983. Short fiction.

063.2 Lover's Choice. Seattle: Seal Press, 1987.

064. BISKIN, MIRIAM.

064.1 "Saga of a Schoolmarm." Negro Digest 13 (September
1964): 63.

065. BLAKE, MARGARET JANE.

065.1 Memoirs of Margaret Jane Blake of Baltimore, Md. and
Selections in Prose and Verse by Sarah R. Leavering.
Baltimore: Press of Innes and Son, 1897.

066. BLANTON, KATHRYN FRANKLIN (1921-).

066.1 A Dictionary of Poetry. New York: Vantage Press,
1974.

067. BOGUS, DIANE (1946-).

067.1 "Blind, Cripple and Crazy." "Gabble Gourmet."
"Slavery." "Translation." "Woman, Perception Poem 1."
Author, 1977. Five broadsides.

067.2 Her Poems. College Corner, OH: W.I.M., 1980.

067.3 _I'm Off to See the Goddamn Wizard, Alright!_ Chicago:
Author, 1971. Poetry.

067.4 _Lady Godiva_. Author, 1981. Broadside.

067.5 "Mayree." _Black American Literature Forum_ 14 (4): 175
(Winter 1980).

067.6 _Sapphire's Sampler_. College Corner, OH: W.I.M., 1982.

067.7 _W.I.M. Poetry Test_. College Corner, OH: W.I.M., 1979.

067.8 _Woman in the Moon_. Stamford, CT: Soap Box, 1977.

1988-1991 Supplement

A067.9 "After the Kiss." _Catalyst_ (Summer 1988): 13.

A067.10 "An Authorial Tie-Up: The Wedding of Symbol and Point
of View in Toni Morrison's _Sula_." _CLA Journal_ 33 (September
1989): 73.

A067.11 "Deep South Passion." _Catalyst_ (Winter 1989): 21.

A067.12 "How Does You Love Me, Sweet Baby?" _Catalyst_ (Winter
1989): 83.

068. BOHANON, MARY.

068.1 _Earth Bosom and Collected Poems_. New York: Carlton
Press, 1973.

068.2 _Poems and Character Sketches_. New York: Greenwich,
1967.

069. BOND, ODESSA.

069.1 _The Double Tragedy_. New York: Vantage Press, 1970.

Bonner, Marita. **SEE** 498. OCCOMY, MARITA BONNER.

070. BOOSE, MARYETTA KELSICK.

070.1 "Somebody Else's Child." _Essence_ 19 (November 1988):
136. Poem.

070.2 "The Teenage Strut." <u>Black American Literature Forum</u>
20 (3): 309 (Fall 1986).

071. BOYD, MELBA JOYCE (1950-).

071.1 "Beer Drops." <u>Obsidian</u> 5 (1-2): 84 (Spring-Summer
1979).

071.2 <u>Cat Eyes and Dead Wood</u>. Highland Park, MI: Fallen
Angel, 1978.

071.3 "The Crowd Wears Sunglasses." <u>Black Scholar</u> 12 (5):
34 (September-October 1981).

071.4 "Detroit Renaissance Sin." <u>First World</u> 2 (Spring
1978): 38.

071.5 "Gramma Wynn." <u>Obsidian</u> 5 (1-2): 83 (Spring-Summer
1979).

071.6 "Like Fine English China." <u>Black Scholar</u> 18 (4-5): 54
(July-August-September-October 1987).

071.7 "Out of the Poetry Ghetto: The Life/Art Struggle of
Small Black Publishing Houses." <u>Black Scholar</u> 16 (4): 12-24
(July-August 1985).

071.8 "Poems." <u>Black Scholar</u> 19 (July/August-
September/October 1988): 75.

071.9 "Silver Lace." <u>Black Scholar</u> 10 (3-4): 46 (November-
December 1978).

071.10 <u>Song for Maya</u>. Highland Park, MI: Fallen Angel, 198?.
Broadside.

071.11 "Sunflowers and Saturdays." <u>Obsidian</u> 5 (1-2): 85
(Spring-Summer 1979).

071.12 "Why?" <u>Obsidian</u> 5 (1-2): 86 (Spring-Summer 1979).

071.13 "Wild Strawberries in the Onion Field (for Maya)."
<u>Black Scholar</u>, 11 (November-December 1980): 76-77.

072. BOYD, SUE ABBOTT.

072.1 <u>How It Is: Selected Poems, 1952-1968</u>. Homestead, FL:
Olivant Press, 1968.

072.2 <u>A Portion of the Fort Root Poems, Volume 1, Act 1</u>.
Fort Smith. AR: South & West, 1973.

073.   BOYER, JILL WITHERSPOON (1947-).

073.1 "Again." <u>Essence</u> 16 (February 1986): 133.

073.2 "Blood Sisters."   <u>Essence</u> 9 (October 1978): 92.

073.3 <u>Breaking Camp</u>. Detroit: Lotus Press, 1984.

073.4 "But I Say." <u>Essence</u> 14 (December 1983): 140.

073.5 <u>Dream Farmer</u>. Detroit: Broadside Press, 1975.

073.6 "Sun Song." In BLACKSONGS,1977.

074.   BRAGG, LINDA BROWN (1939-).

074.1 "And This They Have Done to Their Own." <u>Black Scholar</u>
6 (June 1975): 9.

074.2 "Dream." <u>Black Scholar</u> 10 (November-December 1978):
54.

074.3 <u>A Love Song to Black Men</u>. Detroit: Broadside Press,
1974.

074.4 "My Sisters Speak to Me." <u>Black Scholar</u> 10 (November-
December 1978): 55.

074.5 "Our Blackness Did Not Come to Us Whole." In ADOFF,
pp. 231-232.

074.6 "A Poem About Beauty, Blackness, Poetry (and How to Be
All Three)." In ADOFF, pp. 230-231.

074.7 <u>Rainbow Roun Mah Shoulder</u>. Chapel Hill, NC: Carolina
Wren, 1984.

074.8 "Interview with Linda Brown Bragg." <u>CLA Journal</u> 20
(September 1976): 75-87.

075.   BRAXTON, JOANNE M. (1950-).

075.1 <u>Black Grandmothers: Sources of Artistic Consciousness
and Personal Strength</u>. Wellesley, MA: Wellesley College
Center for Research on Women, 1987.

075.2 <u>Charlotte Forten Grimke (1837-1914)</u>. Wellesley, MA:
Wellesley College Center for Research on Women, 1985.
[working paper no. 153]

075.3 "Harriet Jacobs' Incidents in the Life of a Slave
Girl: The Redefinition of the Slave Narrative Genre."
Massachusetts Review 27 (2): 379-387 (Summer 1986).

075.4 Sometimes I Think of Maryland. Bronx, NY: Sunbury,
1977. Poetry.

075.5 "We Lay There Ageless." Essence 8 (February 1978):54.

                    Secondary Sources

075.6(S) Washington, Edward T. "Joanne M. Braxton." In
HARRIS & DAVIS, pp. 42-47.

Braxton, Jody. SEE 075. BRAXTON, JOANNE M.

076. BREECHWOOD, MARY.

076.1 Memphis Jackson's Son. Boston: Houghton, 1956.

Brent, Linda. SEE 340. JACOBS, HARRIET.

077. BRIGHT, HAZEL V.

077.1 "Mama Pritchett." Black World 22 (October 1973): 54-
58.

077.2 "TV Versus Black Survival." Black World 23 (December
1973): 30-42.

077.3 "When You Dead, You Ain't Done." Black World 22
(January 1973): 60-65.

078. BRITT, ANGELA M.

078.1 "Showered." Essence 18 (August 1987): 122.

079. BRITT, NELLIE.

079.1 My Master and I: Poems That Will Encourage, Inspire
and Strengthen. New York: Carlton Press, 1964.

Britton, Mariah. SEE 314. HOWARD, MARIAH BRITTON.

080. BROOKES, STELLA BREWER (1903-?).

080.1 Joel Chandler Harris, Folklorist. Athens, GA:
University of Georgia Press, 1950.

081. BROOKS, GWENDOLYN (1917-).

081.1 "Adlai Stevenson of Illinois: Poem" Negro Digest 14
(September 1965): 56.

081.2 Aloneness. Detroit: Broadside Press, 1969.

081.3 Annie Allen. New York: Harper, 1949.

081.4 Aurora. Detroit: Broadside Press, 1971.

081.5 The Bean Eaters. New York: Harper, 1960.

081.6 Beckonings. Detroit: Broadside Press, 1975.

081.7 Black Love. Chicago: Brooks Press, 1982.

081.8 "Black Love." Ebony 36 (August 1981): 29; 41
(November 1985): 158.

081.9 The Black Position. Detroit: Broadside Press, 1971.

081.10 "Black Wedding Song: (On the Occasion of the Marriage
of Safisha N. Laini to Haki R. Madhubuti, June 2, 1974)."
Black World 23 (September 1974): 36.

081.11 "Black Writers' Views on Literary Lions and Values."
Negro Digest 17 (January 1967): 29.

081.12 Blacks. Chicago: David Company, 1987.

081.13 "Boy Breaking Glass." Negro Digest 16 (June 1967):
53.

081.14 "Boy Died in My Alley." Black Scholar 8 (June 1975):
8.

081.15 "Boys Black." Ebony 27 (August 1972): 45.

081.16 Broadside Treasury. Detroit: Broadside Press, 1971.

081.17 <u>Bronzeville Boys and Girls</u>. New York: Harper, 1956.

081.18 <u>Family Pictures</u>. Detroit: Broadside Press, 1970.

081.19 "For Dudley Randall: On the Tenth Anniversary of Broadside Press." <u>Black World</u> 25 (January 1976): 91.

081.20 <u>For Illinois 1968: A Sesquicentennial Poem</u>. New York: Harper, 1968.

081.21 "God Works In a Mysterious Way: Poem." <u>Negro Digest</u> 10 (November 1951): 22.

081.22 "How I Told My Child About Race." <u>Negro Digest</u> 9 (June 1951): 29-31.

081.23 <u>In the Mecca</u>. New York: Harper, 1953.

081.24 <u>In the Time of Detachment, In the Time of Cold</u>. Springfield, IL: Civil War Centennial Commission of Illinois, 1965.

081.25 <u>Jump Bad: A New Chicago Anthology</u>. Detroit: Broadside Press, 1971.

081.26 "Langston Hughes: Poem" <u>Negro Digest</u> 16 (September 1967): 31.

081.27 "Line of Leopold: Poem." <u>Negro Digest</u> 13 (September 1964): 70-71.

081.28 "Malcolm X (for Dudley Randall)." <u>Ebony</u> 39 (April 1984): 80.

081.29 "Martin Luther King, Jr: Poem." <u>Negro Digest</u> 17 (September-October 1968): 54.

081.30 <u>Maude Martha</u>. New York: Farrar, Straus & Giroux, 1969.

081.31 <u>Mayor Harold Washington Chicago, the I Will City</u>. Chicago: Brooks Press, 1983.

081.32 <u>The Near-Johannesburg Boy, and Other Poems</u>. Chicago: David Company, 1987.

081.33 "Of Frank London Brown, a Tenant of the World." <u>Negro Digest</u> 11 (September 1962): 44.

081.34 "Piano After War: Poem. <u>Negro Digest</u> 8 (April 1950): 84

081.35 "Poets Who Are Negroes." <u>Phylon</u> 2 (December 1950): 312.

081.36 <u>Primer for Blacks</u>. Chicago: Black Position Press, 1980.

081.37 <u>Report from Part One; an Autobiography</u>. Detroit:
Broadside Press, 1972.

081.38 <u>Riot</u>. Detroit: Broadside Press, 1969.

081.39 <u>Selected Poems</u>. New York: Harper, 1963.

081.40 "Sight of the Horizon: A Centennial Poem." <u>Ebony</u> 18
(September 1963): 27.

081.41 "A Song in the Front Yard." <u>Harper's</u> 269 (August
1984): 47.

081.42 "Speech to the Young, Speech To the Progress-Toward."
<u>Ebony</u> 39 (April 1984): 80.

081.43 <u>A Street in Bronzeville</u>. New York: Harper, 1945.

081.44 "Telephone Conversations." <u>Black American Literature
Forum</u> 17 (Winter 1983): 148.

081.45 "They Call It Bronzeville." <u>Holiday</u> (October 1951):
60-67.

081.46 <u>The Tiger Who Wore White Gloves, or: What You Are You
Are</u>. Chicago: Third World Press, 1974.

081.47 "To a Proper Black Man." <u>Black Scholar</u> 6 (June
1975): 8.

081.48 "To Be in Love." <u>Essence</u> 4 (November 1973): 36

081.49 "To Black Women." <u>Ebony</u> 39 (April 1984): 78.

081.50 <u>To Disembark</u>. Chicago: Third World Press, 1981.

081.51 "Update On Part One: An Interview with Gwendolyn
Brooks." <u>CLA Journal</u> 21 (September 1977): 19-40.

081.52 <u>Very Young Poets</u>. Chicago: Brooks Press, 1983.

081.53 <u>The Wall</u>. Broadside Series # 19. Detroit: Broadside
Press, 1967.

081.54 <u>We Real Cool</u>. Broadside Series #6. Detroit:
Broadside Press, 1966.

081.55 "We Real Cool." <u>Ebony</u> 39 (April 1984): 80.

081.56 "Weaponed Woman." <u>Essence</u> 14 (October 1983): 147.

081.57 "When Handed a Lemon, Make Lemonade." <u>Poetry Now</u> 3
(1): 7 (1976).

081.58 "When You Have Forgotten Sunday: The Love Story."
<u>Ebony</u> 36 (August 1981): 54; 39 (April 1984): 79.

081.59 "Why Negro Women Leave Home. <u>Negro Digest</u> 9 (March 1951): 26-28.

081.60 <u>The World of Gwendolyn Brooks</u>. New York: Harper, 1976. Contains <u>Annie Allen, A Street in Bronzeville</u>, <u>Maud Martha</u> (novel), <u>The Bean Eaters</u> and <u>In The Mecca</u>.

081.61 "Young Afrikans of the Furious." <u>Ebony</u> 39 (April 1984): 82.

081.62 <u>A Capsule Course in Black Poetry Writing</u>. Detroit: Broadside Press, 1975.

Secondary Sources

081.63(S) Andrews, Larry. "Ambivalent Clothes Imagery in Gwendolyn Brooks' <u>The Sundays of Satin-Legs Smith</u>". <u>CLA Journal</u> 24 (December 1980): 150-163.

081.64(S) Baker, Houston. "The Achievement of Gwendolyn Brooks," <u>CLA Journal</u> 16 (September 1972): 23-31.

081.65(S) Bird, Leonard G. "Gwendolyn Brooks: Educator Extraordinaire." <u>Discourse</u> 12 (1969) 158-166.

081.66(S) Brown, Frank London. "Chicago's Great Lady of Poetry." <u>Negro Digest</u> 11 (December 1961): 78-83.

081.67(S) Brown, Martha H. "<u>Great Lakes Review</u> Interview: Gwendolyn Brooks." <u>Great Lakes Review</u> 6 (1): 48-55 (Summer 1979).

081.68(S) Crockett, J. "An Essay on Gwendolyn Brooks" <u>Negro History Bulletin</u> 19 (November 1955): 37-39.

081.69(S) Cutler, B. "Long Reach, Strong Speech." <u>Poetry</u> 103 (1954): 388-389.

081.70(S) Davis Arthur P. "The Black-and-Tan Motif in the Poetry of Gwendolyn Brooks." <u>CLA Journal</u> 6 (December 1962): 90-97.

081.71(S) Davis, Arthur P. "Gwendolyn Brooks: A Poet of the Unheroic." <u>CLA Journal</u> 7 (December 1963): 114-125.

081.72(S) Emanuel, James A. "Gwendolyn Brooks." In VINSON.

081.73(S) Fuller, Hoyt W. "Notes of a Poet." (Gwendolyn Brooks) <u>Negro Digest</u> 11 (August 1962): 50.

081.74(S) Furman, Marva Riley. "Gwendolyn Brooks: The 'Unconditioned Poet.'" <u>CLA Journal</u> 17 (September 1973): 1-10.

081.75(S) Garland, P. "Gwendolyn Brooks: Poet Laureate." <u>Ebony</u> 23 (July 1968): 48-50.

081.76(S) Greasley, Philip A. "Gwendolyn Brooks: The
Emerging Poetic Voice." Great Lakes Review 10 (2): 14-23
(Fall 1984).

081.77(S) Gregory, Carole. "An Appreciation of Gwendolyn
Brooks." Black Collegian 12 (December 1981): 22-23.

081.78(S) Grimes, Nikki. "For Gwendolyn Brooks on Mother's
Day." Greenfield Review 7 (3-4): 14-17 (Spring-Summer 1979).

081.79(S) Guy-Sheftall, Beverly. "The Women of
Bronzeville." In BELL, pp. 157-170.

081.80(S) Hansell, William. "Aestheticism Versus Political
Militancy in Gwendolyn Brooks's 'The Chicago Picasso' and
'The Wall.'" CLA Journal 17 (September 1973): 11-15.

081.81(S) Hansell, William. "Essences, Unifyings, and Black
Militancy: Major Themes in Gwendolyn Brooks's Family Pictures
(1971) and Beckonings (1975)." Black American Literature
Forum 11 (2): 63-66 (Summer 1977).

081.82(S) Hansell, William. "Gwendolyn Brooks's 'In the
Mecca': A Rebirth into Blackness." Negro Literature Forum 8
(Summer 1974): 199-207.

081.83(S) Hansell, William. "The Role of Violence in Recent
Poems of Gwendolyn Brooks." Studies in Black Literature 5
(Summer 1974): 21-27.

081.84(S) Hansell, William H. "The Uncommon Commonplace in
the Early Poems of Gwendolyn Brooks." CLA Journal 30 (3):
261-277 (March 1987).

081.85(S) Harriott, F. "Life of a Pulitzer Poet." Negro
Digest 8 (August 1950): 14-16. Gwendolyn Brooks.

081.86(S) Hoff, Jon N. "Gwendolyn Brooks: A Bibliography."
CLA Journal 17 (1973): 21-32.

081.87(S) Hudson, Clenora F. "Racial Themes in the Poetry
of Gwendolyn Brooks." CLA Journal 17 (September 1973): 16-
20.

081.88(S) Hull, Gloria T. "A Note on the Poetic Technique of
Gwendolyn Brooks," CLA Journal 19 (December 1975): 280-285.

081.89(S) Hull, Gloria T. and Gallagher, Posey. "An
Interview with Gwendolyn Brooks." CLA Journal 21 (September
1977): 19-40.

081.90(S) Jaffee, Dan. "Gwendolyn Brooks: An Appreciation
From the White Suburbs." In BIGSBY. Vol. 2, 89-98.

081.91(S) Kent, George E. "Gwendolyn Brooks: A Portrait, In
Part, of the Artist As a Young Girl and Apprentice Writer."
Callaloo 2 (October 1979): 74.

081.92(S) Kent, George E. "The Poetry of Gwendolyn Brooks."
Black World 2 (September 1971): 30-43; 2 (October 1971): 36-
48.

081.93(S) Kent, George E. "The World of Gwendolyn Brooks."
Black Books Bulletin 2 (Spring 1974): 28-29.

081.94(S) Kunitz, Stanley. "Bronze by Gold." Poetry 76
(1950): 52-56.

081.95(S) Loff, John. "To Be a Black Woman in the Poetry of
Gwendolyn Brooks." Master's Thesis, University of Wisconsin
at Stevens Point, 1972.

081.96(S) Loff, Jon N. "Gwendolyn Brooks: A Bibliography."
CLA Journal 17 (September 1973): 21-32.

081.97(S) McClauren, Irma. "Old Age Sequence (for Gwendolyn
Brooks)." Black American Literature Forum 21 (3): 252 (Fall
1987).

081.98(S) McCluskey, John. "In the Mecca." Studies in Black
Literature 4 (Autumn 1973): 25-30.

081.99(S) Madhubuti, Haki. "The Achievement of Gwendolyn
Brooks." Black Scholar 3 (Summer 1972): 36-48.

081.100(S) Madhubuti, Haki R. Say That the River Turns: The
Impact of Gwendolyn Brooks. Chicago: Third World Press,
1987.

081.101(S) Madhubuti, Safisha N. "Focus on Form in
Gwendolyn Brooks." Black Books Bulletin 2 (Spring 1974): 24-
27.

081.102(S) Mahoney, Heidi L. "Selected Checklist of
Materials By and About Gwendolyn Brooks." Negro American
Literature Forum 8 (1974): 210-211.

081.103(S) Melhem, D.H. Gwendolyn Brooks: Poetry and the
Heroic Voice. Lexington, KY: University of Kentucky Press,
1987.

081.104(S) Melhem, D.H. "Gwendolyn Brooks: The Heroic Voice
of Prophecy." Studies in Black Literature (Spring 1977): 1-
3.

081.105(S) Miller, Jeanne-Marie A. "Poet Laureate of
Bronzeville, U.S.A." Freedomways 10 (1970): 63-75.

081.106(S) Miller, R. Baxter. "Define the Whirlwind: In the
Mecca -Urban Setting, Shifting Narrator and Redemptive
Vision." Obsidian 4 (Spring 1978): 19-31.

081.107(S) Miller, R. Baxter. Langston Hughes and Gwendolyn
Brooks: A Reference Guide. Boston: G.K. Hall, 1978.

081.108(S) Mootry, Maria K. " 'Chocolate Mabbie' and 'Pearl May Lee': Gwendolyn Brooks and the Ballad Tradition." CLA Journal 30 (March 1987): 278-293.

081.109(S) Mootry, Maria K. and Smith, Gary, eds. A Life Distilled: Gwendolyn Brooks, Her Poetry and Fiction. Urbana, IL: University of Illinois Press, 1987.

081.110(S) O'Neale, Sondra. "Race, Sex and Self: Aspects of 'Bildung' in Select Novels by Black American Women Novelists." Melus 9 (4): 25-37 (Winter 1982).

081.111(S) Park, Sue S. "A Study in Tension: Gwendolyn Brooks's 'The Chicago Defender Sends a Man to Little Rock'." Black American Literature Forum 2 (Spring 1977): 32-34.

081.112(S) Park, Sue S. "Social Themes in the Poetry of Gwendolyn Brooks." Ph. D. Dissertation, University of Illinois (Champaigne-Urbana), 1972

081.113(S) Rivers, Conrad Kent. "Poetry of Gwendolyn Brooks." Negro Digest 13 (June 1964): 67-69.

081.114(S) Shands, Annette Oliver. "Gwendolyn Brooks As Novelist." Black World (June 1973): 22-30.

081.115(S) Shaw, Harry. Gwendolyn Brooks. Boston: Twayne, 1980.

081.116(S) Shaw, Harry. "Gwendolyn Brooks: A Critical Study." Ph.D. dissertation, University of Illinois, Champagne-Urbana.

081.117(S) Smith, Gary. "Gwendolyn Brooks's A Street in Bronzeville: The Harlem Renaissance and the Mythologies of Black Women." Melus 10 (3): 33-46 (Fall 1983).

081.118(S) Stavros, George. "An Interview with Gwendolyn Brooks." Contemporary Literary 12 (Winter 1970): 1-20.

081.119(S) Stetson, Erlene. "Songs After Sunset 1935-1936: The Unpublished Poetry of Gwendolyn Elibibeth Brooks." CLA Journal 7 (September 1980): 87-96.

081.120(S) Struthers, Ann. "Gwendolyn Brooks' Children." Iowa English Bulletin: Yearbook 29 (1): 15-16 (1979).

081.121(S) Washington, Mary Helen. "Taming All That Anger Down: Rage and Silence in Gwendolyn Brooks' Maud Martha." Massachusetts Review 24 (2): 453-466 (Summer 1983).

081.122(S) Werner, Craig. "Gwendolyn Brooks: Tradition in Black and White." Minority Voices 1 (2): 27-38 (Fall 1977).

081.123(S) Whitaker, Charles. "A Poet for All Ages." Ebony 42 (June 1987): 154.

081.124(S) Williams, Gladys Margaret. "Gwendolyn Brooks's Way with the Sonnet." CLA Journal 26 (December 1982): 215-240.

1988-1991 Supplement

A081.125 "Henry Dumas: Perceptiveness and Zeal." Black American Literature Forum 22 (Summer 1988): 177.

A081.126 "Poems." Black Scholar 19 (July/August-September/October 1988): 6.

A081.127 "To Those of My Sisters Who Kept Their Naturals." Essence 19 (February 1989): 129. Poem.

Secondary Sources

A081.128(S) Faust, Naomi F. "Ms. Gwendolyn Brooks." Essence 19 (July 1988): 143.

A081.129(S) Jones, Marsha. "Poetry in Motion: The Prose of Gwendolyn Brooks." about...time 16 (June 1988): 8.

A081.130(S) Kent, George E. A Life of Gwendolyn Brooks. Lexington, KY: University Press of Kentucky, 1989.

082. BROOKS, HELEN MORGAN.

082.1 Against Whatever Sky. Provincetown, MA: Advocate Press, 1956.

083. BROOKS, NANCY.

083.1 "Universal Thought." Essence 3 (September 1972): 6.

084. BROWN, BETH.

084.1 "Ancestors." Obsidian 6 (1-2): 206 (Spring-Summer 1980).

084.2 "Blind Music." Black Scholar 11 (5): 72 (May-June 1980).

084.3 "Daily Poems." Obsidian 4 (3): 84-88 (Winter 1978).

084.4 "Eulogy for James Weldon Johnson." Callaloo 9 (1): 16-17 (Winter 1986).

084.5 "Father." <u>Callaloo</u> 9 (1): 15 (Winter 1986).

084.6 "For Whom It Is Too Late Now." <u>Obsidian</u> 4 (3): 83
(Winter 1978).

084.7 "House Arrest." <u>Obsidian</u> 6 (1-2): 205 (Spring-Summer
1980).

084.8 <u>Lightyears: Poems,1973-1876</u>. Detroit: Lotus Press,
1982.

084.9 "Sisters." <u>Black Scholar</u> 11 (5): 73 (May-June 1980).

084.10 "Sunshine and the Troubadors." <u>Black Scholar</u> 9
(July-August 1978): 11-17.

084.11 "Winter's End." <u>Obsidian</u> 6 (1-2): 204 (Spring-Summer
1980).

085. BROWN, CHARLOTTE HAWKINS (1883-1961).

085.1 <u>The Correct Thing To Do, To Say, To Wear</u>. Boston:
Christopher Publishing House, 1941.

085.2 <u>"Mammy": An Appeal to the Heart of the South</u>. Boston:
Pilgrim Press, 1919. Short fiction.

Secondary Sources

085.3(S) Daniel, Sadie Iola. <u>Women Builders</u>. Washington,
DC: Associated Publishers, 1931.

085.4(S) Marteena, Constance H. <u>The Lengthening Shadow of a
Woman: A Biography of Charlotte Hawkins Brown</u>. New York:
Exposition Press, 1977.

085.5(S) Shockley, Ann Allen. "Charlotte Hawkins Brown."
In SHOCKLEY, pp. 363-373.

085.6(S) Smith, Sandra N. and West, Earl H. "Charlotte
Hawkins Brown." <u>Journal of Negro History</u> 51 (Summer 1982):
191-206.

085.7(S) Sulaiman, Madeline. "Charlotte Hawkins Brown:
Pushing for Academic Excellence." <u>about... time</u> 10
(November 1982): 18-20.

085.8(S) Tillman, Elvena. "Charlotte Hawkins Brown." In
LOGAN & WINSTON.

085.9(S) White, Deborah Gray. <u>Ar'n't I a Woman? Female
Slaves in the Plantation South</u>. New York: W. W. Norton,
1985.

086.   BROWN, HALLIE QUINN (1845?-1949).

086.1   Homespun Heroines and Other Women of Distinction.
Xenia, OH: Aldine, 1926. NY: Oxford University Press, 1988.

087.   BROWN, JANE.

087.1   Narrative of the Life of Jane Brown and Her Two
Children. n.p., 1860.

088.   BROWN, JANET.

088.1   Feminist Drama: Definitions and Critical Analysis.
Metuchen, NJ: Scarecrow Press, 1979.

089.   BROWN, LINDA JEAN.

089.1   Kiwi. Author, 1978.

089.2   The Rainbow River. New York: Iridian, 1980.

089.3   To Be More Real. Author, 1976.

090.   BROWN, MATTYE JEANETTE.

090.1   Original Poems and Biblical Information. Nashville,
TN: Author, 1945.

090.2   The Reign of Terror. New York: Vantage Press, 1962.
Novel.

091.   BROWN, WILMETTE.

091.1   "Kwacha." Black World 24 (February 1975): 53.

091.2   "Message." Black World 24 (November 1974): 46.

091.3   "Voices for the Diaspora Home." Black World 24
(November 1974): 24.

092. BROWN-GUILLORY, ELIZABETH (1954-).

092.1 "Alice Childress: A Pioneering Spirit." Sage 4 (1):
66-68 (Spring 1987).

092.2 "Black Women Playwrights: Exorcising Myths." Phylon
48 (Fall 1987): 229.

092.3 "Images of Blacks in Plays by Black Women." Phylon 47
(3): 230-237 (September 1986). African-American playwrights.

092.4 Mam Phillis. In BROWN-GUILLORY.

092.5 Their Place on the Stage: Black Women Playwrights in
America. Westport, CT: Greenwood Press, 1988. A view of the
work of nine black women playwrights.

092.6 Wines in the Wilderness: Plays by African-American
Women from the Harlem Renaissance to the Present. Westport,
CT: Greenwood Press, 1990. Anthology edited by Brown-
Guillory.

093. BROWNING, ALICE C. (1907-).

093.1 Black 'n' Blue. Chicago: Browning Publications, 1973.

                    Secondary Sources

093.2(S) Eddings, H.S. "Essence Woman: Alice C. Browning."
Essence 8 (May 1977): 6.

094. BURGESS, MARIE LOUISE.

094.1 Ave Maria. Boston: Press of the Monthly Review, 1895.
Fiction.

                    Secondary Sources

094.2(S) Shockley, Ann Allen. "Marie Louise Burgess." In
SHOCKLEY, pp. 242-247.

095. BURKE, INEZ M.

095.1 <u>Two Races: A Pageant</u>. In RICHARDSON, pp. 295-302.
One act drama.

096. BURKS, EARLINE.

096.1 "No Time for Getting Up."<u>Essence</u> 8 (September 1977):
56-57.

097. BURRILL, MARY.

097.1 "They That Sit in Darkness." <u>Birth Control Review</u>
(September 1919). One act drama.

Secondary Sources

097.2(S) Abramson, Doris E. "Angelina Weld Grimke, Mary T.
Burrill, Georgia Douglas Johnson, and Marita O. Bonner: An
Analysis of Their Plays." <u>Sage</u> 2 (1): 9-13 (Spring 1985).

098. BURROUGHS, MARGARET TAYLOR G. (1917-).

098.1 <u>Africa, My Africa!</u> Chicago: DuSable Museum Press,
1970.

098.2 "Black Pride." "Everybody But Me." "Only in This
Way." "To Soulfolk." In STETSON, pp. 118-122.

098.3 <u>Did You Feed My Cow?</u> New York: Thomas Crowell, 1955.
rev. ed. Chicago: Follett, 1969.

098.4 "Eric Was Eric; Short Story" <u>Negro Digest</u> 13
(November 1963): 54-63.

098.5 "He Will Always Be a Chicago Artist to Me."
<u>Freedomways</u> 11 (1980): 151-154.

098.6 "Integration of Learning Materials...Now!" <u>Negro
Digest</u> 15 (March 1966): 30-34.

098.7 <u>Jasper the Drummin' Boy</u>. New York: Viking Press,
1947. Rev ed. Chicago: Follett, 1970.

098.8 "Party in Hyde Park; Short Story." <u>Negro Digest</u> 12
(December 1962): 53-60.

098.9 " 'Strawberry Blonde,' That Is." <u>Black World</u> 19 (July
1970): 78-81.

098.10 <u>What Shall I Tell My Children Who Are Black?</u>
Chicago: Museum of African American History Press, 1968.

098.11 <u>Whip Me Whop Me Pudding and Other Stories of Riley</u>
<u>and His Fabulous Friends</u>. Praga Press, 1966. Chicago:
DuSable Museum, n.d.

099. BURROUGHS, NANNIE HELEN (1879-1961).

099.1 <u>The Slabtown District Convention: A Comedy in One Act</u>.
11th ed. Washington, DC: n.p., 1942.

100. BURT, DELLA (1944-).

100.1 "A Little Girl's Dream World." "On the Death of Lisa
Lyman." "Spirit Flowers." In STETSON.

101. BURTON, ANNIE LOUISE.

101.1 <u>Memoirs of Childhood's Slavery Days</u>. n.p., 1909.

102. BUSH, OLIVIA WARD (1869-1944).

102.1 <u>Driftwood</u>. Providence, RI: Atlantic Printing Company,
1914. Poetry.

102.2 <u>Memories of Calvary: An Easter Sketch</u>. Philadelphia:
A.M.E. Book Concern, 1915. One act drama.

102.3 <u>Original Poems</u>. Providence, RI: Press of Louis A.
Basinet, 1899.

Secondary Sources

102.4(S) Guillaume, Bernice F. "Character Names in <u>Indian</u>
<u>Trails</u> by Olivia Ward Bush (Banks): Clues to Afro
Assimilation into Long Island's Native Americans." <u>Afro-</u>
<u>Americans in New York Life and History</u> 10 (2): 45-53 (July
1986).

102.5(S) Guillaume, Bernice F. "The Life and Work of Olivia
Ward Bush (Banks), 1869-1944." Doctoral dissertation, Tulane
University, 1983.

102.6(S) Guillaume, Bernice F. "Olivia Ward Bush: Factors
Shaping the Social and Cultural Outlook of a Nineteenth-
Century Writer." Negro History Bulletin 43 (April-June,
1980): 32-34.

102.7(S) Shockley, Ann Allen. "Olivia Ward Bush Banks." In
SHOCKLEY, pp. 341-345.

103. BUTLER, ANNA LAND (1901-).

103.1 Album of Love Letters -- Unsent. Vol. 1: Morning 'Til
Noon. New York: Margent Press, 1952. Poetry.

103.2 High Noon. Charleston, IL: Prairie Press Books, 1971.
Poetry.

103.3 Touch Stone. Provincetown, MA: Advocate Press, 1961.
Poetry.

104. BUTLER, OCTAVIA ESTELLE (1947-).

104.1 Clay's Ark. New York: St. Martin's, 1984.

104.2 Dawn: Xenogenesis. New York: Warner Books, 1987.

104.3 "Future Forum." Future Life 17 (March 1980): 60.

104.4 Kindred. New York: Doubleday, 1979.

104.5 "Lost Races of Science Fiction." Transmission (Summer
1980): 17-18.

104.6 Mind of My Mind. New York: Doubleday, 1977.

104.7 Patternmaster. New York: Doubleday, 1976.

104.8 "Speech Sounds." Isaac Asimov's Science Fiction
Magazine 7 (December 1983): 26-40.

104.9 Survivor. New York: Doubleday, 1978.

104.10 Wild Seed. New York: Doubleday, 1980.

104.11 "Wild Seed." Essence 11 (January 1981): 86-87.
Excerpt.

                    Secondary Sources

104.12(S) Beal, Francis M. "Black Women and the Science
Fiction Genre." Black Scholar 17 (2): 14-18 (March-April
1986).

104.13(S) Carter, Patricia. "Word Star."   Essence 19
(September 1987): 31.

104.14(S) Govan, Sandra Y. "Connections, Links and Extended
Networks: Patterns in Octavia Butler's Science Fiction."
Black American Literature Forum 18 (Summer 1984): 82-87.

104.15(S) Mixon, Veronica. "Futurist Woman: Octavia
Butler." Essence 9 (April 1979): 12.

104.16(S) O'Connor, Margaret Anne. "Octavia E. Butler." In
DAVIS & HARRIS, pp.35-41.

104.17(S) Salvaggio, Ruth. "Octavia Butler and the Black
Science Fiction Heroine." Black American Literature Forum 18
(Summer 1984): 8-81.

104.18(S) Weixlmann, Joe. "An Octavia Butler Bibliography."
Black American Literature Forum 18 (Summer 1984): 88-89.

104.19(S) Williams, Sherley Anne. "Sherley Anne Williams on
Octavia E. Butler." Ms. 14 (March 1986): 70.

1988-1991 Supplement

A104.20 Adulthood Rites: Xenogenesis. New York: Warner
Books, 1988.

A104.21 "Birth of a Writer." Essence 20 (May 1989): 74.

A104.22 Imago. New York: Warner Books, 1989.

105. BYRD, STEPHANIE.

105.1 A Distant Footstep on the Plain. Author, 1981.

105.2 Twenty-five Years of Malcontent. Boston: Good Gay
Poets, 1976.

106. BYRON, CHERYL.

106.1 Womanwise. New York: Shamal Press, 1979.

Cade, Toni, SEE 42. BAMBARA, TONI CADE.

107.   CAIN, JOHNNIE MAE (1940-).

107.1   <u>Do You Remember...</u>   Philadelphia: Dorrance & Company,
1972.   Poetry.

107.2   <u>White Bastards</u>.   New York: Vantage Press, 1973.
Novel.

108.   CAINE, MARCELLA.

108.1   "Eulogy: Martin Luther King, Jr.: Poem"   <u>Negro Digest</u>
17 (August 1968): 34.

108.2   "Song of Patience: Poem."   <u>Negro Digest</u> 15 (January
1966): 58.

109.   CAPDEVILLE, ANNEYYA ELAM (1925-).

109.1   <u>My Soul Sings: Lyrics</u>.   Washington, DC: Author, 1978.

110.   CAREW, JAN.

110.1   <u>Green Winter</u>.   New York: Stein and Day, 1965.

110.2   <u>The Last Barbarian</u>.   London: Secker & Warburg, 1961.

Carmen, Marilyn   **SEE**   206.   ESHE, AISHA.

111.   CARPENTER, PANDOURA.

111.1   <u>Deal with It</u>!   Denver: She Wolf, 1979.

112.   CARRIGAN, NETTIE W.

112.1   <u>Rhymes and Jingles for the Children's Hour</u>.   Boston:
Christopher Publishing House, 1940.

113.   CARTER, LILLIE BLAND (1919-).

113.1 Whispering Leaves. Toledo, OH: Marcella's
Stenographic Service, 1953.

113.2 "Longest Journey." Negro History Bulletin 36 (May
1973): 106.

113.3 "What Happened to Dreams." Negro History Bulletin 36
(May 1973): 107.

114.   CASSELLE, CORENE FLOWERETTE (1943-).

114.1 Country of the Black People. Chicago: Third World
Press, n.d. Children's stories.

115.   CHAMBERS, MARY SUSAN.

115.1 "Baby Dollies." "Black and White Breakfast."
"Explication." "International House, 1950." "Neon Lights."
"Vignettes, USA: Poems." Midwest Journal 7 (Fall 1955): 235-
240.

116.   CHANEY, BETTY NORWOOD.

116.1 "Matter of Breaking Free." Essence 8 (May 1977): 60-
61.

117.   CHAPMAN, CONSTANCE.

117.1 "For Monte." Essence 15 (November 1984): 45.

118.   CHASE-RIBOUD, BARBARA (1939-).

118.1 Echo of Lions. New York: William Morrow, 1989.

118.2 From Memphis & Peking. New York: Random House, 1974.

118.3 "Life and Death of Josephine Baker." Essence 6
(February 1976): 36-37.

118.4 <u>Portrait of a Nude Woman as Cleopatra</u>. New York: William Morrow, 1987.

118.5 <u>Sally Hemings</u>. New York: Viking Press, 1979.

118.6 <u>Valide: A Novel of the Harem</u>. New York: William Morrow, 1986.

118.7 "Why Paris." <u>Essence</u> 18 (October 1987): 65.

                    Secondary Sources

118.8(S) McHenry, Susan. "Sally Hemings: A Key to Our National Identity" [an interview with Barbara Chase-Riboud]. <u>Ms</u>. (October 1980): 35-40.

118.9(S) Wilson, Judith. "Barbara Chase-Riboud: Sculpting Our History." <u>Essence</u> (December 1979): 12-13.

119. CHERRY, ELLEN.

119.1 "Hope." <u>Black World</u> 21 (September 1972): 65

119.2 "In the Groves." <u>Black World</u> 24 (September 1975): 78.

119.3 "Last/Rites: For Mehalia." <u>Black World</u> 21 (September 1972): 66.

Chesimard, Joanne **SEE** 566. SHAKUR, ASSATA.

120. CHILDRESS, ALICE (1920-).

120.1 <u>Black Scenes: Collection of Scenes from Plays Written by Black People about Black Experience</u>. New York: Doubleday, 1971. Edited by Childress and includes the editor's work.

120.2 "Black Writer's Views on Literary Lions and Values." <u>Negro Digest</u> 17 (January 1968): 36.

120.3 "Florence: A One Act Drama." <u>Masses and Mainstream</u> 3 (October 1950): 34-47.

120.4 "For a Negro Theatre." <u>Masses and Mainstream</u> 4 (February 1951): 61-64.

120.5 "The Health Card." "I Go to a Funeral." In CLARKE.

120.6 <u>A Hero Ain't Nothin' But a Sandwich</u>. New York: Coward, 1973. For children and young adults.

120.7 Let's Hear It for the Queen. New York: Coward, 1979.
Children's drama.

120.8 Like One of the Family. Atlanta: Independence
Publishers, 1956.

120.9 Many Closets. New York: Coward, 1987.

120.10 "Mojo: A Black Love Story." Black World 20 (April
1971): 54-82. New York: Dramatists Play Service, 1971.
Drama.

120.11 "A Negro Playwright Speaks Her Mind." Freedomways 6
(Winter 1966): 14-19. Essay

120.12 "The Negro Woman in American Literature."
Freedomways 6 (Winter 1966): 14-19.

120.13 Rainbow Jordan. New York: Coward, 1980. New York:
Putnam Publishing Group, 1981. Children's stories.

120.14 A Short Walk. New York: Coward, 1979. New York: Avon
Books, 1981.

120.15 "The Soul Man." Essence 2 (October 1971): 68-69.

120.16 String. New York: Dramatists Play Service, 1969.
Drama.

120.17 Wedding Band: A Love/Hate Story in Black and White.
New York: Samuel French, 1973. Drama.

120.18 When the Rattlesnake Sounds. New York: Coward, 1975.
Drama.

120.19 "Why Talk About That?" Negro Digest 14 (April 1967):
17.

120.20 Wine in the Wilderness. New York: Dramatists Play
Service, 1969. Drama.

120.21 "The World on a Hill." In PLAYS. One act drama.

Secondary Sources

120.22(S) Abramson, Doris E. Negro Playwrights in the
American Theater, 1925-1959. New York: Columbia University
Press, 1969. Alice Childress considered pp. 188-204.

120.23(S) Austin, Gayle. "Alice Childress: Black Woman
Playwright as Feminist Critic." Southern Quarterly 25 (3):
52-62 (Spring 1987).

120.24(S) Brown, Elizabeth. "Six Female Black Playwrights:
Images Of Blacks in Plays by Lorraine Hansberry, Alice
Childress, Sonia Sanchez, Barbara Molette, Martie Charles and

Ntozake Shange." Ph. D. dissertation, Florida State University, 1980.

120.25(S) Brown-Guillory, Elizabeth. "Alice Childress: A Pioneering Spirit." Sage 4 (1): 66-68 (Spring 1987).

120.26(S) Curb, Rosemary. "Alice Childress." In CURB, pp. 118-124.

120.27(S) Curb, Rosemary. "An Unfashionable Tragedy of American Racism: Alice Childress' Wedding Band." MELUS 7 (Winter 1980): 57-68.

120.28(S) Evans, Donald. "Bring It All Back Home." Black World 20 (February 1971): 41-45.

120.29(S) Harris, Trudier. "Alice Childress." In DAVIS & HARRIS, 1985, pp. 66-79.

120.30(S) Harris, Trudier. " 'I Wish I Was a Poet': The Character as Artist in Alice Childress's Like One of the Family." Black American Literature Forum 14 (Spring 1980): 24-30.

120.31(S) Hatch, James V. Black Theater, USA: Forty-Five Plays by American Negroes, 1847-1974. New York: Free Press, 1974.

120.32(S) Hay, Samuel A. "Alice Childress's Dramatic Structure." In EVANS, pp. 117-128.

120.33(S) Holliday, Polly. "I Remember Alice Childress." Southern Quarterly 25 (3): 63-65 (Spring 1987).

120.34(S) Killens, John Oliver. "The Literary Genius of Alice Childress." In EVANS, pp. 129-133.

120.35(S) Patterson, Lindsay, ed. Black Theater: A 20th Century Collection of the Work of Its Best Playwrights. New York: Dodd, Mead, 1971.

1988-1991 Supplement

A120.36 Those Other People. NY: Putnam, 1989.

121. CHRISTIAN, ROBIN.

121.1 Lady, These Are for You. New York: Author, 1978.

122. CLARK, CHINA DEBRA (1950-).

122.1 "Perfection in Black." <u>Scripts</u> 1 (May 1972): 81-85.
Drama.

123. CLARK, MAZIE EARHART.

123.1 <u>Garden of Memories</u>. Cincinnati: Eaton Publishing
Company, 1932. Poetry.

123.2 <u>Life's Sunshine and Shadows</u>. Cincinnati: Eaton
Publishing Company, 1940. Poetry.

123.3 <u>Lyrics of Love, Loyalty and Devotion</u>. Cincinnati:
Eaton Publishing Company, 1935.

124. CLARKE, CHERYL.

124.1 "Bulletin." <u>Black Scholar</u> 19 (July/August-September-
October 1988): 28. Poem.

124.2 <u>Living as a Lesbian: Poetry</u>. Ithaca, NY: Firebrand,
1986.

124.3 <u>Narratives: Poems in the Tradition of Black Women</u>.
New York: Kitchen Table: Women of Color, 1982.

Secondary Sources

124.4(S) Hernton, Calvin C. "Black Women Poets: The Oral
Tradition." In HERNTON, pp. 119-155.

125. CLEAGE, PEARL (1948-).

125.1 "Bernice King Carries It On." <u>Essence</u> 19 (January
1989): 69.

125.2 "The Brass Bed." <u>Catalyst</u> (Winter 1988): 19.

125.3 <u>Brass Bed and Other Stories</u>. Chicago: Third World
Press, 1989.

125.4 "Hospice, a Play in One Act." <u>Callaloo</u> 10 (1): 120-
159 (Winter 1987).

125.5 "In My Solitude." <u>Essence</u> 19 (February 1989): 56.

125.6 "In the Time Before Men Came." <u>Catalyst</u> (Winter
1989): 13.

125.7 "Is Your Life Making You Sick?" Essence 21 (June 1990): 55.

125.8 "Let the Church Say Amen." Essence 20 (April 1990):69.

125.9 "Never Say Never." Essence 21 (October 1990): 91.

125.10 "Remembering James Baldwin." Catalyst (Winter 1988): 113.

125.11 "The Ritual Record." Catalyst (Summer 1988): 34.

SEE ALSO 418. LOMAX, PEARL CLEAGE.

Clemmons, Carole G. **SEE** 267. GREGORY, CAROLE CLEMMONS.

126. CLEMONS, DONNA L.

126.1 "Custom-Made Love." Essence 17 (January 1987): 110.

127. CLEVELAND, ODESSA.

127.1 "Life." Black American Literature Forum 21 (4): 450 (Winter 1987).

127.2 "Lifeless Heart." Black American Literature Forum 20 (3): 314 (Fall 1986).

128. CLIFF, MICHELLE.

128.1 Abeng. Trumansburg, NY: The Crossing Press, 1984. New York: Dutton, 1990. Novel.

128.2 Bodies of Water. New York: Dutton, 1990.

128.3 Claiming an Identity They Taught Me to Despise. Watertown, MA: Persephone, 1980. Poetry

128.4 " 'I Found God in Myself and I loved Her/I Loved Her Fiercely': More Thoughts on the Work of Black Women Artists." Journal of Feminist Studies in Religion 2 (1986): 7-39.

128.5 The Land of Look Behind: Poetry and Prose by Michelle Cliff. Ithaca, New York: Firebrand, 1985.

128.6 No Telephone to Heaven. New York: Dutton, 1987.
Novel

128.7 "Travel Notes." Iowa Review 12 (2-3): 32-35 (1981).

128.8 The Winner Names the Age: A Collection of Writings by
Lillian Smith. New York: W. W. Norton, 1978.

129. CLIFFORD, CARRIE WILLIAMS (1882-1958).

129.1 "The Black Draftee from Dixie." In STETSON, pp. 82-
83.

129.2 Race Rhymes. Washington, DC: R.L. Pendleton, 1911.
Poetry.

129.3 The Widening Light. Boston: Walter Reid Company,
1922. New ed. New York: Thomas Crowell, 1971. Poetry.

130. CLIFTON, LUCILLE (1936-).

130.1 "Africa." Black World 19 (August 1970): 82.

130.2 All Us Come Cross the Water. New York: Holt, Rinehart
& Winston, 1973.

130.3 Amifika. New York: Dutton, 1977.

130.4 "Apology (To the Panthers) Poem" Black World 19
(August 1970): 82.

130.5 The Black BC's. New York: Dutton, 1970.

130.6 The Boy Who Didn't Believe in Spring. New York:
Dutton, 1973.

130.7 "Christmas is Something Else." House and Garden 136
(December 1969): 70-71.

130.8 Don't You Remember? New York: Dutton, 1973.

130.9 "The End of Love is Death, the End of Death is Love.
Atlantic 227 (March 1971): 65-67.

130.10 Everett Anderson's Christmas Coming. New York: Holt,
Rinehart & Winston, 1971.

130.11 Everett Anderson's Friend. New York: Holt, Rinehart
& Winston, 1976.

130.12 Everett Anderson's Goodbye. New York: Holt, Rinehart
& Winston, 1983.

130.13 <u>Everett Anderson's Nine Month Long</u>. New York: Holt, Rinehart & Winston, 1978.

130.14 <u>Everett Anderson's 1-2-3</u>. New York: Holt, Rinehart & Winston, 1977.

130.15 <u>Everett Anderson's Year</u>. New York: Holt, Rinehart & Winston, 1974.

130.16 <u>Generations</u>. New York: Random House, 1976.

130.17 <u>Good, Says Jerome</u>. New York: Dutton, 1973.

130.18 <u>Good News about the Earth</u>. New York: Random House, 1972.

130.19 <u>Good Times: Poems</u>. New York: Random House, 1969.

130.20 <u>Good Woman: Poems and Memoir (1969-1980)</u>. New York: BOA Editions, 1987.

130.21 "Harriet." <u>Essence</u> 11 (May 1980): 168.

130.22 "If I Don't Know My Last Name, What is the Meaning of My First? <u>Roots</u>, the Saga of an American Family." <u>Ms.</u> 5 (February 1977): 45.

130.23 "It's All in the Game." <u>Negro Digest</u> 15 (August 1966): 18-19.

130.24 "Leanna's Poem." <u>Essence</u> 10 (December 1979): 20.

130.25 "Listen Children." <u>Essence</u> 14 (October 1983): 88.

130.26 <u>The Lucky Stone</u>. New York: Delacorte Press, 1979.

130.27 "The Magic Mama." <u>Redbook</u> 134 (November 1969): 88-89.

130.28 "My Boys." <u>Essence</u> 10 (December 1979): 20.

130.29 <u>My Brother Fine with Me</u>. New York: Holt, Rinehart & Winston, 1975.

130.30 "My Dream About the Cows." "My Dream About Time." <u>Virginia Quarterly Review</u> 58 (4): 687 (Autumn 1982).

130.31 <u>My Friend Jacob</u>. New York: Dutton, 1980.

130.32 <u>Next: New Poems</u>. New York: BOA Editions, 1987.

130.33 <u>An Ordinary Woman</u>. New York: Random House, 1974.

130.34 "Poem." <u>Black World</u> 19 (August 1970): 82.

130.35 "Sisters (for Elaine Philip on Her Birthday." <u>Essence</u> 3 (May 1972): 26; 11 (May 1980): 102.

130.36 <u>Some of the Days of Everett Anderson</u>. New York:
Holt, Rinehart & Winston, 1969.

130.37 <u>Sonora Beautiful</u>. New York: Dutton, 1981.

130.38 "There is a Girl Inside." <u>American Poetry Review</u> 6
(1): 21 (January-February 1977).

130.39 <u>Three Wishes</u>. New York: Viking Press, 1976.

130.40 <u>The Times They Used to Be</u>. New York: Holt, Rinehart
& Winston, 1974.

130.41 <u>Two-Headed Woman</u>. Amherst, MA: University of
Massachusetts, 1980.

130.42 "Untitled." <u>Essence</u> 3 (May 1972): 26.

130.43 "We Are the Grapevine." <u>Essence</u> 16 (May 1985): 129.

130.44 "We Know This Place." <u>Essence</u> 7 (July 1976).

130.45 <u>My Friend Jacob</u>. New York: Dutton, 1980. Joint
Author: Thomas DiGrazia.

                    Secondary Sources

130.46(S) Baughman, Ronald. "Lucille Clifton." In
GREINER, pp. 132-136.

130.47(S) Bryant, Thelma. "A Conversation with Lucille
Clifton." <u>Sage</u> 2 (1): 52 (Spring 1985).

130.48(S) Madhubuti, Haki. "Lucille Clifton: Warm Water,
Greased Legs, and Dangerous Poetry." In EVANS, pp. 150-160.

130.49(S) Peppers, Wallace R. "Lucille Clifton." In
HARRIS & DAVIS, pp. 55-60.

130.50(S) Scarupa, Harriet Jackson. "Lucille Clifton:
Making the World 'Poem Up'." <u>Ms</u>. 5 (October 1976): 118.

                    1988-1991 Supplement

A130.51 "Eyes." <u>Callaloo</u> 12 (Spring 1989): 379. Poem.

A130.52 "If Our Grandchild Be a Girl." <u>Essence</u> 19 (January
1989):158. Poem.

A130.53 "Letter to Fred." <u>Essence</u> 20 (November 1989): 65.

A130.54 <u>Ten Oxherding Pictures</u>. Santa Cruz, CA: Moving
Parts Press, 1988.

131. CLINTON, DOROTHY RANDLE.

131.1 The Maddening Scar, a Mystery Novel. Boston:
Christopher Publishing House, 1962.

132. CLINTON, GLORIA.

132.1 Trees Along the Highway. New York: Comet Press Books,
1953. Poetry.

133. CLINTON, MICHELLE T.

133.1 High Blood Pressure. Los Angeles: West End, 1986.

133.2 "Poems." Black Scholar 19 (July/August-
September/October 1988): 44.

134. CLOUD, FLYIN' THUNDA.

134.1 A Small Pain. College Corner, OH: W.I.M., 1984.

135. COBB, ALICE S. (1942-).

135.1 "Angela Davis." "The Searching." In STETSON, pp.
146-147.

135.2 "The Searching." Essence 15 (September 1984): 175.

135.3 "To Erroll Garner." "Untitled." "A Vision." Black
American Literature Forum 13 (4) 149-150 (Winter 1979).

136. COBB, JANICE (1952-).

136.1 Yesterdays: The Poems of Janice Cobb. San Francisco:
Julian Richardson, n.d.

137. COBB, PAMELA (1950-).

137.1 "Gerald Cheatom, 1970." "Listen." "Spirit People."
"Uprising: A Day in the History of Revolutionary Warfare."
Black American Literature Forum 18 (1): 8-9 (Spring 1984).

137.2 Inside the Devil's Mouth: First Poems. Detroit: Lotus
Press, 1975.

138. CODLING, BESS.

138.1 Elegy to X. New York: Amuru, 1973. Two act drama.

138.2 Mama's Crazyhorse Rockin Again. New York: Amuru,
1973. Drama.

139. COLEMAN, WANDA (1946-).

139.1 Art in the Court of the Blue Fag. Santa Barbara, CA:
Black Sparrow Press, 1977.

139.2 "At Vital Statistics." Partisan Review 46 (4): 598
(1979).

139.3 "Beneath the Rubble." Obsidian 6 (1-2): 229-233
(Spring-Summer 1980).

139.4 "Boobi Sykes, an Interview." Callaloo 8 (2): 294-303
(Spring/Summer 1985).

139.5 "Casting Call." Michigan Quarterly Review 25 (3): 97
(Summer 1986).

139.6 "El Hajj Malik El-Shabazz." Black American Literature
Forum 17 (Winter 1983): 175.

139.7 "Emmett Till." Callaloo 9 (2): 295-299 (Spring 1986).

139.8 "Ethiopian in the Fuel Supplies." Black American
Literature Forum 17 (Winter 1983): 176.

139.9 Heavy Daughter Blues: Poems and Stories, 1968-1986.
Santa Barbara, CA: Black Sparrow Press, 1987.

139.10 Imagoes. Santa Barbara, CA: Black Sparrow Press,
1983.

139.11 "Indian Summer." Essence 14 (March 1984): 140.

139.12 "Invitation to a Gunfighter." Michigan Quarterly
Review 25 (3): 535 (Summer 1986).

139.13 "Jerry 1967." Partisan Review 46 (4): 601 (1979).

139.14 "Last Grave at Dimbaza." Black American Literature
Forum 13 (1): 34 (Spring 1979).

139.15 "Lessons." Partisan Review 46 (4): 599 (1979).

139.16 Mad Dog, Black Lady. Santa Barbara, CA: Black
Sparrow Press, 1979.

139.17 "Men Lips." Partisan Review 46 (4): 597 (1979).

139.18 "On That Stuf That Ain't Nevah Been Long Enuff for No
Damn Body." Black American Literature Forum 19 (3): 109
(Fall 1985).

139.19 "Queen of the Sinking Sand." Partisan Review 46 (4):
600 (1979).

139.20 "Somewhere There's an Alley with My Name on It."
Black American Literature Forum 13 (1): 35 (Spring 1979).

139.21 A War of Eyes and Other Stories. Santa Rosa, CA:
Black Sparrow Press, 1988.

139.22 "Watching the Sunset." Negro Digest 19 (February
1970): 53-54.

1988-1991 Supplement

A139.23 "Moving Target." Black American Literature Forum 23
(Summer 1989): 231. Short fiction.

A139.24 "Poems." Black Scholar 19 (July/August-
September/October 1988): 43.

A139.25 "Selected Poems." Black American Literature Forum
23 (Fall 1989): 555.

A139.26 A War of Eyes and Other Stories. Santa Rosa, CA:
Black Sparrow Press, 1988.

Secondary Sources

A139.27(S) Magistrale, Tony. "Doing Battle with the Wolf: A
Critical Introduction to Wanda Coleman's Poetry." Black
American Literature Forum 23 (Fall 1989): 539.

140. COLLIER, EUGENIA (1928-).

140.1 "African Presence in Afro-American Literary
Criticism." Obsidian 6 (3): 30-35 (Winter 1980).

140.2 "Afro-American Writers." Black World 19 (September 1970): 92-93.

140.3 "Ain't Supposed to Die a Natural Death." Black World 21 (April 1972): 79-81.

140.4 "Barbados." Black World 25 (March 1976): 53.

140.5 "Black Phoenix." Black World 19 (September 1970): 77.

140.6 "Black Shows for White Viewers." Freedomways 14 (3): 209-217 (1974).

140.7 "The Closing of the Circle: Movement from Division to Wholeness in Paule Marshall's Fiction." In EVANS, p. 295-315.

140.8 "Dimensions of Alienation in Two Black American and Caribbean Novels." Phylon 43 (March 1982): 46-56.

140.9 "The Endless Journey of an Ex-Colored Man." Phylon 32 (Fourth Quarter, Winter 1971): 365-373.

140.10 "The Four-Way Dilemma of Claude McKay." CLA Journal 15(March 1972): 345-353.

140.11 "Heritage from Harlem." Black World 19 (November 1970): 52-59.

140.12 "I Do Not Marvel, Countee Cullen." CLA Journal 11 (1967): 73-87.

140.13 "James Weldon Johnson: Mirror of Change." Phylon 21 (1960): 351-359.

140.14 "Marigold." Black World 14 (November 1969): 54-62.

140.15 "The Nightmare Truth of an Invisible Man." Black World 20 (December 1970): 12-19.

140.16 "A Pain in His Soul: Simple as Epic Hero." In O'DANIEL.

140.17 "The Phrase Unbearably Repeated." Phylon 25 (1964): 288-296.

140.18 "Sinbad the Cat." Black World 19 (July 1971): 53-55.

140.19 "Some Black and Fettered Women." Black World 21 (November 1971): 41.

140.20 "Sweet Potato Pie." Black World 21 (August 1972): 54-62.

140.21 "Thematic Patterns in Baldwin's Essays." Black World 21 (June 1972): 28-34.

1988-1991 Supplement

A140.22 "Elemental Wisdom in Goodbye, Sweetwater:
Suggestions for Further Study." Black American Literature
Forum 22 (Summer 1988): 192.

A140.23 "Wanderers in the Wilderness." Shooting Star Review
3 (Spring 1989): 24.

141. COLLINS, JUNE L.

141.1 "My Poem." Essence 16 (February 1986): 138.

141.2 "This Woman." Essence 16 (December 1985): 128.

141.3 Untitled Poem. Essence 16 (November 1985): 12.

141.4 Untitled Poem. Essence 17 (July 1986): 126.

Conley, Cynthia. SEE 714. ZUBENA, SISTER.

142. CONNER, NELLIE VICTORIA.

142.1 Essence of Good Perfume. Burbank, CA: Ivan Deach,
Jr., 1940.

143. COOLIDGE, FAY LIDDLE.

143.1 Black is White. New York: Vantage Press, 1956.
Novel.

144. COOPER, AFUA PAM.

144.1 Broken Chains. n.p.: Weelahs Publications, 1983.
Poetry.

144.2 "Untitled 2." Essence 15 (February 1985): 122.

145. COOPER, ANNA JULIA HAYWOOD (1859-1964).

145.1   Charlemagne: Voyage a Jerusalem et a Constantinople.
Paris: Lahure, 1925. Old French and modern French verse.
145.2   Christmas Bells: A One Act Play for Children. n.p.,
n.d. Poetic drama.

145.3   Life and Writings of the Grimke' Family. Washington,
DC: Cooper, 1951.

145.4   The Third Step. n.p, n.d.

145.5   A Voice From the South: By a Black Woman of the South.
Xenia, OH: Aldine, 1892. New York: Oxford University Press,
1988.

                        Secondary Sources

145.6(S)   Chateauvert, Melinda. "The Third Step: Anna Julia
Cooper and Black Education in the District of Columbia, 1910-
1960." Sage (Student Supplement 1988): 7.

145.7(S)   Harley, Sharon. "Anna J. Cooper: A Voice for Black
Women." In HARLEY & TERBORG.

145.8(S)   Hutchinson, Louise Daniel. Anna J. Cooper: A Voice
From the South. Washington, DC: Anacostia Neighborhood
Museum of the Smithsonian Institution by the Smithsonian
Institution Press, 1981

145.9(S)   Majors, Monroe Alphus. Noted Negro Women, Their
Triumphs and Activities. New York: Donohue & Henneberry,
1893.

145.10(S)   Shockley, Ann Allen. "Anna Julia Haywood Cooper."
In SHOCKLEY, pp. 204-224.

146.   COOPER, J. CALIFORNIA.

146.1   Homemade Love. New York: St. Martin's, 1986.

146.2   Matter is Life. New York: Doubleday, 1991.
Collection of short fiction.

146.3   A Piece of Mine. Navarro, CA: Wild Trees, 1984. Short
fiction

146.4   Some Soul to Keep. New York: St. Martin's, 1987.

146.5   "Such Good Friends." Essence 21 (May 1990): 150.
Short fiction.

147.   COOPER, LULA.

147.1 A Murmur of Essence. Wilmington, DE: Author, 1972.

148. CORNWELL, ANITA R.

148.1 "And Save a Round for Kamie Brown." Negro Digest 15 (April 1966): 83-92.

148.2 "Attuned to the Energy: Sonia Sanchez." Essence 10 (July 1979): 10-11. Textual criticism of Sanchez's poetry.

148.3 Black Lesbian in White America. Tallahassee, FL: Naiad, 1983. Addresses, essays and lectures on Black feminism.

148.4 "The Boy." Negro Digest 15 (September 1966): 36-40.

148.5 " Memo to Nellie, the Cullud Maid. Negro Digest 15 (November 1965): 30-32.

148.6 "The Negro Woman: America's Unsung Heroine." Negro Digest 14 (October 1965): 15-18.

148.7 "The Rope on the Steps." Negro Digest 14 (May 1965): 56-68.

148.8 "Sound of Crying." Negro Digest 13 (June 1964): 53-61.

148.9 "Strapped on a Sinking Ship." Negro Digest 15 (May 1966): 32-36.

148.10 "Why Can Never Overcome." Negro Digest 14 (July 1965): 3-6.

149. CORTEZ, JAYNE (1936-).

149.1 "Big Fine Women from Ruleville." Black Collegian 5 (May-June 1979): 90; Essence 11 (May 1980): 103; Essence 19 (february 1989): 150.

149.2 "Black Feathered Mules." Black Scholar 12 (5): 32 (September-October 1981).

149.3 "Black Women Writers Visit Cuba." Black Scholar 16 (4): 61 (July/August 1985).

149.4 "Carolina Kingston." Callaloo 5 (2): 70-71 (1979).

149.5 Coagulations: New and Selected Poems. New York: Thunder's Mouth Press, 1984.

149.6 "Cobra Club." Callaloo 5 (2): 51 (1979).

149.7 "Comparative Literature." Black Scholar 18 (4-5): 17
(July/August/September/October 1987).

149.8 Festivals and Funerals. New York: Bola Press, 1973.
Poetry.

149.9 Firespitter. New York: Bola Press, 1982.

149.10 "Global Inequalities." Black Scholar 18 (4-5): 16-17
(July/August/September/October 1987).

149.11 "Ife Night." Essence 5 (September 1974): 19.

149.12 "I'm Not Saying." Callaloo 5 (2): 118 (1979).

149.13 "In the Morning." Black Scholar 10 (November -
December 1978): 11-12.

149.14 "It Came." Black Scholar 12 (5): 31 (September-
October 1981).

149.15 "Lead." Negro Digest 18 (September 1969): 60.

149.16 "Massive Build Up." Black Scholar 18 (4-5): 16
(July/August/September/October 1987).

149.17 "Mercenaries and Minstrels." Black Scholar 10 (3-4):
10 (November-December 1978).

149.18 Mouth on Paper. New York: Bola Press, 1977.

149.19 "Once Upon a Road." Black Scholar 12 (2): 32
(September-October 1981).

149.20 "Opening Act." Essence 11 (May 1980): 102.

149.21 Pissstained Stairs and the Monkey Man's Ware. New
York: Phrase Text, 1969. Poetry.

149.22 "Pray for the Lovers." Essence 4 (November 1973):
36.

149.23 "Rose Solitude (for Duke Ellington). Essence 8
(March 1978): 70.

149.24 Scarifications. New York: Bola Press, 1973.

149.25 "So Long." Essence 5 (September 1974): 19.

149.26 "So Many Feathers." Black Scholar 10 (November-
December 1978): 10.

149.27 "Stockpiling." UNESCO Courier 35 (November 1982):
10-11.

149.28 "Watch Out." Essence 7 (May 1976): 20.

149.29 "When I Look at Wilfredo Lam's Paintings." <u>Callaloo</u> 9 (1): 26-27 (Winter 1986).

149.30 "You Know." <u>Callaloo</u> 5 (2): 92-93 (1979).

149.31 "Poet's World: Jayne Cortez Discusses Her Life and Her Work." <u>Essence</u> 8(March 1978): 76-79. Alexis De Veaux, joint author.

149.32 <u>Merveilleux Coup de Foudre Poetry of Jayne Cortez and Ted Joans</u>. Paris: Handshake Editions, 1982. Ted Joans, joint author.

Secondary Sources

149.33(S) Baraka, Amini. "Looking for the Lyrics (for Jayne Cortez). <u>Black Scholar</u> 12 (July-August 1981): 54.

149.34(S) Melhem, D. H. "Interview with Jayne Cortez." <u>Greenfield Review</u> 11 (1-2): 31-47 (Summer-Fall 1983).

149.35(S) Simmons, Judy Dothard. "Courage: for Jane Cortez." <u>Essence</u> 11 (April 1981): 19.

149.36(S) Woodson, Jon. "Jayne Cortez." In HARRIS & DAVIS.

1988-1991 Supplement

A149.37 "Briefing." <u>Black Scholar</u> 19 (July/August-September/October 1988): 108. Poem.

A149.38 "For the Poets." <u>Black American Literature Forum</u> 22 (Summer 1988): 200.

150. COTTON, ELLA EARLS.

150.1 <u>Queen of Persia, the Story of Esther Who Saved Her People</u>. New York: Exposition Press, 1960. Novel.

151. COWDERY, MAE V. (1910-).

151.1 <u>We Lift Our Voices and Other Poems</u>. Philadelphia: Alpress, 1936.

152. CRAYTON, PEARL.

152.1 "Cotton Alley." Negro Digest 15 (August 1966): 72-80.

152.2 "The Day the World Came To an End." Negro Digest 14
(August 1965): 54-60.

153. CREWS, STELLA (1950-).

153.1 "Push Pawn." Black Scholar 12 (September 1981): 15.

154. CRUMP, PHYLLIS (1955-).

154.1 Poetic Vibrations. New York: Ja-Mac Publishing
Company, 1971.

155. CULVER, ELOISE CROSBY (1915-1972).

155.1 Christmas Around the World. n.p., n.d.

155.2 Great American Negroes in Verse, 1723-1965.
Washington, DC: Associated Publishers, 1966.

156. CULVER, MARJORIE.

156.1 "Black Tuesday." Negro Digest 17 (August 1968): 28.

156.2 "Homology." Negro Digest 18 (1967): 36.

157. CUMBO, KATTIE M. (1938-).

157.1 "Black Sister." "Ceremony." "Domestics." "I'm a
Dreamer." "The Morning After." "Nocturnal Sounds." In
STETSON, pp. 134-138.

Cuney-Hare, Maud. SEE 287. HARE, MAUD CUNEY.

158. CUTHBERT, MARION VERA (1896-).

158.1 April Grasses. New York: Woman's Press, 1936.
Poetry.

158.2 Songs of Creation. New York: Woman's Press, 1949.
Poetry.

159. DAMALI, NIA   [DENISE BURNETT]

159.1 "Dumas: A Man and His Work." Black American
Literature Forum 22 (Summer): 210.

159.2 "Hello Mister..." "Your Song." Black American
Literature Forum 21 (3): 245-246 (Fall 1987).

159.3 I Am That We May Be. Chicago: Third World Press,
1974.

159.4 "Ikons of Love: Love As Power in Poems by Henry
Dumas." Black American Literature Forum 22 (Summer): 213.
Yakini Kemp, joint author.

160. DANCE, DARYL CUMBER (1938-).

160.1 Folklore from Contemporary Jamaicans. Knoxville, TN:
University of Tennessee Press, 1985.

160.2 Long Gone: The Mecklenburg Six and the Theme of Escape
in Black Folklore. Knoxville, TN: University of Tennessee
Press, 1987.

160.3 Shuckin' and Jivin': Folklore from Contemporary Black
Americans. Bloomington, IN: Indiana University Press, 1978.

160.4 Fifty Caribbean Writers: A Bio-Bibliographical
Critical Sourcebook. Westport, CT: Greenwood Press, 1986.

161. DANIEL, EDDIE-MARY.

161.1 "For a Friend." Phat Mama 1 (1970): 29-48. Drama.

162. DANNER, MARGARET (1915-1984).

162.1 "At Home in Dakar." Negro Digest 15 (July 1966): 90.

162.2 "Black Writer's Views on Literary Lions and Values."
Negro Digest 17 (January 1968): 19.

162.3 Brass Horses. Richmond, VA: Virginia Union
University, 1968. Danner edited the book.

162.4 The Down of a Thistle: Selected Poems, Prose Poems,
and Songs. Waukesha, WI: Country Beautiful, 1976.

162.5 Impressions of African Art Forms. Detroit: Broadside
Press, 1960. Poetry.

162.6 Iron Lace. Millbrook, NY: Kriya Press, 1968. Poetry.

162.7 "Like This Jewel-Studded, Carved from Ivory Leopard."
Negro Digest 17 (September-October 1968): 79.

162.8 "Missing Missionaries." Negro Digest 15 (September
1966): 70.

162.9 "Passive Resistance." Negro Digest 12 (September
1963): 58.

162.10 Regroup. Richmond, VA: Virginia Union University,
1969. Danner edited the book.

162.11 "A Sparrow is a Bird." Negro Digest 10 (August
1961): 59.

162.12 To Flower: Poems. Nashville: Hemphill Press, 1963.

162.13 Poem Counterpoem. Detroit: Broadside Press, 1966.
2d ed, 1969. Dudley Randall, joint editor.

                        Secondary Sources

162.14(S) Aldridge, June E. "Benin to Beale Street: African
Art in the Poetry of Margaret Danner." CLA Journal 31
(December 1987): 201-209.

162.15(S) Aldridge, June E. "Langston Hughes and Margaret
Danner. Langston Hughes Review 3 (2): 7-9 (Fall 1984).

162.16(S) Stetson, Erlene. "Dialectic Voices In the Poetry
of Margaret Esse Danner. In MILLER, pp. 93-103.

163. DAVENPORT, DORIS DIOSA.

163.1 Eat Thunder and Drink Rain: Poems. Los Angeles:
Author, 1982.

163.2 It's Like This. Los Angeles: Author, 1981.

163.3 "Teaching Composition in California with My
Grandmother Near Death in Georgia." Black American
Literature Forum 18 (1): 10 (Spring 1984).

164. DAVENPORT, SARAH B.

164.1 "All Of Us and None Of You." Essence 8 (November
1977): 70-71.

165. DAVIS, CHERYL.

165.1 Imani. Madison, WI: Author, [1969?].

165.2 We All Gonna Go Together. Madison, WI: Author, 1971.

166. DAVIS, GLORIA.

166.1 "Ode to Martin de Porres." Negro Digest 12 (September
1963): 60.

166.2 "The Price." Negro Digest 14 (February 1965): 14.

166.3 "The Wall." Negro Digest 15 (August 1966): 59-62.

166.4 "You Promised." Negro Digest 13 (September 1964): 67.

167. DAVIS, JESSICA THORPE.

167.1 "The Spirit Sweep." Essence 16 (August 1985): 58.

168. DAVIS, THADIOUS M. (1944-).

168.1 "Alice Walker." In KIBLER, pp. 350-358. Includes
biography and bibliography.

168.2 "Alice Walker's Celebration of Self in Southern
Generations." Southern Quarterly 31 (4): 39-53 (Summer
1983). Commentaries on some short fiction.

168.3 "Asante, Te Te." Black American Literature Forum 13
(3): 100 (Fall 1979).

168.4   "Asante Sana, Te Te."   "Double Take at Relais de
l"Espadon."   "Honeysuckle Was the Saddest Odor of All, I
Think."   "It's All the Same."   "Remembering Fannie Lou
Hamer."   In   STETSON, pp.276-280.

168.5   "Black Writers on Adventures of Huckleberry Finn One
Hundred Years Later."   Mark Twain Journal 22 (2): 2-3 (Fall
1984).

168.6   "Cloistered in High School."   Black American
Literature Forum 14 (4): 148 (Winter 1983).

168.7   "Crying in the Wilderness: Legal, Racial, and Moral
Codes in Go down, Moses."   Mississippi College Law Review   4
(Spring 1984): 299-318.

168.8   "Double Take at Relais de l"Espadon."   Black American
Literature Forum 13 (3): 100-101 (Fall 1979).

168.9   "Emergence: For Gerry, a Neo-New Yorker."   Black
American Literature Forum 13 (3): 101 (Fall 1979).

168.10   Faulkner's "Negro": Art and the Southern Context.
Baton Rouge, LA: Louisiana State University Press, 1983.

168.11   "For Alice Faye Jackson, from The Vanishing Black
Family In Memoriam (January 1986)."   Black American
Literature Forum 20 (3): 301 (Fall 1986).

168.12   "For Flo Hyman, Captain of the Olympic Volleyball
Team (1984)."   Black American Literature Forum 20 (3): 299
(Fall 1986).

168.13   "For Papa (and Marcus Garvey)."   Obsidian 4 (1): 91
(Spring 1978).

168.14   "For Us: In Hope and Love."   Black Scholar 8 (April
1977): 12.

168.15   "Funeral Sequence."   Black Scholar 8 (April 1977):
12.

168.16   "A Greeting on Tabaski."   Black American Literature
Forum 13 (3): 100 (Fall 1979).

168.17   "Honeysuckle Was the Saddest Odor of All, I Think."
Obsidian 4 (1): 93 (Spring 1978).

168.18   "In Mordiop's Room: Rue Mohamed V, Dakar."   Black
American Literature Forum 13 (3): 100 (Fall 1979).

168.19   "Nella Larsen."   In   HARRIS, 1987, pp. 182-192.

168.20   "New World Griot."   Black American Literature Forum
17 (4): 149 (Winter 1983).

168.21   "Nomzamo."   Black American Literature Forum 20 (3):
302 (Fall 1986).

168.22 "Other Family and Luster in The Sound and the Fury."
CLA Journal 20 (December 1976): 245-261.

168.23 "Ramona Johnson Africa MOVE Survivor." Black
American Literature Forum 20 (3): 300-301 (Fall 1986).

168.24 "Reunion." Black American Literature Forum 17 (4):
149 (Winter 1983).

168.25 "Shirley Graham." In MAINIERO, 1979, pp. 167-169.

168.26 "Strong Women Survive Hurricane Season." Obsidian 4
(1): 92 (Spring 1978).

168.27 "Unfinished Kinship." Black Scholar 8 (April 1977):
13.

168.28 "Wright, Faulkner, and Mississippi as Racial Memory."
Callaloo 9 (3): 469-480 (Summer 1986).

168.29 Afro-American Fiction Writers After 1955.
(Dictionary of Literary Biography, v, 33). Detroit: Gale
Research, 1984. Trudier Harris, joint editor.

168.30 Afro-American Writers After 1955: Dramatists and
Prose Writers. (Dictionary of Literary Biography, v. 38).
Detroit: Gale Research, 1985. Trudier Harris, joint editor.

169. DAVIS, THULANI (1949-).

169.1 All the Renegade Ghosts Rise. Washington, DC: Anemone,
1978. Poetry.

169.2 "Cicatrix." Journal of New Jersey Poets 1 (1): 38
(Spring 1976).

169.3 "He Was Taken." Obsidian 3 (2): 56 (Summer 1977).

169.4 Playing the Changes. Middletown, CT: Wesleyan
University Press, 1985.

169.5 "Song to Some Other Man." "He Was Taken." Obsidian 3
(2): 56-57 (Summer 1977).

Secondary Sources

169.6(S) Hernton, Calvin C. "Black Women Poets: The Oral
Tradition." In HERNTON, pp. 119-155. Criticism of Thulani
Davis.

170. DEAN, BARBARA.

170.1 <u>The Key</u>. Chicago: Free Black Press, 1970. Poetry.

171. DEAN, CORINNE.

171.1 <u>Coconut Suite: Stories of the West Indies</u>. Boston:
Meador, 1952. Short fiction.

172. DEAS, KATHERINE.

172.1 <u>Life Line Poems</u>. Chicago: Edward C. Deas, n.d.

173. DEASE, RUTH ROSEMAN (1911-).

173.1 <u>Scan-Spans</u>. New York: Vantage Press, 1967. Poetry.

174. DEE, RUBY (1923-).

174.1 "For Marvin Gay." <u>Essence</u> 18 (June 1987): 111.

174.2 <u>Glow Child and Other Poems</u>. New York: Third Press,
1973. Anthology edited by Ruby Dee.

174.3 <u>My One Good Nerve</u>. Chicago: Third World Press, 1987.
Poetry.

174.4 <u>Two Ways to Count to Ten</u>. New York: Holt, 1987.

                        Secondary Sources

174.5(S) Norment, Lynn. "Three Great Love Stories."   <u>Ebony</u>
43 (February 1988): 150.

175. DELANY, LUCY A. (1830-?)

175.1 <u>From the Darkness Cometh the Light, or Struggles for</u>
<u>Freedom</u>. St. Louis: Publishing House of J.T. Smith, n.d.

176. DEMOND, ANTOINETTE S.

176.1 "Summer of My Sixteenth Year." <u>Negro Digest</u> 11 (April 1962): 30-35.

177.   DeRAMUS, BETTY.

177.1 "The Addict." <u>Black World</u> 19 (June 1970): 74-77. Short fiction.

177.2 "Anderson's Ordeal." <u>Obsidian</u> 6 (1-2): 98-103 (Spring-Summer 1980). Short fiction.

177.3 "The Neighborhood." In BELL, pp. 371-374. Short fiction.

177.4 "A Time for Burning." <u>Obsidian</u> 3 (2): 28-33 (Summer 1977). Short fiction.

177.5 "Waiting for Beale." <u>Essence</u> 7 (May 1976): 72-73. Short fiction.

178.   DERRICOTTE, TONI (1941-).

178.1 "The Anesthesia is Taking Effect." "Beau Monde." "The House is the Enemy." "The Night She Dreamed She Was Mad." "The Sculpture at Night." <u>Black American Literature Forum</u> 17 (4): 155 (Winter 1983).

178.2 <u>Captivity</u>. Pittsburgh: University of Pittsburgh Press, 1989.

178.3 <u>The Empress of the Death House</u>. Detroit: Lotus Press, 1978.

178.4 "Fears of the Eighth Grade." <u>Callaloo</u> 9 (1): 29 (Winter 1986).

178.5 "Hamtramck: The Polish Women." <u>Callaloo</u> 9 (1): 30 (Winter 1986).

178.6 "Letter to Miss Glasser." <u>Callaloo</u> 9 (1): 28 (Winter 1986).

178.7 <u>Natural Birth</u>. Trumansburg, NY: The Crossing Press, 1983. (selections), <u>Iowa Review</u> 12 (2-3): 63-68 (Spring-Summer 1981). Prose poem on birth of her son.

178.8 "A Note on My Son's Face." <u>Callaloo</u> 10 (4): 561-562 (Fall 1987).

178.9 "On the Turning Up of Unidentified Black Female
Corpses." _Callaloo_ 12 (Spring 1989): 389. Poem.

178.10 "Poems." _Black Scholar_ 19 (July/August-
September/October 1988): 57.

Secondary Sources

178.11(S) Hernton, Calvin C. "Black Women Poets: The Oral
Tradition." In HERNTON, pp. 119-155. Criticism of Toni
Derricotte.

179.   DESHANDS, LOTTIE BELLE.

179.1 _Golden Gems of a New Civilization_. New York:
Exposition Press, 1955. Poetry.

180.   DeVEAUX, ALEXIS (1948-).

180.1 "Alice Walker." _Essence_ 20 (September 1989): 56.

180.2 "Blood Ties." _Essence_ 13 (January 1983): 62-64, 121.

180.3 _Blue Heat: A Portfolio of Poems and Drawings_.
Brooklyn: Diva, 1985.

180.4 "Creating Soul Food: June Jordan." _Essence_ 11 (April
1981): 82, 138-150.

180.5 _Don't Explain: A Song of Billie Holiday_. New York:
Harper, 1980. _Essence_ 12 (June 1981): 72. Excerpts.

180.6 _An Enchanted Hair Tale_. New York: Harper, 1987.

180.7 "Everyone is Nicaragua." _Black Scholar_ 19
(July/August-September/October 1988): 40. Poem.

180.8 _Li Chen/Second Daughter First Son_. Ba Tone Press,
1975.

180.9 "Madeleine's Dreads." _Iowa Review_ 12 (2-3): 62
(Spring-Summer 1981).

180.10 _Na-Ni_. New York: Harper, 1973.

180.11 "New Body, New Life." _Essence_ 19 (June 1988): 57.

180.12 "Paule Marshall -- In Celebration of Our Triumphs."
Essence 11 (May 1980): 70-71,96,98,123-134.

180.13 "Poems." _Hoo-Doo Magazine_. (Spring 1980).

180.14 "Remember Him a Outlaw." <u>Black Creation</u> 4 (Fall 1972): 4-7.

180.15 "The Riddles of Egypt Brownstone." <u>Essence</u> 9 (August 1978): 64-65,96,98.

180.16 "Sister Love." <u>Essence</u> 14 (October 1983): 83.

180.17 "Southern Africa: Listening for the News." <u>Essence</u> 12 (March 1982): 168.

180.18 <u>Spirits in the Streets</u>. New York: Doubleday, 1973.

180.19 "Zimbabwe: Woman Fire." <u>Essence</u> 12 (July 1981): 72-73, 111-112.

                    Secondary Sources

180.20(S) Ramsey, Priscilla R. "Alexis DeVeaux." In DAVIS & HARRIS, 1985, pp. 92-97.

181. DIARA, SCHAVI MALI (1948-).

181.1 "African Woman." "Most Likely to Succeed." "Struggling and Surviving." "To a Special Friend." <u>Black American Literature Forum</u> 16 (2): 71 (Summer 1982).

181.2 "Lament for the Sixties." <u>Black Books Bulletin</u> 7 (2): 50 (1981).

182. DICKENS, DOROTHY LEE.

182.1 <u>Black on the Rainbow</u>. New York: Pageant Press, 1952. Novel.

183. DILBERT, BRENDA C.

183.1 "Falling in Love." <u>About Time</u> 13 (March 1985): 25.

183.2 "Maturity." <u>About Time</u> 13 (March 1985): 25.

183.3 "My Connections." <u>About Time</u> 13 (March 1985): 25.

183.4 "My Poems." <u>About Time</u> 13 (March 1985): 25

184. DIONETTI, MICHELLE.

184.1 <u>The Day Eli Went Looking for Bear</u>. Reading, MA:
Addison-Wesley, 1980.

184.2 <u>Thalia Brown and the Blue Bug</u>. Reading, MA: Addison-
Wesley, 1979.

185. DOUGLAS, GERALDINE.

185.1 "What Are Friends For." <u>Essence</u> 8 (October 1977): 46.

186. DOVE, RITA (1952-).

186.1 "The Abduction." <u>Virginia Quarterly Review</u> 56 (2):
276 (Spring 1980).

186.2 "The Afghani Nomad Coat (Part V)." <u>Northwest Review</u>
22 (1-2): 134-135 (1984).

186.3 "Agosta the Winged Man and Rasha the Black Dove."
<u>Poetry</u> 139 (November 1981): 64-65.

186.4 "Anniversary." <u>Callaloo</u> 9 (1): 46 (Winter 1986).

186.5 "Anti-Father." <u>Massachusetts Review</u> 23 (2): 253
(Summer 1982).

186.6   "The Ants of Argos." <u>Nation</u> (19 December 1981): 664.

186.7 "Aurora Borealis." <u>Ohio Review</u> 28 (1982): 77.

186.8 "Beauty and the Beast." <u>North American Review</u> 264
(4): 47 (Winter 1979).

186.9 "The Bird Frau." <u>Ohio Review</u> 19 (2): 18 (Spring-
Summer 1978).

186.10 "Champagne." <u>Ohio Review</u> 20 (2): 36 (Spring-Summer
1979).

186.11 "La Chapelle. 92nd Division. Ted." <u>Southern Review</u>
21 (3): 849-850 (July 1985).

186.12 "The Charm." <u>Ohio Review</u> 28 (1982): 78.

186.13 "Company." <u>Callaloo</u> 9 (Winter 1986): 50

186.14 "Compendium." "Courtship." "Definition in the Face
of the Unnamed Fury." "The Event." "Jiving." "Refrain."
"The Stroke." "Variation on Guilt." "Variation on Pain."
"The Zeppelin Factory." <u>Ohio Review</u> 28 (1982): 68-78.

186.15 "Courtship, Diligence." New England Review 7 (1): 61
(Autumn 1984).

186.16 "David Walker (1785-1830)." Missouri Review 2 (2):
56 (Spring 1979).

186.17 "Dog Days, Jerusalem." "Fifth Grade Autobiography."
"The Gorge." Southern Review 21 (3): 850-853 (July 1985).

186.18 "Dusting." Poetry 139 (November 1981): 66-67.

186.19 Fifth Sunday. (Callaloo Fiction Series) Lexington,
KY: University of Kentucky Press, 1985.

186.20 "The First Suite." Black American Literature Forum
20 (3): 241-250 (Fall 1986).

186.21 "Five Elephants." Nation (1 March 1980): 253.

186.22 "Flirtation." Poetry 141 (October 1982): 10.

186.23 "Gospel." Georgia Review 38 (3): 618-619 (Autumn
1984). Western Journal of Black Studies 11 (3): 131 (Fall
1987).

186.24 "Headdress." Callaloo 9 (1): 47 (Winter 1986).

186.25 "The Hill Has Something to Say." Georgia Review 35
(3): 554-555 (Autumn 1981).

186.26 "The House on Bishop Street." Callaloo 9 (1): 45
(Winter 1986).

186.27 "The House Slave." Virginia Quarterly Review 56 (2):
275 (Spring 1980).

186.28 "Kentucky, 1833." Paris Review 68 (Winter 1976):
165.

186.29 "The Left-Handed Cellist." New Orleans Review 9 (1):
88 (Spring 1982).

186.30 "Lucille, Post-Operative Years." Georgia Review 40
(4): 937 (Winter 1986).

186.31 Mandolin. Columbus, OH: Ohio Review, 1982.

186.32 "Motherhood." Callaloo 9 (1): 44 (Winter 1986).

186.33 Museum: Poems. Pittsburgh: Carnegie-Mellon
University Press, 1983.

186.34 "Nightmare." Callaloo 9 (1): 49 (Winter 1986).

186.35 "November for Beginners." Poetry 139 (November
1981): 63.

186.36 "O." <u>Ohio Review</u>, 23(1979):37. 30(1983):59.

186.37 "One Volume Missing." <u>Callaloo</u> 9 (1): 39
(Winter 1986).

186.38 <u>The Only Dark Spot in the Sky: Poems</u>. Tempe, AZ:
Porch Publications, 1980.

186.39 "The Oriental Ballerina (Georgianna Magdalena Hord,
1896-1979)." <u>New England Review</u> 7 (1): 62-63 (Autumn 1984).

186.40 <u>The Other Side of the House</u>. Pyracantha Press, 1988.

186.41 "Pomade." <u>Poetry</u> 144 (September 1984): 324-325.

186.42 "Primer for the Nuclear Age." <u>Poetry</u> 145 (October
1984): 49.

186.43 "Promises." <u>Callaloo</u> 9 (1): 43 (Winter 1986).

186.44 "Receiving the Stigmata." <u>Georgia Review</u> 36 (3): 496
(Autumn 1982).

186.45 "Recovery." <u>Callaloo</u> 9 (1): 48 (Winter 1986).

186.46 "Roast Possum." <u>Callaloo</u> 9 (1): 41-42 (Winter 1986).

186.47 "Robert Schumann, or; Musical Genius Begins with
Affliction." <u>Georgia Review</u> 32 (3): 643 (Autumn 1978).

186.48 "Small Town." <u>Georgia Review</u> 33 (4): 805 (Winter
1979).

186.49 "Straw Hat." <u>Callaloo</u> 9 (1): 37 (Winter 1986).

186.50 "Sunday Greens." <u>Western Journal of Black Studies</u> 11
(3): 130 (Fall 1987).

186.51 <u>Ten Poems</u>. Lisbon, IA: Penumbra Press, 1977.

186.52 "This Life." <u>Callaloo</u> 9 (1): 63 (Winter 1986).

186.53 <u>Thomas and Beulah</u>. Pittsburgh: Carnegie-Mellon
University Press, 1986.

186.54 "Three Days of a Forest, a River, Free."
<u>Massachusetts Review</u> 23 (2): 254 (Summer 1982).

186.55 "Under the Viaduct" <u>Callaloo</u> 9 (1): 38 (Winter
1986).

186.56 "Variation on Gaining a Son." <u>Callaloo</u> 9 (1): 40
(Winter 1986).

186.57 "The Wake." <u>Poetry</u> 146 (September 1984): 325-326.

186.58 <u>The Yellow House on the Corner: Poems</u>. Pittsburgh:
Carnegie-Mellon University Press, 1980.

Secondary Sources

186.59(S) Hernton, Calvin C. "Black Women Poets: The Oral
Tradition." In HERNTON, pp. 119-155.

186.60(S) McDowell, Robert. "The Assembling Vision of Rita
Dove." <u>Callaloo</u> 9 (1): 61-70 (Winter 1986).

186.61(S) McKinney, Rhoda E. "Introducing: Pulitzer Prize-
Winning Poet Rita Dove." <u>Ebony</u> 42 (October 1987): 44-46.

186.62(S) Rampersad, Arnold. "Poems of Rita Dove."
<u>Callaloo</u> 9 (1): 52-60 (Winter 1986).

186.63(S) Rubin, Stan Sanvel and Ingersoll, Earl G., eds.
"A Conversation with Rita Dove." <u>Black American Literature
Forum</u> 20 (3): 227-240 (Fall 1986).

1988-1991 Supplement

A186.64 <u>First Sunday</u>. Lexington, KY: University of Kentucky
Press, 1985.

A186.65 <u>Grace Notes</u>. New York: W.W. Norton, 1989.

A186.66 <u>Grace Notes: Poems</u>. New York: W.W. Norton, 1991.

A186.67 "Poems." <u>Black Scholar</u> 19 (July/August-
September/October 1988): 46.

A186.68 <u>Yellow House on the Corner</u>. Pittsburgh: Carnegie-
Mellon, 1989.

187. DRAKE, JEANNETTE.

187.1 "Eating." <u>Catalyst</u> (Spring 1990): 112.

187.2 "Missing Children." <u>Callaloo</u> 10 (3): 480 (Summer
1987).

187.3 "Next Time." <u>Catalyst</u> (Spring 1990): 81.

187.4 "Poems." <u>Obsidian II</u> 3 (Winter 1988): 94.

188. DRUMGOOLD, KATE.

188.1 A Slave Girl's Story: The Autobiography of Kate
Drumgoold. n.p., 1898.

DuBois, Shirley Graham. SEE 258. GRAHAM, SHIRLEY.

189. DuBOIS, SILVIA [C. WILSON LARISON]

189.1 A Biography of the Slave Who Whipt Her Mistress and
Gained Her Freedom. Author, 1883.

190. DUNBAR, ALICE MOORE (1875-1935).

190.1 An Alice Dunbar-Nelson Reader. Ed. by Ora Williams.
Washington, DC: University Press of America, 1979.

190.2 "April Is On the Way." JOHNSON.

190.3 "The Ball Dress." Leslie's Weekly 93 (12 December
1901): 2414.

190.4 "Canto - I Sing." The American International Peace
Committee Bulletin (October 1929).

190.5 "Communion." Opportunity 3 (July 1925): 216

190.6 The Dunbar Speaker and Entertainer: Containing the
Best Prose and Poetic Selections by and about the Negro Race.
Naperville, IL: J.L. Nichols & Co., 1920.

190.7 "Facing Life Squarely." The Messenger 9 (July 1927):
219.

190.8 "Forest Fire." Harlem: A Forum of Negro Life 1
(November 1928): 22.

190.9 Give Us Each Day: The Diary of Alice Dunbar-Nelson.
Ed. by Gloria T. Hull. New York: W. W. Norton, 1984.

190.10 The Goodness of St. Rocque and Other Stories. New
York: Dodd, Mead, 1899.

190.11 "Hope Deferred." Crisis 8 (September 1914): 238-242.

190.12 "I Sit and Sew." "Music." "Snow in October."
"Sonnet." In STETSON, pp. 65-67.

190.13 Masterpieces of Negro Eloquence: The Best Speeches
Delivered By the Negro From the Days of Slavery to the
Present Time. New York: Bookery Publishing Company, 1914.

190.14 "Mine Eyes Have Seen." _Crisis_ (April 1918): 271-275. One act drama.

190.15 "Music." _Opportunity_ 3 (July 1925): 216.

190.16 "Negro Literature for Negro Pupils." _Southern Workman_ 51 (February 1922): 59-63.

190.17 "The Negro Looks at Outworn Tradition." _Southern Workman_ 57 (May 1928): 195-200.

190.18 "Of Old St. Augustine." _Opportunity_ 3 (July 1925): 216.

190.19 "People of Color in Louisiana." Part I. _Journal of Negro History_ 1 (October 1916): 361-376; Part II. 2 (January 1917): 51-78.

190.20 "The Poet and His Song." Paul Laurence Dunbar: Poet laureate of the Negro race. Special Issue, _A.M.E. Church Review_ 21 (October 1914): 5-19.

190.21 "Politics in Delaware." _Opportunity_ 2 (November 1924): 339-340.

190.22 "The Problem of Personal Service." _Meesenger_ 9 (June 1927): 184.

190.23 "Science in Frenchtown - A Short Story." _Saturday Evening Mail_ Magazine section, 7 December 1912, pp. 8-9, 26,27.

190.24 "The Single Standard." _A.M.E. Church Review_ 30 (January 1914): 189-192.

190.25 "Sonnet." _Crisis_ 18 (August 1917): 193.

190.26 "Textbooks in Public Schools: A Job for the Negro Woman." _Messenger_ 9 (May 1927): 149.

190.27 "These 'Colored' United States." Part I. _Messenger_ 6 (August 1924): 244-46; Part II. 6 (September 1924): 276-279.

190.28 "Training of Teachers of English." _Education_ 29 (October 1908): 97-103).

190.29 _Violets and Other Tales_. Boston: Monthly Review, 1895.

190.30 "What Has the Church to Offer the Men of Today?" _A.M.E. Church Review_ 30 (July 1913): 5-13.

190.31 "Woman's Most Serious Problem." _Messenger_ 9 (March 1927): 73, 86.

190.32 "Wordsworth's Use of Milton's Description of
Pandemonium." (letter) Modern Language Notes 24 (April 1909):
124-125.

190.33 The Works of Alice Dunbar-Nelson. NY: Oxford
University Press, 1988. 3 volumes.

Secondary Sources

190.34(S) Hatch, James V. Black Theater, USA: Forty-Five
Plays by American Negroes, 1847-1974. New York: Free Press,
1974.

190.35(S) Hull, Gloria T. "Alice Dunbar-Nelson: Delaware
Writer and Woman of Affairs." Delaware History 17(Fall-
Winter 1976):87-103.

190.36(S) Hull, Gloria T. Color, Sex, and Poetry: Three
Women Writers of the Harlem Renaissance. Bloomington, IN:
Indiana University Press, 1987.

190.37(S) Shockley, Ann Allen. "Alice Ruth Moore Dunbar-
Nelson." In SHOCKLEY, pp. 262-273.

190.38(S) Williams, Ora. "Works By and About Alice Ruth
(Moore) Dunbar-Nelson: A Bibliography." CLA Journal 19(March
1976):322-26.

190.39(S) Young, Pauline A. "Paul Laurence Dunbar: An
Intimate Glimpse." Freedomways 12(Fourth Quarter 1972):319-
29.

191. DUNCAN, THELMA MYRTLE (1902-).

191.1 Black Magic. In YEARBOOK, pp. 215-232. One act
drama.

191.2 The Death Dance. In LOCKE & MONTGOMERY, pp. 323-331.
One act drama.

191.3 Sacrifice. In RICHARDSON, pp.3-24. One act drama.

192. DUNHAM, KATHERINE (1912-).

192.1 Dances of Haiti. Los Angeles: University of
California, Los Angeles, Center African-American Studies,
1983.

192.2 Le Danses d'Haiti. Paris: Fasquelle, 1950. Las
Danzas de Haiti. Mexico: Acta Anthropologica 114, 1947.

192.3 Island Possessed. New York: Doubleday, 1969.

192.4 Kasamance: A Fantasy. New York: Third Press, 1974.

192.5 <u>A Touch of Innocence</u>. New York: Harcourt, 1959, 1969.
Novel.

192.6 <u>Journey to Accompong</u>. New York: Greenwood, 1972.
Autobiography.

                    Secondary Sources

192.7(S) "The Dazzling Color of Alvin Ailey's Dunham
Tribute." <u>Ebony</u> 43 (May 1988): 86.

193. EADY, CORMELIUS.

193.1 "Waffle House Girl." <u>Essence</u> 17 (May 1986): 93.

194. EARLE, VICTORIA (1861-1907).

194.1 <u>Aunt Lindy; a Story Founded on Real Life</u>. New York:
J.J. Little & Co., 1893. Novel.

194.2 <u>The Awakening of the Afro-American Woman</u>. New York:
Author, 1897.

                    Secondary Sources

194.3(S) Brown, Hallie Quinn. <u>Homespun Heroines and Other
Women of Distinction</u>. Xenia, OH: Aldine, 1926.

194.4(S) Davis, Elizabeth Lindsay. <u>Lifting As They Climb</u>.
Chicago, 1933.

194.5(S) Majors, Monroe Alphus. <u>Noted Negro Women, Their
Triumphs and Activities</u>. New York: Donohue & Henneberry,
1893.

194.6(S) Mossell, N.F. [Gertrude Bustill Mossell]. <u>The Work
of the Afro-American Woman</u>. Philadelphia: Geo. S. Ferguson
co., 1894. 2d ed. 1908.

194.7(S) Penn, I. Garland. <u>The Afro-American Press and Its
Editors</u>. Reprint. New York: Arno Press, 1969. 1st published
1891. Victoria Earle p. 376.

194.8(S) Shockley, Ann Allen. "Victoria Earle." In
SHOCKLEY, pp. 181-189.

Easton, Y. W. **SEE** 712. YVONNE.

195.   EATON, ESTELLE ATLEY.

195.1   Out of My Dreams and Other Verses.   Boston:
Christopher Publishing House, 1959.

196.   EBERHARDT, JUANITA BURLESON.

196.1   The World Has Many Doors That I Enter.   Chicago:
DuSable Museum of African American History Press, 1975.

197.   EDWARDS, JEAN.

197.1   "Thanksgiving I'll Never Forget." Sepia 19 (November
1970): 30.

198.   EDWARDS-YEARWOOD, GRACE.

198.1   Shadow of the Peacock.   New York: McGraw-Hill, 1988.

199.   ELAW, ZILPHA (1790-?).

199.1   Memoirs of the Life, Religious Experience, Ministerial
Travels and Labours of Mrs. Zilpha Elaw, an American Female
of Colour; Together with Some Account of the Great Religious
Revivals in America.   London: Author, 1846.

                    Secondary Sources

199.2(S)   Andrews, William L., ed.   Sisters of the Spirit:
Three Black Women's Autobiographies of the Nineteenth-
century.   Bloomington, IN: Indiana University Press, 1986.

199.3(S)   Shockley, Ann Allen.   "Zilpha Elaw."   In SHOCKLEY,
pp. 33-41.

200.   ELDER, ELEANOR HARDEE.

200.1   Me n' de Chillun.   New York: Praeger, 1948.   Poetry.

201. ELDRIDGE, ELLEANOR (1785-1865).

201.1 Elleanor's Second Book. Providence, RI: B.T. Albro, 1842.

201.2 [Francis Harriet Greene McDougall]. Memoirs of Elleanor Eldridge. Providence, RI: B.T. Albro, 1838.

202. ELLETT, M. DEBORAH (1949-).

202.1 From Them I Come. n.p., A Free Will Publication, 1973. Poetry.

203. ELLIOTT, EMILY.

203.1 Still Waters and Other Poems. Cambridge: Author, 1949.

204. ELLIS, TERESA.

204.1 No Way Back: A Novella. New York: Exposition Press, 1973.

Elliston, Maxine Hall SEE 344. JAMILA-RA.

205. EMERUWA, LEATRICE.

205.1 "Black Art and Artists in Cleveland." Black World 22 (January 1973): 23-33.

205.2 Black Girl, Black Girl (Variations on a Theme). Beechwood, OH: Sharaqua, 1976.

205.3 "Black Theater in America: Cleveland, Ohio." Black World 22 (April 1973): 19-26.

205.4 Black Venus in Gemini. n.p., n.d.

205.5 "East 105th and Euclid Street Peddlar's Song." "For What-Sa-Name." "Rage." Pigiron 7(May 1980): 63, 77, 78.

205.6 Ev'ry Shut Eye Ain't Sleep: Ev'ry Goodbye Ain't Gon'.
Beechwood, OH: Sharaqua, 1977.

205.7 "In Memory." Black World 19 (September 1970): 78.

205.8 "Up Against the Black Wall/Pale Critic." Black World
19 (September 1970): 31.

206. ESHE, AISHA (1941-).

206.1 "Birthday Party." "Camp Reilly with Crystall."
"Campside Memory." "For My mother." "Geneva." "Kiss."
"Melting Pot to America." "Signs." Obsidian 7 (2-3): 209-
213 (Summer-Winter 1981).

206.2 "Black Folks." "I Cry When I Return." Black Books
Bulletin 7 (3): 61 (1981).

206.3 "Harrisburg Hospital 1980." Black American Literature
Forum 14 (1): 175 (Winter 1980).

206.4 "He Can Go Home, I Guess We Pulled the Wrong Nigga
This Time." Black American Literature Forum 18 (1): 28
(Spring 1984).

206.5 "Invisible Black Face." "A Vision from Beneath the
Skin." Obsidian 5 (1-2): 77-78 (Spring-Summer 1979).

206.6 "My People on the Run." Shooting Star Review 2
(Summer 1988): 16.

206.7 "Poems." Black American Literature Forum 23 (Fall
1989): 468.

207. EUBANKS, CALLIE MILES.

207.1 I Want to Go Home. New York: Vantage Press, 1971.

208. EVANS, MARI (1923-).

208.1 "...And the Old Women Gathered (the Gospel Singers)."
"Daufuskie (Four Movements)." "How Will You Call Me,
Brother." "Jake." "Janis." "The People Gather." In
STETSON, pp. 142-145.

208.2 (E. Reed) "Behind the Green Door." Black Enterprise
7 (February 1977): 27-32.

208.3   Black Women Writers (1950-1980): A Critical
Evaluation. New York: Anchor/Doubleday, 1984. Mari Evans,
editor.

208.4   "Blackness: A Definition." Negro Digest 19 (November
1969): 19-21.

208.5   "Blues in B flat." Callaloo 5 (2): 47 (1979).

208.6   "Cellblock Blues." Black Scholar 10 (November-
December 1978): 47.

208.7   "Contemporary Black Literature." Black World 19 June
1970): 4, 93-94.

208.8   "Daufuskie (Four Movements)." Black World 23
(September 1974): 42.

208.9   "Daufuskie: Jake." Black World 23 (September 1974):
43.

208.10   "Decolonization as Goal; Political Writing as
Device." First World 2 (November 1979): 34-39.

208.11   "Early in the Morning." "I am a Black Woman."
"Speak the Truth to the People." "Where Have You Gone." In
BARAKA & BARAKA, pp.105-109.

208.12   "Here - Hold My Hand." Essence 4 (November 1973):
37.

208.13   "How Far Away is Not Soon." Black World 23
(September 1974): 44.

208.14   "How Sudden Dies the Blooming." Black Scholar 18 (4-
5): 22 (July/August/Seotember/October 1987).

208.15   "How Will You Call Me, Brother." Black World 21
(September 1972): 71.

208.16   I Am a Black Woman. New York: William Morrow, 1970.

208.17   I Look at Me. Chicago: Third World Press, 1974. A
pre-school reader.

208.18   "In the Time of the Whirlwind: I'm with You." Negro
Digest 17 (May 1968): 31-36, 77-80.

208.19   JD. New York: Doubleday, 1973.

208.20   Jim Flying High. New York: Doubleday, 1979.

208.21   "A Man Without Food." Black Scholar 18 (4-5): 22
(July/August/September/October 1987).

208.22   "Maria Pina and B&G Grill." Callaloo 5 (2): 49
(1979).

208.23 "My Father's Passage." In EVANS, pp. 165-169.

208.24 "The Nature and Methodology of Colonization and its
Relationship to Creativity: A Systems Approach." Black Books
Bulletin 6 (August 1979): 10-17.

208.25 "Nicodemus." Black World 23 (September 1974): 43.

208.26 "Nigger Who is Now Hunting You." Black World 23
(September 1974): 45. Black Scholar 8 (May 1977): 35.

208.27 Nightstar: 1973-1978. Los Angeles: UCLA Center for
Afro-American Studies, 1981.

208.28 "On the Death of Boochie by Starvation." First World
2 (Spring 1978): 11. Callaloo 5 (2): 46 (1979).

208.29 "Political Writing as Device." First World 2 (3):
34-39 (1979).

208.30 "One More Black Belt Gone." Callaloo 5 (2): 50
(1979).

208.31 Rap Stories. Chicago: Third World Press, 1973.

208.32 "Remembering Willie." Black Scholar 10 (November-
December 1978): 47.

208.33 Singing Black. Chicago: Third World Press, 1976.

208.34 "Stations: A Willingness to Be at Risk." Catalyst
(Summer 1987): 70.

208.35 "Street Lady." Callaloo 5 (2): 48 (1979). First
World, 2(Spring 1978):11.

208.36 "Third Stop in Caraway Park." Black World 26 (March
1975): 54-62.

208.37 "To Mother and Steve." Ebony 36 (August 1981): 54.

208.38 Where Is All the Music? London: Paul Breman, 1968.

208.39 Whisper. Berkeley: University of California Center
for African American Studies, 1979.

                    Secondary Sources

208.40(S) Dorsey, David, "The Art of Mari Evans." In
EVANS, pp. 170-189.

208.41(S) Peppers, Wallace R. "Mari Evans." In HARRIS &
DAVIS, pp. 117-123.

208.42(S) Sedlack,, Robert T. "Mari Evans: Consciousness
and Craft." CLA Journal 15 (June 1972): 465-476.

209.   FABIO, SARAH WEBSTER (1928-1979).

209.1 "All Day We've Longed for Night." "Back into the
Garden." "To Turn from Love." In STETSON, pp. 139-141.

209.2 "At Cross Purposes (for SNCC, CORE)." Negro Digest 15
(September 1966): 76.

209.3 "Being Together for Soul Folk." Black Collegian 35
(1980): 22.

209.4 Black Back: Back Black. Oberlin, OH: New Media
Workshop, 1973

209.5 Black Images/Black Resurrection. San Francisco:
Julian Richardson, n.d.

209.6 Black Is/A Panther Caged. San Francisco: Julian
Richardson, n.d.

209.7 "A Black Paper." Negro Digest 18 (July 1969): 26-31.

209.8 Black Talk: Soul, Shield, and Sword. New York:
Doubleday, 1973.

209.9 "Black Writer's Views on Literary Lions and Values."
Negro Digest 17 (January 1968): 39

209.10 "Blowing the Whistle on Some Jive." Black Scholar 10
(May-June 1979): 56-58.

209.11 Boss Soul. Oberlin, OH: New Media Workshop, 1973.

209.12 "A Butts' End Remark Rebuff (a Political Polemic,
1976). Black Scholar 12 (November-December 1981): 64.

209.13 "Estrangement." Black Male/Female Relationships 2
(5): 20 (1981).

209.14 "Free, Freely Free, in Pursuit of Freedom Now."
Black World 24 (July 1975): 88.

209.15 "Going Home." Negro Digest 18 (March 1969): 54-58.

209.16 "Juju for the Known/Unknown Black Woman." Black
Collegian 35 (1980): 22.

209.17 Jujus/Alchemy of the Blues. Oberlin, OH: New Media
Workshop, 1973.

209.18 Jujus and Jubilees: Critical Essays in Rhyme about
Poets/Musicians/Black Heroes, with Introductory Notes.
Oberlin, OH: New Media Workshop, 1973.

209.19 "A Live Celebration." Negro Digest 17 (September-
October 1968): 60-61.

209.20 A Mirror: A Soul. San Francisco: Julian Richardson, 1969.

209.21 My Own Thing. Oberlin, OH: New Media Workshop, 1973.

209.22 "Note to Jomo Kenyatta." Negro Digest 15 (July 1966): 38.

209.23 Rainbow Signs. 7 vols. Privately Printed, 1974.

209.24 Saga of a Black Man. Turn Over Book Stores, 1968.

209.25 "Sassafras Toned, My Grandmother Sat." Black Collegian 35 (1980): 22.

209.26 "Song of the Song in Owen's Song." Black World 24 (July 1975): 89-96.

209.27 Soul Ain't: Soul Is -- The Hurt of it All. Oberlin, OH: New Media Workshop, 1973.

209.28 Together/To Tune of Coltrane's Equinox. Oberlin, OH: New Media Workshop, 1973.

209.29 "Tribute to Owen's Song: Concert Chorus of Black Artistry in Collage." Black World 24 (July 1975): 76-87.

209.30 "Who Speaks Negro? What is Black?" Negro Digest 17 (September-October 1969): 33-37.

210. FAIRLEY, RUTH A.

210.1 Rocks and Roses. New York: Vantage Press, 1970. Novel.

211. FATISHA.

211.1 "Reflective Whimpers in the Banging Silence." Essence 8 (February 1978): 55.

212. FAUSET, JESSIE REDMON (1882-1961).

212.1 "Again It Is September." Crisis 14 (September 1917).

212.2 The Chinaberry Tree: A Novel of American Life. New York: Frederick A. Stokes Company, 1933.

212.3 <u>Comedy, American Style</u>. New York: Frederick A.
Stokes, 1931. Novel.

212.4 " 'Courage!' He Said." <u>Crisis</u> 36 (November 1929):
378.

212.5 "Dilworth Road Revisited." <u>Crisis</u> 24 (August 1922):
167.

212.6 "Double Trouble." <u>Crisis</u> 26 (August 1923): 155-159;
26 (September 1923): 61-63.

212.7 "Emmy." <u>Crisis</u> 5 (December 1912): 134-142.

212.8 "The Gift of Laughter." In LOCKE.

212.9 "Here's April." <u>Crisis</u> 27 (April 1924): 277.

212.10 "Impressions of the Second Pan-African Congress.
<u>Crisis</u> 22 (November 1921): 12-18.

212.11 "Mary Elizabeth." <u>Crisis</u> 19 (December 1919): 51-56.

212.12 "The Meal." In AFRO.

212.13 "My House and a Glimpse of My Life Therein." <u>Crisis</u>
8 (July 1914): 143-145.

212.14 "New Literature on the Negro." <u>Crisis</u> 20 (June
1920): 78-83.

212.15 "Oriflamme." <u>Crisis</u> 24 (July 1920): 128.

212.16 <u>Plum Bun: A Novel Without a Moral</u>. New York:
Frederick A. Stokes, 1929.

212.17 "Rain Fugue." <u>Crisis</u> 28 (August 1924): 155.

212.18 "Rencontre. "<u>Crisis</u> 27 (January 1924): 122.

212.19 "The Return." <u>Crisis</u> 11 (January 1917): 118.

212.20 "Rondeau." <u>Crisis</u> 3 (April 1912): 252.

212.21 "The Sleeper Wakes." <u>Crisis</u> 20 (August 1920): 168-
173; 20 (September 1920): 226-229; 20 (October 1920): 267-
274.

212.22 "Song for a Lost Comrade." <u>Crisis</u> 25 (November
1922): 22.

212.23 "Stars in Alabama." <u>Crisis</u> 35 (January 1928): 14.

212.24 <u>There is Confusion</u>. New York: Boni & Liveright,
1924. Novel.

212.25 " 'There Was One Time,' a Story of Spring." <u>Crisis</u> 13
(April 1917): 272-277; 14 (May 1917): 11-15.

212.26   "Touche." "Oriflamme." In STETSON, pp. 63-64.

212.27   "La Vie C'est la Vie." Crisis 24 (July 1922): 124.

212.28   "What Europe Thought of the Pan-African Congress."
Crisis 22 (December 1921): 60-69.

212.29   "When Christmas Comes." Crisis 25 (December 1922):
61-63.

Secondary Sources

212.30(S)   Ammons, Elizabeth. "New Literary History: Edith
Wharton and Jessie Redmon Fauset." College English 14(1987):
207-218.

212.31(S)   Braithwaite, William Stanley. "The Novels of
Jessie Fauset," In HEMENWAY. Originally appeared in
Opportunity, 12(1934):24-28.

212.32(S)   Carby, Hazel. Reconstructing Womanhood: The
Emergence of the Afro-American Woman Novelist. New York:
Oxford University Press, 1987.

212.33(S)   Christian, Barbara. Black Women Novelists: The
Development of a Tradition, 1892-1976. Westport, CT:
Greenwood Press, 1980.

212.34(S)   Feeney, Joseph. "Black Childhood as Ironic: A
Nursery Rhyme Transformed in Jessie Fauset's Novel, Plum
Bun." Minority Voices 4 (Fall 1980): 65-69.

212.35(S)   Feeney, Joseph. "Greek Tragic Patterns in a Black
Novelist: Jessie Fauset's The Chinaberry Tree." CLA Journal
18 (December 1974): 211-215.

212.36(S)   Feeney, Joseph J. "Jessie Fauset of The Crisis:
Novelist, Feminist, Centenarian." Crisis 90 (June-July
1983): 20.

212.37(S)   Feeney, Joseph J. "Sardonic, Unconventional
Jessie Fauset: The Double Vision of Her Novels." CLA Journal
22 (June 1979): 365-382.

212.38(S)   Huggins, Nathan I. Harlem Renaissance. New York:
Oxford University Press, 1970.

212.39(S)   Johnson, Abby Arthur. "Literary Midwife: Jessie
Redmon Fauset and the Harlem Renaissance." Phylon 39 (June
1978): 143-153.

212.40(S)   Lupton, Mary Jane, "Bad Blood in Jersey: Jessie
Fauset's The Chinaberry Tree (1931)." CLA Journal 27 (June
1984): 383-392.

212.41(S) McDowell, Deborah E. "The Neglected Dimension of Jessie Redmon Fauset." In PRYSE & SPILLERS. Afro-Americans in New York Life and History 5 (July 1981): 33-49.

212.42(S) O'Neale, Sondra. "Race, Sex and Self: Aspects of 'Bildung' in Select Novels by Black American Women Novelists." Melus 9 (4): 25-37 (Winter 1982).

212.43(S) Perry, Margaret. "Jessie Fauset." In PERRY, pp. 77-82.

212.44(S) Sato, Hiroko. "Under the Harlem Shadow: A Study of Jessie Fauset and Nella Larsen," In BONTEMPS.

212.45(S) Shockley, Ann Allen. "Jessie Redmon Fauset Harris." In SHOCKLEY, pp. 415-431.

212.46(S) Sims, Janet L. "Jessie Redmon Fauset (1885-1961): A Selected Annotated Bibliography." Black American Literature Forum 14(Winter 1980):147-52.

212.47(S) Starkey, Marion C. "Jessie Redmon Fauset." Southern Workman 61(May 1932):217-20.

212.48(S) Sylvander, Carolyn Wedin. Jessie Redmon Fauset, Black American Writer. Boston: G.K. Hall, 1980. Troy, New York: Whitston Publishing Company, 1981.

212.49(S) Sylvander, Carolyn Wedin. "Jessie Redmon Fauset (1882-1961). In HARRIS & DAVIS, 1987.

213. FAUST, NAOMI FLOWE.

213.1 All Beautiful Things: Poems. Detroit: Lotus Press, 1983.

213.2 "Ms. Gwendolyn Brooks." Essence 19 (July 1988): 143.

213.3 Speaking in Verse. Boston: Branden Press, 1974.

214. FEELINGS, MURIEL (1938-).

214.1 Jambo Means Hello: Swahili Alphabet Book. n.p., 1974. Children and young adult stories.

214.2 Moja Means One: The Swahili Counting Book. New York: Dial Press, 1971. Children and young adult stories.

214.3 Zamini Goes to Market. Boston: Seabury Press, 1970. Children and young adult stories.

215. FERNANDIS, SARAH COLLINS (1863-).

215.1 Vision. Boston: Gorham, 1925. Poetry.

216. ENTRY OMITTED

217. FIELDS, JULIA (1938-).

217.1 "Alabama Suite - The Letter X." " Sin." " Mary." "
Art." " I Loves a Wig." Black World 24 (February 1975): 41-
47.

217.2 "Aardvark." "Harlem in January." "High on the Hog."
"A Poem for Heroes." In ADOFF, pp. 65, 65-66, 130-132, 185,
190-191.

217.3 "Art." Black World 24 (February 1975): 47.

217.4 "August Heat." Callaloo 4 (October 1978): 37-45.

217.5 "Beginning." Essence 4 (August 1973): 20.

217.6 "Big Momma." Black World 21 (September 1972): 47.

217.7 "Black Students." Negro Digest 17 (December 1967):
47.

217.8 "Black Writer's Views on Literary Lions and Values."
Negro Digest 17 (January 1968): 25.

217.9 "Blood is a River." Black World 22 (September 1973):
88.

217.10 "Boxer." Negro Digest 16 (February 1967) 48.

217.11 East of Moonlight. Charlotte, NC: Red Clay Books,
1973.

217.12 "Flame." Negro Digest 19 (April 1970): 16.

217.13 "For Poets." Negro Digest 14 (September 1965): 60.

217.14 "Georgia Douglas Johnson." Negro Digest 15 (October
1966): 48.

217.15 "Gift." Black World 20 (November 1970): 69.

217.16 The Green Lion of Zion Street. New York: Macmillan
Publishing Company, 1988.

217.17 "High on the Hog." Negro Digest 18 (September 1969):
54-56.

217.18 "The Hypchondriac." <u>Negro Digest</u> 17 (July 1968): 61-65.

217.19 "I Heard a Young Man Saying." <u>Negro Digest</u> 15 (September 1966): 70-72.

217.20 "I Loves a Wig." <u>Black World</u> 24 (February 1975): 47.

217.21 "I, Woman." <u>Essence</u> 4 (November 1973): 37.

217.22 "Jazz." <u>Southern Exposure</u> 6 (3): 49 (Fall 1978).

217.23 "Jonah's Wail." <u>Black World</u> 23 (May 1974): 53.

217.24 "Lily Black Blond from Wig Haven Among the Urinals." <u>Negro Digest</u> 14 (August 1965): 53.

217.25 "Mary." <u>Black World</u> 24 (February 1975): 44.

217.26 "Mr. Tut's House: A Recollection." <u>First World</u> 2 (1979): 38-39.

217.27 "No Great Honor." <u>Black World</u> 19 (June 1970): 66-70.

217.28 "Not Your Singing Dancing Spade." <u>Negro Digest</u> 16 (February 1967): 54-59.

217.29 "The Plot to Bring Back Dunking." <u>Black World</u> 22 (August 1973): 64-71.

217.30 "Poem." <u>Negro Digest</u> 17 (September/October 1968): 62-64.

217.31 "Poem for the Marble 'Negress' Clock." <u>Negro Digest</u> 15 (June 1966): 69.

217.32 <u>Poems</u>. Millbrook, NY: Kriya Press, 1968.

217.33 "The Policeman." <u>Black World</u> 21 (September 1972): 48.

217.34 "Portrait of Pacification." <u>Negro Digest</u> 18 (April 1969): 75.

217.35 "Seizing." <u>Black World</u> 21 (September 1972): 46.

217.36 "Sin." <u>Black World</u> 24 (February 1975): 43.

217.37 <u>Slow Coins: Minted by Julia Fields</u>. Washington, DC: Three Continents Press, 1981.

217.38 "Spring." <u>Black World</u> 23 (September 1974): 76-77.

217.39 <u>A Summoning, a Shining</u>. Scotland Neck, NC: n.p., 1976.

217.40 "Ten to Seven." <u>Negro Digest</u> 15 (July 1966): 79-81.

217.41 "Thoughts is What You Asked For." <u>Callaloo</u> 4
(October 1978): 52.

217.42 "Three Poems -- Seizing, Big Momma, The Policeman."
<u>Black World</u> 21 (September 1972): 46-48.

        Secondary Sources

217.43(S) Burger, Mary Williams. "Julia Fields." In
HARRIS & DAVIS, pp. 123-131.

218   FIELDS, MAMIE.

218.1 <u>Lemon Swamp and Other Places</u>. New York: Free Press,
1983.

219.   FIGGS, CARRIE LAW MORGAN.

219.1 <u>Nuggets of Gold</u>. Chicago: Jaxon Printing Company,
1921. Poetry.

219.2 <u>Poetic Pearls</u>. Jacksonville, FL: Edward Waters
College Press, 1920.

219.3 <u>Select Plays</u>. Chicago: Author, 1923. Includes "Santa
Claus Land." "Jeptha's Daughter." "The Prince of Peace."
"Bachelor's Convention."

220.   FINCH, AMANDA.

220.1 <u>Black Trail: A Novella of Love in the South</u>. New
York: William-Frederick Press, 1951.

221.   FINNEY, NIKKY.

221.1 "Automatic Natural." <u>Essence</u> 17 (April 1987): 120.

221.2 "Blood from a Turnip." <u>Catalyst</u> (Winter 1988): 80.

221.3 "Chariots." <u>Essence</u> 17 (August 1986): 144.

221.4 "Do Write at Last." <u>Essence</u> 16 (January 1986): 128.

221.5 <u>On Wings Made of Gauze</u>. New York: William Morrow,
1985.

221.6 "Uncles." <u>Essence</u> 15 (November 1984): 138.

222. FISHER, GERTRUDE ARQUENE.

222.1 <u>Original Poems</u>. Parsons, KS: Foley Railway Printing
Company, 1910.

223. FLAGG, ANN.

223.1 <u>Great Gettin' Up Mornin'</u>. New York: Samuel French,
1964. Drama.

224. FLEMING, SARAH LEE BROWN (1875-1963).

224.1 <u>Clouds and Sunshine</u>. Boston: Cornhill Company, 1920.
Poetry.

224.2 <u>Hope's Highway</u>. New York: Neale Publishing Company,
1918. Novel.

       Secondary Sources

224.3(S) Shockley, Ann Allen. "Sarah Lee Levy Lindo
McDowell Brown Fleming." In SHOCKLEY, pp. 356-362.

224.4(S) "A Tribute for Mrs. Sarah Lee Fleming."
<u>Congressional Record</u> (27 April 1955): 5186.

225. FORDHAM, MARY WESTON (1862-).

225.1 <u>Magnolia Leaves: Poems</u>. Charleston, SC: Walker, Evans
and Cogswell, 1897.

226. FORTEN, CHARLOTTE L. (1837-1914).

226.1 <u>The Journal of Charlotte L. Forten</u>, ed by R.A.
Billington. New York: Dryden Press, 1953.

226.2 "A Parting Hymn." "Poem." "To W.L.G. on Reading His
'Chosen Queen'." In STETSON, pp. 22-24.

226.3 Two Black Teachers During the Civil War:...Life on the
Sea Islands, ed. by William L Katz. New York: Arno Press,
1969. First published in Atlantic Monthly (May-June 1864).

226.4 "The Forten Family." Negro History Bulletin 10
(January 1947): 75-79, 95.

Secondary Sources

226.5(S) Braxton, Joanne. Charlotte Forten Grimke' (1837-
1914). Wellesley, MA: Wellesley College Center for Research
on Women, 1985. [working paper no. 153]

226.6(S) Brown, William Wells. The Black Man, His Genius
and His Achievements. New York: Thomas Hamilton, Boston:
R.F. Wallcut, 1863. Charlotte Forten, p. 199.

226.7(S) Brown, William Wells. The Rising Sun; or, the
Antecedents and Advancement of the Colored Race. Boston:
A.G. Brown & Co., 1874. Charlotte L. Forten, p. 475.

226.8(S) Cooper, Anna Julia, ed. Life and Writings of the
Grimke' Family. Washington, DC: Cooper, 1951.

226.9(S) Grimke', Angelina Weld   "To Keep the Memory of
Charlotte Forten Grimke'."   In STETSON, pp. 60-63.

226.10(S) Harris, Trudier. "Charlotte L. Forten." In
HARRIS & DAVIS, 1986, pp. 130-139.

226.11(S) Loggins, Vernon. The Negro Author: His
Development in America. New York: Columbia University Press,
1931.

226.12(S) Majors, Gerri, and Saunders, Doris E. Black
Society. Chicago: Johnson Publishing Co., 1976.

226.13(S) Majors, Monroe Alphus. Noted Negro Women, Their
Triumphs and Activities. New York: Donohue & Henneberry,
1893.

226.14(S) Shockley, Ann Allen. "Charlotte L. Forten
Grimke'." In SHOCKLEY, pp. 71-83.

226.15(S) Wilson, Edmund. "Charlotte Forten and Colonel
Higginson." New Yorker 30 (10 April 1945): 132-47.

227 FORTSON, BETTIOLA HELOISE (1890-).

227.1 Mental Pearls: Original Poems and Essays. Chicago:
Author, 1915.

228. FOWLER, CAROLYN.

228.1 "Solid at the Core." <u>Freedomways</u> 14 (First quarter 1974): 59-62.

229. FOSWORTH, NILENE ELIZABETH (1936-).

229.1 <u>If I Were a Miracle Hen</u>. New York: Amuru, 1973. Poetry.

230. FRANKLIN, J[ENNIE] E[LIZABETH] (1937-).

230.1 <u>Black Girl: A Play in Two Acts</u>. New York: Dramatists Play Service, 1971.

230.2 <u>The Prodigal Sister: A New Black Musical</u>. New York: Samuel French, 1975. Musical drama.

            Secondary Sources

230.3(S) Beauford, Fred. "<u>Black Girl</u>'s J.E. Franklin." <u>Black Creation</u> 2 (Fall 1971): 38-40.

231. FRAZIER, RUBY PRIMUS.

231.1 <u>Ruby's Black Emeralds</u>. New York: Rannick Playwrights Company, 1971. New York: Amuru, 1973. Poetry.

232. FREDERICK, KATHERINE WATSON.

232.1 "Hundredfold." <u>Crisis</u>, 8(July 1980):206.

232.2 <u>Where Did You Last Find Me: An Anthology of Prose, Poetry and Songs</u>. Chicago: DuSable Museum of African American History Press, 1975..

233. FREEMAN, CAROL S. (1941-).

233.1 <u>The Poetry of Carol Freeman</u>. San Francisco: Julian Richardson, n.d.

233.2 "The Suicide." In JONES & NEAL, pp. 631-636. One
act drama.

234. FULLER, STEPHANY (1948-).

234.1 "Homeland." _Essence_ 2 (November 1971): 77

234.2 _Moving Deep_. Detroit: Broadside Press, 1969. Poetry.

234.3 "To a Dreamer Comes...." _Black Collegian_ 9 (May-June
1979): 90.

Secondary Sources

234.4(S) Fauntleroy, Mark. "_Essence_ Women: Stephany Inua
Fuller." _Essence_ 9 (October 1978): 7.

235. FULLILOVE, MAGGIE SHAW.

235.1 _Who Was Responsible_. Cincinnati: Abingdon Press,
1919. Novel.

236. GAINES-SHELTON, RUTH A. (1873-).

236.1 "The Church Fight." _Crisis_ 32 (May 1926): 17-21. In
HATCH, pp.189-191. One act drama.

Secondary Sources

236.2(S) Hatch, James V. _Black Theater, USA: Forty-Five
Plays by American Negroes, 1847-1974_. New York: Free Press,
1974.

237. GARNETT, RUTH M.

237.1 "Rites After Victory." _Black Scholar_ 11 (8): 79-80
(November-December 1980).

237.2 "You Want the World Flat Again." _Callaloo_ 12 (Winter
1989): 178. Poem.

238. GARY, MADELEINE SOPHIE.

238.1 Philosophical Essays: Vignettes of the Beam in a
Nigger's Eye. New York: Exposition Press, 1970.

239. GATES, JEANNETTE McPHERSON.

239.1 Reflections. Portland, OR: Press-22, 1971.

239.2 Relevance and Reality: Poetry and Photography. Sandy,
OR: St. Paul's Press, 1973.

239.3 Silhouettes. Sandy, OR: St. Paul's Press, 1972.

240. GAYLES, GLORIA (1940-).

240.1 "Anatomy of an Error: The Color Purple Controversy."
Catalyst 1 (Fall 1986): 50-53.

240.2 "Cracked." "Parade." "Sometimes as Women Only." In
BELL, pp. 361-366.

249.3 "For Our Sons." Catalyst (Fall 1989): 14.

240.4 "Love's Name." Essence 7 (September 1976): 16.

240.5 "The Making of a Permanent Afro." Catalyst (Summer
1988): 20.

240.6 No Crystal Stair: Visions of Race and Sex in Black
Women's Fiction. Boston: Pilgrim Press, 1984.

240.7 "On Hearing and Once Believing." Black Scholar 8
(January-February 1977): 34.

240.8 "Pessimism." Black Scholar 8 (January-February 1977):
34.

240.9   "The Pilgrimage." Catalyst (Summer 1988): 19.

240.10 "Prince Albert Indeed: An Epitaph for My Uncle."
Black Scholar 8 (January-February 1977): 33-34.

240.11 "She Who is Black and Mother: In Sociology and
Fiction, 1940-1970." In RODGERS, pp. 89-106.

240.12 "Soliloquy of a Black Executive Lost." Black World
23 (August 1974): 84-86.

240.13 "The Truths of Our Mothers' Lives: Mother-Daughter
Relationships in Black Women's Fiction." Sage 1 (2): 8-12
(Fall 1984). Textual criticism of Dorothy West and Toni
Morrison.

241. GEE, LETHONIA.

241.1 "By Glistening, Dancing Seas." Essence 15 (February 1985): 29.

242. GIBBS, JOAN.

242.1 Between a Rock and a Hard Place. New York: February 3, 1979. Poetry.

242.2 Top Ranking: A Collection of Articles on Racism and Classism in the Lesbian Community. New York: February 3, 1980. Sara Bennet, joint editor.

243. GIBBS, MICHELE.

243.1 Sketches from Home. Detroit: Broadside Press, 1983.

244. GIBBS, RUTH DUCKETT.

244.1 Black is the Color. Great Neck, New York: Center for Media Development, 1973.

245. GIBSON, P.J.

245.1 Long Time Since Yesterday: A Drama in Two Acts. New York: Samuel French, 1986.

246. GIDDINGS, PAULA (1947-)

246.1 "From a Black Perspective: The Poetry of Don L. Lee." Amistad 2, pp. 297-318.

246.2 "Nikki Giovanni: Taking a Chance on Feeling." In EVANS, pp. 211-217.

246.3 "Raisin Revisited." Encore 4 (7 July 1975): 28-31. Discusses Lorraine Hansberry.

246.4 "A Shoulder Hunched Against a Sharp Concern: Some
Themes in the Poetry of Margaret Walker." <u>Black World</u> 21
(December 1971): 20-25.

246.5 "Sorority Sisters. <u>Essence</u> 19 (July 1988): 36.

246.6 "A Special Vision, a Common Goal." <u>Encore</u> 4 (23 June
1975): 44.

246.7 "Triumph Song of Toni Morrison." <u>Encore</u> 6 (12December
1977): 26-30.

246.8 <u>When and Where I Enter: The Impact of Black Women on
Race and Sex in America</u>. New York: William Morrow, 1984.

246.9 "Woman Warrior: Ida B. Wells, Crusader-Journalist."
<u>Essence</u> 18 (February 1988): 75.

247. GILBERT, MERCEDES (?-1952).

247.1 <u>Aunt Sara's Wooden God</u>. Boston: Christopher
Publishing House, 1938. Novel.

247.2 "Environment." In GILBERT, pp. 53-89. Three act
drama.

247.3 <u>Selected Gems of Poetry, Comedy and Drama</u>. Boston:
Christopher Publishing House, 1931.

                    Secondary Sources

247.4(S) Stewart, Harry T. "The Poet-Actress: A Personal
Interview with Miss Mercedes Gilbert." <u>Education: A Journal
of Reputation</u> 2 (September 1936): 7

248. GIOVANNI, NIKKI (1943-).

248.1 "Aftra: A Rip-Off." <u>Encore</u> 4 (8 September 1975): 28-
29.

248.2 "Ali Outside the Wedding Ring." <u>Encore</u> 4 (3 November
1975): 42.

248.3 "Alone." <u>Essence</u> 1 (February 1971): 47.

248.4 "An Answer to Some Questions on How I Write: In Three
Parts." In EVANS, pp. 205-210.

248.5 "Beautiful Black Men." <u>Ebony</u> 27 (August 1972): 48.

248.6 "Between Consenting Adults." Encore 6 (18 July 1977): 48.

248.7 Black Feeling, Black Talk. Detroit: Broadside Press, 1968; rev 3d ed, 1970.

248.8 Black Feeling, Black Talk, Black Judgement. New York: William Morrow, 1971.

248.9 Black Judgement. Detroit: Broadside Press, 1968.

248.10 "Black Poems, Poseurs and Power. Negro Digest 18 (June 1969): 30-34.

248.11 "Campaign 1976: Hubert Humphrey." Encore 5 (3 May 1976): 18.

248.12 "Celebrating the Human Species." Encore 7 (18 December 1978): 20.

248.13 "Charles White." Freedomways 11 (1980): 155-156.

248.14 "Communication." Ebony 38 (February 1983): 48.

248.15 Cotton Candy on a Rainy Day. New York: William Morrow, 1978.

248.16 "D A and 'Dirty' Harry." Encore 5 (20 September 1976): 48.

248.17 "Decoding Carter's Message." Encore 8 (19 March 1979): 13.

248.18 Ego-Tripping and Other Poems for Young People. New York: Lawrence Hill, 1973.

248.19 "An Emotional View of Lorraine Hansberry." Freedomways 19 (4): 81-82 (1979).

248.20 "Forgotten R." Encore 5 (8 November 1976): 48.

248.21 Gemini, an Extended Autobiographical Statement. Indianapolis: Bobbs-Merrill Company, 1971.

248.22 "Great Stonewaller." Encore 5 (22 March 1976): 36.

248.23 "Housecleaning." Essence 2 (May 1971): 1.

248.24 "I Want to Sing." Essence 1 (February 1971): 47.

248.25 "I Wrote a Good Omelet." Essence 14 (October 1983): 88.

248.26 "Introspection." Encore 7 (18 December 1978): 26.

248.27 "Kennedy: Is Congress a Conspirator." Encore 6 (6 June 1977): 8.

248.28   "Leave it to Cleaver."   _Encore_ 4 (19 May 1975): 26.

248.29   "Loneliest Job in the World."   _Encore_ 6 (17 January 1977): 48.

248.30   "Martin Luther King's Letter from Birmingham Jail." _Encore_ 8 (19 November 1979): 19-21.

248.31   "Mixed Feelings about Mexico."   _Encore_ 6 (7 March 1977): 23.

248.32   _My House_.   New York: William Morrow, 1970.

248.33   "My Own Style."   _Essence_ 16 (May 1985): 60.

248.34   _Night Comes Softly: Anthology of Black Female Voices_. Newark, NJ: Nik-Tom Publications, 1970.   Giovanni, editor.

248.35   "The Planet of Junior Brown."   _Black World_ 21 (March 1972): 70-71.

248.36   _Poem of Angela Davis_.   Newark, NJ: Nik-Tom Publications, 1970.

248.37   _Re:CREATION_.   Detroit: Broadside Press, 1970.

248.38   "Rev. Ike - You Can't Lose with the Stuff I Use." _Encore_ 4 (17 March 1975): 21-22.

248.39   "Poet's Reflections."   _Encore_ 7 (18 September 1978): 39.

248.40   _Sacred Cows...and Other Edibles_.   New York: Willam Morrow, 1988.

248.41   "Same Old Voices, Same Old (Smoke-Filled) Rooms." _Encore_ 5 (21 June 1976): 48.

248.42   "Silent Revolution of the Domestic Worker."   _Encore_ 4 (23 June 1975): 36.

248.43   _Spin a Soft Black Song: Poems for Children_.   New York: Hill & Wang, 1971. Rev. ed.   New York: Farrar, Straus & Giroux, 1987.

248.44   "Symbolism and Reality."   _Encore_ 5 (7 June 1976): 48.

248.45   "They Clapped."   _Essence_ 16 (May 1985): 226.

248.46   _Those Who Ride the Night Winds_.   New York: William Morrow, 1983.

248.47   "Two Families."   _Encore_ 5 (2 August 1976): 31.

248.48   "U.S.A. -- United States of America, Union of South Africa, or Both."   _Encore_ 5 (16 August 1976): 32.

248.49 <u>Vacation Time: Poems for Children</u>. New York: William
Morrow, 1981.

248.50 "What Life is Like Living with a 14-Year Old Son."
<u>Essence</u> 15 (September 1984): 154.

248.51 "Why Landlords Get Relief." <u>Encore</u> 4 (18 August
1975): 32.

248.52 "Why Weren't Our 'Sisters in Liberation' in Boston."
<u>Encore</u> 4 (6 January 1975): 20.

248.53 <u>The Women and the Men</u>. New York: William Morrow,
1975.

248.54 "You Are There." <u>Mademoiselle</u> 84 (October 1978):
228.

248.55 <u>A Dialogue: James Baldwin and Nikki Giovanni</u>.
Philadelphia: Lippincott, 1973. James Baldwin, joint author.

248.56 <u>A Poetic Equation: Conversations between Nikki
Giovanni and Margaret Walker</u>. Washington, DC: Howard
University Press, 1974. Margaret Walker, joint author.

                    Secondary Sources

248.57(S) Bailey, Peter. "Nikki Giovanni: 'I Am Black,
Female, Polite.'" <u>Ebony</u> 27 (February 1972): 48-52,53-54,56.

248.58(S) Bonner, Carrington. "An Interview with Nikki
Giovanni." <u>Black American Literature Forum</u> 18 (Spring 1984):
29-30.

248.59(S) Elder, Arlene. "A <u>Melus</u> Interview: Nikki
Giovanni." <u>Melus</u> 9 (3): 61-75 (Winter 1982).

248.60(S) Giddings, Paula. "Nikki Giovanni: Taking a Chance
on Feeling." In EVANS, pp. 211-217.

248.61(S) Harris, William J. "Sweet Soft Essence of
Possibility: The Poetry of Nikki Giovanni." In EVANS, pp.
218-228.

248.62(S) Mitchell, Mozella G. "Nikki Giovanni." In
HARRIS & DAVIS, pp. 135-151.

248.63(S) Murphy, Frederick B. "Nikki." <u>Encore</u> (5 May
1975): 30-34.

248.64(S) Palmer, R. Roderick. "The Poetry of Three
Revolutionists: Don L. Lee, Sonia Sanchez, and Nikki
Giovanni." <u>CLA Journal</u> 15 (September 1971): 25-36.

248.65(S) Stokes, Stephanie J. "My House: Nikki Giovanni."
<u>Essence</u> 12 (August 1981): 84-86.

248.66(S)   Thompson, M. Cordell.   "Nikki Giovanni: Black
Rebel with ower in Poetry."   Jet (25 May 1972): 18-24.

1988-1991 Supplement

A248.67   "Episodes." Catalyst (Summer 1988): 35.

A248.68   "A Letter from Nikki." Catalyst (Winter 1988): 9.

249 GLASS, MARITA.

249.1   Marvin and Tige. New York: St. Martin's, 1977.

250.   GOLDEN, MARITA (1950-).

250.1   "Autobiography." Catalyst (Winter 1988): 15.

250.2   "Beginnings." Catalyst (Spring 1990): 13.

250.3   "The High Cost of Living." Catalyst (Winter 1989):
36.

250.4   "Keepers of Our Culture." Essence 19 (July 1988):
23.

250.5   Long Distance Life. New York: Doubleday, 1989.

250.6   Migrations of the Heart: A Personal Odyssey. New
York: Doubleday, 1983.

250.7   "My Father, My Mother, Myself." Essence 14 (May
1983): 72-74.

250.8   "Raising Sons Under Siege." Essence 19 (June 1989):
104.

250.9   A Woman's Place. New York: Doubleday, 1986. Essence
17 (August 1986): 88   Excerpt.

251.   GOMEZ, JEWELLE.

251.1   "Black Women Heroes: Here's Reality, Where's the
Fiction?" Black Scholar 17 (2): 8-13 (March-April 1986).

251.2   "For Toi." Essence 16 (February 1986): 136.

251.3   "Golden Song." Essence 8 (February 1978): 26.

251.4 "Housework." Black Scholar 19 (July/August-
September/October 1988): 29.

251.5 The Lipstick Papers. New York: Grace, 1980.

252. GOODWIN, RUBY BERKLEY (1903-?).

252.1 From My Kitchen Window. New York: Wendell Malliet,
1942. Poetry.

252.2 A Gold Star Mother Speaks. Fullerton, CA: Orange
County Printing company, 1944. Poetry.

252.3 It's Good to be Black. New York: Doubleday, 1953.
Autobiography.

253. GORDON, JOAN.

253.1 "Let It Not Be Said." Essence 8 (January 1978): 74.

254. GORDON, SELMA.

254.1 Poems. n.p., n.d.

254.2 Special Poems. n.p., n.d.

Gordon, Vivian V. SEE 558. SATIAFA.

255. GOSSETT, HATTIE.

255.1 "My Soul Looks Back in Wonder." Essence 12 (August
1981): 21.

256. GOVERN, RENA GREENE.

256.1 Democracy's Task. New York: Author, 1945. Poetry.

257. GRAHAM, BERYL.

257.1 "Essence Women: Eloise Greenfield." Essence 10 (June 1979): 32.

258. GRAHAM, SHIRLEY LOLA (1904-1977).

258.1 "After Addis Ababa: A Report on the African Summit Conference." Freedomways 3 (Fall 1963): 471-485.

258.2 "Black Man's Music." Crisis 40 (August 1933): 178-179.

258.3 Booker T. Washington. New York: Julian Messner, 1955.

258.4 DuBois: A Pictorial Biography. Chicago: Johnson Publications, 1978.

258.5 Dust to Earth. Princeton. NJ: Yale Drama School, 1941. Drama.

258.6 "Egypt is Africa." pt.1. Black Scholar 1 (May 1970): 20-22; pt. 2. 2 (September 1970): 28-34.

258.7 Gamal Abdel Nasser, Son of the Nile: A Biography. New York: Third Press, 1972.

258.8 George Washington Carver. New York: Julian Messner, 1944.

258.9 His Day is Marching On: A Memoir of W.E.B. DuBois. Philadelphia: Lippincott, 1971.

258.10 It's Mornin'. In BROWN-GUILLORY. Drama.

258.11 John Baptiste DuSable. New York: Julian Messner, 1953.

258.12 Julius K. Nyerere: Teacher of Africa. New York: Julius Messner, 1975.

258.13 "The Liberation of Africa." Black Scholar 2 (February 1971): 32-37.

258.14 "Nation Building in Ghana." Freedomways 2 (Fall 1962): 371-376.

258.15 "Negroes in the American Revolution." Freedomways (Summer 1961).

258.16 "Oberlin and the Negro." Crisis 42 (April 1935): 118, 124.

258.17 Paul Robeson, Citizen of the World. Westport CT: Greenwood Press. Reprint of 1946 edition.

258.18 A Pictorial History of W.E.B. DuBois. Chicago:
Johnson Publications, 1976.

258.19 "Spirituals to Symphonies." Etude 54 (November
1936): 691.

258.20 The Story of Paul Robeson. New York: Julian Messner,
1967.

258.21 The Story of Phillis Wheatley: Poetess of the
American Revolution. New York: Julian Messner, 1949.

258.22 The Story of Pocahontas. New York: Grosset & Dunlap,
1953.

258.23 "The Struggle in Lesotho." Black Scholar 2 (November
1970): 25-29.

258.24 There Was Once a Slave: The Heroic Story of Frederick
Douglass. New York: Julian Messner, 1966.

258.25 Tom-Tom. Cleveland, n.p., 1932. Opera.

258.26 "Towards an American Theatre." Arts Quarterly
(October-December 1937): 18-20.

258.27 Track Thirteen. Boston: Expression Co., 1940.
Drama.

258.28 "Tribute to Paul Robeson." Freedomways 11 (First
Quarter 1971): 6-7.

258.29 Your Most Humble Servant: The Story of Benjamin
Banneker. New York: Julian Messner, 1949.

258.30 Zulu Heart. New York: Third Press, 1974.

                    Secondary Sources

258.31(S) Davis, Thadious M. "Shirley Graham." In
MAINIERO, 1979, pp. 167-169.

258.32(S) Lewis, Ida. "Conversation: Ida Lewis & Shirley
Graham DuBois." Essence 1 (January 1971): 21-27.

258.33(S) Perkins, Kathy A. "The Unknown Career of Shirley
Graham." Freedomways 25 (1): 6-17 (First Quarter 1985).

258.34(S) Peterson, Bernard L., Jr. "Shirley Graham DuBois:
Composer and Playwright." Crisis 84 (May 1977): 177-179.

259. GREET, ANITA.

259.1   "Aftermath." about... time 9 (March 1981): 23.

259.2   "A Design of Life." about... time 9 (March 1981): 23.

259.3   "Existence." about... time 9 (September 1981): 21.

259.4   "Freedom." about... time 10 (April 1982): 23.

259.5   "The Harvest." about... time 9 (March 1981): 23.

259.6   "Imagination." about... time 10 (April 1982): 23.

259.7   "A Love Song." about... time 9 (March 1981): 23.

259.8   "Maize." about... time 9 (March 1981): 23.

259.9   "A Majestic God." about... time 9 (September 1981):
21.

259.10   "Sepal." about... time 9 (March 1981): 23.

259.11   "The Spirit of the Wind." about... time 10 (April
1982): 23; 10 (December 1982): 19.

259.12   "To Take a Pause." about... time 9 (September 1981):
21.

259.13   "Trust." about... time 10 (April 1982): 23.

260.   GREEN, GERALDINE CLARK.

260.1   "God Bless the Children." About Time 14 (November
1986): 15.

260.2   "Heaven." About Time 14 (November 1986): 15.

260.3   "I Am King of This Castle." About Time 11 (November
1986): 15.

260.4   "Were Only Men Created After God's Image." About Time
11 (November 1986): 15.

261.   GREEN, JAKI SHELTON.

261.1   "A Birthday Tribute III." Essence 18 (December 1987):
137.

261.2   Dead On Arrival and New Poems. Carrboro, NC: Carolina
Wren Press, 1983.

261.3   "Eva I." Essence 17 (March 1987): 122.

261.4 <u>Masks</u>.   Carrboro, NC: Carolina Wren Press, 1981.

262. GREEN, OLIVIA HARRIS.

262.1 "Unsung Melody." <u>Negro History Bulletin</u> 40 (September-October 1977): 750.

263. GREENE, ANN T.

263.1 "Love Letters." <u>Callaloo</u> 10 (4): 563-569 (Fall 1987).

263.2 "The Ugly Man." <u>Callaloo</u> 12 (Winter 1989): 79.   Short fiction.

264. GREENE, EMILY JANE.

264.1 <u>In the Green Pastures</u>. Los Angeles: Author, 1966.

265. GREENFIELD, ELOISE (1929-).

265.1 <u>Africa Dream</u>. New York: John Day, 1972.

265.2 "African American Literature: A New Challenge." <u>Interracial Books for Children Bulletin</u> 17 (2): 4-5 (1986).

265.3 <u>Bubbles</u>. Washington, DC: Drum & Spear, 1972.

265.4 <u>Darlene</u>. New York: Methuen, 1980.

265.5 <u>Daydreamers</u>. New York: Dial Press, 1981.

265.6 <u>First Pink Light</u>. New York: Thomas Crowell, 1976.

265.7 <u>Grandmama's Joy</u>. New York: Philomel, 1980.

265.8 <u>Honey, I Love, and Other Love Poems</u>. New York: Thomas Crowell, 1978.

265.9 "Intrusion." <u>Black World</u> 21 (June 1972): 53-56.

265.10 <u>Mary McLeod Bethune</u>. New York: Thomas Crowell, 1977.

265.11 <u>Me and Neesie</u>. New York: Thomas Crowell, 1975.

265.12 <u>Paul Robeson</u>. New York: Thomas Crowell, 1975.

265.13 <u>Rosa Parks</u>. New York: Thomas Crowell, 1973.

265.14 <u>She Come Bringing Me That Little Baby Girl</u>.
Philadelphia: Lippincott, 1974.

265.15 <u>Sister</u>. New York: Thomas Crowell, 1974.

265.16 <u>Talk About a Family</u>. Philadelphia: Lippincott, 1978.

265.17 "Way to Go Home." <u>Black World</u> 23 (May 1974): 54-58.

265.18 "Writing for Children -- A Joy and a Responsibility."
<u>Interracial Books for Children Bulletin</u> 10 (3): 3-4 (1979).

265.19 <u>Childtimes: A Three-Generation Memoir</u>. New York:
Thomas Crowell, 1979. Lessie Jones Little, joint author.

265.20 <u>I Can Do it by Myself</u>. New York: Thomas Crowell,
1978. Lessie Jones Little, joint author.

265.21 <u>Alesia</u>. New York: Philomel, 1981. Alesia Revis,
joint author.

                    Secondary Sources

265.22(S) Graham, Beryl. "<u>Essence</u> Women: Eloise
Greenfield." <u>Essence</u> 10(June 1979): 32.

265.23(S) Kiah, R.B. "Profile: Eloise Greenfield." <u>Language
Arts</u> 57 (September 1980): 653-659.

                    1988-1991 Supplement

A265.24 <u>Grandpa's Face</u>. New York: Philomel Books, 1988.

A265.25 "I See My Future." <u>Shooting Star Review</u> 3 (Spring
1989): 2. Poem.

A265.26 <u>Nathaniel Talking</u>. New York: Black Butterfly
Children's Books, 1989.

A265.27 <u>Under the Sunday Tree</u>. New York: Harper, 1988.

266. GREENWOOD, THERESA (1936-).

266.1 <u>Psalms of a Black Mother</u>. Anderson, IN: Warner Press,
1970. Poetry.

267. GREGORY, CAROLE.

267.1 "A Freedom Song for the Black Woman." "The Greater
Friendship Baptist Church." "Love Letter." "Revelation."
In STETSON, pp. 185-191.

267.2 "A Letter from Home." "Lotus Women." "Singing
Exercise in the U.S. Army." "Writers and Lovers." Obsidian
7 (2-3): 219-221 (Summer-Winter 1981).

267.3 "Likely Possibility." Black Collegian 35 (1980): 46-
50.

268. GRIFFIN, JUDITH BERRY.

268.1 The Magic Mirrors. New York: Coward McCann, 1971.
Children and young adult stories.

268.2 Nat Turner. New York: Coward McCann, 1970. Children
and young adult stories.

269. GRIFFITH, LOIS ELAINE.

269.1 "Chica." Essence 11 (March 1981): 22.

269.2 "Prince Harlem." In BARAKA & BARAKA, pp. 110-119.

270. GRIMES, NIKKI (1950-).

270.1 "Definition." "Fragments: Mousetrap." "The Takers."
In BARAKA & BARAKA.

270.2 "For Gwendolyn Brooks on Mother's Day." "Niks:1 and
2." "Who Rap for the Dead Lecturer (in Seance)." "The Women
in My Life." Greenfield Review 7 (3-4): 14-17 (Spring-Summer
1979).

270.3 Growin'. New York: Dial Press, 1977. Children's
stories.

270.4 Poems by Nikki. New York: Celebrated Blackness, 1970.

270.5 Something on My Mind. New York: Dial Press, 1978.
Children's poetry.

271. GRIMKE, ANGELINA WELD (1880-1958).

271.1 "At April." "For the Candlelight." "A Mona Lisa."
"To Keep the Memory of Charlotte Forten Grimke." In
STETSON, pp. 60-63.

271.2 "Black Is, As Black Does." Colored American Magazine
1 (August 1900): 160.

271.3 Rachel: A Play in Three Acts. Boston: Cornhill
Company, 1920.

Secondary Sources

271.4(S) Ada. "Lines Suggested on Reading 'An Appeal to
Christian Women of the South' by A.E. Grimke." In STETSON,
pp. 17-19.

271.5(S) Cooper, Anna Julia, ed. Life and Writings of the
Grimke Family. Washington, DC: Cooper, 1951.

271.6(S) Ellington, Mary Davis. "Plays by Negro Authors with
Special Emphasis upon the Period 1916 to 1934." Masters
Thesis, Fisk University, 1934.

271.7(S) Greene, Michael. "Angela Weld Grimke." In HARRIS
& DAVIS, 1986, pp. 149-155.

271.8(S) Hatch, James V. Black Theater, USA: Forty-Five
Plays by American Negroes, 1847-1974. New York: Free Press,
1974.

271.9(S) Hull, Gloria T. Color, Sex, and Poetry: Three
Women Writers of the Harlem Renaissance. Bloomington, IN:
Indiana University Press, 1987.

271.10(S) Hull, Gloria T. " 'Under the Days,' the Buried
Life and Poetry of Angelina Weld Grimke." In SMITH.

271.11(S) Miller, Jeanne-Marie A. "Angelina Weld Grimke."
In QUARTERMAIN, pp. 129-136.

271.12(S) Miller, Jeanne-Marie A. "Angelina Weld Grimke:
Playwright and Poet." CLA Journal 21 (June 1978): 513-524.

271.13(S) Perry, Margaret. "Angelina Weld Grimke." In
PERRY, pp. 86-87.

271.14(S) Shockley, Ann Allen. "Angelina Weld Grimke." In
SHOCKLEY, pp. 373-379.

Grimke, Charlotte Forten SEE 226. FORTEN, CHARLOTTE L.

272. GROSVENOR, VERTA MAE (1939-).

272.1 "Don't Cry for Me, Carolina." <u>Essence</u> 13 (July 1982):
70-72. Short fiction.

272.2 "Nothin' But a Feelin'." <u>Essence</u> 7 (February 1977):
62. Poetry.

272.3 <u>Plain Brown Rapper</u>. New York: Doubleday, 1975.

272.4 "Skillet Blonde." In BARAKA & BARAKA, pp. 124-130.
Short fiction.

272.5 <u>Thursdays and Every Other Sunday Off: A Domestic Rap</u>.
New York: Doubleday, 1972.

272.6 <u>Vibration Cooking: Travels of a Geechee Girl</u>. New
York: Doubleday, 1970. Autobiography.

273. GUINN, DOROTHY.

273.1 <u>Out of the Dark: A Pageant</u>. In RICHARDSON, pp. 305-
330. A four episode pageant.

274. GUNNER, FRANCES.

274.1 <u>The Light of the Women: A Ceremonial for the Use of
Negro Groups</u>. In RICHARDSON, pp. 333-342.

275. GUY, ROSA (1925-).

275.1 <u>And I Heard a Bird Sing</u>. New York: Delacorte Press,
1987.

275.2 <u>Bird at My Window</u>. Philadelphia: Lippincott, 1966.
Novel.

275.3 <u>Children of Longing</u>. New York: Holt, Rinehart &
Winston, 1970.

275.4 <u>The Disappearance</u>. New York: Delacorte Press, 1979.

275.5 <u>Edith Jackson</u>. New York: Viking Press, 1978.

275.6 <u>The Friends</u>. New York: Holt, Rinehart & Winston,
1973. Children and young adult stories.

275.7 <u>A Measure of Time</u>. New York: Holt, Rinehart &
Winston, 1983.

275.8 <u>Mirror of Her Own</u>. New York: Delacorte Press, 1981.

275.9 <u>Mother Crocodile</u>. New York: Delacorte Press, 1981.

275.10 <u>My Love, My Love, or, the Peasant Girl</u>. New York: Henry Holt & Company, 1985.

275.11 <u>New Guys Around the Block</u>. New York: Delacorte Press, 1983.

275.12 <u>Paris, Pee Wee and Big Dog</u>. New York: Delacorte Press, 1985.

275.13 <u>Ruby</u>. New York: Viking Press, 1976.

275.14 <u>The Ups and Downs of Carl Davis, III</u>. NY: Delacorte, 1989.

Secondary Sources

275.15(S) Lawrence, Leota S. "Rosa Guy." In DAVIS & HARRIS, pp. 101-106.

275.16(S) Wilson, Judith. "Rosa Guy: Writing with a Bold Vision." <u>Essence</u> (October 1979): 14,20.

276. GUYTON, MATILDA.

276.1 <u>The Black Woman</u>. Cleveland: Author, 1939.

277. HAGEDORN, JESSICA.

277.1 "Strange Fun." <u>Black Scholar</u> 8 (March 1977): 52.

278. HAINES, CORRIE and ROBERTA.

278.1 <u>As I See It (Prose - Poetry -- Free Verse)</u>. Washington, DC: NuClassics and Science Publishing Company, 1974.

279. HALL, IRMA P. (1935-).

279.1 <u>Pole Moto (Gentle Fire)</u>. Dallas, TX: Akini Isi Publishing Company, 1973.

280. HALL-EVANS, JO ANN (1934-).

280.1 "Cape Coast Castle Revisited." "Seduction." In
STETSON, pp. 191-192.

280.2 "Hope." _Essence_ 17 (April 1987): 131.

281. HAMBRICK, BRENDA.

281.1 "Topaz Lady." _Black American Literature Forum_ 15
(Summer 1981): 72.

282. HAMILTON, SARAH B. EDMONDS.

282.1 _Out of My Heart: Poems_. New York: Exposition Press,
1961.

282.2 _Something to Remember_. New York: Exposition Press,
1961. Poetry.

283. HAMILTON, VIRGINIA (1936-).

283.1 _Arilla Sun Down_. New York: Greenwillow, 1976.

283.2 _Dustland_. New York: Greenwillow, 1980.

283.3 _The Gathering_. New York: Greenwillow, 1981.

283.4 _The House of Dies Drear_. New York: Macmillan
Publishing Company, 1968, reprinted, 1985.

283.5 _Hugo Black: The Alabama Years_. Tuscaloosa, AL:
University of Alabama Press, 1982.

283.6 _Illusion and Reality_. Washington, DC: Library of
Congress, 1976.

283.7 _Jahdu_. New York: Greenwillow, 1980.

283.8 _Junius Over Far_. New York: Harper, 1985.

283.9 _Justice and Her Brothers_. New York: Greenwillow,
1978.

283.10 "Justice Trilogy": _Dustland_. New York: Greenwillow,
1980. _The Gathering_. New York: Greenwillow, 1981. _Justice
and Her Brothers_. New York: Greenwillow, 1978.

283.11 A Little Love. New York: Philomel, 1984.

283.12 M.C. Higgins, the Great. New York: Macmillan
Publishing Company, 1974.

283.13 Magical Adventures of Pretty Pearl. New York:
Harper, 1984.

283.14 The Mystery of Drear House. New York: Greenwillow,
1987.

283.15 Paul Robeson: The Life and Times of a Free Man. New
York: Harper, 1974.

283.16 The People Could Fly: American Black Folktales. New
York: A.A. Knopf, 1987.

283.17 The Planet of Junior Brown. New York: Macmillan
Publishing Company, 1971, reprinted, 1986.

283.18 "Sheema's Journey." Seventeen 43 (April 1984): 202-
203.

283.19 Sweet Whispers, Brother Rush. New York: Philomel,
1982.

283.20 The Time Ago Tales of Jahdu. New York: Macmillan
Publishing Company, 1969.

283.21 Time Ago Lost: More Tales of Jahdu. New York:
Macmillan Publishing Company, 1973.

283.22 W.E.B. DuBois: A Biography. New York: Thomas Crowell,
1972.

283.23 A White Romance. New York: Philomel, 1987.

283.24 Willie Bea and the Time the Martians Landed. New
York: Greenwillow, 1983.

283.25 The Writings of W.E.B. DuBois. New York: Thomas
Crowell, 1972. Edited by Hamilton.

283.26 Zeely. New York: Macmillan Publishing Company, 1967,
reprinted, 1986. New York: Dell, 1978.

                    Secondary Sources

283.27(S) Apseloff, Marilyn. "A Conversation with Virginia
Hamilton." Children's Literature in Education 14 (4): 204-
213 (Winter 1983).

283.28(S) Apseloff, Marilyn. Virginia Hamilton/Ohio
Explorer in the World of Imagination. Columbus, OH: The
State Library of Ohio, 1979.

283.29(S) Ball, Jane. "Virginia Hamilton." In DAVIS &
HARRIS, pp. 107-110.

283.30(S) Dressel, Janice Hartwick. "The Legacy of Ralph
Ellison in Virginia Hamilton's <u>Justice</u> Trilogy." <u>English
Journal</u> 73 (November 1984): 42-48.

283.31(S) Jackson, Harriet. "Virginia Hamilton: A Teller of
Tales." <u>Essence</u> 6 (February 1976): 58-59.

283.32(S) Moss, Anita. "Frontiers of Gender in Children's
Literature: Virginia Hamilton's <u>Arilla Sundown</u>." <u>Children's
Literature Association Quarterly</u> 8 (4): 25-27 (Winter 1983).

283.33(S) Scarupa, Harriet Jackson. "Virginia Hamilton:
Teller of Tales." <u>Essence</u> 6 (January 1976): 58-59.

1988-1991 Supplement

A283.34 <u>Anthony Burns: The Defeat and Triumph of a Fugitive
Slave</u>. NY: A. A. Knopf, 1988.

A283.35 <u>The Mystery of Drear House: The Conclusion of the
Dies Drear Chronicle</u>. NY: Collier, 1988.

A283.36 <u>White Romance</u>. New York: Harbrace, 1989.

284. HANDY, OLIVE LEWIS.

284.1 <u>My Deeply Solemn Thought</u>. n.p., 1939.

285. HANSBERRY, LORRAINE (1930-1965).

285.1 "All the Dark and Beautiful Warriors." <u>Village Voice</u>
28 (16 August 1983): 1, 11-16, 18-19.

285.2 "The Black Revolution and the White Backlash."
<u>National Guardian</u> 26 (4 July 1964): 5-9.

285.3 <u>Les Blancs: The Collected Last Plays of Lorraine
Hansberry</u>. New York: Random House, 1972.

285.4 "The Buck Williams Tennessee Memorial Association."
<u>Southern Exposure</u> 12 (September-October 1984): 28. Excerpt
from uncompleted novel.

285.5 "A Challenge to Artists." <u>Freedomways</u> 3 (Winter
1963): 33-35.

285.6 Collected Last Plays: Les Blancs, The Drinking Gourd, What Use Are Flowers. ed by Robert Nemiroff. New York: New American Library, 1983.

285.7 "The Creative Use of the Unconscious." Journal of American Academy of Psychotherapists 5 (1964): 13-17.

285.8 "Genet, Mailer and the New Paternalism." Village Voice 6 (1 June 1961): 10-15.

285.9 "Images and Essences: 1961 Dialog with an Uncolored Egghead Containing Wholesome Intentions and Some Sass." Urbanite 1 (May 1961): 10, 11, 36.

285.10 "In Defense of the Equality of Men." In GILBERT & GUBAR, pp. 2058-2067.

285.11 "The Legacy of W.E.B. DuBois." Freedomways 5 (Winter 1965): 19-20.

285.12 "A Letter from Lorraine Hansberry on 'Porgy and Bess.'" The Theater (August 1959): 10.

285.13 "Me Tink Me Hear Sounds in de Night." Theatre Arts, 44: 9-11, 69-70.

285.14 The Movement: Documentary of a Struggle for Equality. New York: Simon & Schuster, 1964.

285.15 "My Name is Lorraine Hansberry, I Am a Writer." Esquire 72 (November 1969): 140.

285.16 "The Nation Needs Your Gifts." Negro Digest 13 (August 1964): 26-29.

285.17 "The Negro in American Culture," In BIGSBY. Vol. 1.

285.18 "Negro Writer and His Roots: Toward a New Romanticism." Black Scholar 12 (March-April 1981): 2-12.

285.19 "Ocomogosiay!" Black Collegian 14 (March-April 1984): 48.

285.20 "On Summer." Playbill (27 June 1960): 25-27.

285.21 "Original Prospectus for the John Brown Memorial Theatre of Harlem." Black Scholar 10 (July/August 1979): 14-15.

285.22 A Raisin in the Sun. New York: Random House, 1959.

285.23 The Sign in Sidney Brustein's Window. New York: Random House, 1965.

285.24 "Strange Flower." Liberation 4 (May 1959): 14-15.

285.25 "This Complex of Womanhood." Ebony 15 (August 1960):
40.

285.26 "Three Hundred Years Later." Black Collegian 14
(March-April 1984): 48.

285.27 To Be Young, Gifted and Black: Lorraine Hansberry in
Her Own Words, adapted by Robert Nemiroff. Englewood Cliffs,
NJ: Prentice-Hall, 1969. Autobiography.

285.28 "To Ghana Off the Top of My Head, March 1957." Black
Collegian 14 (March-April 1984): 48.

285.29 "We Are of the Same Sidewalks." Freedomways 11
(1980): 197-198.

285.30 "Willy Loman, Walter Lee Younger and He Who Must
Live." Village Voice 4 (12 August 1959): 7,8.

Secondary Sources

285.31(S) Abramson, Doris E. Negro Playwrights in the
American Theater, 1925-1959. New York: Columbia University
Press, 1969. Lorraine Hansberry, pp. 239-254.

285.32(S) Adams, Michael. "Lorraine Hansberry." In CURB,
pp. 247-254.

285.33(S) Adams, Peter, et al, eds. Afro-American
Literature: Drama. Boston: Houghton, 1969.

285.34(S) Baldwin, James. "Lorraine Hansberry at the
Summit." Freedomways 19 (4): 269-272 (1979).

285.35(S) Baldwin, James. "Sweet Lorraine." Esquire 72
(November 1969): 139-140.

285.36(S) Bennett, Lerone, Jr. and Burroughs, Margaret G.
"A Lorraine Hansberry Rap." Freedomways 19 (4): 226-233
(Fall 1979).

285.37(S) Bond, Jean Corey. "Lorraine Hansberry: To Reclaim
Her Legacy." Freedomways 19 (1): 183-185 (1979).

285.38(S) Bowles, Juliette, ed. In the Memory and Spirit of
Frances, Zora and Lorraine: Essays and Interviews on Black
Women and Writing. Washington, DC: Institute for the Arts
and Humanities, Howard University, 1979.

285.39(S) Bray, Rosemary L. "Work in Progress: The
Definitive Lorraine Hansberry." Ms. 15 (February 1987): 31.

285.40(S) Brown, Lloyd W. "Lorraine Hansberry As Ironist: A
Reappraisal of A Raisin in the Sun." Journal of Black
Studies 4 (March 1974): 237-47.

285.41(S)   Carter, Steven R.   "Commitment Amid Complexity:
Lorraine Hansberry's Life-in-Action."   MELUS 7 (Fall 1980):
39-53.

285.42(S)   Carter, Steven R.   "Images of Men in Lorraine
Hansberry's Writing."   Black American Literature Forum 19
(4): 160-162 (Winter 1985).

285.43(S)   Carter, Steven R.   "John Brown Theatre: Lorraine
Hansberry's Cultural Views and Dramatic Goals."   Freedomways
19 (4): 186-191 (1979).

285.44(S)   Carter, Steven R.   "Lorraine Hansberry."   In
DAVIS & HARRIS, 1985, pp. 120-134.

285.45(S)   Cheney. Anne.   Lorraine Hansberry.   Boston:
Twayne, 1984.

285.46(S)   Childress, Alice, ed. Black Scenes: Collection of
Scenes from Plays Written by Black People about Black
Experience.   New York: Doubleday, 1971.

285.47(S)   Cruse, Harold.   The Crisis of the Negro
Intellectual.   New York: William Morrow, 1967.   Considers
Lorraine Hansberry, p. 267-284

285.48(S)   Davis, Ossie.   "The Significance of Lorraine
Hansberry,"   Freedomways 5 (Summer 1965): 396-402.

285.49(S)   Elder, Lonne, III.   "Lorraine Hansberry: Social
Consciousness and the Will."   Freedomways 19 (4): 213-218
(1979).

285.50(S)   Farrison, W. Edward.   "Lorraine Hansberry's Last
Dramas."   CLA Journal 16 (December 1972): 188-197.

285.51(S)   France, Arthur.   "A Raisin Revisited."
Freedomways 5 (1965): 403-410.

285.52(S)   Freedomways Lorraine Hansberry Issue 19 (Fourth
Quarter 1979).

285.53(S)   Friedman, Sharon.   "Feminism as Theme in Twentieth
Century American Women's Drama."   American Studies 25 (1):
69-89 (Spring 1984).

285.54(S)   Giddings, Paula.   "Raisin Revisited."   Encore 4 (7
July 1975): 28-31.

285.55(S)   Gill, Glenda.   "Techniques of Teaching Lorraine
Hansberry: Liberation from Boredom."   Negro American
Literature Forum 8 (Summer 1974): 226-228.

285.56(S)   Giovanni, Nikki.   "An Emotional View of Lorraine
Hansberry."   Freedomways 19 (4): 81-82 (1979).

285.57(S)   Gresham, Jewell Handy.   "Lorraine Hansberry as
Prose Stylist."   Freedomways 19 (4): 192-204 (1979).

285.58(S)   Hairston, Loyle. "Lorraine Hansberry: Portrait of
an Angry Young Writer." <u>Crisis</u> 86 (April 1979): 123-124.

285.59(S)   Haley, Alex. "Once and Future Vision of Lorraine
Hansberry." <u>Freedomways</u> 19 (4): 277-280 (1979).

285.60(S)   Hatch, James V. <u>Black Theater, USA: Forty-Five
Plays by American Negroes, 1847-1974</u>. New York: Free Press,
1974.

285.61(S)   Isaacs, Harold. "Five Writers and Their African
Ancestors: Part I." <u>Phylon</u> 21 (1960): 66-70.

285.62(S)   Isaacs, Harold. <u>The New World of Negro Americans</u>.
New York: Viking Press, 1964. Considers Lorraine Hansberry,
p. 277-287.

285.63(S)   Kaiser, Ernest and Nemiroff, Robert. "A Lorraine
Hansberry Bibliography." <u>Freedomways</u> 19 (Fourth Quarter
1979): 285-304.

285.64(S)   Killens, John Oliver. "Broadway in Black and
White." <u>African Forum</u> 1 (Winter 1966): 66-70.

285.65(S)   Killens, John Oliver. "Lorraine Hansberry: On
Time." <u>Freedomways</u> 19 (4): 273-276 (1979).

285.66(S)   King, Woodie, Jr. "Lorraine Hansberry's Children:
Black Artists and a <u>Raisin in the Sun</u>." <u>Freedomways</u> 19 (4):
219-22 (1979).

285.67(S)   Lewis, Theophilus. "Social Protest in <u>Raisin in
the Sun</u>." <u>Catholic World</u> 190 (1959): 31-35.

285.68(S)   Mayfield, Julian. "Lorraine Hansberry: A Woman
For All Seasons." <u>Freedomways</u> 19 (4): 263-268 (1979).

285.69(S)   Mootry, Maria K. <u>The Crisis of Feminist
Criticism: A Case Study of Lorraine Hansberry's Feminine
Traits in "Raisin" and "Sign"</u>. (Afro Scholar Working Papers,
v. 16) Urbana, IL: University of Illinois Press, 198?.

285.70(S)   Ness, David. "<u>The Sign in Sidney Brustein's
Window</u>: A Black Playwright Looks at White America."
<u>Freedomways</u>, 11(Fourth Quarter 1971):359-366.

285.71(S)   Ness, David. "Lorraine Hansberry's <u>Les Blancs</u>:
The Victory of the Man Who Must." <u>Freedomways</u> 13 (1974):
294-306.

285.72(S)   Oliver, Clinton and Sills, Stephanie, eds.
<u>Contemporary Black Drama</u>. New York: Charles Scriner's, 1971.

285.73(S)   Patterson, Lindsay, ed. <u>Black Theater: A 20th
Century Collection of the Work of Its Best Playwrights</u>. New
York: Dodd, Mead, 1971.

285.74(S)   Powell, Bertie J. "Black Experience in Margaret Walker's <u>Jubilee</u> and Lorraine Hansberry's <u>The Drinking Gourd</u>." <u>CLA Journal</u> 21 (December 1977): 304-311.

285.75(S)   Rich, Adrienne.   Problem with Lorraine Hansberry." <u>Freedomways</u> 19 (4): 247-255 (1979).

285.76(S)   Riley, Clayton.   "Lorraine Hansberry: A Melody In a Different Key." <u>Freedomways</u> 19 (4): 205-212 (1979).

285.77(S)   Royals, Demetria Brendan.   "The Me Lorraine Hansberry Knew." <u>Freedomways</u> 19 (4): 261-262 (1979).

285.78(S)   Salaam, Kalamu ya.   "What Use Is Writing? Re-reading Lorraine Hansberry." <u>Black Collegian</u> 14 (4): 45-46 (March-April, 1984).

285.79(S)   Scheader, Catherine.   <u>They Found a Way: Lorraine Hansberry</u>.   Chicago: Children's Press, 1978.

285.80(S)   Terkel, Studs.   "An Interview with Lorraine Hansberry." <u>Chicago Five Arts Guide</u> 10 (April 1961): 8-14.

285.81(S)   Ward, Douglas Turner.   "Lorraine Hansberry and the Passion of Walter Lee." <u>Freedomways</u> 19 (4): (1979).

285.82(S)   Weales, Gerald.   "Thoughts On <u>A Raisin in the Sun</u>." <u>Commentary</u> 28 (1959): 527-530.

285.83(S)   Wilkerson, Margaret B.   "The Dark Vision of Lorraine Hansberry: Excerpts From a Literary Biography." <u>Massachusetts Review</u> 28 (4): 642-650 (Winter 1987).

285.84(S)   Wilkerson, Margaret B.   "Lorraine Hansberry: The Complete Feminist." <u>Freedomways</u> 19 (4): 235-245 (1979).

285.85(S)   Wilkerson, Margaret B.   "The Sighted Eyes and Feeling Heart of Lorraine Hansberry." <u>Black American Literature Forum</u> 17 (1): 91-104 (Spring 1983).

285.86(S)   Wright, Sarah Elizabeth.   "Lorraine Hansberry On Film." <u>Freedomways</u> 19 (4): 283-284 (1979).

1988-1991 Supplement

Secondary Sources

A285.87(S)   Carter, Steven R.   "Lorraine Hansberry's <u>Toussaint</u>." <u>Black American Literature Forum</u> 23 (Spring 1989): 139.

A285.88(S)   Washington, J. Charles.   "<u>A Raisin in the Sun</u> Revisited." <u>Black Literature Forum</u> 22 (Spring 1988): 109.

286.   HARDY, JOYCE.

286.1 "Black Woman." about... time 10 (May 1982): 31.

286.2 "Dedication: To the Black Man." about... time 10 (May 1982): 30.

286.3 "My Feelings for You." about... time 10 (May 1982): 30-31.

286.4 "Who." about... time 10 (May1982): 31.

287. HARE, MAUD CUNEY (1874-1936).

287.1 "Antar, the Negro Poet of Arabia." Crisis, 28(June 1924):64. In RICHARDSON, pp.27-74. Four act historical drama.

287.2 "Folk Music of the Creoles." In CUNARD.

287.3 The Message of the Trees: An Anthology of Leaves and Branches. Boston: Cornhill Company, 1918.

287.4 Negro Musicians and Their Music. Washington, DC: Associated Publishers, 1936.

287.5 "Negro Music in Porto Rico." In CUNARD.

287.6 Norris Wright Cuney: A Tribute of the Black People. New York: Crisis Publishing Company, 1913.

                    Secondary Sources

287.7(S) Shockley, Ann Allen. "Maud Cuney Hare." In SHOCKLEY, pp. 334-340.

287.8(S) Southern, Eileen. Biographical Dictionary of Afro-American and African Musicians. Westport, CT: Greenwood Press, 1982.

288. HARPER, FRANCES ELLEN WATKINS (1825-1911).

288.1 The Alabama Martyr and Other Poems. No Imprint. [1890?]

288.2 "An Appeal To My Countrywomen." "The Crocuses." "A Double Standard." "Learning To Read." "The Mission of the Flowers." "She's Free." "Vashti." In STETSON, pp. 27-36.

288.3 Atlanta Offerings: Poems. Philadelphia: Author, 1895.

288.4 "Colored Women of America." Englishwoman's Review (January 1878): 10-15.

288.5 "Duty to Dependent Races." National Council of Women of the United States, Transactions (1891): 86-91.

288.6 Effie Afton. Eventide. Boston: Ferridge, 1895.

288.7 Forest Leaves or Autumn Leaves. Baltimore: Author, 1855.

288.8 Idylls of the Bible. Philadelphia: George S. Ferguson, 1901.

288.9 Iola Leroy; or, Shadows Uplifted. Philadelphia: Garrigues Bros., 1893. 3d ed. Boston: James H. Earle, 1895. Novel.

288.10 Light Beyond the Darkness. Chicago: Donohue and Henneberry, n.d.

288.11 Miscellaneous Poems. Boston: Author, 1854.

288.12 Moses, a Story of the Nile. Philadelphia: Author, 1869.

288.13 "National Woman's Christian Temperance Union." A.M.E. Church Review 5 (1889): 242-245.

288.14 Poems. Boston: Merryhew & Sons, 1871. Philadelphia: Geo. S. Ferguson, 1895.

288.15 Poems on Miscellaneous Subjects. Boston: J.B. Yerrington, 1854. 2d series. Boston: Merryhew & Son, 1864.

288.16 Sketches of Southern Life. Boston: Merryhew & Son, 1872.

288.17 The Sparrow's Fall and Other Poems. n.p., 1890?

288.18 "The Triumph of Freedom -- A Dream." Anglo-African Magazine (January 1860): 21-22.

288.19 "The Two Offers." Anglo-African Magazine (September 1859): 288-291; (October 1859): 311-313.

288.20 "The Woman's Christian Temperance Union and the Colored Woman." A.M.E. Church Review 4 (1888): 313-316.

288.21 "Woman's Political Future." In SEWELL.

Secondary Sources

288.22(S) Bowles, Juliette, ed. In the Memory and Spirit of Frances, Zora and Lorraine: Essays and Interviews on Black Women and Writing. Washington, DC: Institute for the Arts and Humanities, Howard University, 1979.

288.23(S) Brown, Hallie Quinn. <u>Homespun Heroines and Other Women of Distinction</u>. Xenia, OH: Aldine, 1926.

288.24(S) Clark, Alice. "Frances Ellen Watkins Harper." <u>Negro History Bulletin</u> 5 (January 1942): 83.

288.25(S) Daniel, Theodora Williams. "The Poems of Frances E.W. Harper, Edited with a Biographical and Critical Introduction, and Bibliography." M.A. Thesis, Howard University, 1937.

288.26(S) Dempsey, David. "Uncle Tom's Ghost and the Literary Abolitionist." <u>Antioch Review</u> 6 (1946): 442-448.

288.27(S) Graham, Maryemma. "Frances Ellen Watkins Harper." In HARRIS & DAVIS, pp. 164-173.

288.28(S) Hill, Patricia Liggins. " 'Let Me Make the Songs for the People': A Study of Francis Watkins Harper's Poetry." <u>Black American Literature Forum</u> 15 (Summer 1981): 60-65.

288.29(S) Lewis, Vashti Crutcher. "The Near-White Female in Frances Ellen Harper's <u>Iola Leroy</u>." <u>Phylon</u> 45 (4): 314-322 (Winter 1984).

288.30(S) Majors, Monroe Alphus. <u>Noted Negro Women, Their Triumphs and Activities</u>. New York: Donohue & Henneberry, 1893.

288.31(S) O'Neale, Sondra. "Race, Sex and Self: Aspects of 'Bildung' in Select Novels by Black American Women Novelists." <u>Melus</u> 9 (4): 25-37 (Winter 1982).

288.32(S) Riggins, Linda N. "The Works of Frances E.W. Harper." <u>Black World</u> (December 1972): 30-36.

288.33(S) Robinson, William H. <u>Early Black American Poets</u>. Dubuque, IA: Wm. C. Brown Pubs., 1969.

288.34(S) Shockley, Ann Allen. "Frances Watkins Harper." In SHOCKLEY, pp. 56-70, 190-203.

288.35(S) Still, William. <u>The Underground Railroad</u>. Philadelphia: Porter & Coates, 1872. Frances E.W. Harper cited on pp. 750-780.

288.36(S) Washington, Mary Helen. "Uplifting the Women and the Race: The Forerunners -- Harper and Hopkins." In WASHINGTON, pp. 73-86.

1988-1991 Supplement

A288.37 <u>Complete Poems of Frances E. W. Harper</u>. NY: Oxford University Press, 1988.

A288.38 <u>Iola Leroy, or Shadows Uplifted</u>. NY: Oxford University Press, 1988.

Secondary Sources

A288.39(S) Griffin, Farah Jasmine. "Frances Ellen Watkins Harper in the Reconstruction South." _Sage_ (Student Supplement 1988): 45.

289. HARRELD, CLAUDIA WHITE.

289.1 _Remembered Encounters_. Atlanta: Logan Press, 1951. Poetry.

290. HARRELL, LORRAINE.

290.1 "Widow." _Essence_ 18 (June 1987): 110.

291. HARRIS, HELEN WEBB.

291.1 _Genefrede_. In RICHARDSON & MILLER, pp. 219-237. One act dramas for children.

292. HARRISON, DELORIS (1938-).

292.1 "Clarissa's Problem." _Essence_ 8 (October 1977): 50.

292.2 _Journey All Alone_. New York: Dial Press, 1971.

293. HARRISON, EUNICE B.

293.1 _Here is My Heart_. New York: Carlton Press, 1962. Poetry.

294. HART, ESTELLE PUGSLEY.

294.1 _Thoughts in Poetry_. New York: Tobias Press, 1911.

295. HAZZARD, ALVIRA.

295.1 "Little Heads." <u>Saturday Evening Quill</u> No. 2(1929):
42-44. One act drama.

295.2 "Mother Liked It." <u>Saturday Evening Quill</u> No. 1
(1928): 10-14. One act drama.

296. HEARD, JOSEPHINE DELPHINE HENDERSON (1861-1921).

296.1 <u>Morning Glories</u>. Philadelphia: Author 1890.
Atlanta: Franklin Printing Co., 1901. Poetry.

Secondary Sources

296.2(S) Heard, William Henry. <u>From Slavery To the
Bishopric in the A.M.E. Church: An Autobiography</u>.
Philadelphia: A.M.E. Book Concern, 1924.

296.3(S) Majors, Monroe Alphus. <u>Noted Negro Women, Their
Triumphs and Activities</u>. New York: Donohue & Henneberry,
1893.

296.4(S) Robinson, William H. <u>Early Black American Poets</u>.
Dubuque, IO: Wm. C. Brown Pubs., 1969.

296.5(S) Shockley, Ann Allen. "Josephine Delphine Henderson
Heard." In SHOCKLEY, pp. 171-175.

296.6(S) Simson, Renate Maria. "Whoever Heard of Josephine
Heard?" <u>CLA Journal</u> 26 (December 1982): 256-261.

297. HENDERSON, SAFIYA (1950-).

297.1 "Hip Hop Meets Winnie Mandela." <u>Black Scholar</u> 19
(July/August-September/October 1988): 82.

297.2 "Letter to My Father...a Solidarity Long Overdue."
<u>Essence</u> 10 (June 1979): 12.

297.3 "A Memoir to Workers...No Compensation." <u>Black
Scholar</u> 8 (March 1977): 49-50.

297.4 "Portrait of a Woman Artist." In BARAKA & BARAKA,
pp. 131-134.

298. HERSHAW, FAY McKEENE.

298.1 *Verse Along the Way*. New York: Exposition Press, 1954.

299. HILL, ANNE K.

299.1 *Aurora: Poems*. New York: Author, 1948.

300. HILL, LYNDI.

300.1 "Discovery." *Black Scholar* 9 (September 1977): 37.

301. HILL, MILDRED MARTIN.

301.1 *A Traipsin' Heart*. New York: Wendell Malliet, 1942. Poetry.

302. HIRSH, CHARLOTTE TELLER.

302.1 "Hager and Ishmael." *Crisis* 6 (1913): 30-31. One act drama.

303. HODGES, FRENCHY JOLENE (1940-).

303.1 *Black Wisdom*. Detroit: Broadside Press, 1971.

303.2 *For My Guy*. Detroit: Tibi Productions, 1975.

303.3 *Piece De Way Home*. Detroit: Tibi Productions, 1975.

303.4 "Requiem for Willie Lee." *Ms.* 8 (October 1979): 61-62.

304. HOLDEN, ADELE V.

304.1 *Figurine and Other Poems*. Philadelphia: Dorrance Company, 1961.

305. HOLLOWAY, LUCY ARIEL WILLIAMS (1905-).

305.1 Shape Them into Dreams: Poems. New York: Exposition
Press, 1955.

306. HOOKS, BELL.

306.1 Ain't I a Woman: Black Women and Feminism. Boston:
South End Press, 1981. History of African-American women's
attitude toward feminism from the 1950s on.

306.2 And There We Wept: Poems. Los Angeles: Golemics,
1978.

306.3 "Black Is a Woman's Color." Callaloo 12 (Spring
1989): 282. Short fiction excerpt.

306.4 "Black Women Writing: Creating More Space." Sage 2
(1): 44-46 (Spring 1985). African-American women writers.

306.5 "Excerpts from an Autobiography-in-Progress."
Catalyst (Winter 1988): 66.

306.6 Feminist Theory: From Margin to Center. Boston: South
End Press, 1984.

306.7 "Micheaux: Celebrating Blackness." Black American
Literature Forum 25 (Summer 1991): 351.

306.8 "Reflections of a 'Good' Daughter." Sage 1 (2): 28-29
(Fall 1984).

306.9 Talking Back: Thinking Feminist, Thinking Black.
Boston: South End, 1988.

306.10 "Telling the Story." Catalyst (Winter 1988): 63.

306.11 "Whose P---y is This?: A Feminist Comment on 'She's
Gotta Have It.'" Catalyst (Summer 1987): 14.

306.12 Yearning: Race, Gender, and Cultural Politics.
Boston: South End Press, 1991.

307. HOPE, AKUA LEZLI (1957-).

307.1 "Getting to Know, or Stepping Out in an Entirely
Different Way." "Gowanus Canal (Because You Said Look
Again)." Iowa Review 12 (2-3): 89-90 (Spring-Summer 1981).

307.2 "Leaving Is a Little Death." Black American
Literature Forum 20 (3): 262-263 (Fall 1986).

307.3 Lovecycles. New York: Center for New Images, 1976.

307.4 "Poems." Obsidian II 3 (Winter 1988): 21.

307.5 "Revoltillo Bacalao." "Survival is Its Own Reward."
Black Scholar 12 (1): 92-93 (January-February 1981).

307.6 "Songs They Could Sing for Roland." Shooting Star
Review 2 (Winter 1988): 28.

308. HOPKINS, LEA.

308.1 I'm Not Crazy, Just Different. Overland Park, KS:
Author, 1977.

308.2 Womyn I Have Known You. Overland Park, KS: Author,
1978.

                    Secondary Sources

308.3(S) Ebert, Alan. "Lea Hopkins, Just Different."
Essence 10 (April 1980): 88-89.

309. HOPKINS, PAULINE ELIZABETH (1859-1930).

309.1 "As the Lord Lives, He Is of Our Mother's Children."
Colored American Magazine 6 (November 1903): 798-801.

309.2 "Bro'r Abrm Jimson's Wedding: A Christmas Story."
Colored American Magazine 4 (December 1901): 103-112. In
WASHINGTON, pp. 130-149.

309.3 Contending Forces: A Romance Illustrative of Negro
Life North and South. Boston: Colored Co-operative
Publishing Company, 1900. New York: Oxford University Press,
1988.

309.4 "A Dash for Liberty." Colored American Magazine 3
(August 1901): 243-247.

309.5 "Echoes From the Annual Convention of Northeastern
Federation of Colored Women's Clubs." Colored American
Magazine 6 (October 1903): 709-713.

309.6 "Elijah William Smith." Colored American Magazine 6
(December 1902): 96-100.

309.7 Escape from Slavery, a Musical Drama. n.p., 1880.

309.8 "Famous Women of the Negro Race." Colored American
Magazine 4-5 (November 1901-October 1902).

309.9 "General Washington: A Christmas Story." Colored American Magazine 2 (December 1900): 95-104.

309.10 [Sarah A. Allen]. "Hagar's Daughters, a Story of Southern Caste Prejudice." Colored American Magazine 2-4 (March 1901-March 1902).

309.11 "Heroes and Heroines in Black." Colored American Magazine 3 (January 1903): 206-211.

309.12 [Sarah A. Allen]. "Latest Phases of the Race Problem in America." Colored American Magazine 6 (February 1903): 244-251.

309.13 Moses, Story of the Nile. Boston: Merryhew, 1899.

309.14 "Munroe Rogers." Colored American Magazine 6 (November 1902): 20-26.

309.15 "The Mystery Within Us." Colored American Magazine 1 (May 1900): 14-18.

309.16 [Sarah A. Allen]. "A New Profession." Colored American Magazine 6 (September 1903): 661-663.

309.17 "Of One Blood; or, the Hidden Self." Colored American Magazine 6(November 1902-November 1903). Novel.

309.18 A Primer of Facts Pertaining to the Early Greatness of the African Race and the Possibility of Restoration by its Descendants -- With Epilogue. Cambridge: P.E. Hopkins & Company, 1905.

309.19 "Reminiscences of the Life and Time of Lydia Maria Child." Colored American Magazine 6 (February-June 1903).

309.20 "Sappho." In WASHINGTON, pp. 109-129.

309.21 "Talma Gordon." Colored American Magazine 1 (October 1900): 271-290.

309.22 [Sarah Allen]. "The Test of Manhood." Colored American Magazine 6 (December 1902): 113-119.

309.23 "Toussaint L'Overture." Colored American Magazine 2 (November 1900): 9-24.

309.24 "Whittier, the Friend of the Negro." Colored American Magazine 3 (September 1901): 324-330.

309.25 "Winona: A Tale of Negro Life in the South and Southwest." Colored American Magazine 4-5 (May-October 1902). Novel.

Secondary Sources

309.26(S)   Johnson, Abby Arthur and Johnson, Ronald M.   "Away From Accomodation: Radical Editors and Protest Journalism, 1900-1910." Journal of Negro History 62 (July 1977): 325.

309.27(S)   Johnson, Abby Arthur and Johnson, Ronald Maberry. Propaganda and Aesthetics: The Literary Politics of Afro-American Magazines in the Twentieth Century. Amherst, MA: University of Massachusetts, 1979.

309.28(S)   Porter, Dorothy B.   "Pauline Elizabeth Hopkins." In LOGAN & WINSTON.

309.29(S)   Shockley, Ann Allen.   "Pauline Elizabeth Hopkins." In SHOCKLEY, pp. 289-303.

309.30(S)   Shockley, Ann Allen.   "Pauline Elizabeth Hopkins: A Biographical Excursion into Obscurity."   Phylon 33 (Spring 1972): 22-26.

309.31(S)   Tate, Claudia.   "Pauline Hopkins: Our Literary Foremother." In   PRYSE & SPILLERS, pp. 53-66.

309.32(S)   Washington, Mary Helen.   "Uplifting the Women and the Race: The Forerunners -- Harper and Hopkins."   In WASHINGTON, pp. 73-86.

1988-1991 Supplement

A309.33   The Magazine Novels of Pauline Hopkins.   NY: Oxford University Press, 1988.

310.   HOUGH, FLORENZ H.

310.1   Black Paradise.   Philadelphia: Dorrance & Company, 1953.

311.   HOUSE, AMELIA BLOSSOM.

311.1   "Hills."   Essence 18 (December 1987): 138.

House, Gloria Larry SEE 384. KGOSITSILE, ANEB.

312.   HOWARD, ALICE HENRIETTA.

312.1   Onion to Orchard.   New York: William-Frederick Press, 1945. Poetry.

313.   HOWARD, BEATRICE THOMAS.

313.1 <u>Poems and Quotations</u>. New York: Author, 1956.

314.   HOWARD, MARIAH BRITTON.

314.1 "Mabel." <u>Black Forum</u> 1 (1): 13 (January 1976).

314.2 "Reports." "Solution 9 'To Touch You'." "A Using."
In BARAKA & BARAKA, pp. 145-149.

314.3 "A Wellness Has Spoken." <u>Essence</u> 14 (October 1983):
89.

314.4 <u>With Fire</u>. New York: Meta, 1982.

315.   HOWARD, VANESSA (1955-).

315.1 <u>A Screaming Whisper</u>. New York: Holt, Rinehart &
Winston, 1972.

316.   HULL, GLORIA T. (1944-).

316.1 "Alice Dunbar-Nelson: Delaware Writer and Woman of
Affairs." <u>Delaware History</u> 17(Fall-Winter 1976):87-103.

316.2 "Black Woman Writer and the Diaspora." <u>Black Scholar</u>
17 (2): 2-4 (March-April 1986).

316.3 "Black Women Poets from Wheatley to Walker." In
BELL, pp. 69-86. <u>Negro American Literature Forum</u> 9 (Fall
1975): 91-96.

316.4 "Blues Snatch." <u>Obsidian</u> 7 (2-3): 191 (Summer-Winter
1981).

316.5 <u>Color, Sex, and Poetry: Three Women Writers of the
Harlem Renaissance</u>. Bloomington, IN: Indiana University
Press, 1987. Studies of Alice Moore Dunbar, Angelina Weld
Grimke and Georgia Douglas Johnson with bibliographies.

316.6 <u>Healing Heart: Poems 1973-1988</u>. Latham, NY: Kitchen
Table: Women of Color Press, 1989.

316.7 "Movin' and Steppin'." Obsidian 7 (2-3): 188-189 (Summer-Winter 1981).

316.8 "Notes on a Marxist Interpretation of Black American Literature." Black American Literature Forum 12 (4): 148-153 (1978).

316.9 "Poem for Audre Lorde." Callaloo 5 (2): 79-80 (1979).

316.10 "The Prison and the Park." Obsidian 7 (2-3): 189-190 (Summer-Winter 1981).

316.11 "To Be a Black Woman in America: A Reading of Paule Marshall's Reena." Obsidian 4 (3): 5-15 (Winter 1978).

316.12 " 'Under the Days,' the Buried Life and Poetry of Angelina Weld Grimke'." In SMITH.

316.13 All the Women are White, All the Blacks Are Men, But Some of Us Are Brave: Black Women's Studies. Old Westbury, New York: Feminist Press, 1982. Patricia Bell Scott and Barbara Smith, joint editors.

317. HUMPHREY, LILLIE MUSE.

317.1 Aggie. New York: Vantage Press, 1955. Novel.

318. HUMPHREY, MYRTLE "MOSS." (1934-).

318.1 As Much As I Am. Los Angeles: Capricorn House West, 1973. Poetry.

318.2 Be a Man Boy and other Poems. Los Angeles: Capricorn House West, 1973.

319. HUNT, EVELYN TOOLEY.

319.1 Toad-Song: A Collection of Haiku and other Small Poems. New York: Apple Press, 1966.

320. HUNTER, HELEN.

320.1 Magnificent White Men. New York: Vantage Press, 1964.

321. HUNTER, KRISTIN (1931-).

321.1 Africa Speaks to the West. Pittsburgh: Three Rivers,
1976. [Broadside]

321.2 "Bleeding Berries." Callaloo 2 (2): 25-35 (1979).

321.3 Boss Cat. New York: Charles Scribner's Sons, 1971.

321.4 God Bless the Child. New York: Charles Scribner's
Sons, 1964. New York: Bantam Books, 1970. Washington, DC:
Howard University Press, 1986. Novel.

321.5 Guests in the Promised Land. New York: Charles
Scribner's Sons, 1973.

321.6 "Honor Among Thieves." Essence 1 (April 1971): 34-35.

321.7 "How I Got in the Grocery Business." Black World 21
(June 1972): 58-64.

321.8 The Lakestown Rebellion. New York: Charles Scribner's
Sons, 1978.

321.9 The Landlord. New York: Charles Scribners Sons, 1966.
New York: Avon Books, 1969. Novel.

321.10 Lou in the Limelight. New York: Charles Scribner's
Sons, 1981.

321.11 "Love, African Style." Shooting Star Review 2
(Winter 1988): 14. Short fiction.

321.12 The Pool Table War. Boston: Houghton, 1972.

321.13 The Soul Brothers and Sister Lou. New York: Avon
Books, 1968.

321.14 The Survivors. New York: Charles Scribner's Sons,
1975.

321.15 Uncle Daniel and the Raccoon. Boston: Houghton,
1972.

Secondary Sources

321.16(S) Early, Gerald. "Working Girl Blues: Mothers,
Daughter, and the Image of Billie Holiday in Kristin Hunter's
God Bless the Child." Black American Literature Forum 20
(4): 423-442 (Winter 1986).

321.17(S) Malone, Gloria Snodgrass. "The Nature and Causes
of Suffering in the Fiction of Paule Marshall, Kristin
Hunter, Toni Morrision, and Alice Walker." Dissertation,
Kent State University, 1979.

321.18(S) O'Neale, Sondra. "Kristin Hunter." In DAVIS &
HARRIS, pp. 119-124.

321.19(S) Reilly, John M. "Kristin Hunter." In VINSON.

322. HUNTLEY, ELIZABETH MADDOX.

322.1 "Legion, the Demoniac." In DREER, pp. 306-309.
Drama.

322.2 What Ye Sow. New York: Comet Press, 1955. Drama.

323. HURSTON, ZORA NEALE (1891-1960).

323.1 "Characteristics of Negro Expression." In CUNARD.

323.2 "Color Struck." Fire!! 1 (1926): 7-13.

323.3 "Drenched in Light." Opportunity 2(December 1924):
371-374.

323.4 Dust Tracks on a Road: An Autobiography. 2d ed. ed.
by Robert Hemenway. Urbana, IL: University of Illinois
Press, 1984. (1st ed., Philadelphia: Lippincott, 1942)

323.5 "The First One, a Play." In JOHNSON.

323.6 "Folklore Field Notes from Zora Neale Hurston." Black
Scholar 7 (April 1976): 39-46.

323.7 The Gilded Six-Bits. Minneapolis: Redpath Press,
1986. In BURNETT & FOLEY.

323.8 "How It Feels To Be Colored Me." World Tomorrow 11
(May 1928).

323.9 "I Saw Negro Votes Peddled." American Legion Magazine
(November 1950): 12-13, 45-47, 59-60.

323.10 "John Redding Goes to Sea." Opportunity 4 (January
1926): 16-21.

323.11 Jonah's Gourd Vine. Philadelphia: Lippincott, 1934.
Novel.

323.12 Moses, Man of the Mountain. Philadelphia:
Lippincott, 1939. Republished as The Man of the Mountain.
Dent, 1941. Novel.

323.13 Mules and Men. Philadelphia: Lippincott, 1935.

323.14 "A Negro Voter Sizes Up Taft." Saturday Evening Post
244 (December 8, 1951): 29, 150-152.

323.15 Sanctified Church. Berkeley: Turtle Island
Foundation, 1985.

323.16 Seraph on the Suwanee. New York: Charles Scribner's
Son, 1948. Novel.

323.17 "Spunk." Opportunity (June 1925).

323.18 Spunk, the Selected Stories. Berkeley: Turtle Island
Foundation, 1985.

323.19 "Sweat."   In TURNER,1983.

323.20 Tell My Horse. Philadelphia: Lippincott, 1938.
Republished as Voodoo Gods. Dent, 1939.

323.21 Their Eyes Were Watching God. Philadelphia:
Lippincott, 1937. Novel.

323.22 "What White Publishers Won't Print." Negro Digest 7
(April 1950): 85-89.

Secondary Sources

323.23(S) Blake, E.L. "Zora Neale Hurston: Author and
Folklorist." Negro History Bulletin 29 (April 1966): 149-
150.

323.24(S) Bloom, Harold, ed. Zora Neale Hurston. New York:
Chelsea House, 1986.

323.25(S) Bloom, Harold, ed. Zora Neale Hurston's "Their
Eyes Were Watching God". New York: Chelsea House, 1987.

323.26(S) Bowles, Juliette, ed. In the Memory and Spirit of
Frances, Zora and Lorraine: Essays and Interviews on Black
Women and Writing. Washington, DC: Institute for the Arts
and Humanities, Howard University, 1979.

323.27(S) Brown, Lloyd W. "Zora Neale Hurston and the
Nature of Female Perception." Obsidian 4 (3): 39-45 (Winter
1978).

323.28(S) Burke, Virginia M. "Zora Neale Hurston and Fannie
Hurst As They Saw Each Other." CLA Journal 20(June
1977):435-447.

323.29(S) Byrd, James W. "Zora Neale Hurston: A Novel
Folklorist." Tennessee Folklore Society Bulletin 20 (1955):
35-41.

323.30(S) Carr, Glynis. "Storytelling as 'Bildung' on Zora
Neale Hurston's Their Eyes Were Watching God." CLA Journal
31 (December 1987): 189-200.

323.31(S) Crabtree, Claire. "The Confluence of Folklore,
Feminism and Black Self-Determination in Zora Neale Hurston's
Their Eyes Were Watching God." Southern Literary Journal 17
(September 1985): 54-66.

323.32(S) Dawson, Emma J. Waters. "Images of the Afro-
American Female Character in Jean Toomer's Cane, Zora Neale
Hurston's Their Eyes Were Watching God and Alice Walker's The
Color Purple." Dissertation, University of South Florida,
1987.

323.33(S) Ferguson, Sally Ann. "Folkloric Men and Female
Growth in Their Eyes Were Watching God." Black American
Literature Forum 21 (1-2): 185-197 (Spring-Summer 1987).

323.34(S) Freeman, Alice S. "Zora Neale Hurston and Alice
Walker: A Spiritual Kinship." Sage 2 (1): 37-40 (Spring
1985).

323.35(S) Giles, James. "The Significance of Time in Zora
Neale Hurston's Their Eyes Were Watching God." Negro
American Literature Forum 6 (Spring 1972): 52-54.

323.36(S) Hemenway, Robert E. Zora Neale Hurston: A
Literary Biography. Urbana, IL: University of Illinois
Press, 1977.

323.37(S) Hemenway, Robert E. "Folklore Field Notes from
Zora Neale Hurston." Black Scholar 7 (April 1976): 39-46.

323.38(S) Hine, Darlene Clark. "To Be Gifted, Female and
Black." Southwest Review 4 (Autumn 1982): 357-369.

323.39(S) Holloway, Karla F.C. The Character of the Word:
The Texts of Zora Neale Hurston. Westport, CT: Greenwood
Press, 1987.

323.40(S) Howard, Lillie P. "Marriage: Zora Neale Hurston's
System of Values." CLA Journal 11 (December 1977): 256-268.

323.41(S) Howard, Lillie P. "Nanny and Janie: Will the
Twain Ever Meet? (a Look at Zora Neale Hurston's Their Eyes
Were Watching God)." Journal of Black Studies 6 (Fall 1982):
159-165.

323.42(S) Howard, Lillie P. "Zora Neale Hurston." In
HARRIS & DAVIS, 1987, pp. 133-145.

323.43(S) Howard, Lillie P. Zora Neale Hurston. Boston:
Twayne, 1980.

323.44(S) Howard, Lillie P. "Zora Neale Hurston: Just Being
Herself." Essence 10 (November 1980): 100-101.

323.45(S) Hunter, Charlotte. "Zora Neale Hurston: A Critical Biography." Ph. D. Dissertation, Florida State University.

323.46(S) Hurst, Fannie. "Zora Hurston: A Personality Sketch." Yale University Library Gazette 35 (1961): 17-22.

323.47(S) Jordan, June. "Notes Toward a Balancing Of Love and Hatred: On Richard Wright and Zora Neale Hurston." Black World 23 (August 1974): 4-8.

323.48(S) Kilson, Marian. "The Transformation of Eatonville's Ethnographer." Phylon 33 (Summer 1972): 112-119.

323.49(S) Kubitschek, Missy Dehn. " 'Tuh de Horizon and Back': The Female Quest in Their Eyes Were Watching God." Black American Literatue Forum 17 (Fall 1983): 109-115.

323.50(S) Lee, Valerie Gray. "The Use of Folktale in Novels by Black Women Writers." CLA Journal 23 (March 1980): 266-272.

323.51(S) Lewis, Vashti Crutcher. "The Declining Significance of the Mulatto Female as Major Character in the Novels of Zora Neale Hurston." CLA Journal 28 (2): 127-149 (December 1984).

323.52(S) Lomax, Alan. "Zora Neale Hurston -- A Life of Negro Folklore." Sing Out! 10 (October-November 1960): 12-13.

323.53(S) Love, Theresa R. "Zora Neale Hurston's America." Papers on Language and Literature 12 (4): 422-437 (Fall 1976).

323.54(S) Lupton, Mary Jane. "Clothes and Closure in Three Novels by Black Women." Black American Literature Forum 20 (4): 409-421 (Winter 1986).

323.55(S) Lupton, Mary Jane. "Zora Neale Hurston and the Survival of the Female." Southern Literary Journal 15 (1): 45-54 (Fall 1982).

323.56(S) McCredie, Wendy J. "Authority and Authorization in Their Eyes Were Watching God." Black American Literature Forum 16 (Spring 1982): 25-28.

323.57(S) Marks, Donald R. "Sex, Violence, and Organic Consciousness in Zora Neale Hurston's Their Eyes Were Watching God. Black American Literature Forum 19 (4): 152-157 (Winter 1985).

323.58(S) Mikell, Gwendolyn. "The Anthropoligical Imagination of Zora Neale Hurston." Western Journal of Black Studies 7 (1): 27-35 (Spring 1983).

323.59(S) Mikell, Gwendolyn. "When Horses Talk: Reflections on Zora Neale Hurston's Haitian Anthropology." Phylon 43 (September 1982): 213-230.

323.60(S) Murray, Marian. Jump at the Sun: The Story of Zora Neale Hurston. Chicago: Third World Press, 1975.

323.61(S) Neal, Larry. "Eatonville's Zora Neale Hurston: A Profile." Black Review, No. 1, ed. by Mel Watkins. New York: William Morrow, 1972.

323.62(S) O'Neale, Sondra. "Race, Sex and Self: Aspects of 'Bildung' in Select Novels by Black American Women Novelists." Melus 9 (4): 25-37 (Winter 1982).

323.63(S) Pondrom, Cyrena N. "The Role of Myth in Hurston's Their Eyes Were Watching God." American Literature 58 (May 1986): 181-202.

323.64(S) Pratt, Theodore. "A Memoir: Zora Neale Hurston, Florida's First Distinguished Author." Negro Digest 11 (February 1962): 52-56.

323.65(S) Pratt, Theodore. "Zora Neale Hurston." Florida Historical Quarterly 40 (July 1961): 37-41.

323.66(S) Rayson, Ann L. "Dust Tracks on the Road: Zora Neale Hurston and the Form of Black Autobiography." Negro American Literature Forum 7 (1973): 39-45.

323.67(S) Rayson, Ann L. "The Novels of Zora Neale Hurston." Studies in Black Literature 5 (Winter 1974): 1-10.

323.68(S) Sadoff, Dianne F. "Black Matrilineage: The Case of Alice Walker and Zora Neale Hurston." Signs 11 (1): 4-26 (Autumn 1985).

323.69(S) Sheffey, Ruthe T., ed. Rainbow Round Her Shoulder: The Zora Neale Hurston Symposium Papers. Baltimore: Morgan State University, 1983.

323.70(S) Sheffey, Ruthe T. "Zora Neale Hurston's Moses, Man of the Moutain: A Fictionalized Manifesto of the Imperatives of Black Leadership." CLA Journal 29 (2): 206-220 (December 1985).

323.71(S) Southerland, Ellease. "The Influence of Voodoo in the Fiction of Zora Neale Hurston." In BELL, pp. 172-183.

323.72(S) Southerland, Ellease. "Zora Neale Hurston: The Novelist-Anthropologist's Life/Works." Black World 23 (August 1974): 20-30.

323.73(S) Southerland, Ellease. "Zora Neale Hurston." Encore American & Worldwide News 7 (19 June 1978): 38-39.

323.74(S) Turner, Darwin T. "Zora Neale Hurston: The Wandering Minstrel." In TURNER, 1971.

323.75(S) Walker, Alice, ed. I Love Myself When I Am Laughing, and Then Again When I Am Looking Mean and Impressive: A Zora Neale Hurston Reader. Old Westbury, NY: Feminist Press, 1979.

323.76(S) Walker, Alice. "In Search of Zora Neale Hurston." Ms. 3 (March 1975): 74-79, 85-89.

323.77(S) Walker, S.J. "Zora Neale Hurston's Their Eyes Were Watching God: Black Novel of Sexism." Modern Fiction Studies 20 (Winter 1974-75): 519-527.

323.78(S) Washington, Mary Helen. "The Black Woman's Search for Identity: Zora Neale Hurston's Work." Black World 21 (August 1972): 68-75.

323.79(S) Wideman, John. "Defining the Black Voice in Fiction." Black American Literature Forum 11 (3): 79-82 (Fall 1977).

323.80(S) Willis, Miriam DeCosta. "Folklore and the Creative Artist: Lydia Cabrera and Zora Neale Hurston." CLA Journal 27 (September 1981): 81-90.

323.81(S) Willis, Susan. "Wandering: Zora Neale Hurston's Search For Self and Method." In WILLIS, pp.26-52.

323.82(S) Wilson, Margaret F. "Zora Neale Hurston: Author and Folklorist." Negro History Bulletin 45 (October-December 1982): 109-110.

323.83(S) Wolff, Maria Tai. "Listening and Living: Reading and Experience in Their Eyes Were Watching God." Black American Literature Forum 16 (Spring 1982): 29-33.

1988-1991 Supplement

A323.84 Jonah's Gourd Vine. New York: Perrenial: Harper Collins, 1990. Foreword by Rita Dove. Introduction by Sherley Anne Williams.

A323.85 Mule Bone. New York: Harper-Perennial, 1991. Drama, Langston Hughes, joint author.

A323.86 "The Oconee Riot." Essence 19 (February 1989): 61. Short fiction written in the 1920s, first publication.

A323.87 Seraph on the Suwanee. New York: Perennial: HarperCollins, 1991.

A323.88 Their Eyes Were Watching God. Champaign, IL: University of Illinois Press, 1991.

Secondary Sources

A323.89(S) Benesch, Klaus. "Oral Narrative and Literary
Text: Afro-American Folklore in Their Eyes Were Watching
God." Callaloo 11 (Summer 1988): 627.

A323.90(S) Caputi, Jane. " 'Specifying'Fannie Hurst:
Langston Hughes's 'Limitations of Life,' Zora Neale Hurston's
Their Eyes Were Watching God, and Toni Morrison's The Bluest
Eye as 'Answers' to Hurst's Imitation of Life." Black
American Literature Forum 24 (Winter 1990):697.

A323.91(S) Deck, Alice A. "Autoethnography: Zora Neale
Hurston, Noni Jabavu, and Cross-Disciplinary Discourse."
Black American Literature Forum 24 (Summer 1990): 237.

A323.92(S) Foreman, P. Gabrielle. "Looking Back from Zora,
or Talking Out Both Sides My Mouth for Those Who Have Two
Ears". Black American Literature Forum 24 (Winter 1990): 649

A323.93(S) Fox-Genovese, Elizabeth. "Myth and History:
Discourse of Origins in Zora Neale Hurston and Maya Angelou."
Black American Literature Forum 24 (Summer 1990): 221.

A323.94(S) Hudson-Weems, Clenora. "The Tripartite Plight of
African-American Women as Reflected in the Novels of Hurston
and Walker." Journal of Black Studies 20 (December 1989):
192.

A323.95(S) King, Sigrid. "Naming and Power in Zora Neale
Hurston's Their Eyes Were Watching God." Black American
Literature Forum 24 (Winter 1990): 683.

A323.96(S) Krasner, James. "The Life of Women: Zora Neale
Hurston and Female Autobiography." Black American Literature
Forum 23 (Spring 1989)_: 113.

A323.97(S) Nathiri, N.Y., ed. Zora! Zora Neale Hurston: A
Woman and Her Community. New York: Sentinel Books, 1991.

A323.98(S) Newson, Adele S. Zora Neale Hurston: A Reference
Guide. Boston: G.K. Hall, 1987.

A323.99(S) Robey, Judith. "Generic Strategies in Zora Neale
Hurston's Dust Tracks on a Road." Black American Literature
Forum 24 (Winter 1990): 667.

A323.100(S) Story, Ralph D. "Gender and Ambition: Zora
Neale Hurston in the Harlem Renaissance." Black Scholar 20
(1989): 225.

A323.101(S) Thornton, Jerome E. " 'Goin' On de Muck':The
Paradoxical Journey of the Black American Hero." CLA Journal
31 (March 1988): 261.

A323.102(S) Wall, Cheryl A. "Mules and Men and Women: Zora
Neale Hurston's Strategies of Narration and Visions of Female

Empowerment." <u>Black American Literature Forum</u> 23 (Winter
1989): 661.

324. HYMAN, LATEIFA-RAMONA L.

324.1 "Paraphernalia for Suicide: A Revelation of Life." In
BARAKA & BARAKA, pp. 150-151.

324.2 "Respiration (for Queen Mother Moore)." <u>Black Books</u>
<u>Bulletin</u> 7 (3): 61 (1981).

324.3 "Silhouettes from the Street." <u>Obsidian</u> 6 (1-2): 228
(Spring-Summer 1980).

325. IFETAYO, FEMI FUNMI (1954-).

325.1 <u>We the Black Woman</u>. Detroit: Black Arts Publications,
1970. Poetry.

326. INGRUM, ADRIENNE.

326.1 "Friday the 13th Candlelight March." "Loomit." In
BARAKA & BARAKA, pp. 152-161.

327. ISMAILI, RASHIDAH.

327.1 "Dialogue." "Murderous Intent with a Deadly Weapon."
"Struggle of Class." In BARAKA & BARAKA, pp. 162-167.

327.2 "Epilogue." "Reminiscence." <u>Essence</u> 9 (July 1978):
16.

328. JACKSON, ANGELA (1951-).

328.1 "Awakenings." <u>Black Books Bulletin</u> 7 (3): 60 (1981).

328.2 "Basement Music." "For Our Rising." "From a
Speech...." In FIFTEEN, pp. 57-62.

328.3 "Be This As We May." <u>Black World</u> 23 (October 1974):
53-55.

328.4 "Blackmen: Who Make Morning." Black World 22
(September 1973): 78.

328.5 "The Bloom Amid Alabaster Still." Obsidian 5 (3): 90
(Winter 1979).

328.6 "Divination." Obsidian 5 (3): 88-89 (Winter 1979).

328.7 "Doubting Thomas." Callaloo 5 (February 1979): 85.

328.8 "Dreamer." First World 1 (January 1977): 54-57.

328.9 "Fannie." Black American Literature Forum 19 (3): 101
(Fall 1985).

328.10 "From Treemont Stone." Tri Quarterly 60 (Spring
1984): 154-170.

328.11 "Gathering After Those Years Long Ago: Five Women
Circa: The Last Twenties." Black Scholar 11 (July-August
1980): 78-79.

328.12 "George, After All, Means Farmer." "Doubting
Thomas." "Monroe, Louisiana." Callaloo 5 (February 1979):
84-86.

328.13 The Greenville Club. In FOUR.

328.14 "If I Tole You." Black World 2 (September 1971): 58-
59.

328.15 "In Search of the Bop in the Absence of Antiphonals."
Black Scholar 11 (July-August 1980): 78; Essence 11 (January
1981): 17.

328.16 "Invocation." Obsidian 5 (3): 87 (Winter 1979).

328.17 "Life is Too New." Black World 2 (January 1971): 46-
47.

328.18 The Man with the White Liver. 2d ed. New York,
Contact Two, 1987. Originally published in Contact/II (Fall
1985).

328.19 "One Kitchen." "Divination." "Wave for the Man
Wherever the Song Is." "Invocation." "Who Would Trade It."
"The Bloom Amid Alabaster Still." "Untitled." Obsidian 5
(3): 87-92 (Winter 1979).

328.20 "The Ritual Calendar of Yes." Black Scholar 12
(September-October 1981): 59.

328.21 "A Scattered Song." Black World 22 (January 1973):
34-35.

328.22 "Solo For an Alto." Black Collegian 1 (April/May
1980): 121.

328.23 <u>Solo in the Boxcar Third Floor E</u>. Chicago: OBAhouse,
1985.

328.24 "Solo in the Boxcar Third Floor E." <u>Black Collegian</u>
10 (5): 121 (April-May 1980).

328.25 "The Spider's Mantra." "The House of the Spider."
"Spider Divine." "The Itsy Bitsy Spider Climbs and
Analyzes." "The Spider Speaks On the Need For Solidarity."
"Why I Must Take Language." <u>Open Places</u> 37 (Spring/Summer
1984): 3-11.

328.26 <u>Voo Doo/Love Magic</u>. Chicago: Third World Press,
1974.

328.27 "The War Chant of the Architect (Toni Cade Bambara)."
<u>Black American Literature Forum</u> 19 (3): 100 (Fall 1985).

328.28 "Wares For the Man Wherever the Song Is." <u>Obsidian</u> 5
(3): 92 (Winter 1979).

328.29 "Witchdoctor." <u>Chicago Review</u> 28 (Winter 1977): 76-
82.

328.30 "Woman Walk/n Down a Mississippi Road." <u>Essence</u> 15
(February 1985): 121.

328.31 "Woman Watches Ocean On a Reef Through a Glass-
Bottomed Boat." <u>Black Scholar</u> 12 (September-October 1981):
60.

Secondary Sources

328.32(S) Smith, D.L. "Angela Jackson." In HARRIS &
DAVIS, pp. 176-183.

1988-1991 Supplement

A328.33 "Poems." <u>Black Scholar</u> 19 (July/August-
September/October 1988): 31.

Jackson, Aurilda. **SEE** 367. JONES, AURILDA JACKSON.

329. JACKSON, ELAINE.

329.1 "Toe Jam." In KING & MILNER, pp. 641-671. Two act
drama.

330.   JACKSON, EMMA LOU.

330.1   <u>The Veil of Nancy</u>.   New York: Carlton Press, 1970.

331.   JACKSON, GALE.

331.1   "My Mother Usta Sing Love Songs."   <u>Essence</u> 17 (May
1986): 93.

331.2   "Needles, Threads."   <u>Callaloo</u> 9 (2): 314-323 (Spring
1986).

332.   JACKSON, GLORIA B. (1937-).

332.1   "Hope is His Middle Name: A Tribute to John Hope
Franklin."   <u>National Medical Association Journal</u> 73 (January
1981): 66.

333.   JACKSON, LAURA F.

333.1   <u>Paradise (Cleveland Park) and Other Poems</u>.
Washington, DC: R.L. Pendleton, 1920.

334.   JACKSON, MAE (1946-).

334.1   <u>Can I Poet with You</u>.   Detroit: Broadside Press, 1969.

334.2   "Cleaning Out the Closet."   <u>Black Scholar</u> 8(March
1977):30-35.

334.3   "I Could Rest Forever."   <u>Essence</u> 8 (April 1978): 88-
89.

334.4   "These Ain't All My Tears."   <u>Essence</u> 11 (October
1980): 94-95.

334.5   "Who's Gonna Tell Wilma."   <u>Essence</u> 10 (September
1979): 88-89.

335.   JACKSON, NORLISHIA.

335.1 "Bless the Dead." Essence 8 (December 1977): 70-71.

336. JACKSON, PATTI GAYLE.

336.1 "Orbit." Essence 11 (May 1980): 103.

336.2 "These Loves: Revolution." Obsidian 7 (1): 44 (Spring 1981).

336.3 "This Black Girl Fall." Essence 10 (March 1980): 19.

336.4 Untitled Poem. Black American Literature Forum 15 (Spring 1981): 89-92.

336.5 "What Do You Dream Of." Black American Literature Forum 15 (1): 30 (Spring 1981).

337. JACKSON, RUTH.

337.1 "Myself." Essence 18 (September 1987): 157.

338. JACKSON, SANDRA JOY.

338.1 "Age of Womanhood." Essence 14 (February 1984): 146.

338.2 "Blackbirds." Black World 25 (March 1976): 53.

338.3 "Conversation with a Sister I Do Not Know." Black Books Bulletin 7 (3): 63 (1981).

338.4 "Swamp Fever." Black Books Bulletin 7 (3): 63 (1981).

338.5 "Well, After All What Is There To Say." Essence 14 (October 1983): 89.

339. JACOBS, AUROLYN.

339.1 "I Want To Name My Children After Poems." Freedomways 21 (1): 28 (1981).

340. JACOBS, HARRIET ANN (LINDA BRENT) (1813-1897).

340.1 <u>The Deeper Wrong; or,Incidents in the Life of a Slave Girl</u>. London: W. Tweedie, 1862.

340.2 <u>Incidents In the Life of a Slave Girl, Written by Herself</u>. Ed. and with an introduction by Jean Fagan Yellin. Cambridge: Harvard University Press, 1987.

340.3 <u>Incidents In the Life of a Slave Girl, Written by Herself</u>. Ed. by L. Maria Child, Boston: Author, 1861. New York: Oxford University Press, 1988.

Secondary Sources

340.4(S) Braxton, Joanne M. "Harriet Jacobs' <u>Incidents in the Life of a Slave Girl</u>: The Redefinition of the Slave Narrative Genre." <u>Massachusetts Review</u> 27 (2): 379-387 (Summer 1986).

340.5(S) Child, Lydia Maria. <u>The Freedmen's Book</u>. Boston: Ticknor & Fields, 1865. Harriet Ann Jacobs, p. 218.

340.6(S) Doherty, Thomas. "Harriet Jacobs' Narrative Strategies: <u>Incidents in the Life of a Slave Girl</u>." <u>Southern Literary Journal</u> 19 (1): 79-91 (Fall 1986).

340.7(S) Gwin, Minrose. "Green-Eyed Monsters of the Slavocracy: Jealous Mistresses in Two Slave Narratives." In PRYSE & SPILLERS.

340.8(S) Shockley, Ann Allen. "Harriet Ann Jacobs." In SHOCKLEY, pp. 96-105.

340.9(S) White, Deborah Gray. <u>Ar'n't I a Woman? Female Slaves in the Plantation South</u>. New York: W. W. Norton, 1985.

340.10(S) Yellin, Jean Fagin. "Text and Contexts of Harriet Jacobs' <u>Incidents in the Life of a Slave Girl: Written by Herself</u>." In DAVIS & GATES, pp. 262-282.

340.11(S) Yellin, Jean Fagin. "Written By Herself: Harriet Jacobs' Slave Narrative." <u>American Literature</u> 53 (November 1981): 479-486.

341. JACOBSON, HARRIET PRICE (1879-?).

341.1 <u>Songs in the Night</u>. New York: Exposition Press, 1947. Poetry.

342. JAMES, HAZEL.

342.1 "Ghosts Die Hard at Wounded Knee." <u>Crisis</u> 80 (October 1973): 269-274).

342.2 "Listen My Children." <u>Crisis</u> 80 (March 1973): 90.

342.3 "Lullaby." <u>Crisis</u> 84 (March 1977): 122.

342.4 "Massacre." <u>Crisis</u> 80 (December 1973): 358.

342.5 "Thank You." <u>Crisis</u> 84 (June-July 1977): 331.

342.6 "These Hands." <u>Crisis</u> 8 (February 1980): 68.

343. JAMES, ROSETTA.

343.1 "Givin' Honor to God." <u>Essence</u> 8 (July 1977): 28.

344. JAMILA-RA [MAXINE HALL ELLISTON]

344.1 <u>The Good Book</u>. Chicago: Jamaa Scenes, 1971.

345. JEFFERSON, ANNETTA GOMEZ (1927-).

345.1 <u>Mazes</u>. Cleveland: Ramekha Press, 1972.

345.2 "The Pumpkin Time." <u>Black Scholar</u> 12 (5): 33 (September-October 1981).

346. JEFFERSON, SONIA.

346.1 <u>Thirteenth Child</u>. Concord, NC: Franklin Press, 1973

347. JENRETTE, CORINNE McLEMORE (1903-).

347.1 <u>Just For Fun and Pleasure</u>. New York: Carlton Press, 1970. Poetry.

348. JEWELL, AANDER.

348.1   There Is a Song.   New York: Pageant Press, 1967.
Poetry.

349.   JEWELL, TERRI L. (1954-).

349.1   "Covenant."   Black American Literature Forum 20 (3):
259-260 (Fall 1986).

349.2   "Gasoline On the roof."   Black American Literature
Forum 20 (3): 257-259 (Fall 1986).

349.3   "No News Among Us."   Black American Literature Forum
19 (3): 110 (Fall 1985).

349.4   "Salvaging Blood, January 1983."   Black American
Literature Forum 18 (1): 35 (Spring 1984).

349.5   "Theurgy."   Black American Literature Forum 18 (1): 35
(Spring 1984).

                    1988-1991 Supplement

A349.6   "Child Outside."   Catalyst (Spring 1990): 88.

A349.7   "Ha'nt."   Catalyst (Spring 1990): 80.

A349.8   "Poems."   Obsidian II 3 (Winter 1988): 120.

A349.9   "Salvaging Blood."   Catalyst (Summer 1988): 12.

A349.10   "She Who Bears the Thorn."   Black American
Literature Forum 23 (Fall 1989): 462.   Poem.

350.   JIGGETTS, BESS (1938-).

350.1   Soft Souls.   New York: Baker Enterprises, n.d.
Poetry.

351.   JIMASOM. JOANNE.

351.1   Blowing the Blues Away.   Washington, DC: Common
Ground, 1981.

351.2   "It Has Been a Long Time."   Essence 12 (October 1981):
18.

351.3 <u>Naked Against the Belly of the Earth</u>. Washington, DC:
Common Ground, 1977.

352. JOHNSON, ALICIA JOY (1944-).

352.1 <u>Realities vs Spirits</u>. Carbondale, IL: Author, 1969.
Poetry.

352.2 <u>Two Black Poems</u>. n.p., n.d.

353. JOHNSON, AMELIA ETTA HALL (MRS. A.E. JOHNSON) (1858-
      1922).

353.1 <u>Clarence and Corinne; or, God's Way</u>. Philadelphia:
American Baptist Publication Society, 1890. New York: Oxford
University Press, 1988. Novel.

353.2 <u>The Hazeley Family</u>. Philadelphia: American Baptist
Publication Society, 1894. New York: Oxford University Press,
1988. Novel.

353.3 <u>Martina Meriden; or, What Is My Motive?</u> Philadelphia:
American Baptist Publication Society, 1901. Novel.

                        Secondary Sources

353.4(S) Majors, Monroe Alphus. <u>Noted Negro Women, Their
Triumphs and Activities</u>. New York: Donohue & Henneberry,
1893.

353.5(S) Pegues, A. W. <u>Our Baptist Ministers and Schools</u>.
Springfield, MA: Willey & Co., 1892.

353.6(S) Penn, I. Garland. <u>The Afro-American Press and Its
Editors</u>. Reprint. New York: Arno Press, 1969. 1st published
1891. Amelia E. Johnson, pp. 425-426 .

353.7(S) Shockley, Ann Allen. "Amelia Etta Hall Johnson."
In SHOCKLEY, pp. 162-170.

354. JOHNSON, CHRISTINE C.

354.1 <u>Zwadi Ya Afrika Kwa Dunwa (Africa's Gift to the
World</u>). Chicago: Free Black Press, [196-?]. Historical
drama in two parts.

355. JOHNSON, DORIS J.

355.1 <u>A Cloud of Summer and other New Haiku</u>. Chicago:
Follett, 1967. Poetry.

356. JOHNSON, ELOISE McKINNEY.

356.1 "Langston Hughes and Mary McLeod Bethune." <u>Langston
Hughes Review</u> 2 (1): 1-12 (Spring 1983).

356.2 "Spelman College: One Hundred Years." <u>Spelman
Messenger</u> 97 (3): 38 (Fall 1981).

357. JOHNSON, EMMA MAE DORA.

357.1 <u>Poems</u>. Huntington, WV: Author, 1914.

358. JOHNSON, EVELYN ALLEN.

358.1 <u>My Neighbor's Island</u>. New York: Exposition Press,
1965.

359. JOHNSON, GEORGIA BLANCHE DOUGLAS CAMP (1886-1966).

359.1 <u>An Autumn Love Cycle</u>. New York: Harold Vinal, 1928.
New York: Neale Publishing Compan, 1938. Poetry.

359.2 <u>Blue Blood</u>. New York: Appleton, 1927. Drama.

359.3 "Blue-Eyed Black Boy." In BROWN-GUILLORY. Drama.

359.4 <u>Bronze: A Book of Verse</u>. Boston: B.J. Brimmer
Company, 1922.

359.5 "Carter G. Woodson." <u>Midwest Journal</u> 1 (Summer 1949):
49.

359.6 "Conquest." <u>Essence</u> 9(March 1979): 17.

359.7 "Eaglet, Poem." <u>Midwest Journal</u> 1 (Summer 1949): 81.

359.8 "Frederick Douglass and Ellen Craft." In RICHARDSON
& MILLER.

359.10 <u>The Heart of a Woman and Other Poems</u>. Boston:
Cornhill Company, 1918.

359.11 "I Want to Die While You Love Me." <u>Ebony</u> 35 (August
1981): 56.

359.12 "Omnipresence." <u>Voice of the Negro</u> 2 (June 1905):
387.

359.13 <u>Plumes: A Play in One Act</u>. New York: Samuel French,
1927.

359.14 "Poet Speaks." <u>Essence</u> 9 (March 1979): 17; 12
(January 1982): 14.

359.15 "Safe." In BROWN-GUILLORY,   1990. Drama.

359.16 <u>Share My World: A Book of Poems</u>. Washington, DC:
Half-Way House, 1962.

359.17 "A Song of Courage." <u>Liberator</u> 7 (September 1924):
23

359.18 "A Sonnet in Memory of John Brown." <u>Crisis</u> 88 (March
1981): 87.

359.19 <u>A Sunday Morning in the South</u>. In HATCH & SHINE.

359.20 "Your World." <u>Essence</u> 12 (January 1982): 14.

                        Secondary Sources

359.21(S) Abramson, Doris E. "Angelina Weld Grimke, Mary T.
Burrill, Georgia Douglas Johnson, and Marita O. Bonner: An
Analysis of Their Plays." <u>Sage</u> 2 (1): 9-13 (Spring 1985).

359.22(S) Brawley, Benjamin G. <u>The Negro Genius: A New</u>
<u>Appraisal of the Achievement of the American Negro in</u>
<u>Literature and the Fine Arts</u>. New York: Dodd, Mead, 1937.

359.23(S) <u>Catalog of Writings by Georgia Douglas Johnson</u>.
Washington, DC: Half-Way House, n.d.

359.24(S) Davis, Theresa Scott and Freeman, Charles Y. "A
Biographical Sketch of Georgia Douglas Johnson and Some of
Her Works." Nashville: YMCA Graduate School, 1931.

359.25(S) Dover, Cedric. "The Importance of Georgia Douglas
Johnson." <u>Crisis</u> 59 (December 1952): 633-636, 674.

359.26(S) Ellington, Mary Davis. "Plays by Negro Authors
with Special Emphasis upon the Period 1916 to 1934." Masters
Thesis, Fisk University, 1934.

359.27(S)   Fields, Julia.   "Georgia Douglas Johnson."   Negro Digest 15 (October 1966): 48.

359.28(S)   Fletcher, Winona.   "From Genteel Poet to Revolutionary Playwright: Georgia Douglas Johnson as a Symbol of Black Success, Failure and Fortitude."   Theatre Annual 40 (February 1985): 40-64.

359.29(S)   Fletcher, Winona.   "Georgia Douglas Johnson."   In HARRIS & DAVIS, 1987, pp.153-164

359.30(S)   "Georgia Douglas Johnson."   Crisis 32 (1926): 193.

359.31(S)   Hatch, James V.   Black Theater, USA: Forty-Five Plays by American Negroes, 1847-1974.   New York: Free Press, 1974.

359.32(S)   Hoytt, Eleanor Hinton.   "A Letter (With Poem) from Georgia Douglas Johnson to Lugenia Burns Hope."   Sage 2 (1): 62-63 (Spring 1985).

359.33(S)   Hull, Gloria T.   Color, Sex, and Poetry: Three Women Writers of the Harlem Renaissance.   Bloomington, IN: Indiana University Press, 1987.

359.34(S)   Locke, Alain LeRoy and Gregory, Montgomery, eds. Plays of Negro Life: A Source-Book of Native American Drama. New York: Harper, 1927.   Reprint Westport, CT: Negro Universities Press, 1970.

359.35(S)   Richardson, Willis and Miller, May.   Negro History in Thirteen Plays.   Washington, DC: Associated Publishers, 1933.

359.36(S)   Shockley, Ann Allen.   "Georgia Blanche Douglas Camp Johnson."   In   SHOCKLEY, pp. 346-355.

359.37(S)   Stetson, Erlene.   "Rediscovering the Harlem Renaissance: Georgia Douglas Johnson, 'The Negro Poet'." Obsidian 5 (Spring 1979): 26-34.

360.   JOHNSON, HELENE HUBBLE (1907-) .

360.1   "The Road." "Sonnet to a Negro in Harlem." "Remember Not." "Invocation."   In   JOHNSON, 1931, pp. 279-282.

360.2   "Summer Matures." "Fulfillment." "Magalu." "Remember Not." "Invocation." "The Road."   In   HUGHES & BONTEMPS, 1970, pp. 261-266.

360.3   "What Do I Care For Morning." "Sonnet to a Negro In Harlem." "Summer Matures." "Poem'" "Fulfillment," "The Road," "Bottled," and "Magalu."   In   CULLEN, pp.216-223.

Secondary Sources

360.4(S) Shockley, Ann Allen. "Helene Hubble Johnson." In
SHOCKLEY, pp. 451-452.

360.5(S) Patterson, Raymond R. "Helene Johnson." In
HARRIS & DAVIS, 1987, pp. 164-167.

361. JOHNSON, JESSIE DAVIS.

361.1 Christmas Poems. Washington, DC: Author, 1937.

362. JOHNSON, MAGGIE POGUE.

362.1 Fallen Blossoms. Parkersburg, WV: n.p., 1951.

362.2 Thoughts for Idle Hours. Roanoke, VA: Stone Printing
& Mfg. Company, 1915.

362.3 Virginia Dreams: Lyrics for the Idle Hour, Tales of
the Time Told in Rhyme. n.p.: John Leonard, 1910.

363. JOHNSON, PAULETTE S.

363.1 "Introduction." Black Scholar 9 (March 1978): 15.

363.2 "Sugah Blue." Black Scholar 10 (November-December
1978): 48.

364. JONES, ABIGAIL ROBERTS (1932-).

364.1 Where I Have Walked. Philadelphia: Dorrance &
Company, 1974.

365. JONES, ANNA ARMSTRONG.

365.1 A Mother's Musings. Edwardsville, IL: Author, 1933.

366. JONES, ANNE R.

366.1 "The Littlest Warrior." _Essence_ 2 (December 1971): 2.

367. JONES, AURILDA JACKSON.

367.1 _Echo Calls of Laughter Over Greener Years_. Los
Angeles: Trident Shop, 1975.

367.2 _Love Touches the Earth (Love Poems)_. Los Angeles:
Trident Shop, 1975.

367.3 _Untangled_. New York: Vantage Press, 1956. Poetry.

368. JONES, GAYL (1949-) .

368.1 "Almeyda." _Massachusetts Review_ 18 (4): 689-691
(Winter 1977).

368.2 "Alternative." _Callaloo_ 5 (2): 111 (1979).

368.3 "Chance." _Callaloo_ 5 (2): 112 (1979).

368.4 _Chile Woman_. New York: Shubert Foundation, 1974.

368.5 "Composition with Guitar and Apples." _Callaloo_ 5 (3):
85-88 (1982).

368.6 _Corregidora_. New York: Random House, 1975.

368.7 "The Day of the God." _Callaloo_ 5 (3): 54-58 (1982).

368.8 _Eva's Man_. New York: Random House, 1976.

368.9 "Foxes." _Callaloo_ 7 (1): 39-42 (1984).

368.10 "Fur Station." _First World_ 2 (4): 23 (1980).

368.11 "Goosens." _Callaloo_ 5 (3): 54-58 (1982).

368.12 _Hermit-Woman_. Detroit: Lotus Press, 1983.

368.13 "Interview with Lucille Jones." _Obsidian_ 3 (3): 26-
35 (Winter 1977). [Lucille Jones is mother of Gayl Jones]

368.14 "Jevata." _Essence_ 4 (November 1973): 66-67.

368.15 "Lovers." _Essence_ 5 (May 1974): 89.

368.16 "Mr. River's Love Story." _Callaloo_ 7 (1): 43-45
(1984).

368.17 "Prophet Powers." _Callaloo_ 5 (3): 80-84 (1982).

368.18 "Sense of Security." _Essence_ 4 (August 1973): 62-63.

368.19 "The Siege." _Callaloo_ 5 (3): 89-94 (1982).

368.20 _Song for Anninho_. Detroit: Lotus Press, 1981.

368.21 "Spaces." _Black Scholar_ 6 (June 1975): 53-55.

368.22 "Sticks and Witches Brooms." _Michigan Quarterly Review_ 17 (2): 205-208 (Spring 1978).

368.23 "Those Rock People." _Callaloo_ 5 (3): 59-65 (1982).

368.24 "Waiting for the Miracle." _Callaloo_ 5 (3):66-72 (1982).

368.25 _White Rat: Stories_. New York: Random House, 1977.

368.26 "Xarque." _First World_ 2 (3): 13 (1979).

368.27 _Xarque and Other Poems_. Detroit: Lotus Press, 1985.

Secondary Sources

368.28(S) Bell, Roseann P. "Gayl Jones Takes a Look at _Corregidora_ -- An Interview" In BELL, pp. 282-287.

368.29(S) Beyerman, Keith E. "Black Vortex: The Gothic Structure of _Eva's Man_." _MELUS_ 7 (Winter 1980): 93-100.

368.30(S) Beyerman, Keith E. "Intense Behaviors: The Use of the Grotesque in _Eva's Man_ and _The Bluest Eye_. _CLA Journal_ 25 (June 1982): 447-457.

368.31(S) Harper, Michael S. "Gayl Jones: An Interview." In HARPER & STEPTOE, pp. 352-375. _Massachusetts Review_ 18 (4): 692-715 (Winter 1977).

368.32(S) Harris, Trudier. "A Spiritual Journey: Gayl Jones's _Song for Anninho_." _Callaloo_ 5 (October 1982): 105-111.

368.33(S) Lee, Valerie Gray. "The Use of Folktale in Novels by Black Women Writers." _CLA Journal_ 23 (March 1980): 266-272.

368.34(S) Mano, D.K. "How to Write Two First Novels with Your Knuckles." _Esquire_ 80 (December 1976): 62.

368.35(S) O'Neale, Sondra. "Race, Sex and Self: Aspects of 'Bildung' in Select Novels by Black American Women Novelists." _Melus_ 9 (4): 25-37 (Winter 1982).

368.36(S) Rowell, Charles, ed. "Gayl Jones, Poet and Fictionist." _Callaloo_ 5 (October 1982): 31-111. [special section]

368.37(S) Rowell, Charles "An Interview with Gayl Jones.
Callaloo 5 (October 1982): 89-99.

368.38(S) Tate, Claudia. "Corregidora: Ursa's Blues
Medley." Black American Literature Forum 13 (Fall 1979):
139-141.

368.39(S) Tate, Claudia. "Gayl Jones." In TATE, pp. 89-
99.

368.40(S) Tate, Claudia. "An Interview with Gayl Jones."
Black American Literature Forum 13 (Winter 1979): 142-148.

368.41(S) Updike, John. "Eva and Eleanor and Everywoman."
New Yorker (9 August 1976): 74-77.

368.42(S) Ward, Jerry W. "Escape from Trublem: The Fiction
of Gayl Jones." Callaloo 5 (October 1982): 95-104. In
EVANS, pp. 249-257.

369. JONES, GLADYS B.

369.1 Times, Things and Stuff. Montclair, NJ: Lewis
Business Service, 1972.

370. JONES, JOYCE.

370.1 "Pome To My Lover." Black American Literature Forum
18 (Spring 1984): 36.

371. JONES, LUCILLE (1924-).

371.1 "The Boyish Bob." "Twenty-One B Street." Obsidian 6
(3): 82-97 (Winter 1980).

371.2 "A Dinner for Luther and Louis." "Everybody Get Into
the Act." "John and Nancy." "The Salesman." Obsidian 5
(3): 64-74 (Winter 1979).

371.3 "Luther." "Vestina." Excerpt. Obsidian 3 (3): 43-53
(Winter 1977).

372. JONES, MARSHA.

372.1 "Change." About Time 13 (2): 26 (February 1985).

372.2 "The Hurt." About Time 13 (2): 26 (February 1985).

372.3 "Invisible Man." About Time 13 (2): 26 (February 1985).

372.4 "Kaleidoscope Lady: The Wonderful Words of Sonia Sanchez." about...time 16 (July 1988): 14.

372.5 "Maya Angelou: On Mastering Language." about...time 17 (December 1989): 20.

372.6 "Poetry in Motion: The Prose of Gwendolyn Brooks." about...time 16 (June 1988): 8.

373. JONES, PATRICIA (1951-).

373.1 "Dedicated to Lori Sharpe." "Eagle Rock." "It Must Be Her Heartbreak Talking." "LP." "Poem Written On Rosh Hashanah/For Ted Greenwald." ""The Woman Who Loved Musicians." Obsidian 5 (1-2): 113-119 (Spring-Summer 1979).

373.2 "Feeling Evil." Essence 11 (September 1980): 14.

373.3 "In Like Paradise/Out Like the Blues." Black Scholar 12 (May-June 1981): 48-49.

373.4 Mythologizing Always: Seven Sonnets. Guilford, CT: Telephone Books, 1981.

373.5 "Poem for Dad." Black Collegian 6 (January-February 1976): 28.

374. JONES, ROSIE LEE LOGAN (1924-).

374.1 Rain Drops and Pebbles. n.p., Chance-Foster, n.d.

374.2 Tender Clusters. San Antonio, TX: Naylor Co., 1969.

374.3 Treasures of Life. n.p., Riesel Russel, 1945.

Jones, Sylvia. SEE 046. BARAKA, AMINA.

375. JORDAN, ELSIE.

375.1 Strange Sinner. New York: Pageant Press, 1954. Novel.

376.   JORDAN, JUNE (1936-).

376.1   "Ah, Momma." Redbook 150 (December 1977): 74.

376.2   "An Always Lei of Ginger Blossoms for the First Lady
of Hawaii: Queen Lili'uokalani." Callaloo 9 (1): 79-80
(Winter 1986).

376.3   "The Beirut Jokebook." Freedomways 22 (4): 223
(1982).

376.4   "Black Folks and Foreign Policy." Essence 14 (June
1983): 162.

376.5   "The Black Poet Speaks of Poetry." [column]. American
Poetry Review (1974-1977).

376.6   "Black Women Haven't 'Got It All.'" Black Scholar 10
(May-June 1979): 39-40.

376.7   Civil Wars. Boston: Beacon Press, 1981.

376.8   "DeLiza Spend the Day In the City." Freedomways 23
(4): 234-235 (1983).

376.9   "The Difficult Miracle of Black Poetry in America or
Something Like a Sonnet for Phillis Wheatley." Massachusetts
Review 27 (2): 252-262 (Summer 1986). Textual criticism.

376.10   "Don't You Talk About My Mama!" Essence 18 (December
1987): 53.

376.11   Dry Victories. New York: Avon Books, 1975.

376.12   Fannie Lou Hamer. New York: Thomas Crowell, 1972.

376.13   "For Beautiful Mary Brown." Freedomways 11 (Second
Quarter, 1971): 191.

376.14   "Free Flight," Essence 10 (October 1979): 16.

376.15   "From 'The Talking Back of Miss Valentine Jones: Poem
Number One'." Ms. 6 (April 1978): 58.

376.16   "Getting Down To Get Over: Dedicated To My Mother."
Essence 4 (October 1973): 54-55.

376.17   "Grace." Essence 14 (August 1983): 124.

376.18   "Greensboro: North Carolina." Freedomways 23 (4):
235 (1983).

376.19   High Tide-Marea Alta. Willimantic, CT: Curbstone,
1987.

376.20   His Own Where. New York: Dell, 1971.

376.21 "In Our Hands." Essence 16 (May 1985): 50.

376.22 "It's About: Poem on the Beach." Black World 22 (September 1973): 59.

376.23 Kimako's Story. Boston: Houghton, 1981.

376.24 Living Room: New Poems. New York: Thunder's Mouth Press, 1985.

376.25 "May 27, 1971 - No Poem." Essence 2 (September 1971): 1.

376.26 "Memorandum Towards the Spring of Seventy-Nine." Callaloo 5 (2): 98 (1979).

376.27 "The Name Of the Poem Is." Transatlantic Review 58-59 (February 1977): 98.

376.28 New Days: Poems of Exile and Return. New York: Emerson Hall Publishers, 1973.

376.29 New Life: New Room. New York: Thomas Crowell, 1975.

376.30 Niagara Falls. Huntington, NY: Poem a Month Club, 1977. Broadside.

376.31 "Nicaragua: 'Why I Had to Go There.'" Essence 14 (January 1984): 76-78.

376.32 "Nineteen Seventy-Eight." Black Scholar 10 (November-December 1978): 22.

376.33 "Notes Toward a Balancing of Love and Hatred: On Richard Wright and Zora Neale Hurston." Black World 23 (August 1974): 4-8.

376.34 Okay Now. New York: Simon & Schuster, 1977.

376.35 On Call: Political Essays. Boston: South End Press, 1985.

376.36 Passion: New Poems Nineteen Seventy-Seven to Nineteen Eighty. Boston: Beacon Press, 1980.

376.37 "Poem." Black World 22 (March 1973): 63-65.

376.38 "Poem About My Rights." Essence 9 (November 1978): 22

376.39 "Poem For Buddy." Callaloo 9 (2): 341-344 (Spring 1986).

376.40 "Poem For Granville Ivanhoe Jordan." Black World 24 (September 1975): 58-60.

376.41 "Poem In Honor of South African Women." Ms. 9 (November 1980): 47.

376.42 "Poem In Memory of Kimako Baraka (1936-1984)."
Essence 15 (July 1984): 130.

376.43 "Problems of Translation: Problems of Language."
Iowa Review 12 (2-3): 194-197 (Spring-Summer 1981).

376.44 "Relativity." Essence 17 (May 1986): 169.

376.45 "Roman Poem Number Thirteen For Eddie." Essence 2
(August 1971): 11.

376.46 "Roman Poem Twelve." Essence 2 (August 1971): 11.

376.47 "Second Thoughts of a Black Feminist." Ms. 5
(February 1977): 113-115.

376.48 "Sojourner Truth." Black Collegian 9 (May-June
1979): 92.

376.49 Some Changes. New York: Dutton, 1971.

376.50 Soulscript: Afro-American Poetry. New York:
Doubleday, 1970. Anthology. June Jordan, editor.

376.51 "South Africa: Bringing It All Back Home." New York
Times (26 September 1981): 23.

376.52 Things That I Do in the Dark: Selected Poems. New
York: Random House, 1977.

376.53 "Where Is the Love." Essence 9 (October 1978): 62.

376.54 "White English: The Politics of Language." Black
World 22 (August 1973): 4-10.

376.55 Who Look At Me. New York: Thomas Crowell, 1969.

376.56 "Who Would Be Free, Themselves Must Strike the Blow."
Northwest Review 22 (1-2): 38 (1984).

376.57 The Voice of the Children. New York: Holt, Rinehart
& Winston, 1970. Torri Bush, joint author.

                    Secondary Sources

376.58(S) DeVeaux, Alexis. "Creating Soul Food: June
Jordan." Essence 11 (April 1981): 82, 138-150.

376.59(S) Dong, Stella. "PW Interviews June Jordan."
Publishers Weekly (1 May 1981): 12-13.

376.60(S) Erickson, Peter. "June Jordan." In DAVIS &
HARRIS, 1985, pp. 146-162.

376.61(S) Erickson, Peter. "The Love Poetry of June
Jordan." Callaloo 9 (1): 221-234 (Winter 1986).

1988-1991 Supplement

A376.62 "For My Brother." Essence 20 (November 1989): 107.

A376.63 Naming Our Destiny: New and Selected Poems. New
York: Thunder's Mouth Press, 1989.

A376.64 "Poem from Taped Testimony in the Tradition of the
Very Rt. Reasonable Bernhard Goetz." Black Scholar 19
(July/August-September/October 1988): 131. Poem.

Secondary Sources

A376.65(S) Greene, Cheryl Y. and Brown Marie, eds. "Woman
Talk: A Conversation Between June Jordan and Angela Davis."
Essence 21 (May 1990): 92.

377. JOURDAIN, ROSE (1932-).

377.1 Those the Sun Has Loved. New York: Doubleday, 1978.
Novel.

378. KECKLEY, ELIZABETH (1824-1907).

378.1 Behind the Scenes; Formerly a Slave, but Recently
Modiste and Friend to Mrs. Abraham Lincoln, or Thirty Years a
Slave and Four Years in the White House. New York: G.W.
Carleton, 1868.

Secondary Sources

378.2(S) Brown, Hallie Quinn. Homespun Heroines and Other
Women of Distinction. Xenia, OH: Aldine, 1926.

378.3(S) Gwin, Minrose. "Green-Eyed Monsters of the
Slavocracy: Jealous Mistresses in Two Slave Narratives." In
PRYSE & SPILLERS.

378.4(S) Majors, Monroe Alphus. Noted Negro Women, Their
Triumphs and Activities. New York: Donohue & Henneberry,
1893.

378.5(S) Shockley, Ann Allen. "Elizabeth Hobbs Keckley."
In SHOCKLEY, 134-143.

378.6(S) Washington, John E. They Knew Lincoln. New York:
Dutton, 1942.

1988-1991 Supplement

A378.7 <u>Behind the Scenes, Or, Thirty Years a Slave, and Four
Years in the White House</u>. NY: Oxford University Press, 1988.

Secondary Sources

A378.8(S) Andrews, William L. "Reunion in the Postbellum
Slave Narrative: Frederick Douglass and Elizabeth Keckley."
<u>Black American Literature Forum</u> 23 (Spring 1989): 5.

379. KEIN, SYBIL (1939-).

379.1 "Bessie Smith." <u>Essence</u> 17 (July 1986): 121.

379.2 "Billie." <u>Essence</u> 16 (July 1985): 107.

379.3 "Chestnut Lilies." <u>Beloit Poetry Journal</u> 29 (2): 26
(Winter 1978-1979).

379.4 <u>Delta Dancer: New and Selected Poems</u>. Detroit: Lotus
Press, 1984.

379.5 "Flowers." <u>Essence</u> 18 (September 1987): 157.

379.6 "Get Together." In BROWN-GUILLORY. Drama.

379.7 <u>Gombo People: New Orleans Creole Poetry</u>. New Orleans:
Leo J. Hall, 1981.

379.8 "Mo Oule mourri dan lac la." <u>Beloit Poetry Review</u> 29
(2): 25 (Winter 1978-1979).

379.9 "The River." "Shame." "To the Widow Paris." <u>Obsidian</u>
7 (2-3): 142-145 (Summer-Winter 1981). [translated from
Creole French of Louisana]

379.10 <u>Visions From the Rainbow</u>. Flint, MI: N.D. Hosking,
1979.

380. KELLEY, EMMA DUNHAM.

380.1 <u>Four Girls at Cottage City</u>. Boston: James H. Earle,
Publisher, 1898. New York: Oxford University Press, 1988.
Novel.

380.2 <u>Megda</u>. Boston: James H. Earle, 1891. New York:
Oxford University Press, 1988. Novel.

Secondary Sources

380.3(S) Shockley, Ann Allen.   "Emma Dunham Kelley-Hawkins." In SHOCKLEY, pp. 176-180.

381 KENDRICK, DOLORES (1927-).

381.1 "Frustrated Genius." "Josephine in the Jeu de Paume." Beloit Poetry Journal 29 (2): 46-47 (Winter 1978-1979).

381.2 Now Is the Thing to Praise: Poems. Detroit: Lotus Press, 1984.

381.3 Through the Ceiling. London: Paul Breman, 1975.

382. KENNEDY, ADRIENNE (1931-).

382.1 "A Beast Story" In HARRISON, pp. 192-201.   One act drama.

382.2 Cities in Bezique. New York: Samuel French, 1969.

382.3 "Funnyhouse of a Negro." In BRASMER.

382.4 Funnyhouse of a Negro. New York: Samuel French, 1969. Drama.

382.5 The Lennon Play: In His Own Write. New York: Simon and Schuster, 1969.

382.6 "A Lesson in Dead Language." In PARONE, pp. 35-40. Drama.

382.7 "The Owl Answers." In HOFFMAN.

382.8 People Who Led to My Plays. New York: A.A. Knopf, 1987.

382.9 "A Rat's Mass." In COUCH, pp. 83-92. One act drama.

382.10 "Sun: A Poem for Malcolm X Inspired by His Murder." Scripts 1 (November 1971): 51-56. one scene drama.

Secondary Sources

382.11(S) Benston, Kimberly W. "Cities in Bezique: Adrienne Kennedy's Expressionistic Vision." CLA Journal 20 (December 1976): 235-244.

382.12(S) Brasmer, William and Consolo, Dominick, eds. Black Drama: An Anthology. Columbus, OH: Charles E. Merrill, 1970.

382.13(S)   Couch, William, Jr., ed.   New Black Playwrights.
Baton Rouge: Lousiana State University Press, 1968.

382.14(S)   Curb, Rosemary K.   "Fragmented Selves in Adrienne
Kennedy's Funnyhouse of a Negro and The Owl Answers."
Theatre Journal 32 (May 1980): 180-195.

382.15(S)   Harrison, Paul Carter, ed.   Kuntu Drama: Plays of
the African Continuum.   New York: Grove Press, 1973.

382.16(S)   In HATCH.

382.17(S)   Oliver, Clinton and Sills, Stephanie, eds.
Contemporary Black Drama.   New York: Charles Scribner's,
1971.
382.18(S)   Tener, Robert L.   "Theatre of Identity: Adrienne
Kennedy's Portrait Of the Black Woman."   Studies in Black
Literature 6 (Summer 1975): 1-5.

382.19(S)   Wilkerson, Margaret B.   "Adrienne Kennedy."   In
DAVIS & HARRIS, 1985, pp. 162-169.

1988-1991 Supplement

A382.20   Adrienne Kennedy: In One Act. Minneapolis, MN:
University of Minnesota Press, 1988.

A382.21   Deadly Triplets: A Theater Mystery and Journal.
Minneapolis, MN: University of Minnesota Press, 1990.

383.   KENNEDY, BEATRICE BURTON.

383.1   Deep Within.   Philadelphia: Dorrance & Company, 1975.

384.   KGOSITSILE, ANEB.

384.1   Blood River.   Detroit: Broadside Press, 1983.

385.   KIMBALL, KATHLEEN.

385.1   "Meat Rack."   Scripts 1 (May 1972): 5-28.   One act
drama.

386.   KINAMORE, ANGELA H.

386.1 "African American Woman." Essence 19 (February 1989):
142. Poem.

386.2 " 'Home' Girls (The Spirit of Sisterhood)." Essence
19 (January1989): 112. Poem.

386.3 "Remember Him." Essence 12 (February 1982): 20.

386.4 "The Warrior Spirit." Essence 19 (February 1989):
152. Poem.

386.5 "Women Raise Men." Essence 19 (November 1988): 134.

387. KINCAID, JAMAICA (1949-).

387.1 Annie John. New York: Farrar, Straus & Giroux, 1985.

387.2 At the Bottom of the River. New York: Farrar, Straus
& Giroux, 1984.

387.3 "The Circling Hand." New Yorker (21 November 1983):
50-57.

387.4 "Columbus in Chains." New Yorker (10 October 1983):
48-52.

387.5 "Figures in the Distance." New Yorker (9 May 1983):
40-42.

387.6 "Gwen." New Yorker (16 April 1984): 45-51.

387.7 "The Long Rain." New Yorker (30 July 1984): 28-36.

387.8 "The Red Girl." New Yorker (8 August 1983): 32-38.

387.9 "Somewhere, Belgium." New Yorker (14 May 1984): 44-
51.

387.10 "A Walk to the Jetty." New Yorker (5 November 1984):
45-51.

                    1988-1991 Supplement

A387.11 Lucy. New York: Farrar, 1990.

A387.12 A Small Place. New York: Farrar, 1988.

                    Secondary Sources

A387.13(S) Cudjoe, Selwyn R. "Jamaica Kincaid and Modernist
Project: An Interview." Callaloo 12 (Spring 1989): 396.

388.   KING, HELEN H. (1931-).

388.1 <u>Soul of Christmas</u>. Chicago: Johnson, 1972. Children
and young adult stories.

388.2 <u>Willy</u>. New York: Doubleday, 1971. Children and young
adult stories.

389.   KNOX, FAYE MILLER.

389.1 "Forgive Me Child." <u>Crisis</u> 82 (November 1975): 35.

390.   KNOX, JACQUELINE LLOYD.

390.1 <u>Bittersweets: A Book of Verse</u>. Philadelphia: Dorrance
& Company, 1938.

391.   KNOX, JEAN LINDSAY.

391.1 <u>A Key to Brotherhood</u>. New York: Paebar, 1932.
Poetry.

Kunjufu, Johari M. **SEE** 018. AMINI, JOHARI.

392.   KYTLE, ELIZABETH.

392.1 Kytle, Elizabeth. <u>Willie Mae</u>. New York: A.A. Knopf,
1958.

393.   LaHON, VYOLA THERESE.

393.1 <u>The Big Lie</u>. New York: Vantage Press, 1964.

394.   LAKIN, MATTIE T. (1917-).

394.1 Portico to the Temple. Gastonia, NC: Minges Printers,
1970. Poetry.

395. LaMARRE, HAZEL WASHINGTON (1917-).

395.1 Breath in the Worldwind. Los Angeles: Print Rite
Printing Co., 1955. Poetry.

395.2 Half-Past Tomorrow. Hollywood: Swordsman Press, 1973.
Poetry.

395.3 Il Silenzio. Hollywood: Swordsman Press, 1972.
Poetry.

396. LAMBERT, MARY ELIZA PERINE TUCKER (1838-).

396.1 Loew's Bridge, a Broadway Idyll. New York: M.
Doolady, 1867.

396.2 Poems. New York: M. Doolady, 1867.

397. LA MONS, YVONNE C.

397.1 "Night Student." Essence 16 (July 1985): 115.

398. LANE, PINKIE GORDON (1923-).

398.1 "Baton Rouge No. 2." Southern Review 13 (April 1977):
352.

398.2 "Betrayal: On the Loss of a Friend." Callaloo 5
(February 1979): 96.

398.3 "Breathing." Black Scholar 15 (November-December
1984): 55.

398.4 "Children." "Poems to My Father." Black American
Literature Forum 20 (3): 289-293 (Fall 1986).

398.5 "Children." "For Bill." Pembroke Magazine 4 (1973):
26-28.

398.6 Discourses on Poetry. Fort Smith, AR: South & West,
1972. Edited by Gordon.

398.7   "Eulogy on the Death of Trees." Poet: India 14 (May 1973): 477.

398.8   "Finis." Black Scholar 15 (November-December 1984): 31.

398.9   "Flight." "Two Poems." "I Never Scream." Southern Review 10 (Fall 1974): 947-950.

398.10 "Four Love Poems." Black Scholar 15 (November-December 1984): 60.

398.11 "Girl at the Window." Black Scholar 10 (November-December 1978): 17.

398.12 "Gordon." Black Scholar 15 (November-December 1984): 6.

398.13 I Never Scream: New and Selected Poems. Detroit: Lotus Press, 1985.

398.14 "Lake Murry." "Baton Rouge #2." "Southern University." Southern Review 13 (Spring 1977): 351-354.

398.15 "Leaves." "Listenings."   "Opossum." Obsidian 3 (3): 54-56 (Winter 1977).

398.16 "Listenings." "Migration." "The Mystic Female." SouTh aNd WesT: An International Literary Quarterly 14 (Fall 1977): 18-21.

398.17 A Literary Profile to 1977. Baton Rouge: Author, 1977. Bibliography.

398.18 "Love Poem." Black Scholar 12 (November-December 1981): 57.

398.19 "Message." "Who is My Brother?" "Nocturne." "Love Poem." Obsidian 1 (Winter 1975): 87-89.

398.20 "Mid-Summer Thoughts." "Telephone Call." Hoodoo 1 (1973): 477.

398.21 "Midnight Song." "When You Read This Poem." "Love Poem: Thoughts Run Wild." Black Scholar 9 (November 1977): 28-29.

398.22 "Migration."   "The Mystic Female." Callaloo 3 (February 1978): 6, 90.

398.23 The Mystic Female. Fort Smith, AR: South & West, 1978.

398.24 "The Mystic Female." Callaloo 3 (February 1978): 90.

398.25 "Old Photo from a Family Album: 1915." Southern Review 21 (July 1985): 862-863.

398.26 "On This Louisiana Day." "Poem Extract." Louisiana
Review 1 (Summer 1972): 105-106.

398.27 "Poem for Lois: An Elegy." Callaloo 1 (December
1976): 18.

398.28 Poems by Blacks. Fort Smith, AR: South & West, 1973.
2 vols. Edited by Pinkie Lane.

398.29 "Poems to My Father." Black American Literature
Forum 20 (3): 289-293 (Fall 1986).

398.30 "Portrait." Negro American Literature Forum (1972).

398.31 "The Privacy Report." Ms. 7 (January 1980): 29.

398.32 "A Quiet Poem." (Broadside no. 80). Detroit:
Broadside Press, (February 1974).

398.33 "Rain Ditch." "Reaching." Journal of Black Poetry 1
(Fall-Winter 1971): 38-39.

398.34 "Renewal." "Betrayal: On the Loss of a Friend."
Callaloo 2 (February 1979): 88, 96.

398.35 "Sexual Privacy of Women on Welfare."
"Kaleidoscope." Nimrod 21 (1978): 140-141.

398.36 "Silence." Black Scholar 10 (November-December
1978): 17.

398.37 "Survival Poem." "Incident in a Black Ghetto."
"Rain Ditch." "Telephone Call." Confrontation: A Journal of
Third World Literature 1 (1974): 54-57.

398.38 "Two Poems for Gordon." Southern Review 21 (July
1985): 860-861.

398.39 "Waiting." "Spring." New Orleans Review 4 (1974):
272-273.

398.40 "When You Read This Poem." Black Scholar 9 (November
1977): 29.

398.41 "While Sitting in the Airport Waiting Room."
Callaloo 1 (December 1976): 15.

398.42 Wind Thoughts. Fort Smith, AR: South & West, 1972.

Secondary Sources

398.43(S) Craig, Marilyn B. "Pinkie Gordon Lane." In
HARRIS & DAVIS, pp. 212-216.

398.44(S) Newman, Dorothy W. "Lane's Mystic Female."
Callaloo 2 (February 1979): 153-155. Pinkie Gordon Lane.

1988-1991 Supplement

A398.45 "Poems." Black American Literature Forum 23 (Fall
1989): 451.

A398.46 "Reading Poetry by Henry Dumas While Listening to
Cool Jazz." Black American Literature Forum 22 (Summer
1988): 275.

A398.47 "Reflections on Dumas's 'Love Song'." Black
American Literature Forum 22 (Summer 1988): 270.

399.   LARSEN, NELLA MARIAN (1893-1964).

399.1 "The Author's Explanation." Forum (Supp. 4) 83 (April
1930): 4142.

399.2 "Correspondence." Opportunity 4 (September 1926):
295.

399.3 Passing. New York: A.A. Knopf, 1929. Reprint, New
York: Arno Press, 1969. New York: Collier Books, 1971.
Novel.

399.4 "Playtime: Danish Fun." The Brownies' Book 1 (July
1920): 219. Children's stories.

399.5 "Playtime: Three Scandinavian Games." The Brownies'
Book 1 (June 1920): 191-192. Children's stories.

399.6 Quicksand. New York: A.A. Knopf, 1928. Reprint, New
York: Negro Universities Press, 1969. New York: Collier
Books, 1971. Novel.

399.7 Quicksand and Passing. Edited with an introduction by
Deborah E. McDowell. American Women Writers Series. New
Brunswick, NJ: Rutgers University Press, 1986.

399.8 "Sanctuary." Forum 83 (January 1930): 15-18.

Secondary Sources

399.9(S) Clark, William Bedford. "The Letters of Nella
Larsen to Carl Van Vechten: A Survey." Resources for
American Literary Study 8 (Fall 1978): 193-199.

399.10(S) Davis, Thadious M. "Nella Larsen." In HARRIS &
DAVIS, 1987, pp. 182-192.

399.11(S) DuBois, William E.B. "Two Novels." Crisis 35
(June 1928): 202.

399.12(S) Joyce, Joyce Ann. "Nella Larsen's Passing: A
Reflection of the American Dream." Western Journal of Black
Studies 7 (2): 68-73 (Summer 1983).

399.13(S) Lay, Mary M. "Parallels: Henry James's The
Portrait of a Lady and Nella Larsen's Quicksand." CLA Journal
20 (June 1977): 475-486.

399.14(S) Lewis, Vashti Cruthcher. "Nella Larsen's Use of
the Near-White Female in Quicksand and Passing. Western
Journal of Black Studies 10 (3): 137-142 (Fall 1986).

399.15(S) Mays, Benjamin Elijah. The Negro's God As
Reflected In His Literature. Boston: Chapman and Grimes,
1938. Reprint. New York: Russell & Russell, 1968 and New
York: Antheneum, 1968.

399.16(S) Ramsey, Priscilla R. "Freeze the Day: A Feminist
Reading of Nella Larsen's Quicksand and Passing." Afro-
Americans in New York Life and History 9 (1): 27-41 (1985).

399.17(S) Ramsey, Priscilla R. "A Study of Black Identity
in 'Passing' Novels of the 19th and Early 20th Century."
Studies in Black Literature 7 (Winter 1976): 1-7.

399.18(S) Sato, Hiroko. "Under the Harlem Shadow: A Study
of Jessie Fauset and Nella Larsen," In BONTEMPS.

399.19(S) Shockley, Ann Allen. "Nella Marian Larsen Imes."
In SHOCKLEY, pp. 432-445.

399.20(S) Tate, Claudia. "Nella Larsen's Passing: A Problem
of Interpretation." Black American Literature Forum 14
(Winter 1980): 142-46.

399.21(S) Thornton, Hortense E. "Sexism as Quagmire: Nella
Larsen's Quicksand." CLA Journal 16 (March 1973): 285-301.

399.22(S) Wall, Cheryl. "Nella Larsen." In MAINIERO, pp.
505-509.

399.23(S) Wall, Cheryl. "Passing For What? Aspects of
Identity in Nella Larsen's Novels." Black American
Literature Forum 20 (1-2): 97-111 (Spring/Summer 1986).

399.24(S) Washington, Mary Helen. "Lost Woman: Nella Larsen
-- Mystery Woman of the Harlem Renaissance." Ms. 9 (December
1980): 44-50.

399.25(S) Youman, Mary Mabel. "Nella Larsen's Passing: A
Study in Irony." CLA Journal 18(December 1974):235-41.

400. LATIMORE, JEWEL C. (1935-).

400.1 "Compliment." Black World 23 (September 1974): 60

400.2 <u>Images in Black</u>. Chicago: Third World Press, 1967.

400.3 <u>Let's Go Some Where</u>. Chicago: Third World Press, 1970.

400.4 "On the Naming Day." <u>Black World</u> 22 (September 1973): 75.

400.5 "Statement on the Black Arts." <u>Black World</u> 24 (February 1975): 80-81.

400.6 "Unity." <u>Black World</u> 23 (September 1974): 61.

400.7 Untitled Poem. <u>Black World</u>, 23(September 1974):60.

401. LAUDERDALE, BEVERLY.

401.1 "First Comes Touch." <u>Essence</u> 9 (August 1978): 78-79.

401.2 "Gift Exchange." <u>Essence</u> 10 (November 1980): 86-87.

402. LaVAN, MAUDE PEARL.

402.1 <u>Colored Boys in Khaki</u>. n.p.: Cosmo-Advocate Publishing Co., 1918.

403. LAWSON, JENNIFER BLACKMAN.

403.1 <u>Blackbird in My Tree: A Collection of Poems</u>. Palo Alto, CA: Zikawuna, 1979.

403.2 "Early Morning Calls." <u>Essence</u> 7 (August 1976): 54-55.

403.3 "Ella Mae." <u>Essence</u> 11(May 1980): 102.

403.4 <u>High Expectations: Poems for Black Women</u>. Pittsburgh, CA: Los Medans, 1977. Anthology. Dorothy Randall-Tsuruta, joint editor.

404. LEE, ANDREA (1953-).

404.1 "The Days of the Thunderbirds." <u>New Yorker</u> (9 July 1984): 34-42.

404.2 "Fine Points." New Yorker (21 May 1984): 38-41.

404.3 "Gypsies." New Yorker (18 June 1984): 37-39.

404.4 "Negatives." New Yorker (1 October 1984): 34-38.

404.5 "Russia Observed -- The Real Life." Vogue 171 (August 1981): 288-289.

404.6 Russian Journal. New York: Random House, 1981.

404.7 Sarah Phillips. New York: Random House, 1984.

405. LEE, AUDREY.

405.1 "Alienation." Black World 21 (November 1971): 64-66.

405.2 "Antonio Is a Man." Essence 2 (January 1972): 44-45.

405.3 "The Block." Black World 19 (October 1970):65-72.

405.4 The Clarion People. New York: McGraw-Hill, 1968. Novel.

405.5 "Eulogy for a Public Servant." Black World 25 (January 1976): 54-57.

405.6 "Her Private Moment." Essence 2(November 1971): 77.

405.7 "I'm Going To Move Out of This Emotional Ghetto." Negro Digest 19 (December 1969): 63-68.

405.8 "A Man Is a Man." Essence 1 (February 1971): 4-41.

405.9 "The Maudlin Mist of Morning." Essence 2 (May 1971): 1.

405.10 "Moma." Negro Digest 18 (February 1969): 53-65.

405.11 "Nostalgia." Essence 2 (May 1971): 77.

405.12 "Something Sweet." Essence 2 (March 1872): 41.

405.13 "Two Tales." Black American Literature Forum 23 (Summer 1989): 307. Short fiction.

405.14 The Workers. New York: McGraw-Hill, 1969. Novel.

Lee, Don. SEE MADHUBUTI, HAKI R.

406. LEE, JARENA (1783-?).

406.1 Religious Experiences and Journal of Mrs. Jarena Lee,
Giving an Account of Her Call to Preach the Gospel.
Philadelphia: Author, 1849.

Secondary Sources

406.2(S) Andrews, William L., ed. Sisters of the Spirit:
Three Black Women's Autobiographies of the Nineteenth-
century. Bloomington, IN: Indiana University Press, 1986.

406.3(S) Foster, Frances Smith. "Adding Color and Contour
to Early Self-Portraiture: Autobiographical Writings of Afro-
American Women." In PRYSE & SPILLERS, pp. 25-39.

406.4(S) McMahon, Jean, ed. Gifts of Power: The Writings of
Rebecca Jackson, Black Visionary, Shaker Eldress. Amherst,
MA: University of Massachusetts, 1981.

406.5(S) Mason, Mary Grimley, and Green, Carol Hurd, eds.
Journeys: Autobiographical Writings of Women. Boston: G.K.
Hall, 1979. Jarena Lee on p. 74.

406.6(S) Payne, Daniel Alexander. History of the African
Methodist Episcopal Church. Ed. by C.S. Smith. Nashville:
Publishing House of the A.M.E. Church, 1891. Jarena Lee cited
on p. 190.

406.7(S) Shockley, Ann Allen. "Jarena Lee." In SHOCKLEY,
pp. 41-47.

1988-1991 Supplement

Secondary Sources

A406.8(S) Houchins, Sue E., ed. Spiritual Narratives. NY:
Oxford University Press, 1988.

407. LEE, MARY HOPE.

407.1 "Jasmine." Essence 9 (October 1978): 60.

408. LEIA, SANDI.

408.1 The Silhouette of a Pen. Milwaukee: Shore Publishing
Co., 1971.

409. LEWIS, CAROL ANITA.

409.1 "Ask Winnie Mandela." <u>Essence</u> 17 (November 1986): 151.

409.2 "Lula's Chil Grown." <u>Essence</u> 17 (November 1986): 151.

410. LEWIS, CARRIE LOUISE.

410.1 <u>Polished Pebbles: Poems</u>. New York: Exposition Press, 1960.

411. LEWIS, DENISE Y.

411.1 Untitled Poem. <u>Essence</u> 9 (February 1979): 60.

412. LEWIS, IOLA ELIZABETH.

412.1 <u>Life Can Be Beautiful and Other Poems and Songs</u>. Bethesda, MD: Author, 1966.

413. LIGHTS, RIKKI (1952-).

413.1 <u>Dog Moon</u>. Bronx, NY: Sunbury, 1976. Poetry.

413.2 "Gut Riddle." "Lyriclicks." <u>Essence</u> 8 (December 1977): 32.

414. LINCOLN, ABBEY (1930-).

414.1 "A Streak o' Lean." In CHILDRESS, pp. 49-56. Drama. Excerpt.

415. LINDEN, CHARLOTTE E. (1859-).

415.1 <u>Autobiography and Poems</u>. 3d ed. Springfield, OH: Author, 1907?

415.2 <u>Scraps of Time</u>. Springfield, OH: Author, n.d.

416.   LIVINGSTON, MYRTLE S. (1901-).

416.1 "For Unborn Children." _Crisis_ 32 (1926): 122-125.

                    Secondary Sources

416.2(S) Hatch, James V. _Black Theater, USA: Forty-Five Plays by American Negroes, 1847-1974_. New York: Free Press, 1974.

417.   LOFTIN, ELOUISE (1950-).

417.1 _Barefoot Necklace_. Brooklyn: Jamima House Press, 1975.

417.2 "Deeper." _Essence_ 8 (November 1977): 34.

417.3 _Jumbish_. New York: Emerson Hall, 1972.

417.4 "Jumbish-One." _Essence_ 8 (November 1977): 34.

417.5 "Who Are the Happy." _Essence_ 8 (November 1977): 112.

Logan, Rosie Lee. **SEE** 374. JONES, ROSIE LEE LOGAN.

418.   LOMAX, PEARL CLEAGE (1948-).

418.1 "Jesus Drum." "Mississippi Born." "Poem." In ADOFF, pp. 28-29, 47-48, 118-119.

418.2 "Street Dreams." _Essence_ 4 (July 1973): 22.

418.3 _We Don't Need No Music_. Detroit: Broadside Press, 1972. Poetry.

Long, Naomi Cornelia **SEE** 438. MADGETT, NAOMI LONG.

419.   LORDE, AUDRE (1934-1992).

419.1   "Abortion." <u>Iowa Review</u> 12 (2-3): 223-231 (1981).

419.2   <u>Apartheid U.S.A.</u> New York: Kitchen Table: Women of Color, 1986.

419.3   "Bazaar." <u>Denver Quarterly</u> 16 (1): 35 (Spring 1981).

419.4   "Berlin is Hard on Colored Girls." <u>Callaloo</u> 9 (1): 89 (Winter 1986).

419.5   <u>Between Ourselves</u>. Pointe Reyes, CA: Eidolon Editions, 1976.

419.6   "Between Ourselves." <u>Denver Quarterly</u> 16 (1): 29-31 (Spring 1981).

419.7   <u>The Black Unicorn</u>. New York: W. W. Norton, 1978.

419.8   "Black Women's Anger." <u>Essence</u> 14 (October 1983): 90-92.

419.9   <u>Burst of Light</u>. Ithaca, NY: Firebrand Books, 1988.

419.10   <u>Cables to Rage</u>. London: Paul Breman, 1970.

419.11   <u>The Cancer Journals</u>. Argyle, NY: Spinsters, Ink, 1980.

419.12   "Chorus." <u>Denver Quarterly</u> 16 (1): 28 (Spring 1981).

419.13   <u>Chosen Poems, Old and New</u>. New York: W. W. Norton, 1982.

419.14   "Coal." <u>Negro Digest</u> 15 (March 1966): 21.

419.15   <u>Coal</u>. New York: W. W. Norton, 1968.

419.16   "Conclusion." <u>Essence</u> 3 (January 1973): 15.

419.17   "Conference Keynote Address: Sisterhood and Survival." <u>Black Scholar</u> 17 (2): 5-7 (March-April 1986).

419.18   "Coniagui Women." <u>New Yorker</u> (28 November 1977): 84.

419.19   "Contact Lenses." <u>Denver Quarterly</u> 16 (1): 32 (Spring 1981).

419.20   "Equal Opportunity." <u>Black Scholar</u> 15 (May-June 1984): 16-17.

419.21   "Erotic as Power." <u>Ms.</u> 11 (December 1982): 78.

419.22   "The Evening News." <u>Denver Quarterly</u> 16 (1): 34 (Spring 1981).

419.23   "Feminism and Black Liberation." <u>Black Scholar</u> 10 (May-June 1979): 17-20.

419.24 <u>The First Cities</u>. New York: Poets Press, 1968.

419.25 <u>From a Land Where Other People Live</u>. Detroit: Broadside Press, 1973.

419.26 "From the House of Yamanja." <u>American Poetry Review</u> 6 (6): 35 (November-December 1977).

419.27 "Grenada Revisited: An Interim Report." <u>Black Scholar</u> 15 (January-February 1984): 21-29.

419.28 "Harriet: For My Sisters." <u>Essence</u> 8 (June 1977): 48.

419.29 <u>I Am Your Sister: Black Women Organizing Across Sexualities</u>. New York: Kitchen Table: Women of Color, 1980. (Freedom Organizing Series, No.3)

419.30 <u>Litany for Survival</u>. Watsonville, CA: Blackwells, 1981. [Broadside]

419.31 "Mexico." <u>Negro Digest</u> 14 (October 1965): 46.

419.32 "Movement Song." <u>Black World</u> 22 (September 1073): 77.

419.33 "Naturally." <u>Negro Digest</u> 17 (September-October 1968): 71.

419.34 "Need." <u>Black Collegian</u> 35 (1980): 17-19. <u>Black Scholar</u> 12 (May-June 1981): 37-40, (November-December 1981): 35-38.

419.35 "New York City 1970." <u>Black World</u> 19 (July 1970): 26-27.

419.36 <u>The New York Head Shop and Museum</u>. Detroit: Broadside Press, 1974.

419.37 "Now." <u>Black World</u> 22 (June 1973): 32.

419.38 "Of Sisters and Secrets." <u>Callaloo</u> 2 (3): 67-73 (1979).

419.39 <u>Our Dead Behind Us: Poems</u>. New York: W. W. Norton, 1986.

419.40 "Our Sisters in Arms." <u>Callaloo</u> 9 (1): 87-88 (Winter 1986).

419.41 "Outside." <u>American Poetry Review</u> 6 (1): 26 (January-February 1977). <u>Essence</u> 11 (May 1980): 103.

419.42 "Pirouette." <u>Essence</u> 9 (February 1979): 88.

419.43 "A Poem for Women in Rage." <u>Iowa Review</u> 12 (2-3): 220-222 (Spring-Summer 1981).

419.44 "Prologue." Freedomways 12 (1): 31-33 (1972).

419.45 "Scratching the Surface: Some Notes on Barriers to Women and Loving." Black Scholar 9 (April 1978): 31-35.

419.46 "The Seventh Sense." Essence 14 (December 1983): 17.

419.47 Sister Outsider: Essays and Speeches. Trumansburg, NY: Crossing Press, 1982.

419.48 "Sisterhood and Survival." Black Scholar 17 (2): 5-7 (March-April 1986).

419.49 "Sisters in Arms." Parnassus 12-13 (2-1): 225-226 (Spring-Summer-Fall-Winter 1985).

419.50 "Suffer the Children." Negro Digest 13 (January 1964): 15.

419.51 "A Summer Oracle." Negro Digest 18 (1969): 41.

419.52 "Teacher." Negro Digest 14 (September 1965): 64.

419.53 "There is No Hierarchy of Oppressions." Interracial Books for Children Bulletin 14 (3-4): 9 (1983).

419.54 "Timepiece." Denver Quarterly 16 (1): 33 (Spring 1981).

419.55 "To Desi as Joe as Smokey the Lover of 115th Street." Black World 22 (June 1973): 31-32.

419.56 "To My Daughter the Junkie on a Train." Black World 22 (June 1973): 33.

419.57 Uses of the Erotic: The Erotic as Power. Brooklyn: Out & Out, 1979.

419.58 Zami: A New Spelling of My Name. Trumansburg, NY: Crossing Press, 1984.

419.59 "Revolutionary Hope: A Conversation Between James Baldwin and Audre Lorde." Essence 15 (December 1984): 72-74.

419.60 " 'In Memory of Our Children's Blood': Sisterhood and South African Women." Sage 3 (2): 40-43 (Fall 1986). Gloria I. Joseph, joint author.

419.61 Apartheid U.S.A. and Our Common Enemy, Our Common Cause: Freedom Organizing in the Eighties. New York: Kitchen Table: Women of Color, 1986. (Freedom Organizing Series, No. 2). Merle Woo, joint author.

                    Secondary Sources

419.62(S) Avi-ram, Amitai F. "Apo Koinou in Audre Lorde and the Moderns." Callaloo 9 (1): 193-208 (Winter 1986).

419.63(S)   Gilbert, Sandra M.   "On the Edge of the Estate."
Poetry 129 (February 1977): 296-301.

419.64(S)   Hammond, Karla.   "Audre Lorde: Interview."   Denver
Quarterly 16 (1): 20-27 (Spring 1981).

419.65(S)   Hammond, Karla.   "An Interview with Audre Lorde."
American Poetry Review 9 (2): 18-21 (1980).

419.66(S)   Hull, Gloria T.   "Poem for Audre Lorde."   Callaloo
5 (2): 79-80 (1979).

419.67(S)   McClauren-Allen, Irma. "Audre Lorde."   In   HARRIS
& DAVIS, pp. 217-222.

1988-1991 Supplement

A419.68   A Burst of Light: Essays.   Ithaca, NY: Firebrand,
1988.

420.   LOUISE, ESTHER.

420.1   "Equity."   Essence 16 (October 1985): 124.

420.2   "Jesus' Song."   Essence 9 (April 1979): 17.

420.3   "On Predestination."   Essence 9 (April 1979): 18.
Obsidian 6 (1-2): 169 (Spring-Summer 1980).

420.4   "Swinging Doors of Knocking-Wood Cowards."   Essence 11
(December 1980): 20.   Obsidian 6 (1-2): 170-173 (Spring-
Summer 1980).

421.   LOUISE, FANNIE.

421.1   Allow Me To Say.   Washington, DC: Author, [1972?]

422.   LOVE, ROSE LEARY.

422.1   Nebraska and His Granny.   Tuskegee, AL: Tuskegee
Institute Press, 1936.   Poetry.

423.   LYN (1946-).

423.1 <u>Singing Sadness Happy</u>. Detroit: Broadside Press, 1972. Poetry.

424. LYNN, EVE [pseud. of Evelyn Crawford Reynolds]

424.1 <u>No Alabaster Box and Other Poems</u>. Philadelphia: Alpress, 1936.

424.2 <u>Put a Daisy in Your Hair</u>. Philadelphia: Dorrance & Company, 1963.

424.3 <u>To No Special Land</u>. New York: Exposition Press, 1953.

McBain, Barbara Mahone. **SEE** 440. MAHONE, BARBARA.

425. McBROWN, GERTRUDE PARTHENIA.

425.1 "Birthday Surprise." <u>Negro History Bulletin</u> 16 (February 1953): 16. Dramatic sketch on the life of Paul Laurence Dunbar.

425.2 "Bought with Cookies." <u>Negro History Bulletin</u> 12 (April 1949). Drama for children.

425.3 <u>The Picture-Poetry-Book</u>. Washington, DC: Associated Publishers, 1935.

426. McCALL, VALAIDA POTTER.

426.1 <u>Sunrise Over Alabama</u>. New York: Comet Press Books, 1959. Novel.

McCall, W.J. **SEE** 426. McCALL, VALAIDA POTTER.

427. McCLAUREN, IRMA (1952-).

427.1 "Audre Lorde." In HARRIS & DAVIS, pp. 217-222.

427.2 <u>Black Chicago</u>. New York: Amuru, 1973. Poetry.

427.3 "Caribbean Interlude." <u>Essence</u> 19 (April 1989): 114.

427.4 "Harriet Tubman." *Essence* 19 (March 1989): 117.
Catalyst (Spring 1990): 75. Poem.

427.5 "I Woman." *Obsidian* 3 (2): 55 (Summer 1977).

427.6 "Love Poem $ 6." *Essence* 19 (March 1989): 130. Poem.

427.7 "Old Age Sequence (for Gwendolyn Brooks)." *Black American Literature Forum* 21 (3): 252 (Fall 1987).

427.8 *Poems I*. New York: Rannick Playwrights Company, 1971.
Rev. ed. published as *Black Chicago*. New York: Rannick, 1971.

427.9 *Song in the Night*. Chicago: Pearl Press, 1974.

427.10 "Song in the Night," *Essence* 19 (March 1989): 127.
Poem.

428. McCRAY, CHIRLANE.

428.1 "I Am a Lesbian." *Essence* 10 (September 1979): 90-91.

428.2 "Two Love Poems for Sekou: 2." *Essence* 10 (February 1980): 59.

429. McCRAY, NETTIE [SALIMU]

429.1 "Growin' Into Blackness." *Black Theatre* (2): 195-200 (1969). One act drama.

430. McELROY, COLLEEN (1935-).

430.1 *Bone Flames*. New York: Harper, 1987.

430.2 "The Circus of the City." *Southern Poetry Review* 24 (2): 61-62 (Autumn 1984).

430.3 "Day Help." *Essence* 5 (March 1975): 87.

430.4 "Dreams of Johnson Grass." *Southern Poetry Review* 20 (1): 11 (Spring 1980).

430.5 "The Female as Taken from Freshman Essays."
Massachusetts Review 24 (2): 314-316 (Summer 1983).

403.6 "From Blue Waters." *Southern Poetry Review* 20 (1) :13 (Spring 1980).

430.7 _Jesus and Fat Tuesday and Other Short Stories_.
Berkeley: Creative Arts Book Company, 1987.

430.8 "Landscapes and Still Life." _Callaloo_ 1 (4): 77
(1978).

430.9 _Lie and Say You Love Me_. Tacoma, WA: Cincinatum,
1981.

430.10 _Looking for a Country Under its Original Name_.
Yakima, WA: Blue Begonia Press, 1985.

430.11 "Moon, Razor, Eye." _Georgia Review_ 39 (3): 523 (Fall
1985).

430.12 _The Mules Done Long Since Gone_. Seattle: Harrison-
Madrona Center, 1973.

430.13 _Music from Home: Selected Poems_. Carbondale, IL:
Southern Illinois University Press, 1976.

430.14 _Queen of the Ebony Isles_. New York: Harper, 1984.

430.15 "Remember Me to Harris." _Callaloo_ 2 (3): 9-21
(1979).

430.16 "Runners." _Callaloo_ 1 (4): 1 (1978).

430.17 "Shelley at Sequim Inlet." _Manhattan Review_ 3 (2):
72 (Winter 1984-1985).

430.18 "Silence." _Black World_ 25 (November 1975): 27.

430.19 "Singer." _Essence_ 7 (May 1976): 78.

430.20 _Speech and Language Development of the Preschool
Child: A Survey_. Springfield, IL: C.C. Thomas, 1972.

430.21 "Sun, Wind and Water." _Callaloo_ 4 (1-3): 39-46
(1981).

430.22 "To the Lady Holding the MGM Torch." _Callaloo_ 1 (4):
82-83 (1978).

430.23 "Try to Understand Papa." _Encore_ 6 (17 January
1977): 47.

430.24 "What I'd Least Like to Remember." _Manhattan Review_
3 (2): 73 (Winter 1984-1985).

430.25 "When Poets Dream." _Essence_ 10 (November 1980): 22.

430.26 "With Bill Pickett at the 101 Ranch." _Callaloo_ 9
(1): 100 (Winter 1986).

430.27 _Winters Without Snow_. New York: I. Reed, 1980.

430.28 "A Woman's Song." <u>Obsidian</u> 3 (1): 57-58 (Spring 1977).

Secondary Sources

430.29(S) Hernton, Calvin C. "Black Women Poets: The Oral Tradition." In HERNTON, pp. 119-155.

431. McGHEE, MAUDE.

431.1 <u>To Get My Name in the Kingdom Book</u>. Atlanta: Author, 1963.

432. McGINNIS, JULIETTE.

432.1 "Breathe In." <u>Essence</u> 5 (January 1975): 58-59.

432.2 "Mental Gardening." <u>Essence</u> 5 (January 1975): 38-39.

433. McKANE, ALICE WOODBY (1865-1948).

433.1 <u>Clover Leaves</u>. Boston: Still & Still, 1914.

434. McLEARY, EDNA TUBBS.

434.1 <u>Tomorrow's Yesterday</u>. n.p., [196?].

McMichael, Michelle **SEE** 713. ZIMEME-KEITA. NZADI.

435. McMILLAN, TERRY.

435.1 <u>Disappearing Acts</u>. New York: Viking Press, 1990.

435.2 "Every 28 Days." <u>Catalyst</u> (Winter 1989): 41.

435.3 "Franklin." <u>Catalyst</u> (Fall 1989): 66.

435.4 "Ma'Dear (for Estelle Ragsdale)." <u>Callaloo</u> 10 (1): 71-78 (Winter 1987).

435.5 <u>Mama</u>. Boston: Houghton, 1987. <u>Essence</u>, 17(April 1987):72. Excerpt.

435.6 "Zora and Franklin." <u>Essence</u> 20 (August 1989): 67. Excerpt from <u>Disappearing Act</u>.

436. McNEIL, DEE DEE.

436.1 <u>Dee Dee Doodles: Riddles, Poetry and Pictures to Color</u>. Los Angeles: Al-Bait Haram Publishing Company, 1972.

436.2 "Poppy's House." <u>Catalyst</u> (Spring 1990): 74.

436.3 "Some Don't Believe in Demons." <u>Catalyst</u> (Spring 1990): 57.

437. MACK, DONNA.

437.1 "If That Mocking Bird Don't Sing." <u>Essence</u> 8 (July 1977): 44-45.

438. MADGETT, NAOMI LONG (1923-).

438.1 "Alabama Centennial." <u>Negro Digest</u> 12 (October 1963): 65.

438.2 "Autumn Prelude." <u>Negro Digest</u> 12 (September 1963): 54.

438.3 "Black Poet." <u>Obsidian</u> 7 (1): 36 (Spring 1981).

438.4 "Croix du Sud." <u>Negro History Bulletin</u> 36 (April 1973): 88

438.5 <u>Exits and Entrances</u>. Detroit: Lotus Press, 1978.

438.6 "Fifth Street Exit, Richmond." <u>Callaloo</u> 5 (2): 81-83 (1979).

438.7 "In Memoriam: Omualowiba." <u>Negro Digest</u> 17 (September-October 1968): 94.

438.8 "Memorial." <u>Great Lakes Review</u> 6 (1): 73 (Summer 1979).

438.9 "Midway." <u>Freedomways</u> 1 (Fall 1961): 258.

438.10 <u>Octavia and Other Poems</u>. Chicago: Third World Press, 1988.

438.11 "Offspring." Essence 15 (September 1984): 176.

438.12 One and the Many. New York: Exposition Press, 1956.

438.13 "Packrat." Callaloo 5 (2): 52 (1979).

438.14 Phantom Nightingale: Juvenilia. Detroit: Lotus Press, 1981.

438.15 "Phillis." Ebony 29 (March 1974): 96.

438.16 Pink Ladies in the Afternoon. Detroit: Lotus Press, 1972. 1990. Enlarged edition.

438.17 Songs to a Phantom Nightingale. New York: Fortuny's, 1941.

438.18 "Soon I Will Be Done." Callaloo 5 (2): 27 (1979).
Great Lakes Review 6 (1): 72 (1979).

438.19 Star by Star. Detroit: Harlo Press, 1965.

438.20 A Student's Guide to Creative Writing. Detroit: Lotus Press, 1980.

438.21 "The Sun Do Move." Obsidian 7 (1): 37 (Spring 1981).

438.22 Sunny. (Broadside Series) Detroit: Broadside Press, n.d.

438.23 "Sunny." Negro Digest 15 (September 1966): 82.

438.24 "The Survivors." Callaloo 5 (2): 78 (1979).

438.25 "Ten." Obsidian 7 (1): 36 (Spring 1981).

438.26 "Twice a Child (for My Mother at Ninety)." Great Lakes Review 6 (1): 74 (Summer 1979).

438.27 "White Cross." Negro Digest 12 (April 1963): 73.

438.28 "Woman with Flower." In BLACKSONGS.

Secondary Sources

438.29(S) Robinson, Louise. Blacksongs, Series I: Four Poetry Broadsides by Black Women. Detroit: Lotus Press, 1977. Includes Jill Boyer ("Sun Song), Louise Robinson ("Woman-song."), Paulette C. White ("Lost Your Momma.") and Naomi Long Madgett ("Woman with Flower")

439. MAHIRI, JABARI.

439.1 <u>The Day They Stole the Letter J</u>. Chicago: Third World
Press, 1981.

440.   MAHONE, BARBARA (1944-).

440.1 "Colors for Mama." "Sugarfields." In ADOFF, pp. 36-
37.

440.2 <u>Sugarfield Poems</u>. Detroit: Broadside Press, 1970.

                    Secondary Sources

440.3(S) Eanes, Marcie. "<u>Essence</u> Woman: Barbara J. Mahone."
<u>Essence</u> 14 (December 1983): 56.

441.   MAJOR, DEBORAH.

441.1 <u>Ascension II</u>. San Francisco: San Francisco African
American Historical and Cultural Society, 1983. Anthology of
contemporary African-American poetry. Deborah Major, editor.

441.2 "An Open Weave." <u>Callaloo</u> 12 (Summer 1989): 476.
Short fiction.

441.3 "Progress Report." <u>Black Scholar</u> 12 (September-
October 1981): 17.

441.4 "Two Young Men Meet Oppression One Last Time." <u>Black
Scholar</u> 11 (5): 71 (May-June 1980).

Malcolm, Barbara. SEE 487. NAYO.

442.   MALVEAUX, JULIANNE (1953-).

442.1 "Black Women on White Campuses." <u>Essence</u> 10 (August
1979): 78.

442.2 "Don't Take Up with Nobody You Meet on a Train."
<u>Essence</u> 11 (February 1981): 19.

442.3 "Political and Historical Aspects of Black Male/Female
Relationships." <u>Black Scholar</u> 10 (May-June 1979): 32-35.

442.4 <u>Slipping Through the Cracks: The Status of Black
Women</u>. New Brunswick, NJ: Transaction, 1986. Margaret C.
Simms, joint editor.

443. MARCUS, LORRAINE.

443.1 "Bridal Shower." _Essence_ 7 (August 1976): 68-69.

444. MARSHALL, FLORENCE E.

444.1 _Are You Awake?_ Lansing, MI: Shaw Publishing Company,
1936.

445. MARSHALL, PAULE (1929-).

445.1 _Brown Girl, Brownstones_. New York: Random House,
1959. Novel.

445.2 _The Chosen Place, the Timeless People_. New York:
Harcourt, 1969. Novel.

445.3 "Kenya: Variety and Spice on Africa's East Coast."
Essence 13 (July 1982): 51-52

445.4 _Merle: A Novella and Other Stories_. New York:
Feminist Press, 1983.

445.5 "The Negro Woman in American Literature." _Freedomways_
6 (Winter 1966): 20-25.

445.6 _Praisesong for the Widow_. New York: Putnam's Sons,
1983. _Ms._ 11 (February 1983): 49. Excerpt. Novel.

445.7 "Reena." In CLARKE, 1966.

445.8 _Reena and other Stories_. New York: Feminist Press,
1984. Short fiction.

445.9 "Shaping the World of My Art." _New Letters_ 40
(October 1973): 97-112. _Womens's Studies Quarterly_ 9 (4):
23-24 (Winter 1981).

445.10 "Some Get Wasted." In CLARKE.

445.11 _Soul Clap Hands and Sing_. New York: Atheneum, 1961.
In CHAPMAN.

445.12 "Ties That Bind." _Essence_ 16 (May 1985): 64.

445.13 "To Da-Dah, in Memoriam." _New World Magazine_ (1967).

445.14 "Return of a Native Daughter: An Interview with Paule
Marshall and Maryse Conde" translated by John Williams in

Politique Africaine (September 1984). Sage 3 (Fall 1986):
52-53.

                         Secondary Sources

445.15(S) Benston, Kimberly. "Architectural Imagery and
Unity in Paule Marshall's Brown Girl, Brownstones." Negro
American Literature Forum 9 (Fall 1975): 67-70.

445.16(S) Braithwaite, Edward. "West Indian History and
Society in the Art of Paule Marshall's Novel." Journal of
Black Studies 1 (December 1970): 225-238.

445.17(S) Brock, Sabine. "Transcending the 'Loophole of
Retreat': Paule Marshall's Placing of Female Generations."
Callaloo 10 (1): 79-90 (Winter 1987).

445.18(S) Brown, Lloyd W. "Mannequins and Mermaids -- The
Contemporary Writer and Sexual Images in the Consumer
Culture." Women's Studies 5 (1): 1-12 (1977).

445.19(S) Brown, Lloyd W. "The Rhythms of Power in Paule
Marshall's Fiction." Novel 7 (Winter 1974): 159-167.

445.20(S) Christian, Barbara. "Paule Marshall."   In
DAVIS & HARRIS, pp. 161-170.

445.21(S) Christian, Barbara. "Ritualistic Process and the
Structure of Paule Marshall's Praisesong for the Widow."
Callaloo 18 (6): 74-84 (Spring-Summer 1983).

445.22(S) Christian, Barbara. "Sculpture and Space: The
Interdependence of Chaucer and Culture in the Novels of Paule
Marshall." In CHRISTIAN, pp. 80-136.

445.23(S) Collier, Eugenia. "The Closing of the Circle:
Movement from Division to Wholeness in Paule Marshall's
Fiction." In EVANS, pp. 295-315.

445.24(S) Conde, Maryse. "Return of a Native Daughter: An
Interview with Paule Marshall and Maryse Conde." John
Williams, translator. Sage 3 (2): 52-53 (Fall 1986).

445.25(S) Cook, John. "Whose Child?: The Fiction of Paule
Marshall." CLA Journal 7 (September 1980): 1-10.

445.26(S) Denniston, Dorothy. "Early Short Fiction by Paule
Marshall." Callaloo 18(6): 31-45 (Spring-Summer 1983).

445.27(S) DeVeaux, Alexis. "Paule Marshall -- In
Celebration of Our Triumphs." Essence 11 (May 1980): 70-
71,96,98,123-134.

445.28(S) Eko, Ebele O. "Oral Tradition: The Bridge to
Africa in Paule Marshall's Praisesong for the Widow."
Western Journal of Black Studies 10 (3): 143-147 (Fall 1986).

445.29(S) Gayles, Gloria. "The Truths of our Mothers'
Lives: Mother-Daughter Relationships in Black Women's
Fiction." Sage 1 (2): 8-12 (Fall 1984).

445.30(S) Harris, Trudier. "No Outlet for the Blues: Silla
Boyce's Plight in Brown Girl, Brownstones." Callaloo 18(6):
57-67 (Spring-Summer 1983).

445.31(S) Hull, Gloria T. "To Be a Black Woman in America:
A Reading of Paule Marshall's Reena." Obsidian 4 (3): 5-15
(Winter 1978).

445.32(S) Kapai, Seela. "Dominant Themes and Techniques in
Paule Marshall's Fiction." CLA Journal 26 (September 1972):
49-59.

445.33(S) Keiza, Marcia. "Themes and Style In the Works of
Paule Marshall." Negro American Literature Forum 9 (Fall
1975): 67-76.

445.34(S) Kubitschek, Missy Dehn. "Paule Marshall's Women
On Quest." Black American Literature Forum 21 (1-2): 43-60
(Spring-Summer 1987).

445.35(S) Lacovia, R.M. "Migration and Transmutation in the
Novels of McKay, Marshall, and Clarke." Journal of Black
Studies 7 (June 1977): 437-454.

445.36(S) Lodge, S.A. "Publishers Weekly Interviews Paule
Marshall." Publishers Weekly (20 January 1984): 90-91.

445.37(S) McCluskey, John. "And Called Every Generation
Blessed: Theme Setting and Ritual in the Works of Paule
Marshall." In EVANS, pp. 316-334.

445.38(S) Malone, Gloria Snodgrass. "The Nature and Causes
of Suffering in the Fiction of Paule Marshall, Kristin
Hunter, Toni Morrision, and Alice Walker." Dissertation,
Kent State University, 1979.

445.39(S) Nazaruh, Peter. "Paule Marshall's Timeless
People." New Letter 40 (Autumn 1973): 116-131.

445.40(S) Ogunyemi, Chikwenye Okonjo. "The Old Order Shall
Pass: The Examples of Flying Home and Barbados." CLA Journal
25 (March 1982): 303-314.

445.41(S) Pannill, Linda. "From the 'Wordshop': The Fiction
of Paule Marshall." Melus 12 (2): 63-73 (Summer 1985).

445.42(S) Sandiford, Keith A. "Paule Marshall's Praisesong
For the Widow: The Reluctant Heiress, or Whose Life Is It
Anyway?" Black American Literature Forum 20 (4): 371-392
(Winter 1986).

445.43(S) Schneider, Deborah. "A Search for Selfhood: Paule
Marshall's Brown Girl, Brownstones." In BRUCK, pp. 53-72.

445.44(S) Skerrett, Joseph T, Jr. "Paule Marshall and the Crisis of the Middle Years: The Chosen Place, The Timeless People." Callaloo 18(6): 68-73 (Spring-Summer 1983).

445.45(S) Stoeltling, Winifred. "Time Past and Time Present: The Search for Viable Links in The Chosen Place, The Timeless People." CLA Journal 16 (September 1972): 60-71.

445.46(S) Talbert, E. Lee. "The Poetics of Prophecy in Paule Marshall's Soul Clap Hands and Sing. Melus 5 (1): 49-56 (Spring 1978).

445.47(S) Troester, Rosalie Riegle. "Turbulence and Tenderness: Mothers, Daughters, and 'Othermothers' in Paule Marshall's Brown Girl, Brownstones." Sage 1 (2): 13-16 (Fall 1984).

445.48(S) Waniek, Marilyn Nelson. "Paltry Things: Immigrants and Marginal Men in Paule Marshall's Short Fiction." Callaloo 18 (6): 46-56 (Spring Summer 1983).

445.49(S) Washington, Mary Helen. "Afterword," Brown Girl, Brownstones. New York: Feminist Press, 1981. Paule Marshall, pp. 311-324.

1988-1991 Supplement

A445.50 Daughters. New York: Atheneum, 1991.

446. MARTIN, ROSE HINTON.

446.1 Endearing Endeavours. New York: Pageant Press, 1960. Poetry.

447. MASON, JUDI ANN (1955-).

447.1 "A Hollywood Success Story." Essence 19 (March 1989): 79. Short fiction.

447.2 "I Wrote for the Soaps." Essence 19 (August 1988): 59.

447.3 "Smells That Go Boom." Essence 10 (August 1980): 86-87. Short fiction.

448. MAST, VERNETTA (1955-).

448.1 Chained. Dallas, TX: Akini Isi Publishing Co., 1973.

449.   MATANAH [DOROTHY JUNE WATKINS]

449.1 <u>Bits and Pieces</u>. Rev. ed. Dallas, TX: Author, 1974.

449.2 <u>Love Bones</u>. Dallas, TX: Author, 1974.

450.   MATHIS, SHARON BELL (1937-).

450.1 "Arthur." <u>Essence</u> 2 (March 1972): 50-51.

450.2 <u>Brooklyn Story</u>. New York: Hill & Wang, 1970.

450.3 <u>Cartwheels</u>. New York: Scholastic, 1977.

450.4 "Ernie's Father." <u>Black World</u> 22 (June 1973): 57-59.

450.5 <u>The Hundred Penny Box</u>. New York: Viking Press, 1975.

450.6 <u>Listen for the Fig Tree</u>. New York: Viking Press, 1973.

450.7 "My." <u>Negro History Bulletin</u> 35 (March 1972): 67.

450.8 <u>Ray Charles</u>. New York: Thomas Crowell, 1973.

450.9 <u>Sidewalk Story</u>. New York: Viking Press, 1971.

450.10 <u>Teacup Full of Roses</u>. New York: Viking Press, 1972.

Secondary Sources

450.11(S) Foster, Frances Smith. "Sharon Bell Mathis."   In DAVIS & HARRIS, pp. 170-173.

450.12(S) Washington, Brenda M. "<u>Essence</u> Women: Sharon Bell Mathis." <u>Essence</u> 6 (November 1975): 6.

451.   MATTHEWS, BETTIE J.

451.1 "Anxiety." <u>About Time</u> 15 (May 1987): 33.

451.2 "To Be Happy." <u>About Time</u> 15 (May 1987): 33.

451.3 "Waste Not a Moment." <u>About Time</u> 15 (May 1987): 33.

Matthews, Victoria Earle. SEE 194. EARLE, VICTORIA.

452. MAYS, RAYMINA.

452.1 "Lerna's Mother, Verda Lee." _Essence_ 11 (March 1981): 76.

453. MEALY, ROSEMARI.

453.1 _Lift These Shadows From Our Eyes: Poems_. Cambridge: West End, 1978.

454. MERIWETHER, LOUISE (1923-).

454.1 "The Black Family in Crisis: Teenage Pregnancy." _Essence_ 15 (April 1984): 94-96,144,147,151.

454.2 _Daddy Was a Number Runner_. Englewood Cliffs, NJ: Prentice-Hall, 1970. _Antioch Review_ 27 (Fall 1967): 325-337. _Ebony_ 25 (July 1970): 98-103. Excerpts. Novel.

454.3 _Don't Ride the Bus on Monday: The Rosa Parks Story_. Englewood Cliffs, NJ: Prentice-Hall, 1973.

454.4 _The Freedom Ship of Robert Smalls_. Englewood Cliffs, NJ: Prentice-Hall, 1971.

454.5 "A Happening in Barbados." _Antioch Review_ 28 (Spring 1968): 43-52. _Essence_ 2 (June 1971): 58-59.

454.6 _The Heart Man: Dr. Daniel Hale Williams_. Englewood Cliffs, NJ: Prentice-Hall, 1972.

454.7 "James Baldwin: The Fiery Voice of the Negro Revolt." _Negro Digest_ 12 (August 1963): 3-7.

454.8 "Lydia." _Freedomways_ 25 (2): 81-89 (1985).

454.9 "The Negro: Half a Man in a White World." _Negro Digest_ 14 (October 1965): 4-13.

454.10 "The New Face of Negro History." _Frontier_ 16 (October 1965): 5-7.

454.11 "No Race Pride." _Bronze America_ 1 (June 1964): 6-9.

454.12 "Robert and Hannah." _Essence_ 16 (February 1986): 70-72.

454.13 "That Girl from Creektown." In WATKINS, pp. 79-92.

454.14 "The Thick End Is for Whipping." _Negro Digest_ 28 (November 1968): 55-62.

Secondary Sources

454.15(S) Dandridge, Rita B. "From Economic Insecurity to Disintegration: A Study of Character in Louise Meriwether's _Daddy Was a Number Runner_." _Negro American Literature Forum_ 9 (Fall 1975): 82-85.

454.16(S) Dandridge, Rita B. "Louise Meriwether." In DAVIS & HARRIS, pp. 182-186.

1988-1991 Supplement

A454.17 "I Loves You Rain." _Black Scholar_ 19 (July/August-September/October 1988): 25. Fiction.

455. MERRITT, ALICE HADEN (1905-).

455.1 _Dream Themes and Other Poems_. Philadelphia: Dorrance Company, 1940.

455.2 _Psalms and Proverbs: A Poetical Version_. Philadelphia: Dorrance & Company, 1941.

455.3 _Whence Waters Flow: Poems for All Ages From Old Virginia_. Richmond, VA: Dietz Press, 1948.

456. MEYER, JUNE.

456.1 "A Poem." _Negro Digest_ 18 (September 1969): 19.

Micou, Regina **SEE** 325. IFETAYO, FEMI FUNMI.

457. MIGHTY, JULIA GAINES.

457.1 "Chitterlings for Breakfast." _Negro Digest_ 11 (August 1962): 59-62.

458.   MILLER, MAY (1899-).

458.1 "Blazing Accusation." "Love on the Cape." "Nuptual
Calendar." Beloit Poetry Journal 29 (2): 14-16 (1978-1979).

458.2 "The Bog Guide." In BROWN-GUILLORY. Drama.

458.3 "Christophe's Daughter." In RICHARDSON & MILLER, pp.
241-264. Drama.

458.4 The Clearing and Beyond. Washington, DC: Charioteer
Press, 1974. Poetry.

458.5 "Don't Touch." Essence, 4(August 1973):20.

458.6 Dust of Uncertain Journey. Detroit: Lotus Press,
1975. Poetry.

458.7 "Graven Images." In RICHARDSON, pp.109-137. One act
drama for children.

458.8 Green Wind. Washington, D.C.: Commission of Arts and
Humanities, 1978.

458.9 Halfway to the Sun. Washington, DC: Washington
Writers' Publishing House, 1981. Children's poetry.

458.10 "Harriet Tubman." In RICHARDSON & MILLER, pp. 265-
288. Drama.

458.11 Into the Clearing. Washington, DC: Charioteer Press,
1959. Poetry.

458.12 Lyrics of Three Women: Katie, Lyle, Maud Rubin and
May Miller. Baltimore: Linden Press, 1964.

458.13 My World. Charleston, WV: Fine Arts Commission,
1979.

458.14 Not That Far. San Luis Obispo, CA: Solo Press, 1973.

458.15 Poems. Thetford, VT: Cricket Press, 1962.

458.16 The Ransomed Wait. Detroit: Lotus Press, 1983.
Poetry.

458.17 "Riding the Goat." In BROWN-GUILLORY. Drama.

458.18 "Samory." In RICHARDSON & MILLER, pp. 289-311.
Drama.

458.19 "Scratches." Carolina Magazine 59 (April 1929): 36-
44. Drama.

458.20 "Sojourner Truth." In RICHARDSON & MILLER, pp. 313-
333. One act drama.

Secondary Sources

458.21(S) Hatch, James V. Black Theater, USA: Forty-Five
Plays by American Negroes, 1847-1974. New York: Free Press,
1974.

458.22(S) Richardson, Willis and Miller, May. Negro History
in Thirteen Plays. Washington, DC: Associated Publishers,
1933.

458.23(S) Richardson, Willis, ed. Plays and Pageants from
the Life of the Negro. Washington, DC: Associated
Publishers, 1930.

458.24(S) Shockley, Ann. "May Miller." In SHOCKLEY, p.
452.

458.25(S) Stoelting, Winifred. "May Miller." In HARRIS &
DAVIS, pp. 241-247.

Millican, Arthenia Jackson. SEE 049. BATES, ARTHENIA
     JACKSON.

459. MILLS, THELMA.

459.1 A Book of Commonsense Poems. Book No. 1. n.p., n.d.

459.2 A Book of Six Common Sense Poems. New York: Gaillard
Press, n.d.

459.3 Six Poems. Book Three. New York: Type-Art Press,
1942.

460. MILTON, NERISSA LONG.

460.1 "We Have the New Year." Negro History Bulletin 39
(January 1976): 504.

461. MISS GARRISON.

461.1 "Ray of Light." A.M.E. Church Review 6 (July 1889-
90): 74-489.

Secondary Sources

461.2(S) Coppin, Levi J. "Editorial: One Year in
Journalism." A.M.E. Church Review 6 (July 1889): 110-111.

461.3(S) Shockley, Ann Allen. "Miss Garrison." In
SHOCKLEY, pp. 151-161.

462. MITCHELL, KAREN.

462.1 Blackberry Pickin'. Columbia, MO: Mitchell, 1976.

462.2 "For Michael." Essence, 11 (July 1980): 15.

462.3 "My Mother Bakes Cookies." "Visit." "Where Have All
the Black Sheep Gone? They Have Gone Grazing in the Fields."
Obsidian 6 (1-2): 217-220 (Spring-Summer 1980).

463. MITCHELL, KATHRYN.

463.1 "A Dangerous Thing." Negro Digest 14 (October 1965):
72-78.

464. MITCHELL, MARGARET L.

464.1 "Knowing Your Niggers." Black American Literature
Forum 19 (3): 126 (Fall 1985).

464.2 "When Midday Is." Black American Literature Forum 19
(3): 126 (Fall 1985).

465. MOBLEY, EVELYN.

465.1 Something for Everyone. Philadelphia: Dorrance &
Company, 1974.

466. MOLETTE, BARBARA (1940-).

466.1 "Black Heroes and Afriocentric Values in the Theatre."
Journal of Black Studies 15 (4): 447-462 (June 1985).
African-American women playwrights from a historical stance.

466.2 "They Speak. Who Listens?: Black Women Playwrights."
Black World 25 (April 1976): 28-34.

466.3 Black Theatre: Premise and Presentation. Bristol, IN:
Wyndham Hall, 1986. Carlton W. Molette, joint author.

466.4 Rosalee Pritchett. New York: Dramatists Play Service,
197?. Drama. Carlton W. Molette, joint author.

Secondary Sources

466.5(S) Brown, Elizabeth. "Six Female Black Playwrights:
Images Of Blacks in Plays by Lorraine Hansberry, Alice
Childress, Sonia Sanchez, Barbara Molette, Martie Charles and
Ntozake Shange." Ph. D. dissertation, Florida State
University, 1980.

467. MONROE, MARY.

467.1 The Upper Room. New York: St. Martin's, 1985.

468. MOODY, ANNE (1940-).

468.1 Coming of Age in Mississippi. New York: Dial Press,
1969.

468.2 Mr. Death: Four Stories. New York: Harper, 1975.

469. MOODY, CHRISTINA.

469.1 The Story of East St. Louis Riot. n.p., n.d.

469.2 A Tiny Spark. Washington, DC: Murray Brothers, 1910.
Poetry.

Moore, Alice Ruth. SEE 190. DUNBAR, ALICE MOORE.

470. MOORE, CYNTHIA.

470.1 "A Reflection." Essence 17 (February 1987): 123.

471. MOORE, JENNIE DOUGLASS.

471.1 The Rhyme of a Race and Other Poems. New York:
Exposition Press, 1978.

472. MOORE, LaNESE B.

472.1 Can I Be Right? New York: Vantage Press, 1971.
Poetry.

473. MOORE, OPAL.

473.1 "A Happy Story." Callaloo 12 (Spring 1989): 274.
Short fiction/

473.2 "Landscapes: Shakin'" Black American Literature Forum
19 (3): 113 (Fall 1985).

473.3 "Poems." Obsidian II 3 (Spring 1988): 68.

473.4 "A Small Insolence." Callaloo 8 (2): 304-309
(Spring/Summer 1985).

474. MOORER, LIZELIA AUGUSTA JENKINS.

474.1 Prejudice Unveiled and Other Poems. Boston: Roxburgh
Publishing Co., 1907.

475. MOOTRY, MARIA K.

475.1 " 'Chocolate Mabbie' and 'Pearl May Lee': Gwendolyn
Brooks and the Ballad Tradition." CLA Journal 30 (March
1987): 278-293.

475.2 The Crisis of Feminist Criticism: A Case Study of
Lorraine Hansberry's Feminine Traits in "Raisin" and "Sign".
(Afro Scholar Working Papers, v. 16) Urbana, IL: University
of Illinois Press, 198?.

475.3 "Love and Death in the Black Pastoral." Obsidian 3
(2): 5-11 (Summer 1977).

475.4   A Life Distilled: Gwendolyn Brooks, Her Poetry and
Fiction. Urbana, IL: University of Illinois Press, 1987.
Gary Smith, joint editor.

475.5 The Otherwise Room. Carbondale, IL: Poetry Factory,
1981. Anthology. Joyce Jones and Mary McTaggart, joint
editors.

475.6 Sestine: Six Women Poets. Carbondale, IL: Poetry
Factory, 1983. Anthology. Joyce Jones and Mary McTaggart,
joint editors.

476. MORGAN, DEBRA JEAN.

476.1 "Leaving the Nest." Essence 17 (May 1986): 164.

477. MORRISON, TONI (1931-).

477.1 "Behind the Making of The Black Book." Black World
23 (February 1974): 86-90.

477.2 Beloved. New York: A.A. Knopf, 1987.

477.3 "The Big Box." Ms. 8 (March 1980): 57-58.

477.4 Black Book. New York: Random House, 1974.

477.5 The Bluest Eye. New York: Holt, Rinehart & Winston,
1970.

477.6 "Cooking Out." New York Times Book Review (10 June
1973): 4, 16.

477.7 "A Knowing So Deep." Essence 16 (May 1985): 230.

477.8 "Reading." Mademoiselle 81 (May 1975): 14.

477.9 "Rediscovering Black History." The New York Times
Magazine (11 August 1974).

477.10 "Slow Walk of Trees (as Grandmother Would Say)
Hopeless (as Grandfather Would Say)". New York Times
Magazine (4 July 1976): 104,150,152,160,162,164.

477.11 Song of Solomon. New York: A.A. Knopf, 1977.

477.12 Sula. New York: A.A. Knopf, 1974.

477.13 Tar Baby. NY: A.A. Knopf, 1981.

477.14 "Toni Morrison on Cinderella's Stepsisters." Ms. 8
(September 1979): 41-42.

477.15 "What the Black Woman Thinks about Women's Lib." The
New York Times Magazine (22 August 1971).

477.16 "Writers Together."   Nation (24 October 1981): 396-397.

                        Secondary Sources

477.17(S) Abel, Elizabeth. "(E)merging Identities: The Dynamics of Female Friendship in Contemporary Fiction by Women." Signs 6 (3): 413-435 (Spring 1981).

477.18(S) Atlas, Marilyn J. "The Darker Side of Toni Morrison's Song of Solomon." Society for the Study of Midwestern Literature Newsletter 10 (2): 1-13 (1980).

477.19(S) Atlas, Marilyn J. "A Woman Both Shiny and Brown: Feminist Strength in Toni Morrison's Song of Solomon." Society for the Study of Midwestern Literature Newsletter 9 (3): 8-12 (1979).

477.20(S) Bakerman, Jane. "Failures of Love: Female Initiation in the Novels of Toni Morrison." American Literature 52 (January 1981): 541-563.

477.21(S) Bakerman, Jane. "The Seams Can't Show: An Interview with Toni Morrison." Black American Literature Forum 12 (Summer 1978): 56-60.

477.22(S) Banyiwa-Horne, Naana. "The Scary Face of the Self: An Analysis of the Character of Sula in Toni Morrison's Sula." Sage 2 (1): 28-31 (Spring 1985).

477.23(S) Bischoff, Joan. "The Novels of Toni Morrison: Studies in Thwarted Sensitivity." Studies in Black Literature 6 (Fall 1975):21-23.

477.24(S) Blake, Susan L. "Folklore and Community in Song of Solomon." MELUS 7 (Fall 1980): 77-82.

477.25(S) Blake, Susan L. "Toni Morrison." In DAVIS & HARRIS, pp. 187-199.

477.26(S) Brenner, Gerry. "Song of Solomon: Morrison's Rejection of Rank's Monomyth and Feminism." Studies in American Fiction 15 (1): 13-24 (Spring 1987).

477.27(S) Byerman, Keith E. "Intense Behaviors: The Use of the Grotesque in the Bluest Eye and Eva's Man." CLA Journal 25 (June 1982): 447-457.

477.28(S) Christian, Barbara. "Community and Nature: The Novels of Toni Morrison." Journal of Ethnic Studies 7 (4): 65-78 (Winter 1980).

477.29(S) Clark, Norris B. "Flying Black: Toni Morrison's The Bluest Eye, Sula, and Song of Solomon." Minority Voices 4 (2): 51-63 (1980).

477.30(S) Coleman, James. "The Quest for Wholeness in Toni Morrison's _Tar Baby_." _Black American Literature Forum_ 20 (1-2): 63-73 (Spring/Summer 1986).

477.31(S) Davis, Cynthia. "Self, Society. and Myth in Toni Morrison's Fiction." _Contemporary Literature_ 23 (3): 323-342 (Summer 1982).

477.32(S) de Weever, Jacqueline. "The Inverted World of Toni Morrison's _The Bluest Eye_ and _Sula_." _CLA Journal_ 22 (June 1979): 402-414.

477.33(S) Edelberg, Cynthia Dubin. "Morrison's Voices: Formal Education, the Work Ethic, and the Bible." _American Literature_ 58 (May 1986): 217-237.

477.34(S) Erickson, Peter B. "Images of Nurturance in Toni Morrison's _Tar Baby_." _CLA Journal_ 28 (1): 11-32 (September 1984).

477.35(S) Fikes, Robert, Jr. "Echoes from Small Town Ohio: A Toni Morrison Bibliography." _Obsidian_ 5 (Spring/Summer 1979): 142-148.

477.36(S) Fishman, Charles. "Naming Names: Three Recent Novels by Women Writers." _Names_ 32 (March 1984): 33-44.

477.37(S) Gaston, Karen Carmean. "The Theme of Female Self-discovery in the Novels of Judith Rossner, Gail Godwin, Alice Walker and Toni Morrison." Dissertation, Auburn University, 1980.

477.38(S) Gayles, Gloria. "The Truths of our Mothers' Lives: Mother-Daughter Relationships in Black Women's Fiction." _Sage_ 1 (2): 8-12 (Fall 1984).

477.39(S) Giddings, Paula. "Triumph Song of Toni Morrison." _Encore_ 6 (12December 1977): 26-30.

477.40(S) Gillespie, Marcia Ann. "Toni Morrison : (_Ms._ Magazine Woman of the Year)." _Ms._ 16 (January 1988): 80.

477.41(S) Harris, A. Leslie. "Myth as Structure in Toni Morrison's _Song of Solomon_." _MELUS_, 7 (Fall 1980): 69-76.

477.42(S) Harris, Norman. "The Black University in Contemporary Afro-American Fiction." _CLA Journal_ 30 (September 1986): 1-13.

477.43(S) Holloway, Karla F.C. and Demetrakopoulos, Stephanie A. _New Dimensions of Spirituality: A Biracial and Bicultural Reading of the Novels of Toni Morrison_. Westport: CT: Greenwood Press, 1987.

477.44(S) House, Elizabeth B. "The 'Sweet' Life in Toni Morrison's Fiction." _American Literature_ 56 (May 1984): 181-202.

477.45(S) Hovet, Grace Ann and Lounsberry, Barbara. "Flying as Symbol and Legend in Toni Morrison's The Bluest Eye, Sula, and Song of Solomon." CLA Journal 27 (December 1983): 119-140.

477.46(S) Howard, Maureen. "A Novel of Exile and Home." New Republic 184 (21 March 1981): 29-30,32.

477.47(S) Hudson-Withers, Clenora. "Toni Morrison's World of Topsy-Turvydom: A Methodological Explication of New Black Literary Criticism." Western Journal of Black studies 10 (3): 132-136 (Fall 1986).

477.48(S) Iannone, Carol. "Toni Morrison's Career." Commentary 84 (December 1987): 59-63.

477.49(S) Jones, Bessie W. and Vinson, Audrey L. The World of Toni Morrison: Explorations in Literary Criticism. Dubuque, IA: Kendall, 1985.

477.50(S) Klotman, Phyllis Rauch. "Dick-and-Jane and the Shirley Temple Sensibility in The Bluest Eye." Black American Literature Forum 13 (Winter 1979): 123-125.

477.51(S) Lange, Bonnie Shipman. "Toni Morrison's Rainbow Code." Critique 24 (3): 173-181 (Spring 1983).

477.52(S) LeClair, Thomas. " 'Language Must Not Sweat': A Conversation with Toni Morrison." New Republic 184 (21 March 1981): 25-29.

477.53(S) Lee, Dorothy. "Song of Solomon: To Ride the Air" Black American Literature Forum 16 (Summer 1982): 64-70.

477.54(S) Lee, Valerie Gray. "The Use of Folktale in Novels by Black Women Writers." CLA Journal 23 (March 1980): 266-272.

477.55(S) Lewis, Vashti Crutcher. "African Tradition in Toni Morrison's Sula." Phylon 48 (March 1987): 91-97.

477.56(S) Lounsberry, Barbara and Hovet, Grace Ann. "Principles of Perception in Toni Morrison's Sula." Black American Literature Forum 13 (Winter 1979): 126-129.

477.57(S) Lupton, Mary Jane. "Clothes and Closure in Three Novels by Black Women." Black American Literature Forum 20 (4): 409-421 (Winter 1986).

477.58(S) McKay, Nellie. "An Interview with Toni Morrison." Contemporary Literature 24 (4): 413-429 (Winter 1983).

477.59(S) Mano, D.K. "How to Write Two First Novels with Your Knuckles." Esquire 80 (December 1976): 62.

477.60(S) Martin, Odette C. "The Novels of Toni Morrison: Sula." First World 1 (Winter 1977): 34-44.

477.61(S) Medwick, Cathleen. "Oh, Albany! What's Toni
Morrison's First Play Doing At the 'Wrong End' of the
Hudson?" Vogue 176 (January 1986): 56.

477.62(S) Medwick, Cathleen. "Toni Morrison: A Great
American Author, a Spirit of Love and Rage...." Vogue 117
(April 1981): 288-289,330-332.

477.63(S) Mekkawi, Mod. Toni Morrison: A Bibliography.
Washington, DC: Howard University Founders Graduate Library,
1986.

477.64(S) Mickelson, Anne Z. "Winging Upward: Black Women:
Sarah E. Wright, Toni Morrison, Alice Walker." In
MICKELSON, pp. 112-124.

477.65(S) Middleton, Victoria. "Sula: An Experimental
Life." CLA Journal 28 (June 1985): 367-381.

477.66(S) Miller, Adam David. "Breedlove, Peace and the
Dead: Some Observations on the World of Toni Morrison."
Black Scholar 9 (March 1978): 47-50.

477.67(S) Mobley, Marilyn E. "Narrative Dilemma: Jadine As
Cultural Orphan in Toni Morrison's Tar Baby." Southern
Review 23 (4): 761-770 (October 1987).

477.68(S) Munro, Lynn. ""The Tatooed Heart and the
Serpentine Eye: Morrison's Choice of an Epigraph for Sula."
Black American Literature Forum 18 (Winter 1984): 150-154.

477.69(S) Naylor, Gloria and Morrison, Toni. "A
Conversation." Southern Review 21 (July 1985): 567-593.

477.70(S) Ogunyemi, Chikwenye Okonjo. "Order and
Disorganization in Toni Morrison's The Bluest Eye."
Critique: Studies in Modern Fiction 19 (1977): 112-120.

477.71(S) Ogunyemi, Chikwenye Okonjo. "Sula: 'A Nigger
Joke.'" Black American Literature Forum 13 (Winter 1979):
130-133.

477.72(S) O'Meally, Robert G. " 'Tar Baby, She Don Say
Nothin'.'" Callaloo 4 (October-February 1981): 1-3.

477.73(S) Ordonez, Elizabeth J. "Narrative Texts by Ethnic
Women: Rereading the Past, Reshaping the Future." Melus 9
(3): 19-28 (Winter 1982).

477.74(S) Parker, Bettye J. "Complexity: Toni Morrison's
Women -- An Interview Essay." In BELL, pp. 251-257.

477.75(S) Reyes, Angelita. "Ancient Properties In the New
World: The Paradox of the "Other" in Toni Morrison's Tar
baby." Black Scholar 17 (2): 1925 (March-April 1986).

477.76(S)   Rosenburg, Ruth.   "Seeds in Hard Ground: Black
Girlhood in The Bluest Eye." Black American Literature Forum
21 (4): 435-445 (Winter 1987).

477.77(S)   Royster, Philip M. "The Bluest Blue." First World
1 (Winter 1977): 34-44.

477.78(S)   Royster, Philip M. "Milkman's Flying: The
Scapegoat Transcended in Toni Morrison's Song of Solomon."
CLA Journal 24 (June 1981): 419-440.

477.79(S)   Royster, Philip M.   "A Priest and a Witch Against
the Spiders and the Snakes: Scapegoating in Toni Morrison's
Sula." Umoja 2 (1978): 149-168.

477.80(S)   Rubin, H.   "Working Both Sides of the Desk:
Editors Who Write...Writers Who Edit." Publishers Weekly (7
November 1980): 28-31.

477.81(S)   Schultz, Elizabeth. "African and Afro-American
Roots in Contemporary Afro-American Literature: The Difficult
Search for Family Origins." Studies in American Fiction 8
(2): 127-145 (1980).

477.82(S)   Smith, Valerie. "The Quest For and Discovery of
Identity in Toni Morrison's Song of Solomon."   Southern
Review 21 (July 1985): 721-732.

477.83(S)   Sokoloff, Janice M.   "Intimations of Matriarchal
Age: Notes On the Mythical Eva in Toni Morrison's Sula."
Journal of Black Studies 16 (4): 429-434 (June 1986).

477.84(S)   Spallino, Chiara. "Song of Solomon: An Adventure
in Structure." Callaloo 8 (3): 510-524 (Fall 1985).

477.85(S)   Stein, Karen F.   "Toni Morrison's Sula: A Black
Woman's Epic." Black American Literature Forum 18 (Winter
1984): 146-150.

477.86(S)   Stepto, Robert B.   " 'Intimate Things In Place': A
Conversation with Toni Morrison." Massachusetts Review 18
(Autumn 1977): 473-489.

477.87(S)   Stepto, Robert B. "The Phenomenal Woman and the
Severed Daughter." Poetry in Review 8 (Fall/Winter 1979):
312-320.

477.88(S)   Strouse, Jean. "Toni Morrison's Black Magic."
Newsweek 97 (30 March 1981): 52-57.

477.89(S)   Tate, Claudia. "Toni Morrison." In TATE, pp.
117-131.

477.90(S)   Umeh, Marie A. "A Comparative Study of the Idea
of Motherhood in Two Third World Novels." CLS Journal 31
(September 1987): 31-43.

477.91(S) Washington, Elsie. "Toni Morrison Now." Essence
18 (October 1987): 58.

477.92(S) Watkins, Mel. "Talk with Toni Morrison." New
York Times Book Review (11 September 1977): 48,50.

477.93(S) Willis, Susan. "Eruptions of Funk: Historicizing
Toni Morrison." Black American Literature Forum 16 (Spring
1982): 34-42.

477.94(S) Wilson, Judith. "A Conversation with Toni
Morrison." Essence 12 (July 1981): 84-86.

1988-1991 Supplement

A477.95 "On Behalf of Henry Dumas." Black American
Literature Forum 22 (Summer1988): 310.

Secondary Sources

A477.96(S) Alexander, Harriet S. "Toni Morrison: An
Annotated Bibliography of Critical Articles and Essays, 1975-
1984." CLA Journal 33 (September 1989): 81.

A477.97(S) Berret, Anthony J. "Toni Morrison's Literary
Jazz." CLA Journal 32 (March 1989): 267.

A477.98(S) Bogus, S. Diane. "An Authorial Tie-Up: The
Wedding of Symbol and Point of View in Toni Morrison's Sula."
CLA Journal 33 (September 1989): 73.

A477.99(S) Bryant, Cedric Gael. "The Orderliness of
Disorder: Madness and Evil in Toni Morrison's Sula." Black
American Literature Forum 24 (Winter 1990): 731.

A477.100(S) Butler-Evans, Elliott. Race, Gender, and
Desire: Narrative Strategies in the Fiction of Toni Cade
Bambara, Toni Morrison and Alice Walker. Philadelphia:
Temple University Press, 1989.

A477.101(S) Caputi, Jane. " 'Specifying'Fannie Hurst:
Langston Hughes's 'Limitations of Life,' Zora Neale Hurston's
Their Eyes Were Watching God, and Toni Morrison's The Bluest
Eye as 'Answers' to Hurst's Imitation of Life." Black
American Literature Forum 24 (Winter 1990):697.

A477.102(S) Cooper, Barbara. "Milkman's Search for Family
in Toni Morrison's Song of Solomon." CLA Journal 33
(December 1989): 145.

A477.103(S) Gillespie, Diane and Miss Dehn Kubitschek. "Who
Cares? Women-Centered Psychology in Sula." Black American
Literature Forum 24 (Spring 1990): 21.

A477.104(S) Guerrero, Edward. "Tracking 'The Look' in the
Novels of Toni Morrison." Black American Literature Forum 24
(Winter 1990): 761.

A477.105(S) Hawthorne, Evelyn. "On Gaining the Double
Vision Tar Baby as Diasporean Novel." Black American
Literature Forum 22 (Spring 1988): 97.

A477.106(S) McKay, Nellie Y., Critical Essays on Toni
Morrison. Boston: G.K. Hall, 1988.

A477.107(S) Middleton, David L. Toni Morrison: An Annotated
Bibliography. NY: Garland, 1987.

A477.108(S) Montgomery, Maxine Lavon. "A Pilgrimage to the
Origins: The Apocalypse as Structure in Toni Morrison's
Sula." Black American Literature Forum 23 (Spring 1989):
127.

A477.109(S) Otten, Terry. The Crime of Innocence in the
Fiction of Toni Morrison. Columbia, MO: University of
Missouri Press, 1989.

A477.110(S) Powell, Timothy B. "Toni Morrison: The Struggle
to Depict the Black Figure on the White Page." Black
American Literature Forum 24 (Winter 1990): 747.

A477.111(S) Randolph, Laura B. "The Magic of Toni
Morrison." Ebony 43 (July 1988): 100.

A477.112(S) Reddy, Maureen T. "The Tripled Plot and Center
of Sula." Black American Literature Forum 22 (Spring 1988):
29.

A477.113(S) Story, Ralph. "An Excursion in the Black World:
The "Seven Days" in Toni Morrison's Song of Solomon." Black
American Literature Forum 23 (Spring 1989): 149.

A477.114(S) Walther, Malin LaVon. "Out of Sight: Toni
Morrison's Revision of Beauty." Black American Literature
Forum 24 (Winter 1990): 775.

A477.115(S) Wessling, Joseph H. "Narcissism in Toni
Morrison's Sula." CLA Journal 31 (March 1988): 281.

478. MOSS, THYLIAS.

478.1 "Acceptance of the Grave." Indiana Review 7 (1): 66-
67 (Winter 1984).

478.2 "The Barren Midwife Speaks of Duty." North Dakota
Quarterly 52 (2): 98 (Spring 1984).

478.3 "A Child's Been Dead a Week." <u>Texas Review</u> 3 (1-2):
138-139 (Spring-Summer 1984).

478.4 <u>Hosiery Seams on a Bowlegged Woman: Poems</u>. Cleveland:
Cleveland State University Poetry Center, 1983.

478.5 "The Owl in Daytime." <u>Indiana Review</u> 7 (1): 63
(Winter 1984).

478.6 "Poems." <u>Black American Literature Forum</u> 23 (Spring
1989): 271.

478.7 <u>Pyramid of Bone</u>. Charlotteville, VA: University Press
of Virginia, 1989.

478.8 "Rush Hour." <u>Essence</u> 14 (December 1983): 134.

478.9 "Secrets Behind the Names." <u>Indiana Review</u> 7 (1): 68-
69 (Winter 1984).

478.10 "Taluca, Twenty Years Later." <u>Texas Review</u> 5 (1-2):
138 (Spring-Summer 1984).

478.11 "The Undertaker's Daughter (for M. Egolf)." <u>Indiana
Review</u> 7 (1): 64-65 (Winter 1984).

479. MULLEN, HARRYETTE.

479.1 "Alabama Memories." <u>Southern Exposure</u> 9 (3): 73 (Fall
1981).

479.2 "Basic Need." <u>Negro History Bulletin</u> 39 (November-
December 1976): 638.

479.3 "A Black Woman Never Faints (for Gertrude Wilks)."
<u>Greenfield Review</u> 7 (3-4): 25 (Spring-Summer 1979).

479.4 "Circle of Arms." <u>Black Collegian</u> 35 (1980): 20.

479.5 "Cold Storage." <u>Black American Literature Forum</u> 13
(4): 149 (Winter 1979).

479.6 "Daughters in Search of Mothers or a Girl Child in a
Family of Men." <u>Catalyst</u> 1 (Fall 1986): 45-49.

479.7 "Fable." <u>Callaloo</u> 9 (1): 108 (Winter 1986).

479.8 "The Gene for Music." <u>Catalyst</u> (Summer 1987): 85.

479.9 "Jump City." <u>Obsidian</u> 3 (2): 49 (Summer 1977).

479.10 "Madonna." <u>Greenfield Review</u> 7 (3-4): 25 (Spring
Summer 1979).

479.11 "No More Arguments, No More Anything." Black American Literature Forum 13 (4): 149 (Winter 1979).

479.12 "Recipe." Callaloo 5 (2): 31 (1979).

479.13 "Roadmap." Greenfield Review 7 (3-4): 24 (Spring-Summer 1979).

479.14 "Saturday Afternoon, When Chores are Done." Essence 13 (July 1982): 17. Southern Exposure 9 (4): 4 (Winter 1981).

479.15 "Sugar Sandwiches." Catalyst (Winter 1988): 100.

479.16 "A Summer in School with Mother." Sage 2 (1): 60-61 (Spring 1985).

479.17 "They Are Bloated with Power." Negro History Bulletin 39 (November-December 1976): 638.

479.18 Tree Tall Woman: Poems. Galveston, TX: Energy Earth Communications, 1981.

479.19 "Unspoken." Callaloo 9 (2): 345-346 (Spring 1986).

479.20 "Women and the Roses." Black Collegian 35 (1980): 20.

480. MURPHY, BEATRICE M. (1908-).

480.1 An Anthology of Contemporary Verse: Negro Voices. New York: Henry Harrison, 1928. Beatrice Murphy, ed.

480.2 Catching the Editor's Eye. n.p., 1947.

480.3 Ebony Rhythm: An Anthology of Contemporary Negro Verse. New York: Exposition Press, 1948. Beatrice Murphy, ed.

480.4 Get With It, Lord. n.p., 1977.

480.5 Love Is a Terrible Thing. New York: Hobson Book Press, 1945.

480.6 Today's Voices: An Anthology by Young Negro Poets. New York: Julius Messner, 1970. Beatrice Murphy, ed.

480.7 The Rock Cry Out. Detroit: Broadside Press, 1969. Poetry. Nancy L. Arnez, joint author.

481. MURPHY, RUTH.

481.1 Jordan Get Back. Author, 1964.

482. MURRAY, PAULI (1910-1985).

482.1 Dark Testament and Other Poems. Norwalk, CT:
Silvermine, 1970.

482.2 "The Fourth Generation of Proud Shoes." Southern
Exposure 4 (Winter 1977): 4-9. An account of her family.

482.3 Human Rights USA, 1948-1966. Nashville: Service
Center, Board of Missions, Methodist Church, 1967.

482.4 "The Negro Woman in the Quest for Equality." Address
delivered to Leadership Conference of the National Council of
Negro Women, Washington, D.C., November 14, 1963.

482.5 "Prophecy." Essence 16 (October 1985): 124.

482.6 Proud Shoes: The Story of an American Family. New
York: Harper, 1956.

482.7 Song in a Weary Throat: An American Pilgrimage. New
York: Harper, 1987. Autobiography.

482.8 "To the Negro School Children of the American South."
Crisis 74 (October 1967): 406.

Secondary Sources

482.9(S) McKay, Nellie. "Pauli Murray." In HARRIS &
DAVIS, pp. 248-251. Biography and bibliography.

482.10(S) Miller, Casey and Swift, Kate. "Pauli Murray."
Ms. 8 (March 1980): 63-64. Biography and criticism.

1988-1991 Supplement

Secondary Sources

A482.11(S) Humez, Jean M. "Pauli Murray's Histories of
Loyalty and Revolt." Black American Literature Forum 24
(Summer 1990): 315.

483. MURRELL, VIRGINIA.

483.1 Burnt Icarus. Whittier, CA: Stockton Trade Press,
1962.

484.   MUSGRAVE, MARIAN E. (1923-1988).

484.1 "Four Unabashedly Political Poems." _Crisis_ 83
(November 1976): 313.

Secondary Sources

484.2(S) Johnson, Robert C. and Wilkins, Heanon M.   "A
Tribute to Marian Musgrave (1923-1988)." _CLA Journal_ 33
(December 1989): 233.

485.   NATELEGE, SCHAARAZETTA.

485.1 "The Violin's Song." _Obsidian_ 7 (1): 61 (Spring
1981).

486.   NAYLOR, GLORIA (1950-).

486.1 _Centennial_. New York: Pindar Press, 1986.

486.2 "Life on Beekman Place." _Essence_ 10 (March 1980): 82-
83.

486.3 _Linden Hills_. New York: Ticknor & Fields, 1985.

486.4 _Mama Day_. New York: Ticknor & Fields, 1988. _Southern
Review_ 23 (4): 836-873 (October 1987). Excerpt.

486.5 "Until Death Do Us Part." _Essence_ 16 (May 1985): 133.

486.6 "When Mama Comes to Call." _Essence_ 13 (August 1982):
66-68.

486.7 _The Women of Brewster Place: A Novel in Seven Stories_.
New York: Viking Press, 1982.

486.8 "A Conversation." _Southern Review_ 21 (July 1985):
567-593. Toni Morrison, joint author.

Secondary Sources

486.9(S) Goldstein, W. "A Talk with Gloria Naylor."
Publishers Weekly (9 September 1983): 35-36.

1988-1991 Supplement

Secondary Sources

A486.10(S) Andrews, Larry R. "Black Sisterhood in Gloria Naylor's Novels." CLA Journal 33 (September 1989): 1.

A486.11(S) "The Catalyst Interviews: Gloria Naylor." Catalyst (Summer 1988): 56.

A486.12(S) Matus, Jill L. "Dream, Deferral, and Closure in The Women of Brewster Place." Black American Literature Forum 24 (Spring 1990): 49.

487. NAYO [BARBARA MALCOM].

487.1 I Want Me a Home. New Orleans: BlkArtSouth, 1969.

488. NEALS BETTY H.

488.1 Move the Air. East Orange, NJ: Stonechat, 1985. Poetry.

488.2 Spirit Weaving. New York: Sesame, 1977.

489. NEELY, BARBARA.

489.1 "Passing the Word." Essence 12 (October 1981): 104-105.

490. NELSON, ANNIE GREENE (1902-).

490.1 After the Storm. Columbia, SC: Hampton Publishing Company, 1942. Spartansburg, SC: Author, [1974]. Novel.

490.2 The Dawn Appears. Columbia, SC: Hampton Publishing Company, 1944. Novel.

490.3 Don't Walk on My Dream. Author, 1961. Spartansburg, SC: Reprint Company, 1976. Novel.

491. NELSON, RHOBENA.

491.1 Jus' Black. Detroit: 5 Points Printers, 1966.

492. NELSON, SANDRA.

492.1 "Fire." Black American Literature Forum 20 (3): 315
(Fall 1986).

492.2 "The Mate." Black American Literature Forum 20 (3):
316 (Fall 1986).

492.3 "Message To the Country." Black American Literature
Forum 20 (3): 316 (Fall 1986).

493. NEWSOME, EFFIE LEE (1885-1979).

493.1 "Arctic Tern in a Museum." Phylon 3 (1942): 45.

493.2 "The Bird in the Cage." Crisis 33 (February 1927):
190.

493.3 "Bronze Legacy: To a Brown Boy." Crisis 24 (October
1922): 265.

493.4 "Cantibile." Crisis 31 (December 1925): 65.

493.5 "Chocolate Rabbits." Opportunity 4 (April 1926): 127.

493.6 "Capriccio." Crisis 32 (September 1926): 247.

493.7 "Charcoal, Leddy, Charcoal: An Idyl of the South."
Crisis 24 (August 1922): 158-160.

493.8 "Christmas Tree Land." Opportunity 3 (December 1925):
373.

493.9 Come Ye Apart. Indianapolis: Inter-Racial Missionary
Association, [195?].

493.10 "Commodore Bonbon." Opportunity 3 (December 1925):
373.

493.11 "Early Figures in Haitian Methodism." Phylon 5
(1944): 51-61.

493.12 "Ecce Ancilla Domini: An Old Colored Woman Goes to
Prayer." Crisis 41 (June 1934): 180.

493.13 "Exodus." Crisis 29 (January 1925): 113.

493.14 "Father and Son." Crisis 48 (September 1941): 295.

493.15 Gladiola Garden: Poems of Outdoors and Indoors for
Second Grade Readers. Washington, DC: Associated Publishers,
1940. Children's poetry.

493.16 "A Great Prelate: Bishop Lee at Home." Crisis 32
(June 1926): 69-71.

493.17 "He Will Come Back at Easter." Opportunity 4 (April
1926): 126-127.

493.18 "In Winter." Phylon 2 (1941): 75.

493.19 "The Loss of Ashlee Cottage." Crisis 24 (June 1922):
28-85.

493.20 "Magnificat." Crisis 25 (December 1922): 57.

493.21 "Morning Light: the Dew-Drier." Crisis 17 (November
1918): 17.

493.22 "Negro Street Serenade." Crisis 32 (July 1926): 136.

493.23 "Night of Great Holiness." Opportunity 3 (December
1925): 373.

493.24 "O Autumn, Autumn!" Crisis 16 (October 1918): 269.

493.25 "O Sea, That Knowest Thy Strength." Crisis 13 (March
1917): 219.

493.26 "Punchinello on the Tree." Opportunity 3 (December
1925): 373.

493.27 "Spring Rain." Crisis 40 (May 1933): 110.

493.28 "Sun Disk." Crisis 26 (June 1923): 68.

493.29 "The Wind's Christmas Story." Opportunity 3
(December 1925): 372.

493.30 "Wings Away." Phylon 1 (1940): 336.

                    Secondary Sources

493.31(S) Shockley, Ann Allen. "Effie Lee Newsome." In
SHOCKLEY, pp. 452-453.

                    1988-1991 Supplement

                    Secondary Sources

A493.32(S) MacCann, Donnarae. "Effie Lee Newsome: African
American Poet of the 1920s." Children's Literture
Association Quarterly 13 (1988): 60-65.

494. NICHOLES, MARION (1944-).

494.1 **Life Styles**. Detroit: Broadside Press, 1971. Poetry.

495. NJERI, NURU.

495.1 "All Afrikans Ain't Afrikan." "Atlanta Poem Number
1." "Atlanta Poem Number 2." "Bonding." "Little Deaths
Hurt Especially." Black American Literature Forum 18 (1):
15-17 (Spring 1984).

Nkabinde, Thulani. **SEE** 169. DAVIS, THULANI.

496. NOBLE, JEANNE (1926-).

496.1 **Beautiful, Also, Are the Souls of My Black Sisters: A
History of the Black Woman in America**. Englewood Cliffs, NJ:
Prentice-Hall, 1978.

497. NORMAN, FRAN.

497.1 "An Empty Stocking." About Time 14 (December 1986):
25.

498. OCCOMY, MARITA BONNER (1899-1971).

498.1 "Black Fronts." Opportunity 16 (July 1938): 210-214.

498.2 "Drab Rambles." Crisis 34 (December 1927): 335-336,
354-356.

498.3 **Exit -- An Illusion**. Crisis 36 (October 1929):
335,336,352. Drama.

498.4 **Frye Street and Environs: The Collected Works of Maria
Bonner Occomy**. Boston: Beacon Press, 1987.

498.5 "The Hands -- A Story." Opportunity 3 (August 1925):
235-237.

498.6 [Joyce N. Reed]. "Hate is Nothing." Crisis 45
(December 1938): 388-390,394,403-404.

498.7 "Hongry Fire." Crisis 46 (December 1939): 360-362,
376-377.

498.8 "Nothing New." _Crisis_ 33 (November 1926): 17-20.

498.9 "On Being Young -- A Woman -- And Colored." _Crisis_ 31
(December 1925): 225-226.

498.10 [Joseph Maree Andrews]. "One Boy's Story." _Crisis_
34 (November 1927): 297-299, 326-320.

498.11 "One True Love." _Crisis_ 48 (February 1941): 46-47,
58-59.

498.12 "Patch Quilt." _Crisis_ 47 (March 1940): 71,72,92.

498.13 "A Possible Triad on Black Notes." Part I,
Opportunity 11 (July 1933): 205-207; Part II, _Opportunity_ 11
(August 1933): 242-244; Part III, _Opportunity_ 11 (September
1933): 269-271.

498.14 _The Pot Maker (A Play to be Read)_. _Opportunity_ 5
(February 1927): 43-46.

498.15 "The Prison-Bound." _Crisis_ 32 (September 1926): 225-
226.

498.16 "The Purple Flower." In HATCH & SHINE. _Crisis_ 35
(January 1928).

498.17 "A Sealed Pod." _Opportunity_ 14 (March 1936): 88-91.

498.18 "The Skerrett Makin's." _Opportunity_ 17 (January
1939): 18-21.

498.19 "Tin Can. _Opportunity_ 12 (July 1934): 202-205; 12
(August 1934): 236-240.

498.20 "The Whipping." _Crisis_ 46 (June 1939): 172-174.

498.21 "The Young Blood Hungers." _Crisis_ 35 (May 1928):
151, 172.

                    Secondary Sources

498.22(S) Abramson, Doris E. "Angelina Weld Grimke, Mary T.
Burrill, Georgia Douglas Johnson, and Marita O. Bonner: An
Analysis of Their Plays." _Sage_ 2 (1): 9-13 (Spring 1985).

498.23(S) Flynn, Joyce. "Marita Bonner Occomy." In HARRIS
& DAVIS, 1987., pp. 222-228. Biography and bibliography.

498.24(S) Hatch, James V. _Black Theater, USA: Forty-Five
Plays by American Negroes, 1847-1974_. New York: Free Press,
1974.

498.25(S) Roses, Lorraine Elena and Randolph, Ruth
Elizabeth. "Marita Bonner: In Search of Other Mothers'

Gardens." Black American Literature Forum 21 (1-2): 165-183
(Spring-Summer 1987).

499. ODEN, GLORIA (1923-).

499.1 "Bonsai." Negro History Bulletin 40 (4): 716-717
(July-August 1977). Essay on Black writers.

499.2 The Naked Frame: A Love Poem and Sonnets. New York:
Exposition Press, 1952.

499.3 "The Other Side of the Blanket." Ms. 14 (August
1985): 86. Autobiographical.

499.4 Resurrections. Homestead, FL: Olivant, 1978. Poems.

499.5 The Tie That Binds. Homestead, FL: Olivant, 1980.
Poems.

499.6 "Twenty-three." Ms. 11 (1-2): 74 (July-August 1982).

Secondary Sources

499.7(S) Kessler, Jascha. "Reconsiderations and Reviews."
Melus 7 (3): 83-87 (Fall 1980). Commentary on Gloria Oden's
Resurrections.

500. OLIVER, KITTY.

500.1 "Mama." Essence 7 (October 1976): 80-81.

501. O'NEAL, REGINA.

501.1 And Then the Harvest: Three Television Plays.
Detroit: Broadside Press, 1974. Includes the title drama,
"Night Watch" and "Walk a Tight Rope."

502. OSBEY, BRENDA MARIE.

502.1 "Another Time and Farther South." Southern Review 23
(4): 804-805 (October 1987).

502.2 "The Bone Step-Women." <u>Southern Review</u> 21 (3): 831
(July 1985).

502.3 <u>Ceremony for Minneconjoux</u>. Lexington, KY: University
of Kentucky Press, 1983. (Callaloo Poetry Series). <u>Southern
Exposure</u> 12 (3): 48-51 (May-June 1984). Excerpt.

502.4 "Devices of Icons." <u>Southern Review</u> 21 (3): 834-836
(July 1985).

502.5 "Family History." <u>Essence</u> 16 (May 1985): 188.

502.6 "The Godchild." <u>Southern Review</u> 23 (4): 805-807
(October 1987).

502.7 <u>In These Houses</u>. Middletown, CT: Wesleyan University
Press, 1987.

502.8 "In These Houses of Swift Easy Women." <u>Southern
Review</u> 21 (3): 832-833 (July 1985).

502.9 "The Wastrel-Woman Poem." <u>Southern Review</u> 21 (3):
832-833 (July 1985).

Secondary Sources

502.10(S) Hernton, Calvin C. "Black Women Poets: The Oral
Tradition." In HERNTON, pp. 119-155.

1988-1991 Supplement

A502.11 "Faubourg Study No. 3: The Seven Sisters of New
Orleans." <u>Callaloo</u> 11 (Summer 1988): 464.

503. PALMER, OPAL.

503.1 "De Boys." <u>Black Scholar</u> 15 (May-June 1984): 21.

504. PARKER, PAT.

504.1 <u>Child of Myself</u>. San Lorenzo, CA: Shameless Hussy
Press, 1972.

504.2 <u>Jonestown and Other Madness</u>. Ithaca, NY: Firebrand,
1985. Poetry.

504.3 <u>Movement in Black: Collected Poems, 1978-1981</u>.
Trumansburg, NY: Crossing Press, 1983.

504.4 <u>Movement in Black: The Collected Poetry of Pat Parker,</u>
<u>1961-1978</u>. Trumansburg, NY: Crossing Press, 1978.

504.5 <u>Pit Stop</u>. Oakland, CA: Women's Press Collective,
1975.

504.6 <u>Womanslaughter</u>. Oakland, CA: Diana, 1978.

505. PARKERSON, MICHELLE.

505.1 "Aftermath (for Vicki)." <u>Obsidian</u> 6 (1-2): 192
(Spring-Summer 1980).

505.2 "Bama: The Voyage Home." <u>Catalyst</u> (Winter 1989): 33.

505.3 "Dawn in Soweto." <u>Obsidian</u> 6 (1): 189 (Spring-Summer
1980).

505.4 "Epilogue 3." <u>Essence</u> 10 (November 1979): 19.

505.5 "Epilogue: Romance 3." <u>Obsidian</u> 6 (1-2): 186 (Spring-
Summer 1980).

505.6 "Evening Constitutional." <u>Obsidian</u> 6 (1-2): 188
(Spring-Summer 1980).

505.7 "Memo to James Hampton, Builder of the Third Millenium
Altars." <u>Obsidian</u> 6 (1-2): 191-192 (Spring-Summer 1980).

505.8 "Resume." <u>Obsidian</u> 6 (1-2): 192-193 (Spring-Summer
1980).

505.9 "Reunion." <u>Obsidian</u> 6 (1-2): 189 (Spring-Summer
1980).

505.10 "Then as Now..." <u>Obsidian</u> 6 (1-2): 190 (Spring-
Summer 1980).

505.11 <u>Waiting Rooms</u>. Washington, DC: Common Ground, 1983.
Poetry.

505.12 "You Done Us Proud." <u>Obsidian</u> 6 (1-2): 187 (Spring-
Summer 1980).

506. PATTERSON, LUCILLE J.

506.1 "Black Children Cry." <u>Western Journal of Black</u>
<u>Studies</u> 1 (September 1977): 184.

506.2 "Black Drummers." <u>Western Journal of Black Studies</u> 1
(September 1977): 185.

506.3 Sapphire. Chicago: Author, 1972.

507. PATTERSON, VIVIAN.

507.1 Cries from the Chicago Ghetto. Chicago: n.p.,
[1973?].

508. PEKTOR, IRENE MARI.

508.1 Golden Banners. Boston: Christopher Publishing House,
1941.

508.2 War -- Or Peace? Oceano, CA: Harbison & Harbison,
1939.

509. PENDLETON, LEILA AMOS.

509.1 Fragments of Rhyme. Washington, DC: Author, 1921.

510. PERKINS, MINNIE LOUISE.

510.1 A String of Pearls. Chicago: Author, 1945. Poetry.

511. PERRY, MARGARET (1933-).

511.1 "Angelina Weld Grimke." In PERRY, pp. 86-87.

511.2 Bio-Bibliography of Countee Cullen, 1903-1946. New
York: Negro Universities Press, 1970.

511.3 "Dawn of a Doom of a Dream." Phylon 34 (March 1973):
17-29.

511.4 The Harlem Renaissaance: An Annotated Bibliography and
Commentary. New York: Garland Publishing, 1982.

511.5 Silence to the Drums: A Survey of the Literature of
the Harlem Renaissance. Westport, CT: Greenwood Press, 1976.

511.6 "The World of Light." Obsidian II 3 (Winter 1988):
31. Short fiction.

512. PERRY, THELMA D.

512.1 "Inheritance." Negro History Bulletin 36 (March 1973): 62.

512.2 "Melvin J. Chisum, Pioneer Newsman." Negro History Bulletin 36 (December 1973): 24.

512.3 "Race-Conscious Aspects of the John Brown Affair." Negro History Bulletin 37 (October-November 1974): 312-317.

513. PETRY, ANN LANE (1911-).

513.1 The Common Ground. New York: Thomas Y. Crowell, 1964.

513.2 "The Common Ground." Horn Book 41 (April 1965): 147-151.

513.3 Country Place. Boston: Houghton, 1947. Novel.

513.4 The Drugstore Cat. New York: Thomas Crowell, 1949. Boston: Beacon Press, 1988.

513.5 "Harlem." Holiday (April 1949).

513.6 Harriet Tubman: Conductor of the Underground Railway. New York: Thomas Crowell, 1955.

513.7 "In Darkness and Confusion." In CHAPMAN. Novella.

513.8 Legends of the Saints. New York: Thomas Y. Crowell, 1964.

513.9 "Like a Winding Sheet." In FOLEY.

513.10 "Miss Muriel" and Other Stories. Boston: Houghton, 1971. Boston: Beacon Press, 1989. Short fiction.

513.11 The Narrows. Boston: Houghton, 1953. Boston: Beacon Press, 1988.
Novel.

513.12 "The Novel as Social Criticism." In HULL.

513.13 The Street. Boston: Houghton, 1946. Novel.

513.14 Tituba of Salem Village. New York: Thomas Y. Crowell, 1964. Boston: Beacon Press, 1988.

Secondary Sources

513.15(S) Adams, George R. "Riot as Ritual: Ann Petry's In Darkness and Confusion" Negro Literature Forum 6 (Summer 1968): 54-57, 60.

513.16(S) Emanuel, James A. "Ann Petry." In VINSON.

513.17(S) Greene, Marjorie. "Ann Petry Planned to Write." Opportunity 24 (April-June 1946): 78-79.

513.18(S) Ivy, James. "Ann Petry Talks About Her First Novel." Crisis 53 (January 1946): 48-49.

513.19(S) Ivy, James. "Mrs. Petry's Harlem." Crisis 53 (January 1946): 43-46.

513.20(S) Joyce, Joyce Ann. "Ann Petry." Nethula 2 (1982).

513.21(S) Lattin, Vernon E. "Ann Petry and the American Dream." Black American Literature Forum 12 (2): 69-72 (Summer 1978).

513.22(S) McDowell, Margaret. "The Narrows, a Fuller View of Ann Petry." Black American Literature Forum 14 (Winter 1980): 135-141.

513.23(S) Shinn, Thelma. "Women In the Novels of Ann Petry." Critique 16 (1): 110-120.

513.24(S) Washington, Gladys J. "A World Made Cunningly: A Closer Look at Ann Petry's Short Fiction." CLA Journal 30 (1): 14-29 (September 1986).

513.25(S) Weir, Sybil. "The Narrows, a Black New England Novel." Studies in American Fiction, 15(Spring 1987):81-93.

513.26(S) Yarborough, Richard. "The Quest for the American Dream in Three Afro-American Novels: If He Hollers Let Him Go, The Street, and Invisible Man." Melus 8 (4): 33-59 (Winter 1981).

514. PHILLIPS, JANE (1944-).

514.1 "For Nat Turner." Black World 22 (August 1973): 21.

514.2 Mojo Hand. New York: Simon & Schuster, 1966. Novel.

514.3 "Spirit Said the Serpent Was Loosened." Black World 22 (August 1973): 21.

514.4 "Transformational Grammar." Black World 24 (December 1974): 23.

514.5 Untitled Poem. Black World 23 (September 1974): 62.

515. PITTS, GERTRUDE.

515.1 Tragedies of Life. Newark, NJ: Author, 1939. Novel.

516. PLATO, ANN (1820?-?).

516.1 Essays: Including Biographies and Miscellaneous Pieces
in Poetry and Prose. Hartford, CT: Author, 1841. New York:
Oxford University Press, 1988.

516.2 "The Natives of America." "Reflections, Written on
Visiting the Grave of a Venerated Friend." "To the First of
August." In STETSON, pp. 43-46.

Secondary Sources

516.3(S) Loggins, Vernon. The Negro Author: His Development
in America. New York: Columbia University Press, 1931.

516.4(S) Shockley, Ann Allen. "Ann Plato." In SHOCKLEY,
pp. 26-32.

517. PLUMMER, MARGERY.

517.1 "Everlasting Glow." About Time 14 (5): 29 (May 1986).

518.   POLITE, CARLENE HATCHER (1932-).

518.1 Les Flagellents, translated by Pierre Alien. Paris:
Christian Bourgois Editeur, 1966; republished as The
Flagellants. New York: Farrar, Straus & Giroux, 1967. Novel.

518.2 Sister X and the Victims of Foul Play. New York:
Farrar, Straus & Giroux, 1975. Novel.

Secondary Sources

518.3(S) Worthington-Smith, Hammett. "Carlene Hatcher
Polite," In HARRIS & DAVIS, pp. 215-218. Biography and
bibliography.

519. POLK, ELAINE D.R.

519.1 <u>Dreams at Twilight: Religious Meditations in Verse and</u>
<u>Prose</u>. New York: Exposition Press, 1957. Poetry.

520. POPEL, ESTHER A. W.

520.1 <u>A Forest Pool</u>. Washington, DC: Modernistic Press,
1934. Poetry.

520.2 <u>Thoughtless Thinks by a Thinkless Thoughter</u>.
Washington, DC: n.p., [192?].

Potter, Valaida. **SEE** 426. McCALL, VALAIDA POTTER.

521. PRESTWIDGE, KATHLEEN J. (1927-).

521.1 <u>Wisdom Teeth</u>. New York: Author, 1973.

522. PRETTO, CLARITA C.

522.1 <u>The Life of Autumn Holliday</u>. New York: Exposition
Press, 1958.

523. PRICE, DORIS D.

523.1 "The Bright Medallion." In ROWE, pp. 275-315. One
act drama.

523.2 "The Eyes of Old." In ROWE, pp. 317-338. One act
drama.

523.3 "Two Gods: A Minaret." <u>Opportunity</u> 10 (1932): 380-
383, 389. One act drama.

524. PRIME, CYNTHIA.

524.1 <u>The Sour and the Sweet</u>. New York: Williams Frederick,
1972.

525. PRINCE, MARY.

525.1 The History of Mary Prince, a West Indian Slave,
Related by Herself. F. Westley & A.H. Davis, 1831.

526. PRINCE, NANCY GARDENER (1799-?).

526.1 A Narrative of the Life and Travels, of Mrs. Nancy
Prince. Boston: Author, 1850.

526.2 A Narrative of the Life and Travels of Mrs. Nancy
Prince. 3d ed. Boston: Author, 1856.

526.3 The West Indies: Being a Description of the Islands,
Progress of Christianity, Education, and Liberty Among the
Coloured Population Generally. Boston: Dow & Jackson
Printers, 1841.

Secondary Sources

526.4(S) Foster, Frances Smith. "Adding Color and Contour
to Early Self-Portraiture: Autobiographical Writings of Afro-
American Women." In PRYSE & SPILLERS, pp. 25-39.

526.5(S) Shockley, Ann Allen. "Nancy Gardener Prince." In
SHOCKLEY, pp. 48-55.

1988-1991 Supplement

A526.6 A Black Woman's Odyssey Through Russia and Jamaica:
The Narrative of Nancy Prince. NY: Marcus Wiener, 1989.

527. PRITCHARD, GLORIA CLINTON.

527.1 Trees Along the Highway. New York: Comet Press Books,
1953. Poetry.

528. PULLEY, LINA G.

528.1 "Bus Ride." Black Scholar 12 (September-October
1981): 60.

529. RAHMAH, AISHAH.

529.1 "The Lady and the Tramp." In BARAKA & BARAKA, pp.
284-299. Drama.

529.2 "The Mojo and the Tramp." Massachusetts Review 28
(4): 561-608 (Winter 1987). Drama.

529.3 "Transcendental Blues." In BARAKA & BARAKA, pp. 265-
284. Drama.

530. RANDALL, FLORENCE E.

530.1 The Almost Year. New York: Atheneum, 1971. Children
and young adult stories.

530.2 Haldane Station. New York: Harcourt, 1973. Children
and young adult stories.

530.3 Place of Sapphires. New York: Fawcett, 1971.
Children and young adult stories.

531. RANDALL-TSURTA, DOROTHY.

531.1 "An African-American in Ghana to Visit," Negro
History Bulletin 42 (2): 54 (April-May-June 1979).

531.2 "Bicentennial Woman." Black Scholar 11 (8): 78
(November-December 1980). Negro History Bulletin 40 (3): 704
(May-June 1977).

531.3 "Bicentennial Woman II." Black Scholar 11 (8): 78
(November-December 1980). Negro History Bulletin 40 (3): 704
(May-June 1977).

531.4 "Grandma." Negro History Bulletin 42 (2): 54 (April-
May-June 1979).

531.5 "Grandmaw, 1889-1976." Negro History Bulletin 42 (2):
54 (April-May-June 1979).

531.6 "In Ghana." Black Scholar 11 (8): 78 (November-
December 1980).

531.7 "Ready Yet Unresigned." Essence, 15(January
1985):130. Black Scholar 11 (8): 79 (November-December
1980).

532. RANKINE, CLAUDIA.

532.1 "Island Politics." Black Scholar 18 (4-5): 28
(July/August/September/October 1987).

532.2 "Mo Bay." Black Scholar 18 (4-5): 28
(July/August/September/October 1987).

533. RAWLS, ISETTA CRAWFORD (1941-).

533.1 Flashbacks. Detroit: Lotus Press, 1977. Poetry.

534. RAY, EMMA J. (1859-?).

534.1 Twice Sold, Twice Ransomed: Autobiography of Mr. and
Mrs. L.P. Ray. Chicago: Free Methodist Publishing House,
1926.

535. RAY, HENRIETTA CORDELIA (1849?-1916).

535.1 "Antigone and Oedipus." "The Dawn of Love." "Idyl:
Sunrise." "Milton." "Robert G. Shaw." "To my Father." In
STETSON, pp. 37-41.

535.2 Commemoration Ode: On Lincoln. New York: J.J. Little,
1893.

535.3 Poems. New York: Grafton Press, 1910.

535.4 Poems. New York: J.J. Little, 1887.

535.5 Sonnets. New York: J.J. Little, 1893.

Secondary Sources

535.6(S) Brown, Hallie Quinn. Homespun Heroines and Other
Women of Distinction. Xenia, OH: Aldine, 1926.

535.7(S) Shockley, Ann Allen. "Henrietta Cordelia Ray." In
SHOCKLEY, pp. 327-333.

535.8(S) Wilson, Joseph Thomas. Emancipation: Its Course
and Progress, from 1481 B.C. to A.D. 1875. Hampton, VA:
Hampton Normal School Steam Power Press Point, 1882.

1988-1991 Supplement

A535.9 "Poems." <u>Collected Black Women's Poetry</u>. Joan R.
Sherman, editor. New York: Oxford University Press, 1988.
Separately paginated.

536. REESE, SARAH CAROLYN.

536.1 <u>Songs of Freedom: Poems</u>. Detroit: Lotus Press, 1983.

537. REID, ALICE.

537.1 "And Shed a Murderous Tear." <u>Negro Digest</u> 13
(December 1963): 54-63.

537.2 "At This Party Someone Said: 'Miles Don't Feel Nothin'
When He Blows His Horn.'" <u>Negro Digest</u> 18 (September 1069):
84.

537.3 "Corinna." <u>Negro Digest</u> 11 (August 1962): 53-58.

537.4 "Give Us This Day." <u>Black World</u> 23 (June 1974): 72-
75.

537.5 "Harlem." <u>Negro Digest</u> 14 (December 1964): 82-83.

537.6 "Jojo Banks and the Treble Clef." <u>Essence</u> 5 (October
1974): 88-89.

537.7 "Night of the Senior Ball." <u>Negro Digest</u> 12 (November
1962): 58-61.

537.8 "Prima Facie Domestica." <u>Negro Digest</u> 11 (June 1962):
61.

537.9 "Yes, We Are Afraid." <u>Negro Digest</u> 11 (October 1962):
11-14.

538. REID, OLIVIA FOREMAN.

538.1 "Good Times with Grandpa and Grandma." <u>about... time</u>
10 (July 1982): 19.

538.2 "Neighborhood Action Alert." <u>about... time</u> 10
(September 1982): 22.

538.3 "Youthful Impressions of Good Friends and Companions."
<u>about... time</u> 10 (December 1982): 20-21.

Reynolds, Evelyn Crawford **SEE** 424. LYNN, EVE.

Richards, Beah **SEE** 540. RICHARDSON, BEULAH.

539. RICHARDS, ELIZABETH DAVIS (1884-?).

539.1 <u>The Peddler of Dreams and Other Poems</u>. New York: W.A.
Bodler, 1928.

540. RICHARDSON, BEULAH (1926-)

540.1 <u>A Black Woman Speaks of White Womanhood, of White
Supremacy, of Peace</u>. New York: American Women for Peace,
1951. Los Angeles: Inner City Press, 1974. (Published under
Beah Richards).

541. RICHARDSON, CLAUDETTE.

541.1 "Especially Fi San." <u>Essence</u> 11 (June 1980): 22.

541.2 "What Kinda Centre." <u>Essence</u> 11 (June 1980): 22.

542. RICHARDSON, MARILYN.

542.1 "Banner." <u>Callaloo</u> 9 (2): 347-348 (Spring 1986).

542.2 "Barbara-Chase Riboud." In DAVIS & HARRIS, pp. 43-
48.

543. RICHARDSON, NOLA (1936-).

543.1 <u>Even in a Maze</u>. Los Angeles: Crescent Publications,
1975.

543.2 <u>When One Loves: The Black Experience in America</u>.
Millbrae, CA: Celestial Arts, 1974. Poetry.

544. ROBERSON, SADIE.

544.1 <u>Killer of the Dream</u>. New York: Carlton Press, 1963.
Short fiction.

545. ROBINSON, AMELIA P. BOYNTON.

545.1 <u>Bridge Across Jordan</u>. New York: Carlton Press, 1980.

546. ROBINSON, JEANNETTE.

546.1 "Lady Dressed in Blue." <u>Obsidian</u> 3 (1): 66 (Spring
1977).

547. ROBINSON, LOUISE.

547.1 "Woman-Song." In BLACKSONGS.

548. RODGERS, CAROLYN (1945-).

548.1 "Antique Cradle of the Blues." <u>Black World</u> 24 (June
1975): 82.

548.2 "Blackbird in a Cage." <u>Negro Digest</u> 16 (August 1967):
66-71.

548.3 "Black Poetry - Where It's At." <u>Negro Digest</u>
(September 1969): 7-16.

548.4 "Central Standard Time Blues." <u>Essence</u> 6 (November
1975): 68-69.

548.5 "The Children of Their Sin." <u>Black World</u> 2 (October
1971): 78-80.

548.6 <u>Finite Forms: Poems</u>. Cheektowaga, NY: Eden Press,
1985.

548.7 <u>For Flip Wilson</u>. Detroit: Broadside Press, 1971.

548.8 <u>For H.W. Fuller</u>. Detroit: Broadside Press, 1970.

548.9 "For H.W. Fuller." <u>Essence</u> 12 (November 1981): 16.

548.10 <u>For Love of Our Brothers</u>. Chicago: Third World
Press, 1970. Carolyn Rodgers, editor.

548.11 "For Our Fathers." <u>Ebony</u> 27 (August 1972): 46.

548.12 "For Sapphires (For Mamma and Daddy)." _Essence_ 6
(May 1975): 92.

548.13 "For Some Black Men." _Essence_ 14 (September 1983):
20.

548.14 "Grace." _Black World_ 24 (June 1975):83.

548.15 _The Heart as Ever Green_. New York: Anchor/Doubleday,
1978.

548.16 _How I Got Ovah_. New York: Anchor/Doubleday, 1975.

548.17 "How I Got Ovah." _Black World_ 22 (June 1973): 77.
Essence 6 (May 1975): 92.

548.18 "It Is Deep." _Essence_ 6 (May 1975): 39.

548.19 "The Literature of Black." _Black World_ (June 1970):
5-11.

548.20 _A Little Lower Than Angels_. Cheektowaga, NY: Eden
Press, 1984.

548.21 _Long Rap/Commonly Known as a Poetic Essay_. Detroit:
Broadside Press, 1971.

548.22 "Love." _Ebony_ 33 (February 1983): 48.

548.23 _Love Raps_. Chicago: Third World Press, 1969.

548.24 "New Poems." _Black World_ 24 (June 1975): 82-83.

548.25 "No Such Thing as a Witch, Just a Woman, Needing Some
Love." _Essence_ 7 (May 1976): 78. _Ebony_ 36 (August 1981):
54. Excerpt from _How I Got Ovah_.

548.26 _Now Ain't That Love_. Detroit: Broadside Press, 1970.

548.27 "One Time." _Essence_ 6 (November 1975).

548.28 _Paper Soul_. Chicago: Third World Press, 1961.

548.29 "Poem for Some Black Men." _Essence_ 6 (May 1975): 95.

548.30 "Poem for Some Black Women." _Essence_ 6 (May 1975):
93.

548.31 "Poetic Regeneration." _Black World_ 24 (June 1975):
83.

548.32 "Portrait." _Essence_ 6 (May 1975): 95.

548.33 _Roots_. Bloomington, IN: Indiana University Press,
1973. Edited by Carolyn Rodgers.

548.34 "Sacrament." Black World 24 (June 1975): 82.

548.35 Songs of a Black Bird. Chicago: Third World Press,
1969.

548.36 "A Statistic, Trying to Make it Home." Negro Digest
18 (June 1969): 68-71.

548.37 Translations: Poems. Cheektowaga, NY: Eden Press,
1980.

548.38 "Translations." Black Scholar 11 (5): 71 (May-June
1980).

548.39 2 Love Raps. Chicago: Third World Press, 1969.

548.40 "Walk Wid Jesus." Essence 2 (April 1972): 39

Secondary Sources

548.41(S) Davis, Jean. "Carolyn Rodgers." In HARRIS &
DAVIS, pp. 287-295. Includes bibliography and biography.

548.42(S) Mberi, Antar Sudan Katara. "Reaching for Unity
and Harmony. Freedomways 20 (First Quarter 1980): 48-49.

548.43(S) Sales, Estella M. "Contractions in Black Life:
Recognized and Reconciled in How I Got Ovah." CLA Journal 25
(September 1981): 74-81.

549. ROE, HELENE.

549.1 Teach Me to Live. n.p., [1963?].

550. ROLLIN, FRANCES ANNE (1845/47?-1901).

550.1 [Frank A. Rollin]. Life and Public Service of Martin
R. Delaney. Boston: Lee & Shepard, 1868.

Secondary Sources

550.2(S) Bovoso, Carole. "Discovering My Foremothers." Ms.
6(September 1977): 56-59.

550.3(S) Majors, Gerri, and Saunders, Doris E. Black
Society. Chicago: Johnson Publishing Co., 1976.

550.4(S) Shockley, Ann Allen. "Frances Anne Rollin
Whipper." In SHOCKLEY, pp. 123-133.

550.5(S) Sterling, Dorothy. <u>The Making of an Afro-American:</u>
<u>Martin Robison Delany, 1812-1885</u>. Boston: Beacon Press,
1971.

550.6(S) Ullman, Victor. <u>Martin R. Delany: The Beginning of</u>
<u>Black Nationalism</u>. Boston: Beacon Press, 1971. Frances A.
Rollin, p. 410.

550.7(S) Williamson, Joel. <u>After Slavery: The Negro in</u>
<u>South Carolina During Reconstruction, 1861-1877</u>. Chapel
Hill, NC: University of North Carolina Press, 1965. Cites
Frances A. Rollin, p. 176.

551. ROSEBROUGH, DOROTHY.

551.1 <u>Wasted Travail</u>. New York: Vantage Press, 1951.
Novel.

552. ROWLAND, IDA.

552.1 <u>Lisping Leaves</u>. Philadelphia: Dorrance & Company,
1939. Poetry.

553. ROYSTER, SANDRA (1942-).

553.1 "Desert Island." <u>Black World</u> 21 (April 1972): 15.

553.2 <u>Woman Talk</u>. Chicago: Third World Press, 1974.

554. RUST, EDNA.

554.1 Untitled Poem. <u>Essence</u> 17 (January 1987): 101.

554.2 Untitled Poem. <u>Essence</u> 17 (January 1987): 110.

555. RUTLEDGE, DORIS.

555.1 <u>The Weeping Poet</u>. New York: Carlton Press, 1975.

556. SALIMU.

556.1 "Growin' into Blackness." In BULLINS, 1969.

557. SANCHEZ, SONIA (1934-).

557.1 The Adventures of Fathead, Smallhead and Squarehead.
Chicago: Third Press, 1973.

557.2 "After Saturday Night Comes Sunday." Black World 2
(March 1971): 53-59.

557.3 "Black Magic." Black Scholar 18 (1): 54 (January-
February 1987).

557.4 "Black Pow-Wow: Jazz Poems." Black World 21 (January
1972): 86-89.

557.5 "Blk/Rhetoric." Black Scholar 18 (1): 33
(January/February 1987).

557.6 A Blues Book for Blue Black Magical Women. Detroit:
Broadside Press, 1974.

557.7 "The Bronx is Next." Drama Review 12 (Summer 1968)
78-83. One act drama.

557.8 Crisis in Culture -- Two Speeches by Sonia Sanchez.
New York: Black Liberation Press, 1983.

557.9 "Depression." Callaloo 5 (2): 30 (1979).

557.10 "Dialogue." Black World 23 (January 1974): 22

557.11 "Dirty Hearts." Scripts 1 (November 1971): 46-50.
Drama.

557.12 "Father and Daughter." Black Scholar 6 (June 1975):
19.

557.13 "The Final Solution - the Leaders Speak" Negro
Digest 17 (December 1967): 40.

557.14 "5 Haiku." Black Collegian 9 (May-June 1979): 93.
Black Scholar 12 (September-October 1981): 29.

557.15 Generations: Poetry, 1969-1985. London: Karnak
House, 1986.

557.16 "Haiku." Western Journal of Black Studies 9 (3): 174
(Fall 1985).

557.17 "Haiku and Tanka." Black Scholar 10 (November-
December 1978): 49.

557.18 Homecoming. Detroit: Broadside Press, 1968.

557.19   Homegirls & Handgrenades: A Collection of Poetry and
Prose.   New York: Thunder's Mouth Press, 1984.

557.20   "I Have Walked a Long Time."   Callaloo 5 (2): 19-20
(1979).

557.21   "I WaaAANNT to Know; I NeeeeEEEEDS to Know."   Black
World   19 (September 1970): 53.

557.22   Ima Talken Bout the Nation of Islam.   Astoria, NY:
TruthDel, 1972.

557.23   "Indianapolis/Summer/1969/Poem."   Black Scholar 18
(1): 34 (January/February 1987).

557.24   It's a New Day (Poems for Young Brothas and Sistuhs).
Detroit: Broadside Press, 1971.

557.25   I've Been a Woman: New and Selected Poems.
Sausalita, CA: Black Scholar Press, 1981.

557.26   Liberation Poem.   Detroit: Broadside Press, 1970.

557.27   "Life is Not a Dream."   "The Inmate."   Minnesota
Review 2 (Summer 1962): 460-461.

557.28   "Love Poem Written for Sterling Brown After Reading a
N.Y. Times Article Re: A Mummy Kept Preserved for About 3000
Years."   Black Scholar 8 (March 1977): 45.

557.29   Love Poems.   Chicago: Third World Press, 1973.

557.30   "Love Poems, II."   Black Scholar 8 (March 1977): 45.

557.31   "Malcolm."   Black Scholar 18 (1): 32
(January/February 1987).

557.32   "Malcolm/Man Don't Live Here No Mo'".   Black Theatre
6 (1972): 24-27.   Call-Response drama.

557.33   "Nefertiti: Queen to a Sacred Mission."   Journal of
African Civilizations 6 (1): 49-55 (Fall 1984).

557.34   "Notes from a Journal."   American Poetry Review 6
(5): 30 (September-October 1977).

557.35   "Personal Letter No. 2."   Black Scholar 18 (1): 31
(January/February 1987).

557.36   "Personal Letter No. 3."   Black Scholar 18 (1): 31
(January/February 1987).

557.37   "Poem."   Negro Digest 15 (September 1966): 83.

557.38   "Poem (for DCS 8th Graders 1966-67)."   Black Scholar
18 (1): 32 (January/February 1987).

557.39 "Poem for Jesse Jackson." Essence 15 (July 1984):
18.

557.40 "Poem for My Father." Black Scholar 18 (1): 51
(January/February 1987).

557.41 "Poem for Sterling Brown." Black Scholar 8 (March
1977): 45.

557.42 "Poem No. 8 (I've Been a Woman...)." Callaloo 5 (2):
20 (1979).

557.43 "Poem No. 12." Essence 7 (May 1976): 20.

557.44 "Poem No. 14." Black World 23 (January 1974): 23.

557.45 "Poem of Praise." Black Scholar 6 (June 1975): 18-
19. Callaloo 5 (2): 21-23 (1979).

557.46 "The Poet as Creator of Social Values." In HOLLIS.
Black Scholar 16 (1): 20-28 (January/February 1985). Essay.

557.47 "Queens of the Universe." Black Scholar 1 (January-
February 1970) 29-34.

557.48 "Re Death." Black Scholar 9 (October 1977): 55-57;
13 (Summer 1982): 41-43.

557.49 "Rebirth." American Poetry Review 6 (1): 27
(January-February 1977).

557.50 "Right On: White America." Negro Digest 17
(September-October 1968): 57.

557.51 "Role of the Black Woman in a Changing Society."
Black Collegian 35 (1980): 28-30.

557.52 "Ruminations/Reflections." In EVANS.

557.53 "Sister Son/Ji." In BULLINS, 1969, pp. 97-108.
Dramatic monolog.

557.54 "Six Haiku and Two Tankas." Beloit Poetry Journal 29
(1): 34-35 (Winter 1978-1979).

557.55 "Small Comment." Black Scholar 18 (1): 34
(January/February 1987).

557.56 "So Strange." Callaloo 5 (2): 21 (1979).

557.57 A Sound Investment: Short Stories for Young Readers.
Chicago: Third World Press, 1980. Children's stories.

557.58 "Summer Words of Sistah Addict." Black Scholar 18
(1): 32 (January/February 1987).

557.59 Three Hundred and Sixty Degrees of Blackness Comin'
at You. New York: 5X Publishing Company, 1972. Edited by
Sonia Sanchez.

557.60 "To All Brothers; from All Sisters." Western Journal
of Black Studies 9 (3): 174 (Fall 1985).

557.61 "Uh, Uh, But How Do It Free Us?" In BULLINS, pp.
165-219. Series of dramatic vignettes.

557.62 Under a Soprano Sky. New York: Thunder's Mouth,
1986.

557.63 "Untitled Poem." Black World 21 (September 1972):
76-77.

557.64 We a BaddDDD People. Detroit: Broadside Press, 1970.

557.65 "We Are Muslim Women." Black World 23 (January
1974): 24-25. Essence 6 (October 1975): 55.

557.66 We Be Word Sorcerers: 25 Stories by Black Americans.
New York: Bantam Books, 1973. Anthology. Sanchez, editor.

Secondary Sources

557.67(S) Bullins, Ed, ed. The New Lafayette Theatre
Presents: Plays with Aesthetic Comments by 6 Black
Playwrights. New York: Anchor/Doubleday, 1974.

557.68(S) Bullins, Ed, ed. New Plays from the Black
Theatre. New York: Doubleday, 1969.

557.69(S) Brown, Elizabeth. "Six Female Black Playwrights:
Images Of Blacks in Plays by Lorraine Hansberry, Alice
Childress, Sonia Sanchez, Barbara Molette, Martie Charles and
Ntozake Shange." Ph.D. dissertation, Florida State
University, 1980.

557.70(S) Clarke, Sebastian. "Sonia Sanchez and Her Work."
Black World 2 (June 1971): 45-48, 96-98. Also in Presence
Africaine 78 (1971): 253-261.

557.71(S) Cornwell, Anita R. "Attuned to the Energy: Sonia
Sanchez." Essence 10 (July 1979): 10-11.

557.72(S) Joyce, Joyce. "The Development of Sonia Sanchez:
A Continuing Journey." Indiana Journal of American Studies
13 (July 1983): 37-71.

557.73(S) Palmer, R. Roderick. "The Poetry of Three
Revolutionists: Don L. Lee, Sonia Sanchez, and Nikki
Giovanni." CLA Journal 15 (September 1971): 25-36.

557.74(S) Salaam, Kalamu ya. "Sonia Sanchez." In HARRIS &
DAVIS, pp. 295-306. Biographical and bibliographical
material.

557.75(S) Walker, Barbara. "Sonia Sanchez Creates Poetry
for the Stage." Black Creation 5 (Fall, 1973): 12-14.

1988-1991 Supplement

A557.76 "Poems." Black Scholar 19 (July/August-
September/October 1988): 47.

A557.77 "Poems." Callaloo 12 (Spring 1989): 350.

A557.78 "A Remembrance." Essence 18 (March 1988): 52.

Secondary Sources

A557.79(S) Jones, Marsha. "Kaleidoscope Lady: The Wonderful
Words of Sonia Sanchez." about...time 16 (July 1988): 14.

558. SATIAFA.

558.1 "For Dark Women and Others." Western Journal of Black
Studies 7 (3): 146-147 (Fall 1983).

558.2 For Dark Women and Others: Poems. Detroit: Lotus
Press, 1982.

559. SAUNDERS, RUBIE.

559.1 Marilyn Morgan, R.N. New York: Amsterdam Library,
1969.

560. SAVAGE, EUDORA V.

560.1 Vibrations of My Heartstrings. New York: Exposition
Press, 1944. Poetry.

561. SCHUYLER, PHILIPPA DUKE (1932-1967).

561.1 Adventure in Black and White. New York: Robert
Speller, 1960.

561.2 Good Men Die. New York: Twin Circle Publishers, 1969.

561.3 Jungle Saints. New York: Herder and Herder, 1963.

561.4 "Meet the George Schuyler's." Our World 6 (April 1951): 22-26.

561.5 "Music of Modern Africa." Music Journal 18 (October 1960): 60-63.

561.6 Who Killed the Congo? New York: Devin-Adair Company, 1962.

561.7 "Why I Don't Marry." Ebony 13 (July 1958): 78-80.

561.8 Kingdom of Dreams. New York: Robert Speller, 1966. Josephine Schuyler, joint author.

Secondary Sources

561.9(S) "Philippa Duke Schuyler." Who's Who in Colored America, 7th ed. Yonker-on-Hudson, NY: Christian E. Burckel & Associates, 1950. p. 455.

561.10(S) Schuyler, Josephine. Philippa: The Beautiful American. New York: The Philippa Schuyler Memorial Foundation, 1969.

562. SCOTT, ANNE.

562.1 Case 999: A Christmas Story. Boston: Meador, 1953.

563. SCOTT, CAROLYN PATRICIA.

563.1 The Boogaloo Child. San Francisco: Julian Richardson, n.d. Poetry and short fiction.

564. SCOTT, SHARON.

564.1 "Poem, Because We Would Be Stronger." Black World 2 (September 1971): 54.

565. SEACOLE, MARY.

565.1 Wonderful Adventures of Mrs. Seacole in Many Lands. Published in 1857. New York: Oxford University Press, 1988. (The Schomburg Library of Nineteenth-Century Black Women Writers).

Sele, Baraka. **SEE** 137. COBB, PAMELA.

566. SHAKUR, ASSATA.

566.1 <u>Assata: An Autobiography</u>. Westport, CT: L. Hill,
1987.

566.2 "Women in Prison: How We Are." <u>Black Scholar</u> 9 (7):
8-15 (April 1978). An essay.

Secondary Sources

566.3(S) Angola, Bibi, compiler and ed. <u>Assata Speaks: And
the People Speak on Assata</u>. Brooklyn: Black News, 1980.

566.4(S) Greene, Cheryl Y. "Words from a Sister in Exile."
<u>Essence</u> 18 (February 1988): 60.

567. SHANDS, ANNETTE OLIVER.

567.1 <u>Black Volume</u>. Mount Vernon, NY: A&J Press, 1973.

567.2 "Gwendolyn Brooks As Novelist." <u>Black World</u> (June
1973): 22-30.

568. SHANGE, NTOSAKE (1948-).

568.1 "Aw, Babee, You So Pretty." <u>Essence</u> 9 (April 1979):
87. Short fiction.

568.2 <u>Betsey Brown</u>. New York: St. Martin's, 1985. Novel.

568.3 "Black and White Two-dimensional Planes." <u>Callaloo</u> 5
(2): 56-62 (1979).

568.4 "Christmas for Sassafrass, Cypress and Indigo."
<u>Essence</u> 13 (December 1982): 68-70. Excerpt from <u>Sassafrass,
Cypress and Indigo: A Novel</u>.

568.5 <u>A Daughter's Geography</u>. New York: St. Martin's, 1984.
Drama.

568.6 <u>For Colored Girls Who Have Considered Suicide/When the
Rainbow is Enuf: A Choreopoem</u>. San Lorenzo, CA: Shameless
Hussy Press, 1975. New York: Macmillan Publishing Company,
1977. Drama.

568.7   From Okra to Greens: A Different Kinda Love Story.
New York: Samuel French, 1985.   Drama.

568.8   From Okra to Greens: Poems.   St. Paul, MN: Coffee
House Press, 1984.

568.9   "Get It and Feel Good."   Essence 9 (February 1979): 88

568.10   "Gray."   Callaloo 5 (2): 63 (1979).

568.11   "Is Not So Good to Be Born a Girl."   Black Scholar 10
(May-June 1979): 28-29.

568.12   "Like the Fog & the Sun Teasin the Rapids."
Mademoiselle 82 (September 1976): 28.

568.13   Mellisa & Smith.   St. Paul, MN: Bookslingers Edition,
1976.

568.14   "Memory (for Philip Wilson, Oliver Lake, David Murray
& Julius Hemphill)."   Mademoiselle 82 (September 1976): 28.

568.15   Nappy Edges.   New York: St. Martin's, 1978. Poetry.

568.16   Natural Diasters and Other Festive Occasions.   San
Francisco: Heirs, 1977.   Poetry and prose.

568.17   "Ntozake Shange Interviews Herself."   Ms. 6 (December
1977): 35, 70, 72.

568.18   "Oh She Gotta Head Fulla Hair."   Black Scholar 10
(November-December 1978): 13-14.

568.19   "On Becoming Successful."   Mademoiselle 82 (September
1976): 28.

568.20   "Otherwise I Would Think It Odd To Have Rape
Prevention Month."   Black Scholar 10 (May-June 1979): 29-30.

568.21   A Photograph: Lovers in Motion. Poemplay.   New York:
Samuel French, 1981.   Drama.

568.22   Ridin' the Moon in Texas: Word Paintings.   New York:
St. Martin's, 1987.   Poetry and prose.

568.23   Sassafrass.   Berkeley: Shameless Hussy, 1976.

568.24   Sassafras, Cypress and Indigo: A Novel.   New York:
St. Martin's, 1983.

568.25   "A Scene from Boogie Woogie Landscapes."   Ms. 10
(August 1981): 70-71.   From Three Pieces.

568.26   See No Evil: Prefaces, Essays and Accounts, 1976-
1983.   San Francisco: Momo's Press, 1984.

568.27   "She Bleeds."   Essence 11 (May 1980): 103.

568.28   Some Men. [St. Louis, MO] n.p., 1981. Pamphlet of
poems.

568.29   Spell # 7: A Theatre Piece in Two Acts. New York:
Samuel French, 1981.

568.30   "Three (For International Women's Day). Black
Scholar 6 (June 1975): 56-61.

568.31   Three Pieces. New York: St. Martin's, 1981. New
York: Penguin Books, 1982. Short plays.

568.32   Three Pieces: Spell # 7. New York: St. Martin's,
1981.

568.33   Tween Itaparica y Itapua. New York: Basement
Editions, 1978. Broadside.

568.34   "Unrecovered Losses/Black Theatre Traditions."
Black Scholar 10 (July-August 1979): 7-9.

568.35   "We Are Just Kinda That Way." Beloit Poetry Journal
29 (2): 22 (Winter 1978-1979).

568.36   "With No Immediate Cause." Essence 11 (June 1980):
140.

568.37   "Wow, Yr Just Like a Man!" Ms. 7 (December 1978):
52. From Nappy Edges.

                    Secondary Sources

568.38(S) Allen, Bonnie. "A Home Instinct." Essence 11
(August 1980): 17.

568.39(S) Bambara, Toni Cade. "For Colored Girls -- And
White Girls Too." Ms. 5 (September 1976): 36,38.

568.40(S) Blackwell, Henry. "An Interview with Ntozake
Shange." Black American Literature Forum 13 (4): 134-138
(Winter 1979).

568.41(S) Brown, Elizabeth. "Ntozake Shange." In DAVIS &
HARRIS, 1985, pp. 240-250. Biography and bibliography.

568.42(S) Brown, Elizabeth. "Six Female Black Playwrights:
Images Of Blacks in Plays by Lorraine Hansberry, Alice
Childress, Sonia Sanchez, Barbara Molette, Martie Charles and
Ntozake Shange." Ph. D. dissertation, Florida State
University, 1980.

568.43(S) Daniels, Bonnie. "For Colored Girls...A
Catharsis." Black Scholar 10 (8-9): 61-62 (May-June 1979).

568.44(S) Dong, Stella. "PW Interviews Ntozake Shange."
Publishers Weekly (3 May 1985): 227.

568.45(S) Elliot, Jeffrey M. "Ntozake Shange: Genesis of a
Choreopoem." Negro History Bulletin 41 (January-February
1978): 797-800.

568.46(S) Fleming, Robert. "A Conversation with the
Author." Encore American and Worldwide News 9 (June 1980):
35-37.

568.47(S) Flowers, Sandra Hollins. "Colored Girls: Textbook
for the Eighties." Black American Literature Forum,
15(Summer 1981):51-54.

568.48(S) Gillespie, Marcia Ann. "Ntozake Shange Talks with
Marcia Ann Gillespie." Essence 16 (May 1985): 122.

568.49(S) Harris, Jessica. "For Colored Girls Who Have
Considered Suicide/When the Rainbow Is Enuf -- The Women Who
Are the Rainbow." Essence 7 (November 1976): 87-89, 102-104,
120-122, 147.

568.50(S) Jones, Terry. "The Need to Go Beyond
Stereotypes." Black Scholar 10 (8-9): 48-49 (May-June 1979).

568.51(S) Latour, Martine. "Ntozake Shange: Driven
Poet/Playwright." Mademoiselle 82 (September 1976): 182,
226. An interview.

568.52(S) Lewis, Barbara. "The Poet." Essence 7 (November
1976): 86, 119-120.

568.53(S) Peters, Erskine. "Some Tragic Propensities of
Ourselves: The Occasion of Nzotake Shange's For Colored Girls
Who Have Considered Suicide/When the Rainbow Is Enuf."
Journal of Ethnic Studies 6 (1): 79-85 (Spring 1978).

568.54(S) Rhys, Jean. "Ntozake Shange: Interviews." New
Yorker (2 August 1976): 17-19. In the "Talk of the Town"
column.

568.55(S) Ribowsky, Mark. "Poetess Scores a Hit with Play
On 'What's Wrong with Black Men.'" Sepia 25 (December 1976):
42-46. On Ntosake Shange's For Colored Girls....

568.56(S) Richards, Sandra L. "Conflicting Impulses in the
Plays of Ntozake Shange." Black American Literature Forum 17
(Summer 1983): 73-78.

568.57(S) Rushing, Andrea Benton. "For Colored Girls,
Suicide or Struggle." Massachusetts Review 22 (3): 539-550
(Autumn 1981).

568.58(S) Smith, Yvonne. "Ntozake Shange a 'Colored Girl'
Considers Success." Essence 12 (February 1982): 12.

568.59(S) Talbert, Linda Lee. "Ntozake Shange: Scarlet
Woman and Witch/Poet." Umoja 4 (1980) 5-10.

568.60(S) Valentine, Dean. New Leader (2 January 1978): 29.
On a presentation of Shange's play A Photograph: A Study in
Cruelty.

568.61(S) Vallely, Jean. "Trying To Be Nice." Time 198 (19
July 1976): 44-45.

568.62(S) Webster, Ivan. "Ntozake Shange's Bold Brechtian
Gamble." Encore American and Worldwide News 9 (June 1980):
34. On Shange's adaptation of Bertolt Brecht's play Mother
Courage and Her Children.

1988-1991 Supplement

A568.63 Love Space Demands (a continuing saga). New York:
St. Martins Press, 1991.

Secondary Sources

A568.64(S) Lester, Neal A. "At the Heart of Shange's
Feminism: An Interview." Black American Literature Forum 24
(Winter 1990): 717.

Shange, Ntozake SEE 586. SHANGE, NTOSAKE.

569. SHANK, DOROTHY.

569.1 "Blindness Is But a State of Mind." Crisis 91
(November 1984): 34.

570. SHARP, SAUNDRA (1942-).

570.1 From the Windows of My Mind. New York: Togetherness
Productions, 1970. Poetry.

570.2 "Growing up Integrated. (Did Momma Do the Right
Thing?)" Crisis (March 1988): 8.

570.3 "Hollywood Blacks Fighting Back." Black Collegian 35
(November 1980): 202-204.

570.4 In the Midst of Change. Los Angeles: Togetherness
Productions, 1972. Poetry.

570.5 "Long Distance." Essence 17 (March 1987): 132.

570.6 Soft Song. Los Angeles: Poets Pay Rent Too, 1978.
Poetry.

570.7 "Thirty and a Half." _Essence_,17 (October 19086): 123.

570.8 "This Last Piece of Paper." _Crisis_ 94 (November 1987): 39. _Essence_ 17 (February 1987): 116.

571.   SHAW, LETTIE M.

571.1 _Angel Mink_. New York: Comet Press Books, 1937. Novel.

572.   SHAWN, KAREN.

572.1 "Rape." _Essence_ 10 (October 1979): 94.

573.   SHERROD, LENA.

573.1 "Absence." _Essence_ 6 (February 1976): 38-39.

574.   SHIELDS, ANNA E.

574.1 _Ethiopia's Petition_. Cambridge: Author, 1918.

574.2 _Passion Week_. Cambridge: Author, 1924.

574.3 _Unpolished Truths_. Cambridge: Author, [192?]

574.4 _When God's Fire Comes_. New York: Carlton Press, 1969. Poetry.

575.   SHOCKLEY, ANN ALLEN (1927-).

575.1 "Abraham and the Spirit." _Negro Digest_ 8 (July 1950): 85-91.

575.2 _Afro-American Women Writers, 1746-1933: An Anthology and Critical Guide_. Boston: G.K. Hall, 1988. Edited by Shockley.

575.3 "Ah: The Young Black Poet." _New Letters_ 41 (Winter 1974): 45-60.

575.4 "Ain't No Use in Crying." _Negro Digest_ 17 (December 1967): 69-78.

575.5 "American Anti-Slavery Literature: An Overview --
1693-1859." Negro History Bulletin 37 (April/May 1974): 232-
235.

575.6 The Black and White of It. Tallahassee, FL: Naiad
press, 1980. Short fiction.

575.7 "Black Lesbian Biography: Lifting the Veil." Other
Black Woman 1 (1982): 5-9.

575.8 "The Black Lesbian in American Literature."
Conditions Five 11 (Autumn 1979): 133-142.

575.9 "Black Publishers and Black Librarians: A Necessary
Union." Black World 26 (March 1975): 38-44.

575.10 "A Case of Telemania." Azalea 1 (Fall 1978): 1-5.
Short fiction.

575.11 "Crying for Her Man." Liberator 11 (January-February
1971): 14-17.

575.12 "Does the Negro College Library Need a Special Negro
Collection?" Library Journal 86 (1 June 1961): 2049-2050.

575.13 "End of an Affair." Liberator 9 (June 1969): 14-16.

575.14 "Faculty Party." Black World 21 (November 1971): 54-
63.

575.15 "A Far Off Sound." Umbra 2 (December 1963): 11-17.

575.16 "The Funeral." Phylon 28 (Spring 1967): 95-101.

575.17 A Handbook for the Administration of Special Black
Collections. Nashville: Fisk University Library, 1970.

575.18 "Her Own Thing." Black America 2 (August 1972): 58-
61, 54.

575.19 "Is She Relevant?" Black World 20 (January 1971):
58-65.

575.20 "Joseph S. Cotter, Sr.: Biographical Sketch of a
Black Louisville Bard." CLA Journal 18 (March 1975): 327-
340.

575.21 "Living in Fear, Is a Slow Death." Fisk University
Herald 40 (January 1947): 8-10, 24.

575.22 Loving Her. Indianapolis: Bobbs-Merrill, 1974.
Novel.

575.23 "A Meeting of the Sapphic Daughters." Sinister
Wisdom 9 (Spring 1979): 54-59. Short fiction.

575.24 "Monday Will Be Better." Negro Digest 13 (May 1964):
54-65.

575.25 "The More Things Change." Essence 8 (October 1977):
78-79, 93-94, 97-99. Short fiction.

575.26 "A Necessary Union: Black Publishers and Librarians."
Black World 26 (March 1975): 38-44.

575.27 "The Negro Woman in Retrospect: Blueprint for the
Future." Negro History Bulletin 24 (December 1965): 55-56,
62.

575.28 "The New Black Feminists." Northwest Journal of
African and Black American Studies 2 (Winter 1974): 1-5.

575.29 "On Lesbian/Feminist Book Reviewing." Sojourner: The
Women's Forum (April 1984): 18.

575.30 "Oral History: A Research Tool for Black History."
Negro History Bulletin 41 (January-February 1978): 787-789.
An essay.

575.31 "Pauline Elizabeth Hopkins: A Biographical Excursion
into Obscurity." Phylon 33 (Spring 1972): 22-26.

575.32 "The Picture." Fisk University Herald 39 (November
1945): 15-16.

575.33 "The Picture Prize." Negro Digest 11 (October 1962):
53-60.

575.34 "The President." Freedomways 10 (Fourth Quarter
1970): 343-349.

575.35 "Red Jordan Arobateau: A Different Kind of Black
Lesbian Writer." Sinister Wisdom 21 (Fall 1982): 35-39.

575.36 "The Saga of Private Julius Cole." Black World 23
(March 1974): 54-70.

575.37 "The Salsa Soul Sisters." Off Our Backs 11 (November
1979): 13. Essay.

575.38 Say Jesus and Come To Me. New York: Avon Books,
1982.

575.39 "Song of Hope." Fisk University Herald 40 (October
1945): 26-29.

575.40 "A Soul Cry for Reading." In JOSEY, pp. 225-233.

575.41 "A Special Evening." Sisters 4 (August 1973): 18-28.

575.42 "Tell It Like It Is: A New Criteria for Children's
Books in Black and White." Southeastern Libraries 30 (Spring
1970): 30-33.

575.43 "To Be a Man." Negro Digest 18 (July 1969): 54-65.

575.44 "The Waiter." Fisk University Herald 39 (December 1945): 16-17.

575.45 "Women In a Southern Time." Feminary 11 (1982): 45-56.

575.46 "The World of Rosie Polk." Black American Literature Forum 21 (1-2): 133-146 (Spring-Summer 1987). Short fiction.

575.47 Living Black American Authors: A Biographical Directory. New York: R.R. Bowker Company, 1973. Sue P. Chandler, joint editor.

575.48 A Handbook of Black Librarianship. Littleton, CO: Libraries Unlimited, 1977. E.J. Josey, joint editor.

575.49 "Black Women Discuss Today's Problems: Men, Families, Society." Southern Voices 1 (August/September 1974): 16-19. Veronica E. Tucker, joint author.

Secondary Sources

575.50(S) Dandridge, Rita B., Compiler. Ann Allen Shockley: An Annotated Primary and Secondary Bibliography. Westport, CT: Greenwood Press, 1987.

575.51(S) Dandridge, Rita B. "Gathering Pieces: A Selected Bibliography of Ann Allen Shockley." Black American Literature Forum 21 (1-2): 133-146 (Spring-Summer 1987). Includes work and reviews of Shockley, biographical and critical articles about her work.

575.52(S) Houston, Helen R. "Ann Allen Shockley." In DAVIS & HARRIS, pp. 232-236.

575.53(S) White, Evelyn C. "Comprehensive Oppression: Lesbians and Race In the Work of Ann Allen Shockley." Backbone 3 (1981): 38-40.

1988-1991 Supplement

A575.54 "When Poets Collide: A Story of the Seventies." Catalyst (Summer 1988): 70.

576. SHOKUNBI, MAE GLEATON.

576.1 Songs Of the Soul. Philadelphia: Dorrance & Company, 1945.

577. SHORES, MINNIE T.

577.1 <u>Americans in America</u>. Boston: Christopher Publishing
House, 1960. Novel.

577.2 <u>Publicans and Sinners</u>. New York: Comet Press Books,
1960. Novel.

578. SIMMONS, JUDY DOTHARD (1944-).

578.1 "The Clock Turns Backwards." <u>Essence</u> 17 (April 1987):
118.

578.2 "A Conversation with Isaac Hayes, the First Man of
Rap, About His Life." <u>Essence</u> 18 (July 1987): 33.

578.3 "Courage: For Jane Cortez." <u>Essence</u> 11 (April 1981):
19.

578.4 <u>Decent Intentions</u>. Bronx, New York: Blind Beggar,
1983. Poetry.

578.5 <u>Judith's Blues</u>. Detroit. MI: Broadside Press, 1973.
Poetry.

578.6 "Marriage Talk." <u>Essence</u> 18 (July 1987): 57.

578.7 "A Matter of Choice." <u>Essence</u> 18 (October 1987): 55.

578.8 "Sexual Ease." <u>Essence</u> 19 (December 1988): 48.

578.9 "Spirituality: An African View." <u>Essence</u> 18 (December
1987): 61.

578.10 "Staying Power in Publishing: Militant Book Lover
Marid Brown Battles for Black Expression and Publishing
Profits." <u>Essence</u> 18 (May 1987): 135.

578.11 "Your Chest is a Creamy Beige Sky." <u>Essence</u> 11
(April 1981): 19.

579. SIMMONS. VIRGINIA LEE.

579.1 <u>Whitecaps</u>. Yellowsprings, OH: Antioch Press, 1942.

580. SIMS, LILLIAN.

580.1 Collection of Poems. Chicago: Author, 1971.

581. SKINNER, THEODOSIA B.

581.1 Ice Cream from Heaven. New York: Vantage Press, 1962.
Short fiction.

582. SLAUGHTER, EMMA.

582.1 "All Because of Emily." Essence 9 (May 1978): 94-95.

Smart-Grosvenor, Verta Mae SEE 272. GROSVENOR, VERTA MAE.

583. SMITH. AMANDA BERRY (1837-1915).

583. 1 An Autobiography; the Story of the Lord's Dealings
with Mrs. Amanda Smith, the Colored Evangelist; Containing an
Account of Her Life Work of Faith, and Her Travels in
America, England, Ireland, Scotland, India and Africa, As an
Independent Missionary. Chicago: Meyer & Brother, 1893. New
York: Garland, 1987. New York: Oxford University Press,
1988.

                    Secondary Sources

583.2(S) Brown, Hallie Quinn. Homespun Heroines and Other
Women of Distinction. Xenia, OH: Aldine, 1926.

583.3(S) Shockley, Ann Allen. "Amanda Berry Smith." In
SHOCKLEY, pp. 225-232.

584. SMITH, ANN ODENE.

584.1 God's Step Chilluns. Detroit: Harlo Press, 1981.

585. SMITH, CHERYL.

585.1 "Just Give Me a Little Piece of the Sun." Essence 9
(June 1978): 39.

586. SMITH, FRANCES LAURENCE.

586.1 <u>Wishful Thinking</u>. Baltimore: Garland Publishing,
1953. Poetry.

587. SMITH, J. PAULINE.

587.1 <u>"Exceeding Riches" and Other Verse</u>. Detroit: n.p.,
1922. Poetry.

588. SMITH, JEAN.

588.1 "O.C.'s Heart." <u>Black World</u> 19 (April 1970): 56-76.
Excerpts from a three act drama.

588.2 "Somethin-To-Eat." <u>Black World</u> 2 (June 1971): 7-76.

589. SMITH, LUCY.

589.1 <u>Give Me A Child</u>. Philadelphia: Kraft Publishing Co.,
1955. Written with Sarah Wright.

589.2 <u>No Middle Ground: A Collection of Poems</u>.
Philadelphia: Philadelphia Council of the Arts, Sciences and
Professions, 1952.

590. SMITH, MARGARET L.

590.1 <u>Creative Poems</u>. New York: Vantage Press, 1974.

591. SMITH, MARY CARTER.

591.1 <u>Heart to Heart</u>. Columbia, MD: C.H. Fairfax, 1980.
Poetry.

591.2 "The Lions and the Rabbits: A Fable." <u>Crisis</u> 85
(March 1978): 194-205. Short fiction.

591.3 <u>Town Child</u>. Columbia, MD: Nordika, 1976. Poetry.

592. SMITH, RHUBERDIA K.

592.1 "Needin'"   Essence 7 (May 1976): 64-65.

593. SOUTHERLAND, ELLEASE (1943-).

593.1 "Beck-Junior and the Good Shepherd."   Massachusetts Review 15 (Autumn 1974): 719-732.

593.2 "Black Is."   Black World 21(May 1972): 45.

593.3 "Ibo Man."   Presence Africaine 91 (Third Quarter 1974): 56.

593.4 "The Influence of Voodoo in the Fiction of Zora Neale Hurston."   In   BELL, pp. 172-183.

593.5 Let the Lion Eat Straw.   New York: Charles Scribner's Sons, 1979. Novel.

593.6 The Magic Sun Spins.   London: Paul Breman, 1975.

593.7 "The Red Bridge."   Black World 24 (September 1975): 57.

593.8 "Rerun."   Black World 20 (March 1971): 3.

593.9 "The Retelling."   Poet Lore 67 (Summer 1972): 145-146.

593.10 "Seconds."   Presence Africaine 93 (First Quarter 1975): 73.

593.11 "Seventeen Days in Nigeria."   Black World 21 (January 1972): 29-41.

593.12 "Shells."   Journal of Black Poetry 1 (Fall, Winter 1971): 67-68.

593.13 "Soldiers."   Black World 22 (June 1973): 54-56.

593.14 "Zora Neale Hurston: The Novelist-Anthropologist's Life/Works."   Black World 23 (August 1974): 20-30.

593.15 "Zora Neale Hurston."   Encore American & Worldwide News 7 (19 June 1978): 38-39.

Secondary Sources

593.16(S) Brookhart, Mary Hughes.   "Ellease Southerland." In   DAVIS & HARRIS, pp. 239-244. Biography and bibliography.

593.17(S) Fuller, Hoyt W., Jackson, Angela and Kilgore, James C. "Two Views: Let the Lion Eat Straw." First World 2 (3): 49-52 (1979).

593.18(S) Southgate, Robert L. Black Plots and Black Characters: A Handbook for Afro-American Literature. Syracuse, NY: Gaylord Professional, 1979.

1988-1991 Supplement

A593.19 "Ancient as the World: Egyptian Symbols and Contemporary Black Literature." Black Scholar 19 (July/August-September/October 1988): 13.

594. SPEARMAN, AURELIA L.P. CHILDS.

594.1 What Christmas Means To Us. New York: Carlton Press, 1964. Poetry.

596. SPENCE, EULALIE (1894-1981).

596.1 "Episode." "Hot Stuff." In BROWN-GUILLORY. Drama.

596.2 Fool's Errand. New York: Samuel French, 1927. One act drama.

596.3 Foreign Mail. New York: Samuel French, 1927. Drama.

596.4 "The Hunch." Opportunity (1927).

596.5 "The Starter" In LOCKE & MONTGOMERY, pp. 205-214. One act drama.

596.6 "Undertow." Carolina Magazine (April 1929): 5-15. One act drama.

Secondary Sources

596.7(S) Hatch, James V. Black Theater, USA: Forty-Five Plays by American Negroes, 1847-1974. New York: Free Press, 1974.

596.8(S) Locke, Alain LeRoy and Gregory, Montgomery, eds. Plays of Negro Life: A Source-Book of Native American Drama. New York: Harper, 1927. Reprint New York: Negro Universities Press, 1970.

597. SPENCER, ANNE (1882-1975).

597.1 "At the Carnival." "Before the Feast of Shushan."
"Lady, Lady." "Letter to My Sister." "Substitution." In
STETSON, pp. 68-72.

597.2 "Before the Feast at Shushan." Crisis 19 (February
1920): 186.

597.3 "Dunbar." Crisis 21 (November 1920): 32.

597.4 "Grapes: Still-Life." Crisis 36 (April 1929): 124.

597.5 "Lady, Lady." Survey Graphic 6 (March 1925): 661.

597.6 "Lines to a Nasturtium (A Lover Muses)." Palms 4
(October 1926): 13.

597.7 "The Poems." In GREENE, pp.175-197.

597.8 "Requiem." Lyric (Spring 1931): 3.

597.9 "Rime for the Christmas Baby (At 48 Webster Place,
Orange)." Opportunity 5 (December 1927): 368.

597.10 "White Things." Crisis 25 (March 1923): 204.

Secondary Sources

597.11(S) Dean, Sharon G. "Anne Spencer." In QUARTERMAIN,
pp. 420-427. Biography and bibliography.

597.12(S) Greene, J. Lee. "Anne Spencer." In HARRIS &
DAVIS, 1987, pp. 252-259. Biography and bibliography
included.

597.13(S) Greene, J. Lee. Time's Unfading Garden: Anne
Spencer's Life and Poetry. Baton Rouge: Louisiana State
University Press, 1977.

597.14(S) Shockley, Ann Allen. "Anne Spencer." In
SHOCKLEY, pp. 453-455.

597.15(S) Stetson, Erlene. "Anne Spencer." CLA Journal 21
(March 1978): 400-409.

1988-1991 Supplement

A597.16 "Romance." Shooting Star Review 2 (Winter 1988):
12.

Secondary Sources

A597.17(S) Honey, Maureen, editor. <u>Shadowed Dreams: Women's Poetry of the Harlem Renaissance</u>. New Brunswick, NJ: Rutgers University Press, 1989.

598. SPENCER, MARY ETTA.

598.1 "Beyond the Years." <u>Opportunity</u> 7 (October 1929): 311-13. Short fiction.

598.2 <u>The Resentment</u>. Philadelphia: A.M.E. Book Concern, 1921. Novel.

                        Secondary Sources

598.3(S) Shockley, Ann Allen. "Mary Etta Spencer." In SHOCKLEY, pp. 387-391.

599. SPILLERS, HORTENSE (1942-)

599.1 "Isom." <u>Essence</u> 11 (May 1981): 88-91. Short fiction.

599.2 "A Lament." <u>Black Scholar</u> 8 (5): 12-16 (March 1977). Short fiction.

599.3 "Mama's Baby, Papa's Mamybe: An American Grammar Book." <u>Diacritics</u> 17 (Summer 1987): 65-81.

599.4 "Moving On Down the Line: On African-American Sermons." <u>The American Quarterly</u> 40 (March 1988): 83-109.

600. STEED, OPHELIA DUDLEY.

600.1 <u>"America's Negro" Subtitled "This is Our Country</u>." Cleveland: Author, 1944.

601. STEPHANY [STEPHANY JEAN DAWSON FULLER] (1947-).

601.1 <u>Moving Deep</u>. Detroit: Broadside Press, 1969.

602. STEWART, MARIA MILLER W. (1803-1879).

602.1 <u>Meditations from the Pen of Mrs. Maria Stewart</u>.
Washington, DC: Enterprise Publishing Company, 1879.

Secondary Sources

602.2(S) Richardson, Marilyn, ed. <u>Maria W. Stewart:
America's First Black Woman Political Writer, Essays and
Speeches</u>. Bloomington, IN: Indiana University Press, 1987.

1988-1991 Supplement

Secondary Sources

A602.3(S) Houchins, Sue E., ed. <u>Spiritual Narratives</u>. NY:
Oxford University Press, 1988.

603. STILES, THELMA JACKSON.

603.1 "In Light of What Has Happened." <u>Essence</u> 10 (June
1979): 76.

604. STOREY, PATRICIA.

604.1 "I." <u>Negro History Bulletin</u> 39 (May 1976): 600.

604.2 "Poetry Is..." <u>Negro History Bulletin</u> 39 (May 1976):
600.

605. STUCKEY, ELMA (1907-).

605.1 <u>The Big Gate</u>. Chicago: Precedent Publishers, 1976.

605.2 <u>Collected Poems of Elma Stuckey</u>. Chicago: Precedent
Publishers, 1987.

605.3 "Family or Freedom." <u>Black Collegian</u> 9 (May-June
1979): 93.

605.4 "Reprobate." <u>Black American Literature Forum</u> 17 (4):
171 (Winter 1973).

605.5 "Sally." <u>Black Collegian</u> 9 (May-June 1979): 93.

Secondary Sources

605.6(S) Roediger, David R. "Elma Stuckey: A Poet Laureate of Black History." Negro History Bulletin 4 (March-April 1977): 690-691.

605.7(S) Roediger, David R. "An Interview with Elma Stuckey." Black American Literature Forum 11 (Winter 1977): 151-153.

606. SULLIVAN, DONNA M.

606.1 "Call Me Black." Crisis 79 (March 1972): 9.

607. SUMMERS, LUCY COOPER.

607.1 99 Patches. New York: Carlton Press, 1969. Poetry.

608. TALIAFERRO, JUNE C. WILLIAMS.

608.1 Moods Intermingled. New York: Vantage Press, 1974.

609. TASSIN, IDA MAE.

609.1 Proud Mary: Poems From a Black Sister in Prison. Buffalo, NY: Buffalo Women's Prison Project, 1971.

610. TATE, ELEANORA E. (1948-).

610.1 Just an Overnight Guest. New York: Dial Press, 1980. Children's stories.

610.2 The Secret of Gumbo Grove. New York: F. Watts, 1987. Children's stories.

611. TAYLOR, GLORIA LEE.

611.1 Dreams for Sale. New York: Exposition Press, 1953. Poetry.

612.   TAYLOR, MILDRED D.   (1943-).

612.1 <u>The Friendship</u>. New York: Dial Press, 1987.
Children's stories.

612.2 <u>The Gold Cadillac</u>. New York: Dial Press, 1987.
Children's stories.

612.3 <u>Let the Circle Be Unbroken</u>. New York: Dial Press,
1981. Children's stories. Sequel to <u>Roll of Thunder, Hear
My Cry</u>.

612.4 "Newbery Award Acceptance Speech." <u>Horn Book</u> 53
(August 1977): 401-409. At the American Library Association
meeting in Chicago, 1977, for <u>Roll of Thunder, Hear My Cry</u> as
the outstanding juvenile book of the year.

612.5 <u>Roll of Thunder, Hear My Cry</u>. New York: Dial Press,
1976. Children's stories. Sequel to <u>Song of the Trees</u>.

612.6 <u>Song of the Trees</u>. New York: Dial Press, 1975.
Children's stories.

Secondary Sources

612.7(S) Fogelman, Phyllis J. "Mildred D. Taylor." <u>Horn
Book</u> 53 (August 1977): 410-414.

613.   TAYLOR, STEPHANIE PARRISH.

613.1 "The Albino." <u>Black American Literature Forum</u> 15
(Spring 1981): 30.

614.   TAYLOR, SUSIE BAKER KING (1848-1912).

614.1 <u>Reminiscences of My Life with the 33d United States
Colored Troops Late 1st S.C. Volunteers</u>. Boston: Author,
1902. New York: Arno Press, 1968. New York: Marcus Wiener,
1988.

Secondary Sources

614.2(S) Katz, William Loren. <u>Eyewitness: The Negro in
American History</u>. New York: Pitman Publishing Company, 1967.

614.3(S) McPherson, James M. <u>The Negro's Civil War: How
American Negroes Felt and Acted During the War of the Union</u>.
New York: Vintage Books, 1965.

614.4(S) Quarles, Benjamin. The Negro in the Civil War.
Boston: Little, 1953.

614.5(S) Shockley, Ann Allen. "Susie Baker King Taylor."
In SHOCKLEY, pp. 312-319.

615. TEISH, LUISAH.

615.1 Jambalaya: The Natural Woman's Book of Personal Charms
and Practical Rituals. San Francisco: Harper, 1985. Based
on author's beliefs about voodoo.

615.2 "Ole Black Emelda." Southern Exposure 10 (4): 22-23
(July-August 1982). Short fiction.

616. TERRY, LUCY (1730-1821).

616.1 "Bars Fight, August 28, 1746." In HUGHES & BONTEMPS.
In STETSON, p. 12. In SHOCKLEY, p. 15.

Secondary Sources

616.2(S) Greene, Lorenzo J. The Negro in Colonial New
England, 1620-1776. New York: Columbia University Press,
1959. Lucy Terry is mentioned on p. 315.

616.3(S) Kaplan, Sidney. The Black Presence in the Era of
the American Revolution, 1770-1800. New York: New York
Graphic Society, 1973. Lucy Terry is mentioned on p. 210.

616.4(S) Katz, Bernard. "A Second Version of Lucy Terry's
Early Ballad." Negro History Bulletin 29 (1966): 183-184.

616.5(S) Robinson, William H. Early Black American Poets.
Dubuque, IA: Wm. C. Brown Pubs., 1969.

616.6(S) Sheldon, George. History of Deerfield,
Massachusetts. Greenfield, MA: Press of E.M. Hall, 1895-
1896. 2 vol. Comments on Lucy Terry, p. 545-549.

616.7(S) Sheldon, George. "Negro Slavery in Old Deerfield,"
New England Magazine 8 (March-August, 1893): 49-60.

616.8(S) Shockley, Ann Allen. "Lucy Terry Prince." In
SHOCKLEY, pp. 13-15.

617. THEUS, MARGARET FULLER.

617.1 My Favorite Thoughts. n.p., n.d.

618. THIBODEAUX, MARY ROGER.

618.1 A Black Nun Looks at Black Power. New York: Sheed and Ward, 1972.

619. THOMAS, IANTHE. (1951-).

619.1 Eliza's Daddy. New York: Harcourt, 1976. Children's stories.

619.2 Hi, Mrs. Mallory!. New York: Harper, 1979. Children's stories.

619.3 My Street's a Morning Cool Street. New York: Harper, 1976. Children's stories.

619.4 Wille Blows a Mean Horn. New York: Harper, 1981.

620. THOMAS, JOYCE CAROL (1938-).

620.1 "Aretha." Black Scholar 7 (May 1976): 59.

620.2 Bittersweet. San Jose, CA: Firesign Press, 1973. Poetry.

620.3 Black Child. New York: Zamani Productions, 1981. Poetry.

620.4 Blessing. Berkeley: Jocato Press, 1975.

620.5 Bright Shadow. New York: Avon Books, 1983. Children's stories. Sequel to Marked by Fire.

620.6 Crystal Breezes. San Jose, CA: Firesign Press, 1974.

620.7 "Hide the Children." American Poetry Review 6 (1): 28 (January-February 1977).

620.8 The Golden Pasture. New York: Scholastic, 1986. Children's stories.

620.9 Inside the Rainbow: Poems. Palo Alto, CA: Zikawuna Press, 1982.

620.10 "Lubelle Berries." Black Scholar 10 (November-December 1978): 18-21. Short fiction .

620.11 <u>Marked by Fire</u>. New York: Avon Books, 1982.
Children's stories.

620.12 <u>Water Girl</u>. New York: Avon Books, 1986. Children's
stories.

621. THOMPSON, CAROLYN.

621.1 <u>Frank</u>. Detroit: Broadside Press, 1970.

622. THOMPSON, CATHY.

622.1 "Composition." <u>Essence</u> 7 (October 1976): 18.

623. THOMPSON, CLARA ANN (1869-1949).

623.1 <u>A Garland of Poems</u>. Boston: Christopher Publishing
House, 1926.

623.2 <u>Songs From the Wayside</u>. Rossmoyne, OH: Author, 1900.

Secondary Sources

623.3(S) Dabney, Wendell P. <u>Cincinnati's Colored Citizens,
Historical, Sociological, and Biographical</u>. Cincinnati:
Dabney Publishing Company, 1926.

623.4(S) Shockley, Ann Allen. "Clara Ann Thompson." In
SHOCKLEY, pp. 320-326.

624. THOMPSON, CLARISSA MINNIE.

624.1 "Treading the Winepress; or, A Mountain of
Misfortune." <u>Boston Advocate</u> 1,2 (1885-86).

Secondary Sources

624.2(S) Haley, James T. <u>Afro-American Encyclopedia; or,
Thoughts, Doings, and Sayings of the Race</u>. Nashville: Haley
& Florida, 1895.

624.3(S) Majors, Monroe Alphus. <u>Noted Negro Women, Their
Triumphs and Activities</u>. New York: Donohue & Henneberry,
1893.

624.4(S) Shockley, Ann Allen.   "Clarissa Minnie Thompson."
In SHOCKLEY, pp. 144-50.

625.   THOMPSON. DIANA R.

625.1 "Bourgeois vs Baptist." Essence 17 (May 1986): 93.

626.   THOMPSON, DOROTHENIA.

626.1 Three Slices of Black. Chicago: Free Black Press,
1972.

627.   THOMPSON, E. B.

627.1 "Message from a Mahogany Blond." Negro Digest 8 (July
1950): 29-33.

628.   THOMPSON, ELOISE BIBB (1878-1928).

628.1 "Mademoiselle 'Tasie -- A Story." Opportunity
3(September 1925):272-76.

628.2 "Masks." Opportunity 5 (October 1927): 300-302.

628.3 Poems by Eloise Bibb. Boston: Monthly Review Press,
1895. Reprinted in Sherman, Joan R., editor. Collected
Black Women's Poetry. New York: Oxford University Press,
1988. Vol. 4.

Secondary Sources

628.4(S) Abajian, James de T. Blacks in Selected
Newspapers, Censuses and Subjects. Boston: G.K. Hall, 1977.

628.5(S) Beasley, Delilah L. The Negro Trail Blazers of
California, 1919. Reprint. New York: Negro Universities
Press, 1969.

628.6(S) Scally, Anthony, Sister. Negro Catholic Writer,
1900-1943: A Bio-Bibliography. Grosse Pointe, MI: Walter
Romig, 1945.

628.7(S) Shockley, Ann Allen. "Eloise Bibb Thompson." In
SHOCKLEY, pp. 233-41.

629.   THOMPSON, PRISCILLA JANE (1871-1924).

629.1 Ethiope Lays. Rossmoyne, OH: Author, 1900.

629.2 Gleanings of Quiet Hours. Rossmoyne, OH: Author, 1907.

Secondary Sources

629.3(S) Coyle, William. Ohio Authors and Their Books: Biographical Data and Selective Bibliographies for Ohio Authors, Native and Resident, 1796-1950. Cleveland: World Publishing Company, 1962.

629.4(S) Dabney, Wendell P. Cincinnati's Colored Citizens, Historical, Sociological, and Biographical. Cincinnati: Dabney Publishing Company, 1926.

629.5(S) Shockley, Ann Allen. "Priscilla Jane Thompson." In SHOCKLEY, pp. 304-311.

630.   TILLMAN, KATHERINE DAVIS.

630.1 Aunt Betsy's Thanksgiving. Philadelphia: A.M.E. Book Concern, 191? One act drama.

630.2 Fifty Years of Freedom; or, From Cabin to Congress: A Drama in Five Acts. Philadelphia: A.M.E. Book Concern, 1910. Drama.

630.3 Thirty Years after Freedom. n.p., n.d. Drama.

631.   TONEY, IEDA MAI.

631.1 To Raise the Dead and Foretell the Future. New York: New Lafayette Theatre, 1970.

631.2 The Young Scholar and Other Poems. Boston: Meador, 1951.

632.   TOWNSEND, WILLA A.

632.1 Because He Lives: A Drama of Resurrection. Nashville: Sunday School Publishing Board of the National Baptist Convention, 1924.

633. TRENT, HELEN.

633.1 **My Memory Gems**. Salisbury, NC: Rowan Printing
Company, 1948.

634. TRUTH, SOJOURNER (1797-1883).

634.1 "Ain't I a Woman?" In STETSON, pp. 24-25. Erlene
Stetson adapted poetry of Truth's speech at Women's Rights
Convention at Akron, OH in 1852.

634.2 **Narrative of Sojourner Truth: A Bondswoman of Olden
Time, Emancipated by the New York Legislature in the Early
Part of the Present Century with a History of Her Labors and
Correspondence**. Boston: Author, 1875.

Secondary Sources

634.3(S) Miller, May. "Sojourner Truth." In RICHARDSON &
MILLER, pp. 313-333. One act drama.

1988-1991 Supplement

Secondary Sources

A634.4(S) Ferris, Jeri. **Walking the Road to Freedom: A
Story About Sojourner Truth**. Minneapolis: Lerner
Publications, 1989.

A634.5(S) Krass, Peter. **Sojourner Truth**. New York: Chelsea
House, 1989.

635. TURNER, BESSYE TOBIAS.

635.1 **La Librae: An Anthology of Poetry For the Living**.
Detroit: Harlo Press, 1968.

636. TURNER, FAITH M.

636.1 **Getting to Know Me**. Washington, DC: Author, 1975.

637. TURNER, GLADYS T. (1935-).

637.1 <u>Autobiography of Tammy: A Life Full of Love and Fun</u>.
Dayton, OH: Challenge, 1978. Children's stories.

637.2 <u>Bus Ride in Alabama: A Children's Story</u>. Dayton, OH:
Challenge, 1980.

637.3 <u>Papa Babe's Stamp Collection</u>. New York: Exposition
Press, 1983. Children's stories.

638. TURNER, JONETTA.

638.1 "Beautiful Mississippi." <u>Black World</u> 22 (September
1973): 66.

639. TURNER. LUCY MAE.

639.1 <u>'Bout Cullud Folkses</u>. New York: H. Harrison, 1938.
Poetry.

640. TYNES, BERYL EWEL.

640.1 <u>Penpoint Drippings</u>. Lynchburg, VA: Author, 1935.

641. VAUGHT, ESTELLA V.

641.1 <u>Vengeance Is Mine</u>. New York: Comet Press Books, 1959.

642. VENEY, BETHANY.

642.1 <u>The Narrative of Bethany Veney, or Aunt Betty's Story</u>.
Author, 1889.

643. VROMAN, MARY ELIZABETH (1923-1967).

643.1 <u>Esther</u>. New York: Bantam Books, 1963. Novel.

643.2 <u>Harlem Summer</u>. New York: Putnam, 1967. New York:
Berkeley Publishing Corporation, 1968. Novel.

643.3 "See How They Run." Negro Digest 10 (November 1951)
52-68.

643.4 Shaped To its Purpose: Delta Sigma Theta, the First
Fifty Years. New York: Random House, 1965.

                    Secondary Sources

643.5(S) Blicksilver, Edith. "Mary Elizabeth Vroman." In
DAVIS & HARRIS, pp.255-258.

Wade-Gayles, Gloria. SEE 240. GAYLES, GLORIA.

644. WALKER, ALICE (1944-).

644.1 "Abduction of Saints." Freedomways 15 (4): 266-267
(1975).

644.2 "The Abortion." Mother Jones 5 (August 1980): 30.
Short fiction.

644.3 "Advancing Luna -- And Ida B. Wells." Ms. 5 (July
1977): 75-76. Short fiction.

644.4 "Am I Blue?" Ms. 15 (July 1986): 29-30. Essay on the
feeling of animals.

644.5 "America Should Have Closed Down on the First Day a
Black Woman Observed That the Supermarket Collard Greens
Tasted Like Water." Ms. 5 (April 1977): 46.

644.6 "Anais Nin: 1903-1977." Ms. 5 (April 1977): 46.
Essay.

644.7 "Attentiveness." Essence 15 (October 1984): 90.

644.8 "Beyond the Peacock: The Reconstruction of Flannery
O'Connor." Ms. 4 (December 1975): 77-79.

644.9 "The Black Writer and the Southern Experience." New
South 25 (Fall 1970): 23-26.

644.10 "Black Writer's Views on Literary Lions and Values."
Negro Digest 17 (January 1968): 13.

644.11 "Burial." Harper's Magazine 244 (March 1972): 73.

644.12 "But Yet and Still, the Cotton Gin Kept on Working."
Black Scholar 1 (January/February 1970): 17-21; 14
(September/October 1983.

644.13 "Can I Be My Brother's Sister?" Ms. 4 (October 1975): 64-67.

644.14 "China: A Poet Takes Snapshots in Her Mind, Meets Trees and Relatives, and Learns That She Writes in Chinese." Ms. 13 (March 1985): 51-52, 54, 106-107. Essay.

644.15 "The Civil Rights Movement: What Good Was It?" American Scholar 36 (4): 550-554 (Autumn 1967).

644.16 The Color Purple. New York: Harcourt, 1982. Novel.

644.17 "Cuddling." Essence 16 (July 1985): 74-76. Short fiction.

644.18 "The Diamonds on Liz's Bosom." Vanity Fair 47 (September 1984): 110.

644.19 "Diary of an African Nun." Freedomways 8 (Summer 1968): 226-229.

644.20 "Did This Happen to Your Mother? Did Your Sister Throw Up a Lot?" Ms. 6(February 1978): 41.

644.21 "Each One Pull One." Freedomways 11 (1980): 87-89.

644.22 "Embracing the Dark and the Light." Essence 13 (July 1982): 67, 114, 117-118, 121. Essay.

644.23 "Eudora Welty: An Interview." Harvard Advocate 106 (Winter 1973): 68-72.

644.24 "Every Morning." Ladies Home Journal 192 (May 1985): 103.

644.25 "Facing the Way." Freedomways 15 (4): 265-266 (1975).

644.26 "Family Of." Freedomways 21 (1): 46-47 (1981).

644.27 "Father: For What You Were." Essence 16 (May 1985): 93-94, 96. Essay.

644.28 "Finding Celie's Voice." Ms. 14 (December 1985): 71-72. Essay.

644.29 "First Day (A Fable after Brown)." Freedomways 14 (4): 314-316 (1974).

644.30 Five Poems. Detroit: Broadside Press, 1972.

644.31 "For My Sister Molly." Harper's Magazine 244 (March 1972): 72.

644.32 "Forgive Me If My Praises." Black Scholar 10 (November-December 1978): 78.

644.33 "Forgiveness." Freedomways 15 (4): 267 (1975).

644.34   "From the Alice Walker Journals."   _Sage_ 2 (2): 53
(Spring 1985).

644.35   "Gift."   _Essence_ 3 (July 1972): 6.

644.36   _Good Night Willie Lee, I'll See You In the Morning:_
Poems. New York: Dial Press, 1979

644.37   "Gray."   _Callaloo_ 2 (February 1979): 63.

644.38   _Horses Make a Landscape Look More Beautiful: Poems_.
New York: Harcourt, 1984.

644.39   "How Did I Get Away with Killing One of the Biggest
Lawyers in the State?"   _Ms._ 9 (November 1980): 72, 75.   Short
fiction.

644.40   "How Poems Are Made/a Discredited View."   _Freedomways_
24 (2): 97 (1984).   _Vanity Fair_ 47 (September 1984): 110.

644.41   _I Love Myself When I Am Laughing, and Then Again When_
I Am Looking Mean and Impressive: A Zora Neale Hurston
Reader. Old Westbury, NY: Feminist Press, 1979.   Edited by
Alice Walker.

644.42   "I Must Whistle Like a Woman Undaunted."   _Essence_ 15
(October 1984): 90.

644.43   "If the Present Looks Like the Past, What Does the
Future Look Like?..."   _Heresies_ 4 (3): 56-59 (1982).   Essay.

644.44   "If Those People Like You."   _Ms._ 7 (April 1979): 21.

644.45   "I'm Really Very Fond."   _Ms._ 7 (April 1979): 21.

644.46   _In Love and Trouble: Stories of Black Women_.   New
York: Harcourt, 1973.

644.47   "In Search of Our Mother's Gardens." _Ms._ 2(May
1974):64-70.   _Southern Exposure_ 4 (4): 60-84 (1976). Essay.

644.48   _In Search of Our Mother's Gardens: Womanist Prose_.
New York: Harcourt, 1983.   Essays.

644.49   "In Search of Zora Neale Hurston."   _Ms._ 3 (March
1975): 74-79, 85-89.

644.50   "In the Closet of the Soul: A Letter to an African-
American Friend."   _Ms._ 15 (November 1986): 32-33.   Essay on
the character of "Mister" in _The Color Purple_.

644.51   "In These Dissenting Times."   _Black World_ 20
(November 1970): 60-63.

644.52   "Janie Crawford."   _Black Collegian_ 9 (May-June 1979):
93.

644.53   "Judith Jamisom."   _Ms._ 1 (May 1973): 66-67.

644.54 "Kindred Spirits." _Esquire_ 104 (August 1985): 106-111. Short fiction.

644.55 _Langston Hughes, American Poet_. New York: Thomas Crowell, 1974.

644.56 "Laurel." _Ms._ 7 (November 1978): 64-66, 83-84. Short fiction.

644.57 "A Letter of the Times, or Should This Sado-masochism Be Saved?" _Ms._ 11 (October 1981): 62-64. Short fiction.

644.58 "Letters Forum: Anti-Semitism." _Ms._ 11 (February 1983): 13, 15-16. Essay.

644.59 _The Life of Thomas Lodge_. Folcroft, PA: Folcroft, 1974. (Reprint of 1933 ed.)

644.60 _Living by the Word: Selected Writings, 1973-1987_. New York: Harcourt, 1988.

644.61 "Love Is Not Concerned." _Essence_ 15 (6): 91 (October 1984).

644.62 "The Lover." _Essence_ 12 (April 1981): 87, 132, 135, 137-138. Short fiction.

644.63 "Lulls." _Black Scholar_ 7 (May 1976): 3-12.

644.64 "Lulls -- A Native Daughter Returns To the South." _Ms._ 5 (January 1977): 58-61, 89-90. Essay.

644.65 "Malcolm." _Black Collegian_ 9 (May-June 1979): 93.

644.66 _Meridian_. New York: Harcourt, 1976. Novel.

644.67 "Meridian." _Essence_ 7 (July 1976): 73-78. Novel. Excerpt.

644.68 "Mississippi Winter II." _Vanity Fair_ 47 (September 1984): 110.

644.69 "Mississippi Winter III." _Vanity Fair_ 47 (September 1984): 110.

644.70 "Mississippi Winter IV." _Essence_ 15 (October 1984): 91.

644.71 "My Daughter Is Coming." _Callaloo_ 2 (February 1979): 33.

644.72 "My Father's Country Is the Poor." _Black Scholar_ 8 (Summer 1977): 40-43. Essay.

644.73 "New Face." _Essence_ 14 (November 1983): 122.

644.74 "1955, or, You Can't Keep a Good Woman Down." <u>Ms.</u> 9
(March 1981): 54, 57, 85-87. Short fiction.

644.75 "Nobody Can Watch the Wasichu." <u>Freedomways</u> 24 (2):
99 (1984).

644.76 "Nuclear Exorcism: Beyond Cursing the Day We Were
Born." <u>Mother Jones Journal</u> 7 (8): 20-21 (September-October
1982). Essay.

644.77 "Olive Oil." <u>Ms.</u> 14 (August 1985): 35-36, 78. Short
fiction.

644.78 <u>Once: Poems</u>. New York: Harcourt, 1968.

644.79 "One Child of One's Own: A Meaningful Digression
Within the Work[s]." In STERNBURG, pp. 121-140. <u>Ms.</u> 8
(August 1979): 47-50, 72-75. Essay on childbirth and
creativity.

644.80 "Other Voices, Other Moods." <u>Ms.</u> 7 (February 1979):
50-51, 70. Essay.

644.81 "Overnights." <u>Callaloo</u> 2 (February 1979): 109.

644.82 "Poem At Thirty-Nine." <u>Ms.</u> 11 (June 1983): 101.

644.83 "Redemption Day." <u>Mother Jones</u> 11 (December 1986):
43-45.

644.84 "Remembering Mr. Sweet." <u>New York Times Book Review</u>
(May 1988): 33.

644.85 "Revenge of Hannah Kemhuff." <u>Ms.</u> 2 (July 1973): 70-
72. Short fiction.

644.86 <u>Revolutionary Petunias & Other Poems</u>. New York:
Harcourt, 1973.

644.87 "Rock Eagle." <u>Freedomways</u> 11 (4): 367 (1971).

644.88 "S M." <u>Freedomways</u> 24 (2): 96 (1984).

644.89 "Secrets of the New Cuba." <u>Ms.</u> 5 (September 1977):
71-72, 74, 96-99. Essay.

644.90 "Silver Writes." <u>Perspectives: The Civil Rights
Quarterly</u> 14 (1982): 22-23. Essay on the term "civil
rights."

644.91 "Sojourner." <u>Ms.</u> 4 (May 1976): 67-71.

644.92 "Something You Done Wrong." <u>Mother Jones Journal</u> 7
(5): 32-35 (June 1982).

644.93 "Songless." <u>Freedomways</u> 24 (2): 98 (1984).

644.94 "South." <u>Freedomways</u> 11 (4): 368 (1971).

644.95 "Staying at Home in Mississippi: Ten Years After the March On Washington." New York Times Magazine (26 August 1973): 9.

644.96 "The Strangest Dinner Party I Ever Went To." Ms. 11 (1-2): 58 (July/August 1982).

644.97 "Strong Horse Tea." Negro Digest 17 (June 1968): 53-60.

644.98 "A Sudden Trip Home in the Spring." Essence 2 (September 1971): 58-59. Short fiction.

644.99 A Talk by Alice Walker, '65: Convocation 1972." Sarah Lawrence Alumni Magazine (Summer 1972).

644.100 "Talking To My Grandmother Who Died Poor Some Years Ago (While Listening To Richard Nixon Declare 'I'm Not a Crook')." Black Scholar 6 (June 1965): 62; 12 (November-December 1981): 25.

644.101 The Temple of My Familiar. New York: Harcourt, 1989. Novel.

644.102 "These Mornings of Rain." Essence 15 (October 1984): 91.

644.103 "Thief." Essence 3 (July 1972): 6.

644.104 The Third Life of George Copeland. New York: Harcourt, 1970. Redbook 137 (May 1971): 173-195.

644.105 To Hell with Dying. New York: Harcourt, 1988. Readers Digest (October 1983): 110-114 (condensed). Children's stories.

644.106 "Uncle Remus, No Friend of Mine." Southern Exposure 9 (2): 29-31 (Summer 1981). Essay.

644.107 "The Unglamorous but Worthwhile Duties of the Black Revolutionary Artist, Or of the Black Writer Who Simply Works and Writes." Black Collegian 2 (1): 5 (September/October 1971).

644.108 Untitled Poem. Freedomways 24 (2): 95-96 (1984).

644.109 "View from Rosehill Cemetery: A Tribute to Dr. Martin Luther King, Jr." South Today 4 (1973): 11.

644.110 "Walker." Essence 15 (October 1984): 91.

644.111 "We Alone." Freedomways 24 (2): 97 (1984).

644.112 "When a Tree Falls." Ms. 12 (January 1984): 48, 52-53, 55. Essay.

644.113   "When Golda Meir Was in Africa." Black Scholar 10
(6-7): 8 (March/April 1979). Ms. (April 1979): 21.

644.114   "When the Other Dancer Is the Self." Ms. 11 (May
1983): 70, 72, 142-143. Essay.

644.115   "When We Held Our Marriage." Nimrod 21 (2-22): 296
(1977).

644.116   "When Women Confront Porn at Home." Ms. 8 (February
1980): 67, 69-70. Short fiction.

644.117   "Women." Essence 11 (May 1980): 102.

644.118   You Can't Keep a Good Woman Down: Stories. New
York: Harcourt, 1981.

644.119   "Your Soul Shines." Nimrod 21 (2-22): 296 (1977).

Secondary Sources

644.120(S)   Abramson, Pam.   "Alice Walker Makes the Big Time
with Black Folk Tales." California Living (15 August 1982):
16-20.

644.121(S)   Anello, Ray.   "Characters In Search of a Book."
Newsweek 99 (21 June 1982): 67. Alice Walker's The Color
Purple.

644.122(S)   Babb, Valerie.   "The Color Purple: Writing To
Undo What Writing Has Done." Phylon 47 (2): 107-116 (June
1986).

644.123(S)   Baker, Houston and Pierce-Baker, Charlotte.
"Patches: Quilts and Community in Alice Walker's 'Everyday
Use.' " The Southern Review 21 (3): 706-720 (July 1985).

644.124(S)   Blount, Marcellus.   "A Woman Speaks." Callaloo 6
(1): 118-122 (1983).   On Alice Walker's The Color Purple.

644.125(S)   Brewer, Krista.   "Writing To Survive: An
Interview with Alice Walker." Southern Exposure 9 (2): 12-15
(Summer 1981).

644.126(S)   Buncombe, Marie H.   "Androgyny As Metaphor in
Alice Walker's Novels." CLA Journal 30 (June 1987): 419-427.

644.127(S)   Burnett, Zaron W.   "The Color Purple: Personal
Reaction." Catalyst 1 (Fall 1986): 43-44.

644.128(S)   Byerman, Keith E.   "Women's Blues: The Fiction of
Toni Cade Bambara and Alice Walker." In BYERMAN, pp. 104-
170.

644.129(S)   Byrd, Rudolph P.   "Sound Advice From a Friend:
Words and Thoughts From the Higher Ground of Alice Walker."

<u>Callaloo</u> 6 (1): 123-129 (1983). On <u>In Search of Our Mothers'</u>
<u>Gardens</u>.

644.130(S) Callahan, John. "The Higher Ground of Alice
Walker." <u>The New Republic</u> (September 14, 1974): 21-22.

644.131(S) Chambers, Kimberly R. "Right on Time: History
and Religion in Alice Walker's <u>The Color Purple</u>." <u>CLA</u>
<u>Journal</u> 31 (September 1987): 44-62.

644.132(S) Christian, Barbara. "Alice Walker." In DAVIS &
HARRIS, pp. 258-271. Biography and bibliography.

644.133(S) Christian, Barbara. "The Contrary Black Women of
Alice Walker: A Study of Female Protagonist in <u>In Love and</u>
<u>Trouble</u>." <u>Black Scholar</u> 12 (March, April 1981): 21-30, 70-
71.

644.134(S) Christian, Barbara. "Novels for Everyday Use:
The Novels of Alice Walker." In CHRISTIAN, pp. 190-238.

644.135(S) Christian, Barbara. "We Are the Ones That Have
Been Waiting For: Political Content in Alice Walker's
Novels." <u>Women's Studies International Forum</u> 9 (4): 421-426
(1986).

644.136(S) Coleman, Viralene J. "Miss Celie's Song."
<u>Publication of the Arkansas Philological Association</u> 11
(Spring 1985): 27-34.

644.137(S) Cooke, Michael G. "Recent Novels: Women Bearing
Violence." <u>Yale Review</u> 66 (1): 146-155 (October 1976).

644.138(S) Davis, Thadious M. "Alice Walker." In KIBLER,
pp. 350-358. Includes biography and bibliography.

644.139(S) Davis, Thadious M. "Alice Walker's Celebration
of Self in Southern Generations." <u>Southern Quarterly</u> 31 (4):
39-53 (Summer 1983). Commentaries on some short fiction.

644.140(S) Dawson, Emma J. Waters. "Images of the Afro-
American Female Character in Jean Toomer's <u>Cane</u>, Zora Neale
Hurston's <u>Their Eyes Were Watching God</u> and Alice Walker's <u>The</u>
<u>Color Purple</u>." Dissertation, University of South Florida,
1987.

644.141(S) Dworkin, Susan. "The Strange and Wonderful Story
of the Making of <u>The Color Purple</u>." <u>Ms.</u> 14 (December 1985):
66-70, 94-95.

644.142(S) El Saffar, Ruth. "Alice Walker's <u>The Color</u>
<u>Purple</u>." <u>The International Fiction Review</u> 12 (1): 11-17
(Winter 1985).

644.143(S) Erickson, Peter. "Cast Out Alone/To Heal/and Re-
create/Ourselves: Family Based Identity in the Work of Alice
Walker." <u>CLA Journal</u> 23 (September 1979): 71-94.

644.144(S) Fifer, Elizabeth. "A Bibliography of Writings by
Alice Walker." In RAINWATER, pp. 165-171.

644.145(S) Fishman, Charles. "Naming Names: Three Recent
Novels by Women Writers." Names 32 (March 1984): 33-44.

644.146(S) Fontenot, Chester J. "Alice Walker: 'The Diary
of an African Nun' and DuBois Double Consciousness." Journal
of Afro-American Issues 5 (2): 192-196 (Spring 1977).

644.147(S) Fontenot, Chester J. "Modern Black Fiction from
Tragedy to Romance." Cornell Review 3 (Spring 1978): 115-
123.

644.148(S) Freeman, Alice S. "Zora Neale Hurston and Alice
Walker: A Spiritual Kinship." Sage 2 (1): 37-40 (Spring
1985).

644.149(S) Gaston, Karen Carmean. "The Theme of Female
Self-Discovery in the Novels of Judith Rossner, Gail Godwin,
Alice Walker and Toni Morrison." Dissertation, Auburn
University, 1980.

644.150(S) Gaston, Karen C. "Women in the Lives of Grange
Copeland." CLA Journal 24 (March 1981): 276-286.

644.151(S) Goldstein, William. "Alice Walker on the Set of
The Color Purple." Publishers Weekly (6 September 1985): 46-
48.

644.152(S) Guy-Sheftall, Beverly. "Literary Profile: Alice
Walker, You Can Go Home Again." Black Southerner 1 (June
1984): 9.

644.153(S) Harris, Jessica. "Interview with Alice Walker."
Essence 7 (July 1976).

644.154(S) Harris, Trudier. "The Color Purple as the
Culmination of Alice Walker's Portrayal of Black Women."
Studies in American Fiction 14 (Spring 1986): 1-17.

644.155(S) Harris, Trudier. "Folklore in the Fiction of
Alice Walker: A Perpetuation of Historical and Literary
Traditions." Black American Literature Forum 2 (Spring
1977): 3-8.

644.156(S) Harris, Trudier. "From Victimization to Free
Enterprise: Alice Walker's The Color Purple." Studies in
American Fiction 14 (Spring 1986): 1-17.

644.157(S) Harris, Trudier. "On The Color Purple,
Sterotypes, and Silence." Black American Literature Forum 18
(Winter 1984): 155-161.

644.158(S) Harris, Trudier. "Tiptoeing Through Taboo:
Incest in 'The Child Who Favored Daughter.' " Modern Fiction
Studies 28 (3): 495-505 (Autumn 1982).

644.159(S)   Harris, Trudier. "Violence in The Third Life of Grange Copeland." CLA Journal 19 (December 1975): 238-247.

644.160(S)   Hellenbrand, Harold. "Speech, After Silence: Alice Walker's The Third Life of Grange Copeland." Black American Literature Forum 20 (1-2): 113-128 (Spring/Summer 1986).

644.161(S)   Henderson, Mae G. "The Color Purple: Revisions and Redefinitions." Sage 2 (1): 14-18 (Spring 1985). Comments on the format of Alice Walker's novel.

644.162(S)   Hiers, John T. "Creation Theology in Alice Walker's The Color Purple." Notes on Contemporary Literature 14 (September 1984): 2-3.

644.163(S)   Higgins, Chester A. "Pulitzer Beginning To Do Something Right." Crisis 90 (June-July 1983): 49.

644.164(S)   Hogue, W. Lawrence. "History, the Feminist Discourse, and Alice Walker's The Third Life of Grange Copeland." Melus 12 (2): 45-62 (Summer 1985).

644.165(S)   Kearns, Katherine Sue. "Some Versions of Violence in Three Contemporary American Novels: John Irving's The World According to Garp, Tim O'Brien's Going After Cacciato, and Alice Walker's The Color Purple." Dissertation, University of North Carolina (Chapel Hill), 1982.

644.166(S)   Kirschner, Susan. "Alice Walker's Nonfictional Prose: A Checklist, 1966-1984." Black American Literature Forum 18 (Winter 1984): 162-163.

644.167(S)   Krauth, Leland. "Mark Twain, Alice Walker, and the Aesthetics of Joy." Proteus (Fall 1984): 9-24.

644.168(S)   Lee, Dorothy. "Three Black Plays: Alienation and Paths to Recovery." Modern Drama 19 (December 1976): 397-404. Alice Walker play discussed with plays of Gordone and Elder.

644.169(S)   Lupton, Mary Jane. "Clothes and Closure in Three Novels by Black Women." Black American Literature Forum 20 (4): 409-421 (Winter 2986).

644.170(S)   McDowell, Deborah E. "The Self in Bloom: Alice Walker's Meridian." CLA Journal 24 (March 1981): 262-275.

644.171(S)   McGowan, Martha J. "Atonement and Release in Alice Walker's Meridian." Critique 23 (1): 25-36 (Fall 1981-82).

644.172(S)   Malone, Gloria Snodgrass. "The Nature and Causes of Suffering in the Fiction of Paule Marshall, Kristin Hunter, Toni Morrison, and Alice Walker." Dissertation, Kent State University, 1979.

644.173(S) Mickelson, Anne Z. "Winging Upward: Black Women:
Sarah E. Wright, Toni Morrison, Alice Walker." In
MICKELSON, pp. 112-124.

644.174(S) Nadel, Alan. "Reading the Body: Alice Walker's
Meridian and the Archaeology of Self." Modern Fiction
Studies 34 (Spring 1988): 55.

644.175(S) Nedelhaft, Ruth. "Domestic Violence in
Literature: A Preliminary Study." Mosaic 17 (2): 242-259
(Spring 1984).

644.176(S) Norment, Lunn. "The Color Purple: Controversial
Prize-Winning Book Becomes an Equally Controversial Movie."
Ebony 41 (February 1986): 146, 148, 150, 155.

644.177(S) Nowik, Nan. "Mixing Art and Politics: The
Writings of Adrienne Rich, Marge Piercy, and Alice Walker.
The Centennial Review 30 (2): 208-218 (Spring 1986).

644.178(S) Parker-Smith, Bettye J. "Alice Walker's Women:
In Search of Some Peace of Mind." In   EVANS, pp. 478-493.

644.179(S) Pratt, Louis H. and Pratt, Darnell D. Alice
Malsenior Walker: An Annotated Bibliography: 1968-1986.
Westport, CT: Meckler Corporation, 1988.

644.180(S) Rose, Pat. "Growing Books at Wild Tree Press."
Small Press 4 (2): 30-35 (November-December 1986). On the
establishment of a small press by Alice Walker and Robert
Allen.

644.181(S) Ross, Daniel W. "Celie in the Looking Glass: The
Desire for Selfhood in The Color Purple. Modern Fiction
Studies 34 (Spring 1988): 89.

644.182(S) Royster, Philip M. "In Search of Our Fathers'
Arms: Alice Walker's Persona of the Alienated Darling."
Black American Literature Forum 20 (4): 347-370 (Winter
1986).

644.183(S) Sadoff, Dianne F. "Black Matrilineage: The Case
of Alice Walker and Zora Neale Hurston." Signs 11 (1): 4-26
(Autumn 1985).

644.184(S) Shelton, Frank W. "Alienation and Integration in
Alice Walker's The Color Purple." CLA Journal 28 (4): 383-
392 (June 1985).

644.185(S) Smith, Barbara. "Sexual Oppression Unmasked."
Callaloo 7 (3): 170-176 (1984).

644.186(S) Stade, George. "Womanist Fiction and Male
Characters." Partisan Review 52 (3): 264-270 (1985). .

644.187(S) Stein, Karen F. "Meridian: Alice Walker's
Critique of Revolution." Black American Literature Forum 20
(1-2): 129-141 (Spring/Summer 1986).

644.188(S)   Steinem, Gloria.   "Do You Know This Woman?   She Knows You -- A Profile of Alice Walker."   Ms. 10 (June 1982): 35-37, 89-94.

644.189(S)   Tate, Claudia.   "Alice Walker."   In TATE, pp. 175-187.

644.190(S)   Tavormina, M. Teresa.   "Dressing the Spirit: Clothworking and Language in The Color Purple."   Journal of Narrative Technique 16 (1986): 220-230.

644.191(S)   Turner, Darwin T.   "A Spectrum of Blackness." Parnassys 4 (2): 202-218 (Spring-Summer 1976).   Comparison of works of Alice Walker and Ishmael Reed.

644.192(S)   Walker, Robbie.   "Coping Strategies of the Women in Alice Walker's Novels: Implications for Survival."   CLA Journal 30 (4): 401-418 (June 1987).

644.193(S)   Walsh, Margaret.   "The Enchanted World of The Color Purple."   Southern Quarterly 25 (1987): 89-101.

644.194(S)   Washington, Mary Helen.   "An Essay on Alice Walker."   In BELL, pp.133-149.

644.195(S)   Washington, Mary Helen.   "Her Mother's Gifts." Ms. 10 (June 1982): 38.   Alice Walker and her mother.

644.196(S)   Wesley, Richard.   "The Color Purple: Debate, Reading Bewteen the Lines."   Ms. 13 (September 1986): 62, 90-92.   On Alice Walker's novel movie version.

644.197(S)   Williamson, Alan.   "In a Middle Style."   Poetry 135 (6): 353-354 (March 1980).

644.198(S)   Willis, Susan.   "Alice Walker's Women."   New Orleans Review 12 (1): 33-41 (Spring 1985).

644.199(S)   Winchell, Mark Royden.   "Fetching the Doctor: Shamanistic House Calls in Alice Walker's 'Strong Horse Tea'."   Mississippi Folklore Register 5 (2): 97-101 (Fall 1981).

644.200(S)   Worthington, Pepper.   "Writing a Rationale For a Controversial Common Reading Book: Alice Walker's The Color Purple."   English Journal 74 (January 1985): 48-52.

1988-1991 Supplement

A644.201   Her Blue Body Everything We Know: Earthling Poems 1965-1990 Complete.   New York: Harcourt, 1991.

A644.202   "Marriage vs Freedom."   Essence 20 (May 1989): 81. Excerpt from The Temple of My Familiar.

A644.203   "Notes from My Journal."   Essence 19 (July 1988): 71. Essay.

A644.204 "Turning into Love: Some Thoughts on Surviving and Meeting Langston Hughes." Callaloo 12 (Fall 1989): 663.

Secondary Sources

A644.205(S) Bloom, Harold. Alice Walker. New York: Chelsea House, 1989.

A644.206(S) Bobo, Jacqueline. "Sifting Through the Controversy: Reading The Color Purple." Callaloo 12 (Spring 1989): 332.

A644.207(S) Brown, Joseph A. " 'All Saints Should Walk Away': The Mystical Pilgrimage of Meridian." Callaloo 12 (Spring 1989): 310.

A644.208(S) Butler, Robert James. "Making a Way Out of No Way: The Open Journey in Alice Walker's The Third Life of George Copeland." Black American Literature Forum 22 (Spring 1988): 65.

A644.209(S) Butler-Evans, Elliott. Race, Gender, and Desire: Narrative Strategies in the Fiction of Toni Cade Bambara, Toni Morrison and Alice Walker. Philadelphia: Temple University Press, 1989.

A644.210(S) Byerman, Keith. "Desire and Alice Walker: The Quest for a Womanist Narrative." WPWPCCOM 12 (Spring 1989): 321.

A644.211(S) Byerman, Keith and Banks, Erma, compilers. "Alice Walker: Bibliography, 1968-1988." Callaloo 12 (Spring 1989): 343.

A644.212(S) DeVeaux, Alexis. "Alice Walker." Essence 20 (September 1989): 56.

A644.213(S) Hamilton, Cynthia. "Alice Walker's Politics of The Color Purple." Journal of Black Studies 18 (March 1988): 379.

A644.214(S) Hudson-Weems, Clenora. "The Tripartite Plight of African-American Women as Reflected in the Novels of Hurston and Walker." Journal of Black Studies 20 (December 1989): 192.

A644.215(S) Marsh, Carole. "The Color Purple" and All That Jazz. Bath, NC: Gallopade, 1989.

A644.216(S) Mason, Theodore O., Jr. "Alice Walker's The Third Life of George Copeland: The Dynamics of Enclosure." Callaloo 12 (Spring 1989): 297.

A644.217(S) Roses, Lorraine and Randolph, Ruth E., The Harlem Renaissance and Beyond: 100 Black Women Writers, 1900-1950. Boston: G.K. Hall, 1989.

644.218(S) Tucker, Lindsey. "Alice Walker's <u>The Color
Purple</u>: Emerging Woman, Emergent Text." <u>Black American
Literature Forum</u> 18 (March 1988): 81.

A644.219(S) Washington, J. Charles. "Positive Black Male
Images in Alice Walker's Fiction." <u>Obsidian II</u> 3 (Spring
1988): 23.

645. WALKER, MARGARET (1915-).

645.1 "Ballad for Phillis Wheatley." <u>Ebony</u> 25 (March 1974):
96.

645.2 <u>Ballad of the Free</u>. Detroit: Broadside Press, 1966.

645.3 "Birmingham 1963." "Black Paramour." "My Mississippi
Spring." <u>Southern Review</u> 21 (3): 827-829 (July 1985).

645.4 "Black Writer's Views on Literary Lions and Values."
<u>Negro Digest</u> 17 (January 1968): 23.

645.5 <u>The Daemonic Genius of Richard Wright</u>. New York:
Warner, 1988

645.6 "Daydream." <u>Crisis</u> 77 (November 1970): 368.

645.7 <u>For Farish Streen Green</u>. n.p., 1986.

645.8 <u>For My People</u>. New Haven, CT: Yale University, 1942.
Poetry.

645.9 "For My People." <u>Ebony</u> 35 (September 1980): 151.

645.10 <u>How I Wrote "Jubilee."</u> Chicago: Third World Press,
1972.

645.11 "The Humanistic Tradition of Afro-American
Literature." <u>American Libraries</u> 1 (October 1970): 849-854.

645.12 "I Hear a Rumbling." <u>Great Lakes Review</u> 8-9 (2-1):
96-98 (Fall 1982-Spring 1983).

645.13 "Inflation Blues." <u>Black Scholar</u> 11 (5): 74 (May-
June 1980).

645.14 <u>Jubilee</u>. Boston: Houghton, 1966.

645.15 "Nausea of Sartre." <u>Yale Review</u> 42 (December 1952):
251-261.

645.16 "New Poets." In GAYLE.

645.17 <u>October Journey</u>. Detroit: Broadside Press, 1973.
Poetry.

645.18 <u>Prophets for a New Day</u>. Detroit: Broadside Press,
1970.

645.19 <u>Richard Wright, Daemonic Genius: A Portrait of the
Man, a Critical Look at His Work</u>. New York: Amistad, 1985.

645.20 "Some Aspects of the Black Aesthetic." <u>Freedomways</u>
16 (Second Quarter 1976): 95-103. Essay.

645.21 "They Have Put Us On Hold." <u>Black Scholar</u> 12
(September-October 1981): 25.

645.22 <u>This is My Country: New and Collected Poems</u>. Athens,
GA: University of Georgia Press, 1988.

645.23 "Tribute Robert Hayden." <u>Black Scholar</u> 4 (April
1980): 75.

645.24 "Willing to Pay the Price." In WORMLEY & FENDERSON,
pp. 119-130. Autobiographical statement.

645.25 <u>A Poetic Equation: Conversations Between Nikki
Giovanni and Margaret Walker</u>. Washington, DC: Howard
University Press, 1974. Reprinted with new postscript, 1983.
Nikki Giovanni, joint author.

Secondary Sources

645.26(S) Egejuru, Phanuel and Fox, Robert Elliot. "An
Interview with Margaret Walker." <u>Callaloo</u> 2 (2): 29-35
(1979).

645.27(S) Emanuel, James A. "Margaret Walker." In VINSON.

645.28(S) Freibert, Lucy M. "Southern Song: An Interview
with Margaret Walker." <u>Frontiers</u> 9 (3): 50-56 (1987).

645.29(S) Giddings, Paula. "A Shoulder Hunched Against a
Sharp Concern: Some Themes in the Poetry of Margaret Walker."
<u>Black World</u> 21 (December 1971): 20-25.

645.30(S) Klotman, Phyllis Rauch. "Oh Freedom -- Women and
History in Margaret Walker's <u>Jubilee</u>." <u>Black American
Literature Forum</u> 2 (Winter 1977): 139-145.

645.31(S) Miller, R. Baxter. "The 'Etched Flame' of
Margaret Walker: Biblical and Literary Re-creation in
Southern History." <u>Tennessee Studies in Literature</u> 26
(1981): 157-172.

645.32(S) Powell, Bertie J. "Black Experience in Margaret
Walker's <u>Jubilee</u> and Lorraine Hansberry's <u>The Drinking
Gourd</u>." <u>CLA Journal</u> 21 (December 1977): 304-311.

645.33(S) Rowell, Charles H. "Poetry, History, and Humanism: An Interview with Margaret Walker." Black World 24 (December 1975): 4-17.

645.34(S) Scarupa, Harriet Jackson. "Margaret Walker Alexander." American Visions 1 (2): 48-52 (March-April 1986).

645.35(S) Spears, James E. "Black Folk Elements in Margaret Walker's Jubilee." Mississippi Folklore Register 14 (Spring 1980): 13-19.

645.36(S) Traylor, Eleanor W. " 'Bolder Measures Crashing Through': Margaret Walker's Poem of the Century." Callaloo 10 (4): 570-595 (Fall 1987).

1988-1991 Supplement

A645.37 "Goodbye, Sweetwater." Black American Literature Forum 22 (Summer 1988): 155.

A645.38 How I Wrote "Jubilee" and Other Essays on Life and Literature. New York: Feminist Press, 1990.

A645.39 "The Mysterious Death of Richard Wright." Ebony 44 (February 1989): 116.

A645.40 "The Telly Boob-Tube on the Idiot Box." Black Scholar 19 (July/August-September/October 1988): 56. Poem.

Secondary Sources

A645.41(S) Collier, Eugenia. "Elemental Wisdom in Goodbye, Sweetwater: Suggestions for Further Study." Black American Literature Forum 22 (Summer 1988): 192.

646. WALLACE, ELIZABETH WEST.

646.1 Scandal at Daybreak. New York: Pageant Press, 1954. Novel.

647. WALLACE, MICHELE (1952-).

647.1 "Baby Faith." Ms. 16 (July-August 1987): 154. Biographical essay.

647.2 Black Macho and the Myth of the Superwoman. New York: Dial Press, 1978. Controversial non-fiction on African-American women in America.

647.3 "The Envelope." _Essence_ 14 (August 1983): 93-94.
Short fiction.

647.4 "The Storyteller." _Essence_ 14 (December 1983): 72-74.
Short fiction.

Secondary Sources

647.5(S) Boorstein, Karen. "Beyond _Black Macho_: An
Interview with Michele Wallace." _Black American Literature
Forum_ 18 (4): 163-167 (Winter 1984).

647.6(S) Gillespie, Marcia Ann. "Macho Myths and Michele
Wallace." _Essence_ 10 (August 1979): 76-77, 99-100, 102.
Interview.

1988-1991 Supplement

A647.7 _Invisibility Blues: From Pop to Theory_. New York:
Verso, 1991.

648. WALLER, EFFIE.

648.1 _Rhymes from the Cumberland_. New York: Broadway
Publishing, 1909. Poetry.

648.2 _Songs of the Months_. New York: Broadway Publishing,
1904. Poetry.

649. WALSH, JOY.

649.1 "Praised Be Imagination." _Black American Literature
Forum_ 19 (3): 111 (Fall 1985).

650. WALTER, MILDRED PITTS.

650.1 _Because We Are_. New York: Lothrop, Lee and Shepard,
1983. Children's stories.

650.2 _Brother to the Wind_. New York: Lothrop, Lee and
Shepard, 1985. Children's stories.

650.3 _The Girl on the Outside_. New York: Lothrop, Lee and
Shepard, 1982. Children's stories.

650.4 _Justin and the Best Biscuits in the World_. New York:
Lothrop, Lee and Shepard, 1986. Children's stories.

650.5 <u>Mariah Loves Rock</u>. NY: Bradbury, 1988.

650.6 <u>My Mama Needs Me</u>. New York: Lothrop, Lee and Shepard, 1983. Children's stories.

650.7 <u>Trouble's Child</u>. New York: Lothrop, Lee and Shepard, 1985. Children's stories.

650.8 <u>TY's One-Man Band</u>. New York: Four Winds, 1980. Children's stories.

651. WAMBLE, THELMA (1916-).

651.1 <u>All in the Family</u>. New York: New Voices, 1953. Novel

651.2 <u>Look Over My Shoulder</u>. New York: Vantage Press, 1969. Novel.

652. WANIEK, MARILYN NELSON (1946-).

652.1 "Animals Who Remember." <u>Georgia Review</u> 32 (4): 866 (Winter 1978).

652.2 "The Century Quilt." <u>Southern Review</u> 21 (3): 825-826 (July 1985).

652.3 "The Dream Lover." <u>Essence</u> 14 (February 1984): 139.

652.4 <u>For the Body: Poems</u>. Baton Rouge: Louisiana State University Press, 1978.

652.5 "For the Dead One." <u>Crisis</u> 83 (May 1976): 148.

652.6 "Herbs In the Attic." <u>Georgia Review</u> 33 (4): 898 (Winter 1979).

652.7 "I Decide Not To Have Children." <u>Georgia Review</u> 32 (1): 44 (Spring 1978).

652.8 "I Imagine Driving Across Country." <u>Hudson Review</u> 3 (1): 114 (Spring 1978).

652.9 "I Send Mama Home." <u>Southern Review</u> 21 (3): 23-825 (July 1985).

652.10 "It's All In Your Head." <u>Georgia Review</u> 37 (4): 787-789 (Winter 1983).

652.11 "Light Under the Door." <u>Ohio Review</u> 28 (1982): 46-47.

652.12 "Like a Forgotten Dream." <u>Crisis</u> 87 (April 1980):
151.

652.13 "Mama's Promise." <u>Southern Review</u> 21 (3): 821-823
(July 1985).

652.14 <u>Mama's Promises</u>. Baton Rouge: Louisiana State
University Press, 1985.

652.15 "Miracles." <u>Black Scholar</u> 19 (July/August-
September/October 1988): 52.

652.16 "Other Women's Children." <u>Georgia Review</u> 32 (1): 45
(Spring 1978).

652.17 "Paltry Things: Immigrants and Marginal Men in Paule
Marshall's Short Fiction." <u>Callaloo</u> 18 (6): 46-56 (Spring
Summer 1983).

652.18 "Poem with Sixteen Names." <u>Crisis</u> 85 (November
1978): 310.

652.19 "A Strange Beautiful Woman." <u>Crisis</u> 87 (April 1980):
151.

652.20 "To My Father." <u>Crisis</u> 83 (May 1976): 148.

652.21 <u>Hundreds of Hens and Other Poems: Translations from
the Works of Danish Poet Halfdan Wedel Rasmussen</u>.
Minneapolis: Black Willow, 1982. Pamela Espeland, joint
translator.

653. WARD, ELLA J. MAYO.

653.1 <u>Bougainvillaea and Desert Sand</u>. Charlottesville, VA:
Michie Company, 1942. Poetry,

653.2 <u>Purple Wings</u>. Charlottesville, VA: Michie Company,
1941. Poetry.

654. WARREN, ALYCE (1940-).

654.1 <u>Into These Depths</u>. New York: Vantage Press, 1968.

655. WASHINGTON, DORIS.

655.1 <u>Yulan</u>. New York: Carlton Press, 1964. Novel.

656.   WASHINGTON, LORICE.

656.1 "Good Things Come To Those Who Hustle While They
Wait." _Essence_ 17 (August 1986): 138.

657.   WATERS, SHIRLEY A. (1949-).

657.1 _Psalms of a Black Woman_. Los Angeles: Hopkins-Thomas,
1969. Poetry.

658.   WATKINS, BARBARA (NAYO).

658.1 _I Want Me a Home_. New Orleans: BLKARTSOUTH, 1969.

Watkins, Dorothy June. SEE   449. MATANAH.

Watkins, Frances Ellen. **SEE**   288. HARPER, FRANCES ELLEN
     WATKINS.

659.   WATKINS, PATRICIA D.

659.1 "The Paradoxical Structure of Richard Wright's _The Man
Who Lived Underground_." _Black American Literature Forum_ 23
(Winter 1989): 767.

659.2 "Song To My Black Son." _Crisis_ 80 (June-July 1973):
197.

660.   WATKINS, VIOLET PEACHES.

660.1 _My Dream World of Poetry: Poems of Imagination,
Reality, and Dreams_. New York: Exposition Press, 1955.
Poetry.

661.   WATSON, FRIEDA K.

661.1 _Fellin's_. Los Angeles: Krizna Publication, 1971.
Poetry.

662. WATSON, NANA.

662.1 <u>Reap the Harvest</u>. New York: William-Frederick Press, 1952. Poetry.

663. WATSON, ROBERTA BRUCE (1911-).

663.1 <u>Closed Doors</u>. New York: Exposition Press, 1967. Novel.

664. WEATHERFORD, CAROLE BOSTON.

664.1 "Day's Work." <u>Black American Literature Forum</u> 21 (3): 239 (Fall 1987).

664.2 "Migrant Man." <u>Black American Literature Forum</u> 21 (3): 238-239 (Fall 1987).

664.3 "Shebazz." <u>Black American Literature Forum</u> 21 (3): 237-238 (Fall 1987).

664.4 "This Blood." <u>Black American Literature Forum</u> 21 (3): 237 (Fall 1987).

665. WELCH, LEONA NICHOLAS (1942-).

665.1 <u>Black Gibraltar</u>. San Francisco: Leswing Press, 1971.

666. WELLS, BEVERLY WIGGINS.

666.1 "Bereft of Rainbows." <u>Essence</u> 16 (September 1985): 156.

666.2 "Claiming the Body." <u>Essence</u> 16 (March 1986): 122.

667. WELLS, IDA BELL (1862-1931).

667.1 <u>Crusade for Justice: The Autobiography of Ida B. Wells</u>. Duster, Alfreda M., ed. Chicago: University of Chicago Press, 1970.

667.2 "Lynch Law in America." Arena 23 (January 1900): 15-24.

667.3 "Lynching and the Excuse For It." Independent 53 (May 1901): 1133-1136.

667.4 Mob Rule in New Orleans: Robert Charles and His Fight to the Death. Chicago: Author, 1900.

667.5 On Lynchings: Southern Horrors; A Red Record; Mob Control in New Orleans. New York: Arno Press, 1969 (reprint)

667.6 A Red Record: Tabulated Statistics and Alleged Causes of Lynchings in the United States, 1892-1893-1894. Chicago: Donohue & Henneberry, 1895.

667.7 The Reason Why: The Colored American is Not in the World's Columbian Exposition. Chicago: Author, 1893.

667.8 Southern Horrors: Lynch Law in All Its Phases. New York: New York Age Print, 1892.

667.9 "The White Man's Problem." Arena 23 (January 1900): 1-30.

Secondary Sources

667.10(S) Holt, Thomas C. "The Lonely Warrior: Ida B. Wells and the Struggle for Black Leadership." In FRANKLIN.

667.11(S) Majors, Gerri, and Saunders, Doris E. Black Society. Chicago: Johnson Publishing Co., 1976.

667.12(S) Mossell, N.F. [Gertrude Bustill Mossell]. The Work of the Afro-American Woman. Philadelphia: Geo. S. Ferguson Co., 1894. 2d ed. 1908.

667.13(S) Penn, I. Garland. The Afro-American Press and Its Editors. Reprint. New York: Arno Press, 1969. 1st published 1891. Ida B. Wells, p. 408.

667.14(S) Shockley, Ann Allen. "Ida Bell Wells-Barnett." In SHOCKLEY, pp. 248-261.

667.15(S) Walker, Alice. "Advancing Luna -- And Ida B. Wells." Ms. 5 (July 1977): 75-76. Short fiction.

1988-1991 Supplement
Secondary Sources

A667.16(S) Giddings, Paula. "Woman Warrior: Ida B. Wells, Crusader-Journalist." Essence 18 (February 1988): 75.

A667.17(S) Sterling, Dorothy. Black Foremothers: Three Lives. New York: Feminist Press, 1988. Ida B. Wells considered.

668. WELSH, KARIAMU.

668.1 "God Bless the Cook." Essence 12 (May 1981): 106, 170. Short fiction.

668.2 "I'm Not That Strong." Essence 9 (February 1979): 39. Autobiography.

668.3 "She Was Linda Before She Was Ayesha." Essence 11 (October 1980): 106, 167, 171. Short fiction.

668.4 "Sudeka 1,2,3,4." Obsidian 5 (3): 101-104 (Winter 1979). Poetry.

668.5 "Textured Women." Obsidian 5 (3): 104-105 (Winter 1979).

668.6 Textured Women, Cowrie Shells and Beetle Sticks: Poems. Buffalo, NY: Amulefi, 1978.

669. WEST, DOROTHY (1907-).

669.1 "The Black Dress." Opportunity 12 (May 1934): 140, 158.

669.2 "Elephant's Dance: A Memoir of Wallace Thurman." Black World 20 (November 1970): 77-85.

669.3 "Hannah Byde." Messenger 8 (July 1926): 197-199.

669.4 The Living is Easy. Boston: Houghton, 1948. Novel.

669.5 "Mammy." Opportunity 18 (October 1940): 298-302.

669.6 "Prologue to a Life." Saturday Evening Quill 2 (April 1929): 5-10.

669.7 "The Typewriter." Opportunity, 4 (July 1926): 220-222, 233-234.

669.8 "An Unimportant Man." Saturday Evening Quill 2 (April 1928): 21-32.

Secondary Sources

669.9(S) Gayles, Gloria. "The Truths of Our Mothers' Lives: Mother-Daughter Relationships in Black Women's Fiction." Sage 1 (2): 8-12 (Fall 1984).

669.10(S) Iaciofana, Carol. "The Sun Doesn't Set on Dorothy West." Sojourner 7(April 1982):15.

669.11(S) Roses, Lorraine Elena. "Dorothy West at Oak Bluffs, Massachusetts." Sage 2 (1): 47-49 (Spring 1985).

669.12(S) Shockley, Ann Allen. "Dorothy West." In SHOCKLEY, p. 455.

670. WEST, SANDRA.

670.1 "Vietnam." Essence 18 (October 1987): 134. Catalyst (Winter 1989): 78.

671. WHALING, MARIETTA R.

671.1 Rhyme and Reason. New York: Exposition Press, 1975.

672. WHEATLEY, PHILLIS (1753?-1784).

672.1 A Beautiful Poem on Providence. Boston: E. Gay, 1805.

672.2 An Elegaic Poem, on the Death of That Celebrated Divine...George Whitefield.... Boston: Ezekiel Russell and John Boyles, 1770.

672.3 An Elegy, Sacred to the Memory of That Great Divine, the Reverend and Learned Dr. Samuel Cooper.... by Phillis Peters. Boston: E. Russell, 1784.

672.4 An Elegy to Miss Mary Moorhead, on the Death of Her Father, the Rev. Mr. John Moorhead. [broadside]   Boston: William McAlpine, 1773.

672.5 Liberty and Peace, a Poem. Boston: Warden and Russell, 1784.

672.6 Memoir and Poems of Phillis Wheatley, a Native African and Slave. Boston: George W. Light, 1834. Boston: Issac Knapp, 1838.

672.7 Poems and Letters. Ed. by Charles F. Heartman. New York: Heartman, 1915.

672.8 Poems of Phillis Wheatley. Ed. by Julian D. Mason, Jr. Chapel Hill, NC: University of North Carolina Press, 1966.

672.9 Poems of Phillis Wheatley. Ed. Charlotte Ruth Wright. Philadelphia: The Wrights, 1930.

672.10 Poems of Phillis Wheatley as They Were Originally
Published in London, 1773. Philadelphia: R.R. and C.C.
Wright, 1909.

672.11 Poems on Comic, Serious and Moral Subjects. 2d ed,
corrected. London: J. French, 1787.

672.12 Poems on Various Subjects, Religious and Moral.
London: A. Bell, Bookseller, 1773.

672.13 Six Broadsides Relating to Phillis Wheatley (Phillis
Peters) with Portrait and Facsimile of Her Handwriting. New
York: Charles F. Heartman, 1915.

672.14 To Mrs. Leonard, on the Death of Her Husband.
[broadside]. Boston, 1771.

672.15 To the Hon'ble Thomas Hubbard, Esq., on the Death of
Mrs. Thankful Leonard. [broadside]. Boston, 1773.

672.16 To the Rev. Mr. Pitkin, on the Death of His Lady.
[broadside]. Boston, 1772.

Secondary Sources

672.17(S) Akers, Charles W. "Our Modern Egyptians: Phillis
Wheatley and the Whig Campaign Against Slavery in
Revolutionary Boston." Journal of Negro History 60 (July
1975): 397-410.

672.18(S) Allen, William G. Wheatley, Banneker and Horton.
Boston: Laing, 1849.

672.19(S) Borland, Kathryn Kilby and Speicher, Helen Ross.
Phillis Wheatley: Young Colonial Poet. Indianapolis: Bobbs-
Merrill, 1968.

672.20(S) Brawley, Benjamin G. Early Negro American
Writers, Selections with Biographical and Critical
Introductions. Chapel Hill, NC: University of North Carolina
Press, 1935. Phillis Wheatley, p. 32.

672.21(S) Brawley, Benjamin G. The Negro in Literature and
Art. New York: Duffield & Company, 1929. Phillis Wheatley,
p. 17-18.

672.22(S) Collins, Terence. "Phillis Wheatley: The Dark
Side of the Poetry." Phylon, 36(1975):78-88.

672.23(S) Constanzo, Angelo. "Three Black Poets in
Eighteenth Century America." Shippenburg State College
Review (1973): 89-101.

672.24(S) Davis, Arthur P. "Personal Elements in the Poetry
of Phillis Wheatley." Phylon 14 (1953): 191-198.

672.25(S) Deane, Charles, ed. "Letters of Phillis Wheatley." _Proceedings of the Massachusetts Historical Society_, 7 (1864): 267-79. Privately printed, 1864.

672.26(S) Fuller, Miriam Morris. _Phillis Wheatley: America's First Black Poetess_. Champaign, IL: Garrard Publishing Company, 1971.

672.27(S) Graham, Shirley. _The Story of Phillis Wheatley: Poetess of the American Revolution_. New York: Julian Messner, 1949.

672.28(S) Gregory, Montgomery. "The Spirit of Phillis Wheatley." _Opportunity_ 1 (1923): 374-375.

672.29(S) Heartman, Charles F. _Phillis Wheatley (Phillis Peters): A Critical Attempt and a Bibliography of Her Writings_. New York: Heartman, 1915.

672.30(S) Holmes, Wilfred. "Phillis Wheatley." _Negro History Bulletin_ 6 (1943): 117-118.

672.31(S) Hull, Gloria T. "Black Women Poets from Wheatley to Walker." In BELL, pp. 69-86. _Negro American Literature Forum_ 9 (Fall 1975): 91-96.

672.32(S) Isani, Muktar Ali. "The British Reception of Wheatley's _Poems on Various Subjects_." _Journal of Negro History_ 66 (Summer 1981): 144-149.

672.33(S) Isani, Muktar Ali. "Early Versions of Some Works by Phillis Wheatley." _American Early Literature_ 14 (2): 149-155 (Fall 1979).

672.34(S) Isani, Muktar Ali. " 'An Elegy on Leaving----': A New Poem by Phillis Wheatley." _American Literature_ 58 (4): 609-613 (December 1986).

672.35(S) Isani, Muktar Ali, "The First Proposed Edition of _Poems on Various Subjects_ and the Phillis Wheatley Canon." _American Literature_ 49 (1): 97-103 (March 1977).

672.36(S) Isani, Muktar Ali. " 'Gambia on My Mind': Africa and the African in the Writings of Phillis Wheatley." _Melus_ 16 (1): 64-72 (Spring 1979).

672.37(S) Isani, Muktar Ali. "The Methodist Connection: New Variants of Some Phillis Wheatley Poems." _Early American Literature_ 22 (1): 108-113 (Spring 1987).

672.38(S) Isani, Muktar Ali. "The Original Version of Wheatley's 'On the Death of Dr. Samuel Marshall'." _Studies in Black Literature_ 7 (3): 20 (Autumn 1976).

672.39(S) Jackson, Sara D. "Letters of Phillis Wheatley and Susanna Wheatley." _Journal of Negro History_ 57 (April 1972): 211-215.

672.40(S)   Jamison, Angelene.   "Analysis of Selected Poetry of Phillis Wheatley."   Journal of Negro Education 43 (Summer 1974): 408-416).

672.41(S)   Jordan, June.   "The Difficult Miracle of Black Poetry in America or Something Like a Sonnet for Phillis Wheatley."   Massachusetts Review 27 (2): 252-262 (Summer 1986).

672.42(S)   Kuncio, R.C.   "Some Unpublished Poems of Phillis Wheatley."   New England Quarterly 43 (1970): 287-299.

672.43(S)   Lapansky. Phil.   " 'Deism' -- An Unpublished Poem by Phillis Wheatley."   New England Quarterly 5 (3): 517-520 (September 1977).

672.44(S)   Loggins, Vernon.   The Negro Author: His Development in America.   New York: Columbia University Press, 1931.

672.45(S)   Mason, R. Lynn.   "Phillis Wheatley -- Soul Sister."   Phylon 33 (1972): 222-230.

672.46(S)   Nielsen, A.L.   "Patterns of Subversion in the Works of Phillis Wheatley and Jupiter Hammon."   The Western Journal of Black Studies 6 (Winter 1982): 212-219.

672.47(S)   Ogunyemi, Chikwenye Okonjo.   "Phillis Wheatley: the Modest Beginning."   Studies in Black Literature 7 (3): 16-19 (Autumn 1976).

672.48(S)   O'Neale, Sondra A.   "Challenge to Wheatley's Critics: 'There Was No Other "Game" in Town'."   Journal of Negro Education 54 (4): 500-511 (Fall 1985).

672.49(S)   O'Neale, Sondra.   "A Slave's Subtle War: Phillis Wheatley's Use of Biblical Myth and Symbol."   Early American Literature 21 (2): 144-165 (Fall 1986).

672.50(S)   Petrie, Phil W.   "Phillis Wheatley: Poetry's Child Prodigy."   Encore 5 (6 July 1976): 2.

672.51(S)   Porter, Dorothy B.   North American Negro Poets: A Bibliographical Checklist of Their Writings, 1760-1944.   Hattiesburg. MS: Book Farm, 1945.

672.52(S)   Renfro, G. Herbert.   "A Discourse on the Life and Poetry of Phillis Wheatley."   A.M.E. Church Review 7 (1891): 76-109.

672.53(S)   Renfro, G. Herbert.   Life and Works of Phillis Wheatley, Containing Her Complete Poetical Works, Numerous Letters, a Complete Biography of This Famous Poet of a Century and a Half Ago.   New York: Robert L. Pendleton, 1916.

672.54(S) Richmond, Merle A. Bid the Vassal Soar:
Interpretive Essays on the Life and Poetry of Phillis
Wheatley and George Moses Horton. Washington, DC: Howard
University Press, 1974. Phillis Wheatley is considered p. 3-
83.

672.55(S) Richmond, Merle A. Phillis Wheatley. New York:
Chelsea House, 1987. Children's book with index, chronology
and bibliography.

672.56(S) Rigsby, Gregory. "Form and Content in Phillis
Wheatley's Elegies." CLA Journal 19 (December 1975): 248-
257.

672.57(S) Robinson, William H. Black New England Letters:
The Uses of Writing in Black New England. Boston: Boston
Public Library, 1979.

672.58(S) Robinson, William H. Early Black American Poets.
Dubuque, IA: Wm. C. Brown Pubs., 1969.

672.59(S) Robinson, William H. Phillis Wheatley: A Bio-
Bibliography. Boston: G.K. Hall & Co., 1981.

672.60(S) Robinson, William H. Phillis Wheatley and Her
Writings. New York: Garland Publishing, 1984.

672.61(S) Robinson, William H. "Phillis Wheatley: Colonial
Quandary." CLA Journal 9 (September 19650: 25-38.

672.62(S) Robinson, William H. "Phillis Wheatley in
London." CLA Journal 21 (2): 187-201 (December 1977).

672.63(S) Robinson, William H. Phillis Wheatley in the
Black American Beginnings. (Broadside Critics Series, no. 5,
ed. by James A. Emanuel). Detroit: Broadside Press, 1975.

672.64(S) Rogal, Samuel J. "Phillis Wheatley's Methodist
Connection." Black American Literature Forum 21 (1-2): 85-95
(Spring-Summer 1987).

672.65(S) Scheick, William J. "Phillis Wheatley and Oliver
Goldsmith: A Fugitive Satire." Early American Literature 19
(1): 82-84 (Spring 1984).

672.66(S) Seeber, Edward D. "Phillis Wheatley." Journal of
Negro History 24 (1939): 259-262.

672.67(S) Shields, John C. "Phillis Wheatley and Mather
Byles: A Study in Literary Relationship." CLA Journal 7
(1980): 377-390.

672.68(S) Shields, John C. "Phillis Wheatley's Use of
Classicism." American Literature 52 (1): 97-111 (March
1980).

672.69(S) Shockley, Ann Allen. "Phillis Wheatley. In SHOCKLEY, pp. 17-25.

672.70(S) Shurtlef, N.B. "Phillis Wheatley, the Negro-Slave Poet." Proceedings of the Massachusetts Historical Society 7 (1864): 270-272.

672.71(S) Silverman, Kenneth. "Four New Letters by Phillis Wheatley." Early American Literature (Winter 1974): 257-272.

672.72(S) Sistrunk, Albertha. "Phillis Wheatley: An Eighteenth-Century Black American Poet Revisited." CLA Journal 7 (1980): 391-398.

672.73(S) Slattery, J.R. "Phillis Wheatley, the Negro Poetess. Catholic World 39 (1884): 484-498.

672.74(S) Smith, Eleanor. "Phillis Wheatley: A Black Perspective." Journal of Negro Education 43 (Summer 1974): 401-407.

672.75(S) Steele, Thomas J. "The Figure of Columbia: Phillis Wheatley Plus George Washington." New England Quarterly 54 (2): 264-266 (1981).

672.76(S) Thatcher, Benjamin Bussey. Memoir of Phillis Wheatley, a Native African and a Slave. Boston: Geo. Light, 1834.

672.77(S) Walker, Margaret. "Ballad for Phillis Wheatley." Ebony 25 (March 1974): 96.

672.78(S) Wegelin, Oscar. "Was Phillis Wheatley America's First Negro Poet?" Literary Collector (August 1904): 117-118.

672.79(S) Weight, Glenn S. "The Anniversary of Phillis Wheatley Remains an Inspiration To All." Negro History Bulletin 25 (1962): 91-92.

672.80(S) Williams, George W. History of the Negro Race, 1619-1800. New York: Putnam's Sons, 1883. Phillis Wheatley discussed on p. 198.

672.81(S) Yeocum, William H. "Phillis Wheatley -- The First African Poetess." A.M.E. Church Review 6 (1890): 329-333.

1988-1991 Supplement

A672.82 The Collected Works of Phillis Wheatley. John C. Shields, ed. New York: Oxford University Press, 1989.

A672.83 Poems of Phillis Wheatley. Julian D. Mason, Jr., ed. Revised and enlarged edition. Chapel Hill, NC: University of North Carolina Press, 1989.

Secondary Sources

A672.84(S) Richmond, Merle A., <u>Phillis Wheatley</u>. NY:
Chelsea House, 1988.

A672.85(S) Smith, Cynthia J. " 'To Maecenas': Phillis
Wheatley's Invocation of a Idealized Reader." <u>Black American
Literature Forum</u> 23 (Fall 1989): 579.

673. WHITAKER, CHRISTINE D.

673.1 <u>The Singing Teakettle: Poems for Children</u>. New York:
Exposition Press, 1956.

674. WHITE, LINDA J.

674.1 "Down Home Hospitality." <u>Black Books Bulletin</u> 7 (3):
26-31 (1981).

675. WHITE, PAULETTE CHILDRESS (1948-).

675.1 <u>Lost Your Mama</u>. In BLACKSONGS.

675.2 <u>Love Poem to a Black Junkie</u>. Detroit: Lotus Press,
1975.

675.3 <u>The Watermelon Dress: Portrait of a Woman: Poems and
Illustrations</u>. Detroit: Lotus Press, 1984.

676. WIGGINS, BERNICE LOVE (1897-).

676.1 <u>Tuneful Tales</u>. El Paso, TX: Author, 1925.

677. WILDS, MYRA VIOLA.

677.1 <u>Thoughts of Idle Hours</u>. Nashville: National Baptist
Publishing Board, 1915.

678. WILKINSON, BRENDA (1946-).

678.1 <u>Ludell</u>. New York: Harper, 1975. Children's stories.

678.2 <u>Ludell and Willie</u>. New York: Harper, 1976. Children's stories.

678.3 <u>Ludell's New York Time</u>. New York: Harper, 1980. Children's stories.

678.4 <u>Not Separate, Not Equal</u>. New York: Harper, 1987. Children's stories.

679. WILLIAMS. ELSIE ARRINGTON.

679.1 "Academic Evaporation." "A Lady." "Suburbia Spoke To Us Last Night." "The Teacher Will Come." <u>Obsidian</u> 7 (2-3): 204-205 (Summer-Winter 1981).

680. WILLIAMS, FLORENCE.

680.1 <u>The Guiding Light</u>. Nashville: National Baptist Training School Board, 1963. Poetry.

681. WILLIAMS, JEANETTE MARIS (1946-).

681.1 <u>Soul of a Sapphire</u>. Chicago: Free Black Press, 1970. Poetry.

682. WILLIAMS, JOAN.

682.1 <u>Thoughts of Love and Life</u>. Milwaukee: Shore Publishing Company, 1972.

683. WILLIAMS, JUNE VANLEER.

683.1 <u>Will the Real You Please Stand Up?: Poetry</u>. Philadelphia: Dorrance & Company, 1983.

684. WILLIAMS, LORNA V.

684.1 <u>Jamaica Mento</u>. St. Clair, Trinidad and Tobago:
Publishing Associates, 1978. Short fiction.

685. WILLIAMS, ORA.

685.1 <u>American Black Women in the Arts and Social Studies: A</u>
<u>Bibliographic Survey</u>. Rev. ed. Metuchen, NJ: Scarecrow
Press, 1978.

686. WILLIAMS, SHERLEY ANNE (1944-).

686.1 "The Blues Roots of Contemporary Afro-American
Poetry." <u>Massachusetts Review</u> 18 (Autumn 1977): 542-554.
Essays.

686.2 "D.C. Visions the Verified Tongue." <u>Black Scholar</u> 8
(March 1977): 38.

686.3 <u>Dessa Rose</u>. New York: William Morrow, 1986. New
York: Berkley Publishers, 1987. Novel.

686.4 "Dream Realized." <u>Black Scholar</u> 8 (March 1977): 36.

686.5 <u>Give Birth to Brightness: A Thematic Study in Neo-</u>
<u>Black Literature</u>. New York: Dial Press, 1972.

686.6 "The House of Desire." <u>Essence</u> 14 (January 1984):
112.

686.7 "I See My Life." <u>Essence</u> 6 (December 1975): 65.

686.8 "Juneteenth: The Bicentennial Poem." <u>Black Scholar</u> 8
(March 1977): 36.

686.9 "Kinhouse." <u>Black Scholar</u> 8 (March 1977): 37-38.

686.10 "Letters From a New England Negro." <u>Callaloo</u> 5 (2):
1-16 (1979). <u>Iowa Review</u> 11 (4): 149-188 (1980). Drama.

686.11 "Meditations on History." In WASHINGTON, 1980, pp.
200-248. Short fiction.

686.12 "Middle Passage." <u>Black Scholar</u> 8 (March 1977): 37-
38.

686.13 "Miss Abinetha." <u>Partisan Review</u> 43 (1): 84 (1976).

686.14 "Mother of the Blues." <u>Black Scholar</u> 8 (March 1977):
39.

686.15 "Oral History Project." <u>Callaloo</u> 9 (1): 127-129
(Winter 1986).

686.16 <u>The Peacock Poems</u>. Middletown, CT: Wesleyan University Press, 1975.

686.17 "Sherley Anne Williams on Octavia E. Butler." <u>Ms</u>. 14 (March 1986): 70.

686.18 "Some Implications of Womanist Theory." <u>Callaloo</u> 9 (2): 303-308 (Spring 1986).

686.19 "Some One Sweet Angel Child." <u>Massachusetts Review</u> 18 (3): 567-572 (Autumn 1977).

686.20 <u>Some One Sweet Angel Chile</u>. New York: William Morrow, 1982. Poetry.

686.21 "Soul Saga." <u>American Poetry Review</u> 7 (3): 16-18 (May-June 1978).

Secondary Sources

686.22(S) Howard, Lillie. "Sherley Anne Williams." In HARRIS & DAVIS, pp. 345-350. Biography and bibliography included.

1988-1991 Supplement

A686.23 "An African-American Returns: A Market in Ghana." <u>Callaloo</u> 12 (Spring 1989): 346. Poem.

A686.24 "Remembering Prof. Sterling A. Brown, 1901-1989." <u>Black American Literature Forum</u> 23 (Spring 1989): 106.

Secondary Sources

A686.25(S) Davis, Mary Kemp. "Everybody Knows Her Name: The Recovery of the Past in Sherley Anne Williams's <u>Dessa Rose</u>." <u>Callaloo</u> 12 (Summer 1989): 544.

687. WILLIAMS, SHIRLEY.

687.1 "Straight Talk From Plain Women." <u>Essence</u> 14 (October 1983): 89.

687.2 "This Is a Sad-Ass Poem For a Black Woman to Be Writing." <u>Essence</u> 6 (December 1975): 65.

688. WILLIAMS, SUSAN.

688.1   "To Mother."   _Essence_ 7 (February 1977): 43.

689.   WILLIAMS, SYLVIA DURANT.

689.1   "I Had a Dream."   _Essence_ 15 (January 1985): 133.

690.   WILSON, ALICE T. (1908-).

690.1   _How an American Poet Made Money and Forget-Me-Not_.
New York: Pageant Press, 1968. Drama and poems.

691.   WILSON, FLORA McCULLOUGH (1927-).

691.1   _Not by Bread Alone_.   New York: Carlton Press, 1970.
Poetry.

692.   WILSON, HARRIET E. ADAMS (1828-1870).

692.1   _Our Nig; or, Sketches from the Life of a Free Black,
in a Two-Story White House, North.   Showing That Slavery's
Shadows Fall Even There_. By "Our Nig." Boston: Printed by
George Rand & Avery, 1859. New York: Random House, 1983.

                        Secondary Sources

692.2(S)   Foster, Frances Smith.   "Adding Color and Contour
to Early Self-Portraiture: Autobiographical Writings of Afro-
American Women." In PRYSE & SPILLERS, pp. 25-39.

692.3(S)   Shockley, Ann Allen.   "Harriet E. Adams Wilson."
In SHOCKLEY, pp. 84-95.

693.   WILSON, PAT.

693.1   _The Sign of Keola_. New York: Carlton Press, 1961.
Novel.

694.   WINSTON, BESSIE BRENT.

694.1 <u>Alabaster Boxes</u>. Washington, DC: Review and Herald
Publishing Association, 1947. Poetry.

694.2 <u>Life's Red Sea and Other Poems</u>. Washington, DC:
Review and Herald Publishing Association, 1950.

695. WINSTON, BETTY.

695.1 <u>The Africans</u>. Wayne, PA: Banbury, 1983. Novel.
<u>Essence</u>, 14(October 1983):79-80, 165-166. Excerpt.

Witherspoon, Naomi Long. **SEE** 438. MADGETT, NAOMI LONG.

696. WOLF, SHIRLEY.

696.1 "Terror." <u>Essence</u> 7 (August 1976): 14.

697. WOOD, DEBBIE.

697.1 <u>On Being</u>. Washington, DC: Author, 1976.

698. WOOD, LILLIAN E.

698.1 <u>Let My People Go</u>." Philadelphia: A.M.E. Book Concern,
1922. Fiction.

Secondary Sources

698.2(S) Shockley, Ann Allen. "Lillian E. Woods." In
SHOCKLEY, pp. 392-398.

699. WOOD, ODELLA PHELPS.

699.1 <u>High Ground</u>. New York: Exposition Press, 1945.
Novel.

699.2 <u>Recaptured Echoes</u>. New York: Exposition Press, 1944.
Poetry.

700. WOOLDRIDGE, IRIS.

700.1 A Touch...a Smile...a Memory. New York: Vantage press
Press, 1975.

701. WORRELL, LELIA E.

701.1 Reflections: Past, Present, Future. New York: Carlton
Press, 1972.

702. WORTHAM, ANNE.

702.1 Silence. New York: Pageant Press, 1965. Poetry.

703. WRIGHT, BEATRICE.

703.1 Color Scheme: Selected Poems. New York: Pageant
Press, 1957.

704. WRIGHT, ETHEL WILLIAMS.

704.1 Of Men and Trees. New York: Exposition Press, 1954.

705. WRIGHT, MARTHA R.

705.1 "Bijah's Luce of Guilford." Negro History Bulletin 27
(1965): 152-153, 159.

706. WRIGHT, SARAH ELIZABETH (1928-).

706.1 "Black Writers' Views of America." Freedomways 19
(3): 161-162 (1979). Essay.

706.2 "I Have Known Death." Tomorrow 10 (3 November 1950):
46.

706.3 "Lament for a Harlem Mother." American Pen 4 (Spring
1972): 23-27.

706.4 "Lorraine Hansberry On Film." _Freedomways_ 19 (4):
283-284 (1979).

706.5 "The Negro Woman in American Literature." _Freedomways_
6 (Winter 1966): 8-10.

706.6 "Roadblocks To the Development of the Negro Writer."
In AMERICAN, pp. 71-73.

706.7 _This Child's Gonna Live_. New York: Delacorte Press,
1969. _Black Scholar_ 18 (4-5): 2-9 (July-August-September-
October 1987). Novel. Excerpt.

706.8 "Urgency" and "Window Pictures." In POOL, pp. 184-
185.

706.9 _Give Me a Child_. Philadelphia: Kraft, 1955. Lucy
Smith, joint author.

Secondary Sources

706.10(S) Guilford, Virginia B.   "Sarah Elizabeth Wright."
In DAVIS & HARRIS, pp. 293-300. Biography and bibliography.

706.11(S) Mickelson, Anne Z. "Winging Upward: Black Women:
Sarah E. Wright, Toni Morrison, Alice Walker." In
MICKELSON, pp. 112-124.

706.12(S) Whitlow, Roger. "Sarah E. Wright." In WHITLOW,
pp. 162-65.

707. WRIGHT, ZARA.

707.1 _Black and White Tangled Threads_. Chicago: Privately
Printed, 1920. Reprint. New York: AMS Press, 1975. Novel.

707.2 _Kenneth_. 1920. Reprint. New York: AMS Press, 1975.
Novel.

Secondary Sources

707.3(S) Shockley, Ann Allen.   "Zara Wright." In SHOCKLEY,
pp. 380-386.

708. YANCEY, BESSIE WOODSON (1882-?).

708.1 _Echoes from the Hills_. Washington, DC: Associated
Publishers, 1939.

709.   YARBROUGH, CAMILLE.

709.1   Cornrows. New York: Putnam, 1979. Children's stories.

709.2   The Little Tree Growin' in the Shade. New York: Putnam, 1987. Children's stories.

709.3   The Shimmershine Queens. NY: Putnam, 1989.

710.   YEISER, IDABELLE.

710.1   Lyric and Legend. Boston: Christopher Publishing House, 1947.

710.2   Moods. Philadelphia: Colony Press, 1937. Poetry.

711.   YOUNGBLOOD, SHAY.

711.1   The Big Mama Stories. Ithaca, NY: Firebrand, 1989.

711.2   "The Blues Ain't Nothin' But A Good Woman Feelin' Bad." Catalyst (Summer 1988): 89.

711.3   "Living on the Front Line." Essence 17 (May 1986): 93.

712.   YVONNE.

712.1   "Before the Riots." Ms. 5 (July 1976): 57.

712.2   "Eastwick: Five House." Ms. 6 (November 1977): 72-73.

712.3   Iwilla. Bronx, NY: Sunbury, 1982. Poetry.

712.4   Iwilla Scourge. Bronx, NY: Chameleon, 1986. Poetry.

712.5   Iwilla/Soil. Bronx, NY: Chameleon, 1985. Poetry.

712.6   "Nineteen Forty-Six." Obsidian 2 (2): 49-50 (Summer 1976).

712.7   "Premonition: A Contour Drawing." Obsidian 2 (2): 51-52 (Summer 1976).

712.8   "Receive This White Garment." Ms. 16 (July-August 1987): 52.

712.9 "Severance Pay." _Ms._ 9 (January 1981): 33-35.

712.10 "The Tearing of the Skin (Part I)." _Ms._ 7 (January 1979): 63.

713. ZIMELE-KEITA, NZADI.

713.1 "Birds of Paradise." "Long Road Rhythm." "What We Know." In BARAKA & BARAKA, pp. 396-399.

714. ZUBENA, SISTER [CYNTHIA CONLEY]

714.1 _Calling All Sisters_. Chicago: Free Black Press, 1970. 2d printing: _Callin' All Sisters_. Chicago: Author, 1970. Poetry.

714.2 _Om Black_. Chicago: Author, 1971. Poetry.

Anthologies

715(AN). Abdul, Raoul, ed. <u>The Magic of Black Poetry</u>. New York: Dodd, Mead, 1972. Anthology.

716(AN). Adams, Williams, Conn, Peter and Slepian, Barry, eds. <u>Afro-American Literature: Poetry</u>. Boston: Houghton, 1970. Anthology.

717(AN). Adoff, Arnold, ed. <u>Black Out Loud: An Anthology of Modern Poems by Black Americans</u>. New York: Dell, 1975.

718(AN). Adoff, Arnold, ed. <u>Celebrations: A New Anthology of Black American Poetry</u>. Chicago: Follett, 1977.

719(AN). Adoff, Arnold, ed. <u>The Poetry of Black America: An Anthology of the 20th century</u>. New York: Harper, 1973.

720(AN). <u>Afro-American Voices, 1770s-1970s</u>. New York: Oxford Book Company, 1970.

721(AN). Alhamisi, Ahmed and Wangara, Harun Kofi, eds. <u>Black Arts: An Anthology of Black Creations</u>. Detroit: Black Arts Publications, 1969.

722(AN). Ambrose, Amanda, ed. <u>My Name is Black: An Anthology of Black Poets</u>. New York: Scholastic Book Services, 1973.

723(AN). Baker, Houston A., Jr., ed. <u>Black Literature in America</u>. New York: McGraw-Hill, 1971.

724(AN). Baraka, Amiri and Baraka, Amina, eds. <u>Confirmation: An Anthology of African-American Women</u>. New York: Quill, 1983.

725(AN). Barksdale, Richard and Kinnamon, Kenneth. <u>Black Writers of America: A Comprehensive Anthology</u>. New York: Macmillan Publishing Company, 1972.

726(AN). Bell, Bernard, ed., <u>Afro-American Poetry</u>. Boston: Allyn & Bacon, 1972.

727(AN).   Bell, Bernard.   Modern and Contemporary Afro-
American Poetry. Boston: Allyn & Bacon, 1972.

728(AN).   Bernikow, Louise, ed.   The World Split Open: Four
Centuries of Women Poets in England and America, 1552-1950.
New York: Vintage Books, 1974.

729(AN).   Blacksongs, Series I: Four Poetry Broadsides by
Black Women.   Detroit: Lotus Press, 1977.

730(AN).   Bontemps, Arna W., ed.   American Negro Poetry.   New
York: Hill & Wang, 1963.

731(AN).   Booker, Merrel Daniel, Sr. et al., eds.   Cry at
Birth.   New York: McGraw-Hill, 1971.

732(AN).   Boyd, Sue Abbot, ed.   Poems by Blacks. 2 vols.
Fort Smith, AR: South & West, 1971-72.

733(AN).   Braithwaite, William Stanley, ed.   Anthology of
Magazine Verse for 1927 and Yearbook of American Poetry.
Boston: Brimmer, 1927.

734(AN).   Brasmer, William and Consolo, Dominick, eds.   Black
Drama: An Anthology.   Columbus, OH: Charles Merrill, 1970.

735(AN).   Brawley, Benjamin G., ed.   Early Negro American
Writers: Selections with Biographical and Critical
Introductions.   Chapel Hill, NC: University of North Carolina
Press, 1935.   Reprint: New York: Dover, 1970.

736(AN).   Breman, Paul, ed.   Sixes and Sevens: An Anthology
of New Poetry. Heritage series, 2.   London: Paul Breman,
1963.

737(AN).   Breman, Paul, ed.   You Better Believe It: Black
Verse in English from Africa, the West Indies and the United
States.   Baltimore: Penguin Books, 1973.

738(AN).   Brooks, Gwendolyn, ed.   A Broadside Treasury.
Detroit: Broadside Press, 1971.

739(AN).   Brooks, Gwendolyn, ed.   Jump Bad: A New Chicago
Anthology.   Detroit: Broadside Press, 1971.

740(AN).   Brown, Sterling Allen, Davis, Arthur P. and Lee,
Ulysses, eds. The Negro Caravan: Writings by American
Negroes.   New York: Dryden Press, 1941.

741(AN).   Brown-Guillory, Elizabeth, ed.   Wines in the
Wilderness: Plays by African-American Women from the Harlem
Renaissance to the Present.   Westport, CT: Greenwood Press,
1990.

742(AN).   Bruchac, Joseph, ed.   The Next World: Poems by
Thirty-Two Third World Americans.   Trumansburg, NY: Crossing
Press, 1978.

743(AN). Bulkin, Elly and Larkin, Joan, eds. Lesbian
Fiction: An Anthology. Watertown, MA: Persephone, 1981.

744(AN). Bullins, Ed, ed. The New Lafayette Theatre
Presents: Plays with Aesthetic Comments by 6 Black
Playwrights. New York: Anchor/Doubleday, 1974.

745(AN). Bullins, Ed, ed. New Plays from the Black Theater.
New York: Bantam Books, 1969.

746(AN). Burnett, Whit and Foley, Martha, eds. Story in
America. New York: Vanguard Press, 1934.

747(AN). Calverton, V.F., ed. Anthology of American Negro
Literature. New York: Modern Library, 1929.

748(AN). Carson, Josephine, ed. Silent Voices: The Southern
Negro Woman Today. New York: Delacorte Press, 1969.

749(AN). Chapman, Abraham, ed. Black Voices: An Anthology
of Afro-American Literature. New York: New American Library,
1968.

750(AN). Chapman, Abraham, ed. New Black Voices: An
Anthology of Contemporary Afro-American Literature. New
York: New American Library, 1972.

751(AN). Childress, Alice, ed. Black Scenes. New York:
Doubleday, 1971.

752(AN). Clarke, Cheryl. Narratives: Poems in the Tradition
of Black Women. New Brunswick, NJ: Sister Books, 1982.

753(AN). Clarke, John H., ed. American Negro Short Stories.
New York: Hill & Wang, 1966.

754(AN). Clarke, John Henrik, ed. Harlem, U.S.A. Berlin,
Germany: Seven Seas Publishers, 1964. Camden, ME: 1974.

755(AN). Cohn, Ruby. New American Dramatists: 1960-1980.
New York: Grove Press, 1982.

756(AN). Coombs, Orde, ed. We Speak as Liberators: Young
Black Poets. New York: Dodd, Mead, 1970.

757(AN). Couch, William Jr., ed. New Black Playwrights.
Baton Rouge: LA: Louisiana State University Press, 1968.

758(AN). Cromwell, Otelia, Turner, Lorenzo Dow & Dykes, Eva
B., eds. Readings from Negro Authors for Schools and
Colleges, with a Bibliography of Negro Literature. New York:
Harcourt, 1931.

759(AN). Cullen, Countee, ed. Caroling Dusk: An Anthology
of Verse by Negro Poets. New York: Harper, 1927.

760(AN). Cunard, Nancy. Negro Anthology. Made by Nancy
Cunard, 1931-1933. London: Author at Wishart & Co, 1934.

Reprint: New York: Negro Universities Press, 1969 and New
York: Ungar, 1970.

761(AN). Davis, Arthur P. From the Dark Tower: Afro-
American Writers 1900 to 1960. Washington, DC: Howard
University Press, 1974.

762(AN). Davis, Arthur P. and Redding, J. Saunders.
Cavalcade: Negro American Writing from 1760 to the Present.
Boston: Houghton, 1971.

763(AN). Davis, Charles T. and Gates, Henry Louis, Jr. The
Slave's Narrative. New York: Oxford, 1985.

764(AN). Dee, Ruby., ed. Glow Child and Other Poems. New
York: Third Press, 1973.

765(AN). Dore, Anita, ed. The Premier Book of Major Poets:
An Anthology. New York: Fawcett Publications, 1970.

766(AN). Dreer, Herman, ed. American Literature by Negro
Authors. New York: Macmillan Publishing Company, 1950.

767(AN). Emanuel, James A. and Gross, Theodore L., eds.
Dark Symphony: Negro Literature in America. New York: Free
Press, 1968.

768(AN). Exum, Pat Crutchfield, ed. Keeping the Faith:
Writings by Contemporary Black American Women. New York:
Fawcett Publications, 1974.

769(AN). 15 Chicago Poets. Chicago: Yellow Press, 1976.

770(AN). Fisher, Dexter, ed. The Third Woman: Minority
Women Writers of the United States. Boston: Houghton, 1980.

771(AN). Foley, Martha, ed. The Best American Short Stories
for 1946. Boston: Houghton, 1946.

772(AN). Four Black Poets. Kansas City, MO: Bk Mk Press,
1977.

773(AN). Gibson, Donald, ed. Modern Black Poets. Englewood
Cliffs, NJ: Prentice-Hall, 1973.

774(AN). Gilbert, Mercedes. Selected Gems of Poetry, Comedy
and Drama. Boston: Christopher Publishing House, 1931.

775(AN). Gilbert, Sandra M. and Gubar, Susan. The Norton
Anthology of Literature by Women: The Tradition in English.
New York: W. W. Norton, 1985.

776(AN). Giovanni, Nikki, ed. Night Comes Softly: Anthology
of Black Female Voices. Newark, NJ: Medic Press, 1970.

777(AN). Gould, Jean. Modern American Women Poets. New
York: Dodd, Mead, 1984.

778(AN). Harper, Michael S. and Steptoe, Robert B., eds.
Chant of Saints: A Gathering of Afro-American Literature, Art
and Scholarship. Urbana, IL: University of Illinois Press,
1979.

779(AN). Harris, Marie and Aguero, Kathleen, eds. A Gift of
Tongues: Critical Challenges in Contemporary American Poetry.
Athen, GA: University of Georgia Press, 1987.

780(AN). Harrison, Paul C., ed. Kuntu Drama: Plays of the
African Continuum. New York: Grove Press, 1973.

781(AN). Hatch, James V. Black Theater, USA: Forty-Five
Plays by American Negroes, 1847-1974. New York: Free Press,
1974.

782(AN). Hatch, James and Shine, Ted, eds. Black Theater
USA. New York: Free Press, 1974.

783(AN). Hayden, Robert, ed. Kaleidoscope: Poems by
American Negro Poets. New York: Harcourt, 1967.

784(AN). Hayden, Robert, et al.,eds. Afro-American
Literature: An Introduction. New York: Harcourt, 1971.

785(AN). Hill, Herbert, ed. Soon, One Morning: New Writing
by American Negroes 1940-1962. New York : A.A. Knopf, 1963.

786(AN). Hoffman, William M., ed. New American Plays. New
York: Hill & Wang, 1968.

787(AN). Hollis, Burney, ed. Swords Upon This Hill.
Baltimore: Morgan State University Press, 1984.

788(AN). Huggins, Nathan Irvin, ed. Voices from the Harlem
Renaissance. New York: Oxford University Press, 1976.

789(AN). Hughes, Langston, ed. New Negro Poets, U.S.A.
Bloomington, IN: Indiana University Press, 1964.

790(AN). Hughes, Langston & Bontemps, Arna, eds. The Poetry
of the Negro, 1746-1949. New York: Doubleday, 1949.

791(AN). Hughes, Langston & Bontemps, Arna, eds. The Poetry
of the Negro, 1746-1970. Rev. ed. New York: Doubleday,
1970.

792(AN). Johnson, Charles Spurgeon, ed. Ebony and Topaz: a
Collectanea. New York: National Urban League, 1927.

793(AN). Johnson, James Weldon, ed. The Book of American
Negro Poetry. New York: Harcourt, 1922.

794(AN). Johnson, James Weldon, ed. The Book of American
Negro Poetry. Rev. ed. New York: Harcourt, 1931.

795(AN). Jones, LeRoi and Neal, Larry, eds. Black Fire: An
Anthology of Afro-American Writing. New York: William
Morrow, 1968.

796(AN). Jordan, June, ed. Soulscripts: Afro-American
Poetry. New York: Doubleday, 1970.

797(AN). Kerlin, Robert T. Negro Poets and Their Poems.
Washington, DC: Associated Publishers, 1923.

798(AN). King, Woodie, ed. Blackspirits: A Festival of New
Black Poets in America. New York: Random House, 1972.

799(AN). King, Woodie, ed. The Forerunners: Black Poets in
America. Washington, DC: Howard University Press, 1975.

800(AN). King, Woodie and Milner, Ron, eds. Black Drama
Anthology. New York: Columbia University Press, Signet, New
American Library, 1972.

801(AN). Lawson, Jennifer Blackman and Randall-Tsuruta,
Dorothy, eds. High Expectations: Poems for Black Women.
Pittsburgh, CA: Los Medans, 1977.

802(AN). Lee, A. Robert. Black Fiction: New Studies in the
Afro-American Novel Since 1945. Totawa, NJ: Barnes and
Noble, 1980.

803(AN). Lobo-Cobb, Angela, ed. Winter Nest: A Poetry
Anthology of Midwestern Women Poets of Color. Madison, WI:
Blue Reed, 1987.

804(AN). Locke, Alain LeRoy, ed. The New Negro: An
Interpretation. New York: Albert & Charles Boni, 1925. The
seminal work of the Harlem Renaissance.

805(AN). Locke, Alain LeRoy and Montgomery, Gregory, eds.
Plays of Negro Life: A Sourcebook of Native American Drama.
New York: Harper, 1927.

806(AN). Loewenberg, Bert James and Bogin, Ruth. Black
Women in Nineteenth Century American Life: Their Words, Their
Thoughts, Their Feelings. University Park, PA: Pennsylvania
State University Press, 1976.

807(AN). Lomax, Alan and Abdul, Raoul, eds. 3000 Years of
Black Poetry: An Anthology. New York: Dodd, Mead, 1970.

808(AN). Long, Richard A. and Collier, Eugenia, eds. Afro-
American Writing: An Anthology of Prose and Poetry. New
York: New York University, 1972. 2d ed. University Park,
PA: Pennsylvania State University, 1985.

809(AN). Major, Clarence, ed. The New Black Poetry. New
York: International Press, 1969.

810(AN). Major, Deborah, ed. <u>Ascension II</u>. San Francisco:
San Francisco African American Historical and Cultural
Society, 1983.

811(AN). Menarini, G., ed. <u>I Negri: Poesie e Canti</u>. Rome:
Edizioni Academnia, 1969.

812(AN). Miller, R. Baxter, ed. <u>Black American Literature
and Humanism</u>. Lexington, KY: University Press of Kentucky,
1981.

813(AN). Miller, R. Baxter, ed. <u>Black American Poets
Between Worlds, 1940-1960</u>. Knoxville, TN: University of
Tennessee Press, 1986.

814(AN). Mootry, Maria K., Jones, Joyce and McTaggart, Mary,
eds. <u>The Otherwise Room</u>. Carbondale, IL: Poetry Factory,
1981.

815(AN). Mootry, Maria K., Jones, Joyce, and McTaggart,
Mary, eds. <u>Sestine: Six Women Poets</u>. Carbondale, IL: Poetry
Factory, 1983.

816(AN). Moraga, Cherrie and Anzaldua, eds. <u>This Bridge
Called My Back: Writings by Radical Women of Color</u>.
Watertown, MA: Persephone, 1981.

817(AN). Murphy, Beatrice M., ed. <u>An Anthology of
Contemporary Verse: Negro Voices</u>. New York: Henry Harrison,
1928.

818(AN). Murphy, Beatrice M., ed. <u>Ebony Rhythm: An
Anthology of Contemporary Negro Verse</u>. New York: Exposition
Press, 1948.

819(AN). Ostrow, Eileen J., ed. <u>Center Stage: An Anthology
of Twenty-One Contemporary Black-American Plays</u>. Oakland,
CA: Sea Urchin, 1981.

820(AN). Patterson, Lindsay, ed. <u>Anthology of the Afro-
American in the Theatre: A Critical Approach</u>. Cornwells
Heights, PA: Publishers Agency, 1978.

821(AN). Patterson, Lindsay, ed. <u>A Rock Against the Wind:
Black Love Poems</u>. New York: Dodd, Mead, 1973.

822(AN). Peplow, Michael W. and Davis, Arthur. <u>The New
Negro Renaissance: An Anthology</u>. New York: Holt, Rinehart, &
Winston, 1975.

823(AN). <u>Plays to Remember</u>. Literary Heritage Series. New
York: Macmillan Publishing Company, 1968.

824(AN). Pool, Rosey, ed. <u>Beyond the Blues: New Poems By
American Negroes</u>. Lympne, Kent, England: Hand & Flowers
Press, 1962. Detroit: Broadside Press, 1971.

825(AN). Porter, Dorothy B., ed. Early Negro Writing, 1760-1837. Boston: Beacon Press, 1971.

826(AN). Prenshaw, Peggy Whitman, ed. Women Writers of the Contemporary South. Jackson, MS: University Press of Mississippi, 1984.

827(AN). Randall, Dudley, ed. The Black Poets. New York: Bantam Books, 1971.

828(AN). Randall, Dudley and Burroughs, Margaret, eds. For Malcolm: Poems On the Life and Death of Malcolm X. Detroit: Broadside Press, 1967.

829(AN). Reit, Ann, ed. Alone Amid All This Noise: A Collection of Women's Poetry. New York: Four Winds/Scholastic, 1976.

830(AN). Richardson, Willis, ed. Plays and Pageants from the Life of the Negro. Washington, DC: Associated Publishers, 1930.

831(AN). Richardson, Willis and Miller, May, eds. Negro History in Thirteen Plays. Washington, DC: Associated Publishers, 1935.

832(AN). Robinson, William H., ed. Early Black American Poets. Dubuque, IA: William C. Brown, 1969.

833(AN). Rowe, Kenneth, ed. University of Michigan Plays. Ann Arbor, MI: University of Michigan Press, 1932.

834(AN). Sanchez, Sonia, ed. Three Hundred and Sixty Degrees of Blackness Comin' at You. New York: 5X Publishing Company, 1971.

835(AN). Sanchez, Sonia, ed. We Be Word Sorcerers: 25 Stories by Black Americans. New York: Bantam Books, 1973.

836(AN). Schevill, James, ed. Breakout: In Search of New Theatrical Environments. Athens, OH: Swallow Press, 1973.

837(AN). Sherman, Joan R. Invisible Poets: Afro-Americans of the Nineteenth-Century. Urbana, IL: University of Illinois Press, 1974.

838(AN). Shockley, Ann Allen, ed. Afro-American Women Writers, 1746-1933. Boston: G.K. Hall, 1988.

839(AN). Shuman, R. Baird, ed. Nine Black Poets. Oakpark, IL: Moore Publishing Company, 1968.

840(AN). Singh, Amritjit. The Novels of the Harlem Renaissance. University Park, PA: Pennsylvania State University Press, 1976.

841(AN). Smith, Barbara. Home Girls: A Black Feminist Anthology. New York: Kitchen Table: Women of Color, 1983.

842(AN). Stetson, Erlene. Black Sister: Poetry by Black American Women, 1746-1980. Bloomington, IN: Indiana University Press, 1981.

843(AN). Troupe, Quincy. and Schulte, Rainer, eds. Giant Talk: An Anthology of Third World Writings. New York: Random House, 1975.

844(AN). Turner, Bessye Tobias. La Librae: an Anthology of Poetry For the Living. Detroit: Harlo Press, 1968.

845(AN). Turner, Darwin T., ed. Black American Literature: Essays, Poetry, Fiction, Drama. Columbus, OH: Charles Merrill, 1970. New York: Continuum, 1983.

846(AN). Turner, Darwin T., ed. Black American Literature: Poetry Columbus, OH: Charles E. Merrill, 1969.

847(AN). Wagner, Jean. Black Poets of the United States: From Paul Laurence Dunbar to Langston Hughes. Translated by Kenneth Douglas. Urbana, IL: University of Illinois Press, 1973.

848(AN). Washington, Mary Helen, ed. Black-Eyed Susans: Classic Stories By and About Black Women. New York: Doubleday, 1975.

849(AN). Washington, Mary Helen, ed. Invented Lives: Narratives of Black Women, 1860-1960. New York: Anchor/Doubleday, 1987.

850(AN). Washington, Mary Helen. Midnight Birds: Stories of Contemporary Black Women Writers. New York: Anchor/Doubleday, 1980.

851(AN). Weatherly, Toma and Wilentz, eds. Natural Process: An Anthology of New Black Poetry. New York: Hill & Wang, 1970.

852(AN). White, Newman Ivey and Jackson, Walter C. An Anthology of Verse by American Negroes. Durham, NC: Trinity College Press, 1924.

853(AN). Wilentz, Ted and Weatherly, eds. Natural Process: An Anthology of New Black Poetry. New York: Hill & Wang, 1970.

854(AN). Wilkerson, Margaret B. Nine Plays by Black Women. New York: New American Library, 1986.

855(AN). Yearbook of Short Plays, First Series. Evanston, IL: Row Peterson, 1931.

856(AN). Young, James O. Black Writers of the Thirties. Baton Rouge: Louisiana State University Press, 1973.

General Works

857(G). Abajian, James de T. _Blacks in Selected Newspapers,_
Censuses and Subjects. Boston: G.K. Hall, 1977.

858(G). Abramson, Doris E. _Negro Playwrights in the_
American Theatre, 1925-1969. New York: Columbia University
Press, 1969.

859(G). _The American Negro Writer and His Roots_. Selected
papers from the first conference of American Negro Writers.
American Society of African Culture, 1960.

860(G). Anderson, Jervis. _This Was Harlem_. New York:
Farrar, Straus & Giroux, 1981.

861(G). Arata, Esther Spring and Rotoli, Nicholas John.
Black American Playwrights, 1800 to Present: A Bibliography.
Metuchen, NJ: Scarecrow Press, 1976.

862(G). Ascher, Carol et al, eds. _Between Women:_
Biographers, Novelists, Critics, Teachers and Artists Write
About Their Work on Women. Boston: Beacon Press, 1984.

863(G). Baker, Houston A. _Singers of Daybreak: Studies in_
Black American Literature. Washington, DC: Howard University
Press, 1974.

864(G). Baraka, Amiri and Baraka, Amina, eds. _The Music:_
Reflections on Jazz and Blues. New York: William Morrow,
1987.

865(G). Bardolph, Richard. _The Negro Vanguard_. New York:
Vintage Books, 1961. Collective biographies.

866(G). Barksdale, Richard K. "Castration Symbolism in
Recent American Fiction." _CLA Journal_ 29 (4): 400-413 (June
1986).

867(G). Barthold, Bonnie J. _Black Time: Fiction of Africa,_
the Caribbean and the United States. New Haven, CT: Yale
University Press, 1981.

868(G). Baym, Nina. Woman's Fiction: A Guide to Novels By
and About Women in America, 1820-1870. Ithaca, NY: Cornell
University Press, 1978.

869(G). Beard, Linda Susan. "The Black Woman Writer and the
Diaspora, October 27-30, 1985, Michigan State University,
East Lansing, Michigan." Sage 3 (Fall 1986): 70-71.
Conference report.

870(G). Bell, Bernard W. The Afro-American Novel and Its
Tradition. Amherst, MA: University of Massachusetts, 1987.

871(G). Bell, Roseann P., Parker, Bettye J. and Guy-
Sheftall, Beverly, eds. Sturdy Black Bridges: Visions of
Black Women in Literature. New York: Anchor Books, 1979.
African-American women writers.

872(G). Berry, Faith. "A Question of Publishers and a
Question of Audience." Black Scholar 17 (2): 41-49 (March-
April 1986). African-American women in publishing.

873(G). Berzon, Judith R. Neither white Nor Black: The
Mulatto Character in American Fiction. New York: New York
University, 1978.

874(G). Bevilacqua, Winifred F., ed. Fiction by American
Women: Recent Views. Port Washington, NY: Associated
Faculty, 1983.

875(G). Bigsby, C.W.E., ed. Black American Writers. Vol 1.
New York: Penguin Books, 1971.

876(G). Bigsby, C.W.E. Confrontation and Commitment: A
Study of Contemporary American Drama, 1959-1966. Columbia,
MO: University of Missouri Press, 1968.

877(G). Bigsby, C.W.E. The Second Black Renaissance: Essays
in Black Literature. Westport, CT: Greenwood Press, 1980.

878(G). Birtha, Becky. "Recovering a Literary Heritage:
Black Women's Books." Off Our Backs 9 (6): 14 (June 1979).

879(G). Blicksilver, Edith. The Ethnic American Woman:
Problems, Protests, Lifestyle. Dubuque, IA: Kendall-Hunt,
1979.

880(G). Bone, Robert. Down Home. New York: Putnam's Sons,
1975.

881(G). Bone, Robert A. The Negro Author: His Development
in America. New Haven, CT: Yale University Press, 1958.

882(G). Bone, Robert A. The Negro Novel in America. Rev.
ed. New Haven, CT: Yale University Press, 1965.

883(G). Bontemps, Arna W., ed. The Harlem Renaissance
Remembered. New York: Dodd, Mead, 1972.

884(G). Booth, Martha F. "Black Ghetto Life Portrayed in
Novels for the Adolescent." Ph. D. Dissertation, University
of Iowa, 1971.

885(G). Bowen, Angela. "Sage: A Journal That Fills a Long
Unmet Need." Sojourner 9 (8): 19 (April 1984). On Spelman
College's scholarly African-American women's journal.

886(G). Bowles, Juliette, ed. In the Memory and Spirit of
Frances, Zora, and Lorraine; Essays and Interviews on Black
Women and Writing. Washington, DC: Institute for the Arts
and the Humanities, Howard University, 1979.

887(G). Boyd, Melba Joyce. "Out of the Poetry Ghetto: the
Life/Art Struggle of Small Black Publishing Houses." Black
Scholar 16 (4): 12-24 (July-August 1985).

888(G). Bradley, David. "Telling the Black Woman's Story."
New York Times Magazine (8 January 1984): 25-37.

889(G). Brooks, Russell. "The Motifs of Dynamic Change in
Black Revolutionary Poetry." CLA Journal 15 (September
1971): 7-17.

890(G). Brown, Elizabeth. "Six Female Black Playwrights:
Images of Blacks in Plays by Lorraine Hansberry, Alice
Childress, Sonia Sanchez, Barbara Molette, Martie Charles and
Ntozake Shange." Ph. D. dissertation, Florida State
University, 1980.

891(G). Brown, Janet. Feminist Drama: Definition and
Critical Analysis. Metuchen, NJ: Scarecrow Press, 1979.

892(G). Brown, Sterling Allen. The Negro in American
Fiction. New York: Atheneum, 1969. (Reprint of 1937 ed.)

893(G). Brown-Guillory, Elizabeth. Their Place on Stage:
Black Women Playwrights in America. Westport, CT: Greenwood
Press, 1988.

894(G). Bruck, Peter and Karrer, Wolfgang, eds. The Afro-
American Novel Since 1960. Amsterdam: Gruner, 1982.

895(G). Butcher, Philip. "The Younger Novelist and the
Urban Negro." CLA Journal 4 (March 1961): 196-203.

896(G). Byerman, Keith E. Fingering the Jagged Grain:
Tradition and Form in Recent Black Fiction. Athens, GA:
University of Georgia Press, 1985.

897(G). Campbell, Jane. Mythic Black Fiction: The
Transformation of History. Knoxville, TN: University of
Tennessee Press, 1986.

898(G). Carby, Hazel V. Reconstructing Womanhood: The
Emergence of the Afro-American Woman Novelist. New York:
Oxford University Press, 1987.

899(G).   Cary, Meredith.   _Different Drummers: A Study of_
Cultural Alternatives in Fiction.   Metuchen, NJ: Scarecrow
Press, 1984.

900(G).   Central State College. Hallie Q. Brown Library.
Index to Periodical Articles by and About Negroes.
Wilberforce, OH, 1950-

901(G).   Chapman, Dorothy, compiler.   _Index to Poetry by_
Black American Women.   Westport, CT: Greenwood Press, 1986.
Indexes by author, subject, title and first line.

902(G).   Christian, Barbara.   "Afro-American Women Poets: A
Historical Introduction."   In her _Black Feminist Criticism:_
Perspectives on Black Women Writers.   New York: Pergamon
Press, 1985.   p. 119-125.

903(G).   Christian, Barbara.   _Black Feminist Criticism:_
Perspectives on Black Women Writers.   New York: Pergamon
Press, 1985. African-American women writers.

904(G).   Christian, Barbara.   "The Black Woman Writer as
Wayward."   In Evans, Mari, ed.   _Black Women Writers, 1950-_
_1980_.   New York: Doubleday, 1984., p.457-477.

905(G).   Christian, Barbara.   _Black Women Novelists: The_
Development of a Tradition, 1892-1976.   Westport, CT:
Greenwood Press, 1980.

906(G).   Christian, Barbara.   _"From the Inside Out" Afro-_
American Women's Literature and the State.   Minneapolis:
Center for Humanistic Studies, University of Minnesota, 1987.
African-American women writers.

907(G).   Collins, Patricia Hill.   "The Emerging Theory and
Pedagogy of Black Women's Studies."   _Feminist Issues_ 6 (1):
3-17 (Spring 1986).

908(G).   Cooke, Michael.   _Afro-American Literature in the_
Twentieth Century: The Achievement of Intimacy.   New Haven,
CT: Yale University Press, 1984.

909(G).   Cornwell, Anita.   _Black Lesbian in White America_.
Tallahassee, FL: Naiad,

910(G).   Curb, Rosemary, ed.   Twentieth-Century American
Dramatists.   (Dictionary of Literary Biography, v. 7).
Detroit: Gale Research, 1981.

911(G).   Dabney, Wendell P.   _Cincinnati's Colored Citizens,_
Historical, Sociological, and Biographical.   Cincinnati:
Dabney Publishing Company, 1926.

912(G).   Dandridge, Rita B.   "Male Critics/Black Women's
Novels."   _CLA Journal_ 23 (September 1979): 1-11.

913(G).   Daniel, Sadie Iola.   _Profiles of Negro Womanhood_.
Vol. 2.   Yonkers, NY: Educational Heritage, 1966.

914(G). Dannett, Sylvia G.L. Profiles of Negro Womanhood.
Vol. 1, 1619-1900. Yonkers, NY: Educational Heritage, 1964.

915(G). Davis, Lenwood. The Black Woman in American
Society: A Selected Annotated Bibliography. Boston: G.K.
Hall, 1975.

916(G). Davis, Thadious M. and Harris, Trudier, eds. Afro-
American Fiction Writers After 1955. (Dictionary of Literary
Biography, v, 33). Detroit: Gale Research, 1984.

917(G). Davis, Thadious M. and Harris, Trudier, eds. Afro-
American Writers After 1955: Dramatists and Prose Writers.
(Dictionary of Literary Biography, v. 38). Detroit: Gale
Research, 1985.

918(G). Dill, Bonnie Thornton. "Race, Class and Gender:
Prospects for an All-Inclusive Sisterhood." Feminist Studies
9 (Spring 1983): 131-150.

919(G). Dobbs, Jeanine. "Not Another Poetess: A Study of
Female Experience in Modern American Poetry." Ph. D.
dissertation, University of New Hampshire, 1973.

920(G). Doyle, Sr. Mary Ellen. "The Heroines of Black
Novels." In Johnson, Willa and Green, Thomas, eds.
Perspectives on Afro-American Women. ECCA Publishers, 1975,
pp. 112-125.

921(G). Duke, Maurice et al, eds. American Women Writers:
Bibliographical Essays. Westport, CT: Greenwood Press,
1983.

922(G). Ebert, Roger. "First Novels by Young Negroes."
American Scholar (Autumn 1967): 682-686.

923(G). Evans, Mari, ed. Black Women Writers (1950-1980): A
Critical Evaluation. New York: Anchor/Doubleday, 1984.

924(G). Fairbanks, Carol and Engeldinger, Eugene A.,
compilers. Black American Fiction: A Bibliography.
Metuchen, NJ: Scarecrow Press, 1978.

925(G). Fisk University Library. Dictionary Catalog of the
Negro Collection. 6 vols. Boston: G.K. Hall, 1974.

926(G). Ford, Nick Aaron. The Contemporary Negro Novel.
Boston: Meador, 1936.

927(G). Foster, Frances. "'In Respect to Females...':
Differences in the Portrayal of Women by Male and Female
Narrators." Black American Literature Forum 15 (Summer
1981): 66-70.

928(G). Franklin, John Hope, ed. Black Leaders of the
Twentieth Century. Urbana, IL: University of Illinois Press,
1982.

929(G). Friend, Beverly Oberfield. "Popular Culture." In
Haber, Barbara, ed. The Women's Annual: 1982-83. Boston:
G.K. Hall,1983, p. 149-176.

930(G). Fullinwider, S.P. The Mind and Mood of Black
America: 20th Century Thought. Homewood, IL: Dorsey Press,
1969.

931(G). Gates, Henry Louis, Jr. Black Literature and
Literary Theory. New York: Methuen, 1984.

932(G). Gates, Henry Louis, Jr. "The Black Person in Art:
How Should S/He Be Portrayed?" (Part I) Black American
Literature Forum 21 (1-2): 13-24 (Spring-Summer 1987).
African-American women writers' portrayal of women.

933(G). Gates, Henry Louis, Jr. Figures in Black: Words,
Signs, and the 'Racial' Self. New York: Oxford University
Press, 1987.

934(G). Gayle, Addison, ed. Black Expression. New York:
Weybright Talley, 1969.

935(G). Gayle, Addison. The Way of the New World: The Black
Novel in America. New York: Doubleday, 1975.

936(G). Gilbert, Sandra M. and Gubar, Susan. The Madwoman
in the Attic: The Woman Writer and the Nineteenth-Century
Literary Imagination. New Haven, CT: Yale University Press,
1984.

937(G). Glikin, Ronda. Black American Women in Literature:
A Bibliography, 1976 through 1987. Jefferson, NC: McFarland
& Company, 1989.

938(G). Gloster, Hugh M. Negro Voices in American Fiction.
Chapel Hill, NC: University of North Carolina Press, 1948.

939(G). Greene, J. Lee. Time's Unfading Garden: Anne
Spencer's Life and Poetry. Baton Rouge: Louisiana State
University Press, 1977.

940(G). Gregoire, Henri. An Enquiry Concerning the
Intellectual and Moral Faculties, and Literature of Negroes;
Followed with an Account of the Life and Works of Fifteen
Negroes and Mulattoes, Distinguished in Science, Literature
and the Arts. Brooklyn: Thomas Kirk, 1810.

941(G). Gregory, Montgomery. "The Drama of Negro Life." In
Locke, Alain LeRoy, The New Negro. New York: Albert &
Charles Boni, 1925.

942(G). Greiner, Donald J., ed. American Poets Since World
War II. (Dictionary of Literary Biography, v.5). Detroit:
Gale Research, 1980.

943(G). Gross, Seymour and Hardy, John,eds. Images of the
Negro in American Literature. Chicago: University of Chicago
Press, 1966.

944(G). Gwin, Minrose. Black and White Women of the Old
South: The Peculiar Sisterhood in American Literature.
Knoxville, TN: University of Tennessee Press, 1985.

945(G). Harlem Renaissance Remembered: Essays Edited with a
Memoir. Ed. by Arna W. Bontemps. New York: Dodd, Mead,
1972.

946(G). Harley, Sharon and Terborg-Penn, Rosalyn. The Afro-
American Woman: Struggles and Images. Port Washington, NY:
Kennikat, 1978.

947(G). Harris, Trudier. Exorcising Blackness: Historical
and Literary Lynching and Burning Rituals. Bloomington, IN:
Indiana University Press, 1984.

948(G). Harris, Trudier. From Mammies to Militants:
Domestics in Black America Literature. Philadelphia: Temple
University Press, 1982.

949(G). Harris, Trudier and Davis, Thadious M., eds. Afro-
American Poets Since 1955. (Dictionary of Literary
Biography, v. 42). Detroit: Gale Research, 1985.

950(G). Harris, Trudier and Davis, Thadious M., eds. Afro-
American Writers Before the Harlem Renaissance. (Dictionary
of Literary Biography, v. 50). Detroit: Gale Research, 1986.

951(G). Harris, Trudier and Davis, Thadious, eds. Afro-
American Writers from the Harlem Renaissance to 1940.
(Dictionary of Literary Biography, v. 51). Detroit: Gale
Research, 1987.

952(G). Hatch, James V. Black American Playwrights, 1823-
1977: Annotated Bibliography of Plays. New York: Bowker,
1977.

953(G). Hatch, James V. and Abdullah, Omanii. Black
Playwrights, 1823-1977: An Annotated Bibliography of Plays.
New York: Bowker, 1977.

954(G). Hemenway, Robert, ed. The Black Novelist.
Columbus, OH: Charles Merrill, 1970.

955(G). Henderson, Stephen. Understanding the New Black
Poetry: Black Speech and Black Music as Poetic References.
New York: William Morrow, 1973.

956(G). Hernton, Calvin. "The Sexual Mountain and Black
Women Writers." Black American Literature Forum 18 (4): 139-
145 (Winter 1984). Black Scholar 16 (4): 2-11 (July-August
1985).

957(G). Hernton, Calvin. The Sexual Mountain and Black
Writers: Adventures in Sex, Literature and Real Life. New
York: Anchor/Doubleday, 1987.

958(G). Homans, Margaret. "Her Very Own Howl." Signs 9
(1983): 186-205.

959(G). Hooks, Bell. Ain't I a Woman: Black Women and
Feminism. Boston: South End, 1981.

960(G). Hooks, Bell. "Black Women Writing: Creating More
Space." Sage 2 (1): 44-46 (Spring 1985).

961(G). Hooks, Bell. Feminist Theory: From Margin to
Center. Boston: South End, 1984.

962(G). Horton, Rod W., and Edwards, Herbert. "Black
Writers: Soul and Solidarity." In Backgrounds of American
Literary Thought. Englewood Cliffs, NJ: Prentice-Hall, 1974.

963(G). Howard University Founders Library. Dictionary
Catalog of the Jesse E. Moorland Collection of Negro Life and
History. 9 vols. Boston: G.K. Hall & Co., 1962.

964(G). Huggins, Nathan Irvin. Harlem Renaissance. New
York: Oxford University Press, 1971.

965(G). Hughes, Carl Milton. The Negro Novelist 1940-1950.
New York: Citadel Press, 1953.

966(G). Hughes, Langston. Famous Negro Heroes of America.
New York: Dodd, Mead, 1958.

967(G). Hull, Gloria T. "The Black Woman Writer and the
Diaspora." Black Scholar 17 (2): 2-4 (March-April 1986).

968(G). Hull, Gloria T., Scott, Patricia Bell, and Smith,
Barbara, eds. All the Women Are White, All the Blacks Are
Men, But Some of Us Are Brave: Black Women's Studies. Old
Westbury, New York: Feminist Press, 1982. African-American
women writers

969(G). Hull, Helen, ed. The Writers Book. New York:
Harper, 1950.

970(G). Inge, M. Thomas et al. Black American Writers:
Bibliographical Essays. (The Beginnings Through the Harlem
Renaissance and Langston Hughes Series, v. 1). New York: St.
Martin's, 1978.

971(G). Jackson, Blyden. "Some Negroes in the Land of
Goshen." Tennessee Folklore Society Bulletin 19 (1939): 103-
107.

972(G). Jackson, Blyden, and Rubin, Louis D. Black Poetry
in America: Two Essays in Historical Interpretation. Baton
Rouge: Louisiana State University Press, 1974.

973(G).   Jahn, Janheinz.   A Bibliography of Neo-African
Literature from Africa, America and the Caribbean.   New York:
Praeger, 1965.

974(G).   Johnson, Charles Spurgeon.   "A Note On the New
Literary Movement."   Opportunity 4 (March 1926): 80.
Discusses some women writers of the emerging Harlem
Renaissance.

975(G).   Johnson, James N.   "Blacklisting Poets."   Ramparts
(14 December 1968): 48-54.

976(G).   Joseph, Gloria I. and Lewis, Jill.   Common
Differences: Conflicts In Black and White Feminist
Perspectives.   New York: Doubleday, 1981.

977(G).   Josey, E.J., ed.   The Black Librarian in America.
Metuchen, NJ: Scarecrow Press, 1970.

978(G).   Joyce, Donald Franklin.   Gatekeepers of Black
Culture: Black-Owned Book Publishing in the United States,
1817-1981.   Westport, CT: Greenwood Press, 1983.

979(G).   Kellner, Bruce, ed.   The Harlem Renaissance: a
Historical Dictionary for the Era.   Westport, CT: Greenwood
Press, 1984.

980(G).   Kent, George E.   Blackness and the Adventure of
Western Culture.   Chicago: Third World Press, 1972.

981(G).   Kent, George E. "Notes on the 1974 Black Literary
Scene."   Phylon 36 (June 1975): 197-199. Discusses Black
female writers.

982(G).   Keyssar, Helene.   The Curtain and the Veil:
Strategies in Black Drama.   New York: Franklin, 1981.

983(G).   Kibler, James E., ed.   American Novelists Since
World War II, Second Series.   (Dictionary of Literary
Biography, v. 6).   Detroit: Gale Research, 1980.

984(G).   Lee, Dorothy.   "Black Voices in Detroit."   Michigan
Quarterly Review 25 (2): 313-328 (Spring 1986).   Many
African-American women writers are mentioned.

985(G).   Lerner, Gerda.   Black Women in White America: A
Documentary History.   New York: Pantheon Books, 1972.

986(G).   LeSeur, Geta.   "One Mother, Two Daughters: the Afro-
American and the Afro-Caribbean Female 'Bildungsroman'."
Black Scholar 12 (2): 26-33 (March-April 1986).   Fiction
criticism.

987(G).   Lewis, David Levering.   When Harlem Was in Vogue.
New York: A.A. Knopf, 1981. An account of the Harlem
Renaissance.

988(G). Littlejohn, David. Black on White: A Critical
Survey of Writing by American Negroes. New York: Viking
Press, 1966.

989(G). Logan, Rayford W. and Winston, Michael R.
Dictionary of American Negro Biography. New York: W. W.
Norton, 1982.

990(G). Lomax, Michael. "Fantasies of Affirmation: the
1920's Novel of Negro life." CLA Journal 16 (December 1972):
232-246.

991(G). McDowell, Deborah E. " 'The Changing Same':
Generational Connections and Black Women Novelists." New
Literary History 18 (2): 281-302 (Winter 1987).

992(G). McDowell, Deborah E. "New Directions for Black
Feminist Criticism." Black American Literature Forum 14 (4):
153-159 (Winter 1980).

993(G). Madhubuti, Haki. "The Poets and Their Poetry: There
Is a Tradition." In Dynamite Voices: Black Poets of the
1960's. Detroit: Broadside Press, 1971. Black women writers
are considered.

994(G). Mainiero, Lina, ed. American Women Writers: A
Critical Reference Guide from Colonial Times to the Present.
New York: Ungar, 1979.

995(G). Mainiero, Lina, ed. American Women Writers. Vol. 2.
New York: Ungar, 1980.

996(G). Marr, Warren, II. "Black Pulitzer Awardees."
Crisis 77 (May 1970): 186-188.

997(G). Matthews, Geraldine O., ed. Black American Writers,
1773-1949: Bibliography and Union List. Boston: G.K. Hall,
1975.

998(G). Maund, Alfred. "The Negro Novelist and the
Contemporary American Scene." Chicago Jewish Forum 12
(1954): 28-34.

999(G). Mickelson, Anne Z. Reaching Out: Sensitivity and
Order in Recent American Fiction by Women. Metuchen, NJ:
Scarecrow Press, 1979.

1000(G). Mickelson, Anne Z. "Winging Upward: Black Women:
Sarah E. Wright, Toni Morrison, Alice Walker." In her
Reaching Out: Sensitivity and Order in Recent American
Fiction by Women. Metuchen, NJ: Scarecrow Press, 1979. p.
112-124.

1001(G). Miller, Jeanne-Marie A. "Images of Black Women in
Plays by Black Playwrights." CLA Journal 20 (June 1977):
494-507. African-American playwrights.

1002(G). Miller, Ruth. <u>Backgrounds to Blackamerican</u>
<u>Literature</u>. Scranton, PA: Chandler Publishing Co, 1971.

1003(G). Mitchell, Loften. <u>Black Drama: The Story of the</u>
<u>American Negro in the Theater</u>. New York: Hawthorn Books,
1967.

1004(G). Molette, Barbara J. "Black Heroes amd Afrocentric
Values in the Theatre." <u>Journal of Black Studies</u> 15 (June
1985): 447-462.

1005(G). Molette, Barbara J. "They Speak. Who Listens?
Black Women Playwrights." <u>Black World</u> 6 (April 1976): 28-34.

1006(G). New York Public Library, Schomburg Collection of
Negro Literature and History. <u>Dictionary Catalog</u>. 9 vols.
Boston: G.K. Hall & Company, 1962.

1007(G). Noble, Jeanne. <u>Beautiful, Also, Are the Souls of</u>
<u>My Black Sisters: A History of the Black Woman in America</u>.
Englewood Cliffs, NJ: Prentice Hall, 1978.

1008(G). O'Brien, Jack, ed. <u>Interviews with Black Writers</u>.
New York: Harcourt, 1973.

1009(G). O'Connor, Lillian Mary. <u>Pioneer Women Orators</u>.
New York: Columbia University Press, 1954.

1010(G). O'Daniel, Therman, ed. <u>Langston Hughes: Black</u>
<u>Genius</u>. New York: William Morrow, 1971.

1011(G). Omolade, Barbara. "Black Women and Feminism."   In
Feisenstein, Hester and Jardine, Alice, eds. <u>The Future</u>
<u>Difference</u>. Boston: G.K. Hall, 1980, p. 247-257.

1012(G). O'Neale, Sondra. "Speaking for Ourselves: Black
Women Writers of the '80's." <u>Southern Exposure</u> 9 (2): 16-19
(Summer 1981). African-American women writers.

1013(G). "The <u>Opportunity</u> Dinner." <u>Opportunity</u> 3 (June
1925): 176. Honoring young African American writers of the
1920s.

1014(G). Page, James A. <u>Selected Black American Authors: An</u>
<u>Illustrated Bio-Bibliography</u>. Boston: G.K. Hall, 1977.

1015(G). Parone, Edward, ed. <u>Collision Course</u>. New York:
Random House, 1968.

1016(G). Patterson, Raymond. "What's Happening in Black
Poetry?" <u>Poetry Review</u> 2 (April 1975): 7-11.

1017(G). Perry, Margaret. <u>The Harlem Renaissance: An</u>
<u>Annotated Bibliography and Commentary</u>. New York: Garland
Publishing, 1982.

1018(G). Perry, Margaret. Silence to the Drums: A Survey of
the Literature of the Harlem Renaissance. Westport, CT:
Greenwood Press, 1976.

1019(G). Pool, Rosey. "The Discovery of American Negro
Poetry." Freedomways 3 (1963): 46-51.

1020(G). Porter, Dorothy B. A Working Bibliography of the
Negro in the United States. Ann Arbor, MI: Xerox, University
Microfilms, 1969.

1021(G). Potter, Velma R. "New Politics, New Mothers." CLA
Journal 16 (December 1972): 247-255.

1022(G). Pryse, Marjorie and Spillers, Hortense J., eds.
Conjuring: Black Women, Fiction, and Literary Tradition.
Bloomington, IN: Indiana University Press, 1985.

1023(G). Quartermain, Peter, ed. American Poets, 1880-1945,
Third Series. (Dictionary of Literary Biography, v. 54).
Detroit: Gale Research, 1987.

1024(G). Rainwater, Catherine, ed. Contemporary Women
Writers. Lexington, KY: University Press of Kentucky, 1985.

1025(G). Randall, Dudley. "The Black Aesthetics in the
Thirties, Forties, and Fifties." In Gayle, Addison,Jr., ed.
The Black Aesthetic. New York: Doubleday, 1971.

1026(G). Redding, J. Saunders. To Make a Poet Black. New
York: McGrath, 1939.

1027(G). Redmond, Eugene. Drumvoices: The Mission of Afro-
American Poetry: A Critical History. New York:
Anchor/Doubleday, 1976.

1028(G). Rhodes, Jane. "Heard at Last: Black Female
Voices." Utne Reader 22 (July-August 1987): 118-121, 123.
African-American women in publishing.

1029(G). Roberts, J.R. Black Lesbian: An Annotated
Bibliography. Tallahassee, FL: Naiad, 1981. Writings by
African-American women writers.

1030(G). Robinson, Wilhelmina S. Historical Negro
Biographies. (International Library of Negro Life and
History). New York: Publishers Company, 1967. Includes
biographical sketches of Black women writers.

1031(G). Rodgers-Rose, LaFrances, ed. The Black Woman.
Beverly Hills, CA: Sage, 1980.

1032(G). Rosenblatt, Roger. Black Fiction. Cambridge:
Harvard University Press, 1974.

1033(G). Rush, Theressa Gunn, Myers, Carol Fairbanks and
Arata, Esther Spring. Black American Writers Past and

Present: A Biographical and Bibliographical Dictionary. 2
vols. Metuchen, NJ: Scarecrow Press, 1975.

1034(G). Rushing, Andrea Benton. "An Annotated Bibliography
of Images of Black Women in Black Literature." CLA Journal 25
(December 1981): 234-262. African-American women writers.

1035(G). Rushing, Andrea Benton. "Images of Black Women in
Afro-American Poetry." Black World 24 (September 1975): 18-
30.

1036(G). Schomburg, Arthur A. A Bibliographical Checklist
of Negro Poetry. New York: Heartman, 1916.

1037(G). Schorer, Mark. "Novels and Nothingness." American
Scholar (Winter 1970-71): 169-170.

1038(G). Schraufnagel, Noel. From Apology To Protest: The
Black American Novel. Deland, FL: Everett/Edwards, 1973.

1039(G). Scruggs, Lawson Andrew. Women of Distinction:
Remarkable Works and Invincible Character. Raleigh, NC:
Author, 1893.

1040(G). Segrest, M. "Lines I Dare To Write: Lesbian
Writing In the South." Southern Exposure 9 (Summer 1981):
53-62.

1041(G). Sewell, May Wright, ed. World's Congress of
Representative Women. Chicago: Rand McNally, 1894.

1042(G). Shapiro, Laura. "Discovering a Lost Tradition:
Black Women Writers Win Back Their History." Newsweek 111 (7
March 1988): 70.

1043(G). Shockley, Ann Allen. "The Black Lesbian in
American Literature: An Overview." Conditions 5 2 (2): 133-
142 (Autumn 1979).

1044(G). Shockley, Ann Allen and Chandler, Sue P., eds.
Living Black American Authors: A Biographical Directory. New
York: Bowker, 1973.

1045(G). Showalter, Elaine, ed. The New Feminist Criticism:
Essays on Women, Literature, and Theory. New York: Pantheon
Books, 1985.

1046(G). Sims, Janet L. The Progress of Afro-American
Women: A Selected Bibliography and Resource Guide. Westport,
CT: Greenwood Press, 1980.

1047(G). Sims-Wood, Janet. "African-American Women Writers:
A Selected Listing of Master's Theses and Doctoral
Dissertations." Sage 2 (1) : 69-70 (Spring 1985).

1048(G). Smith, Barbara. "The Souls of Black Women." Ms. 2
(February 1974): 42-43, 78.

1049(G). Sochen, June. The Unbridgeable Gap: Blacks and
Their Quest for the American Dream, 1900-1930. Chicago: Rand
McNally College Publishing Co., 1972.

1050(G). Southgate, Robert L. Black Plots and Black
Characters: A Handbook for Afro-American Literature.
Syracuse, NY: Gaylord Professional, 1979.

1051(G). Spillers, Hortense J. "Kinship and Resemblances."
Feminist Studies 11 (1): 111-125 (Spring 1985).

1052(G). Sterling, Dorothy, ed. We Are Your Sisters: Black
Women in the Nineteenth Century. New York: W. W. Norton,
1984.

1053(G). Sternburg, Janet, ed. The Writer on Her Work. New
York: W. W. Norton, 1980.

1054(G). Stevenson, Rosemary. "Black Women in the United
States: A Bibliography of Recent Works." Black Scholar 16
(2): 45-49 (March/April 1985).

1055(G). Tanner, Laura E. "Self-Conscious Representation in
the Slave Narrative." Black American Literature Forum 21
(4): 415-424 (Winter 1987).

1056(G). Tate, Claudia, ed. Black Women Writers at Work.
New York: Continuum, 1983. African-American women writers.

1057(G). Towns, Saundra. "Black Autobiography and Dilemma
of Western Artistic Tradition." Black Books Bulletin 2
(Spring 1974): 17-23.

1058(G). Turner, Darwin T. A Minor Chord: Three Afro-
American Writers and Their Search For Identity. Urbana, IL:
University of Illinois Press, 1971.

1059(G). Turner, Darwin T. "The Negro Dramatist's Image of
the Universe, 1920-1960." CLA Journal 5 (December 1961):
106-120.

1060(G). Turner, Darwin T. "The Negro Novelist and the
South." Southern Humanities Review 1 (1967): 21-29.

1061(G). Vinson, James, ed. Contemporary Novelists. New
York: St. Martin's, 1972.

1062(G). Wade-Gayles, Gloria. No Crystal Stair: Visions of
Race and Sex in Black Women's Fiction. New York: Pilgrim,
1984.

1063(G). Walker, Cheryl Lawson. "The Women's Tradition In
American Politics." Ph. D. dissertation, Brandeis
University, 1973.

1064(G). Wallace, Michele. Black Macho and the Myth of the
Superwoman. New York: Dial Press, 1979.

1065(G). Ward, Jerry W. Jr. "Selected Bibliography For the
Study of Southern Black Literature in the Twentieth Century."
Southern Quarterly 23 (2): 94-115 (Winter 1985).

1066(G). Washington, Mary Helen. "Black Women Image
Makers." Black World, 23 (August 1974): 10-18.

1067(G). Washington, Mary Helen. "Black Women Myth and
Image Makers." Black World 23 (August 1974): 10-18.

1068(G). Washington, Mary Helen. "New Lives and New
Letters: Black Women Writers at the End of the Seventies."
College English 43 (January 1981): 1-16.

1069(G). Washington, Mary Helen. "Teaching Black-Eyed
Susans: An Approach to the Study of Black Women Writers."
Black American Literature Forum 11 (1): 20-24 (Spring 1977).
African-American women writers.

1070(G). Watkins, Mel, ed. Black Review No. 2. New York:
William Morrow, 1972.

1071(G). Watkins, Mel and David, Joy, eds. To Be a Black
Woman: Portraits In Fact and Fiction. New York: William
Morrow, 1970.

1072(G). Watson, Carole McAlpine. Prologue: The Novels of
Black American Women, 1891-1965. Westport, CT: Greenwood
Press, 1985. Has a chronology of novels and stories from
1859-1964.

1073(G). Weixlmann, Joe and Fontenot, Chester J., eds.
Belief vs. Theory in Black American Literary Criticism.
Greenwood, FL: Penkeville, 1986.

1074(G). White, Vernessa Cecelia. "A Comparative Study of
Alienation, Identity, and the Development of Self in Afro-
American and East German Fiction." Dissertation, State
University of New York at Binghamton, 1981.

1075(G). Whiteman, Maxwell. A Century of Fiction by
American Negroes, 1853-1952: A Descriptive Bibliography.
Philadelphia: Albert Safier, 1955.

1076(G). Whitlow, Roger. Black American Literature: A
Critical History. Chicago: Nelson Hall, 1973.

1077(G). Who's Who in Colored America: A Biographical
Dictionary of Notable Living Persons of African Descent in
America, 1938-1939-1940). 5th ed. Brooklyn: Who's Who in
Colored America, 1940. 7th ed. Yonkers-on-Hudson, NY:
Christian E. Burckel & Associates, 1950.

1078(G). Williams, Delores S. "Women's Oppression and
Lifeline Politics in Black Women's Religious Narratives."
Journal of Feminist Studies in Religion 1 (31): 59-71 (1985).

1079(G). Willis, Robert J. "Anger and the Contemporary
Black Theater." Negro American Literature Forum 8 (Summer
1974): 213-215.

1080(G). Willis, Susan. Specifying: Black Women Writing the
American Experience. Madison, WI: University of Wisconsin,
1987. On African-American women novelists.

1081(G). Work, Monroe Nathan. A Bibliography of the Negro
in Africa and America. Brooklyn: H.W. Wilson, 1928. Reprint.
NY: Octagon Books, 1979.

1082(G). Wormley, Stanton L. and Fenderson, W.H., eds. Many
Shades of Black. New York: William Morrow, 1969.

1083(G). Wright, Odessa Mae. "Achievements of Negro Women
Since 1865." Master's thesis, State University of Iowa,
1931.

Supplement: Additional Writers and Sources, 1988–1991

Anthologies and Collected Works

A1084(AN) McMillan, Terry, ed. <u>Breaking Ice: An Anthology</u> <u>of Contemporary African-American Fiction</u>. New York: Penguin, 1991.

A1085(AN) Nekola, Charlotte and Rabinowitz, Paula, ed. <u>Writing Red: Anthology of American Women Writers, 1930-1940</u>. NY: Feminist Press, 1988.

A1086(AN) Perkins, Kathy A., editor. <u>Black Female</u> <u>Playwrights: An Anthology of Plays Before 1950</u>. Bloomington, IN: Indiana University Press, 1989.

General Works

A1087(G) Awkward, Michael. <u>Inspiriting Influences:</u> <u>Tradition, Revision, and Afro-American Women's Novels</u>. NY: Columbia University Press, 1989.

A1088(G) Braxton, Joanne M. and McLaughlin, Andree Nicola, joint editors. <u>Wild Women in the Whirlwind: Afro-American</u> <u>Culture and the Contemporary Literary Renaissance</u>. New Brunswick, NJ: Rutgers University Press, 1989.

A1089(G) Holloway, Karla F.C. "Revision and (Re)membrance: A Theory of Literary Structures in Literature by African-American Women Writers." <u>Black American Literature Forum</u> 24 (Winter 1990): 617.

A1090(G) Honey, Maureen, editor. <u>Shadowed Dreams: Women's</u> <u>Poetry of the Harlem Renaissance</u>. New Brunswick, NJ: Rutgers University Press, 1989.

A1091(G) Wall, Cheryl A., editor. <u>Changing Our Own Words:</u>
<u>Essays on Criticism, Theory, and Writing by Black Women</u>. New
Brunswick, NJ: Rutgers University Press, 1989.

A1092(G) Werner, Craig Hansen. <u>Black American Women</u>
<u>Novelists: An Annotated Bibliography</u>. Pasadena, CA: Salem,
1989.

Writers and Sources

A1093. ADAMS, FRANKEYE MALIKA.

A1093.1 "Maw-Maw." <u>Catalyst</u> (Spring 1990): 71.

A1094. ADERO, MALAIKA.

A1094.1   "Outta My Name." <u>Catalyst</u> (Winter 1988): 78.

A1095. ALDISA, OPAL PALMER.

A1095.1 "Madness Disguises Sanity." <u>Catalyst</u> (Winter 1988):
33.

A1095.2 "Stubborn." <u>Catalyst</u> (Winter 1989): 62.

A1095.3 "Walking Away. <u>Catalyst</u> (Winter 1989): 77.

A1096. ANDERSON, SUSAN.

A1096.1 "Some People Just Can't Handle Fame." <u>Black Scholar</u>
19 (July/August-September/October 1988): 105. Poem.

A1097. ANSA, TINA McELROY.

A1097.1 <u>Baby of the Family</u>. New York: Harcourt, 1990.

A1098. BATON, MAISHA.

A1098.1 "Born a Drummer." <u>Catalyst</u> (Spring 1990): 66.

A1098.2 "Graduation Day." <u>Catalyst</u> (Fall, 1989): 46

A1098.3 "Love Song." <u>Shooting Star Review</u> 2 (Winter 1988):
24. Poem.

A1098.4 "One Life for Each of Us." <u>Shooting Star Review</u> 3 (Spring 1989): 26. Poem.

A1098.5 "She Gave Him Babies." <u>Catalyst</u> (Fall, 1989): 44. <u>Shooting Star Review</u> 3 (Spring 1989): 7. Poem.

A1098.6 "You Can Dance." <u>Catalyst</u> (Fall, 1989): 44.

A1099. BELGRAVE, MICHELLE.

A1099.1 "Where Are You Going To Brother?" <u>Catalyst</u> (Fall, 1989):28.

A1100. BIKIS, GWENDOLYN.

A1100.1 "My Mother Used to Hold Me (June 22, 1983)". <u>Catalyst</u> (Spring 1990): 40.

A1101. BOWE, VALERIE R.

A1101.1 "Sister and Me." <u>Shooting Star Review</u> 3 (Spring 1989): 30. Poem.

A1102. BOYD, JULIA A.

A1102.1 "She Dances." <u>Essence</u> 19 (July 1988): 136.

A1103. BRAND, TAIKA.

A1103.1 "Sleeping Guard at Dali Exhibit." <u>Catalyst</u> (Spring 1990): 69.

A1104. BURKE, LINDA JOY.

A1104.1 "Poems." <u>Obsidian II</u> 3 (Spring 1988): 76.

A1105. BYER, BEVERLEY.

A1105.1 "Chicopee to Brooklyn." Shooting Star Review 2
(Summer 1988): 14. Short fiction.

A1106. CAMPBELL, BEBE MOORE.

A1106.1 "Good Friends." Essence 20 (September 1989): 91.
Short fiction.

A1106.2 "Holy Music." Essence 21 (December 1990): 58.
Short fiction.

A1106.3 "Mothering: When Words Hurt." Essence 20 (July
1989): 88.

A1106.4 "Myths About Black Female Sexuality." Essence 19
(April 1989): 71.

A1106.5 "Single Women, Married Women: Can We Be Friends?"
Essence 20 (July 1989): 47

A1106.6 "Staying in the Community." Essence 20 (December
1989): 96.

A1106.7 Sweet Summer: Growing Up With and Without My Dad.
New York: Putnam, 1989.

A1106.8 "When Old Men Went Out of My Life." Essence 20
(June 1989): 58. Excerpt from Sweet Summer.

A1106.9 "Women Who Go for It." Essence 20 (August 1989):
48.

A1107. CARLTON-ALEXANDER, SANDRA.

A1107.1 "When the Revolution Comes." Obsidian II 3 (Summer
1988): 120. Excerpt from novel.

A1108. CARY, LORENE.

A1108.1 Black Ice. New York: A.A. Knopf, 1991.

A1109. CHIVERS, CONNEE L.

A1109.1 "Desire." <u>Shooting Star Review</u> 3 (Winter 1989/Spring 1990): 29. Poem.

A1110. CHOPIN, KATE.

A1110.1 "Beyond the Bayou." <u>Shooting Star Review</u> 3 (Winter 1989/Spring 1990): 22. Short fiction.

A1111. CLARK, BARBARA RANDALL.

A1111.1 "Above the Rim." <u>Catalyst</u> (Fall 1989): 32.

A1112. CLAYTOR. APRIL L.

A1112.1 "Double Dutch." <u>Shooting Star Review</u> 3 (Spring 1989): 32. Short fiction.

A1113. COLES, ROSALIND BRADLEY.

A1113.1 "The Proud Rooster." <u>Ebony</u> 44 (February 1989): 188. Short fiction.

A1114. COLLINS, KIMBERLY A.

A1114.1 "Sisters (For Angel)." <u>Catalyst</u> (Winter 1989): 31.

A1115. COLLINS, PATRICIA HILL (1948-   )

A1115.1 <u>Black Feminist Thought: Knowledge, Consciousness, and the Politics of Empowerment</u>. Winchester, MA: Unwin Hyman, 1991.

A1116. COLLINS, RENEE.

A1116.1 "he." <u>Catalyst</u> (Fall 1989): 110.

A1116.2 "the ladies of harlem tea club." <u>Catalyst</u> (Winter 1989): 25.

A1117. CONDE, MARYSE.

A1117.1 "The Breadnut and the Breadfruit." <u>Callaloo</u> 12 (Winter 1989): 134. Short fiction.

A1117.2 <u>Children of Segu</u>. New York: Viking Press, 1989.

A1117.3 "La Vie Scelerate." <u>Callaloo</u> 11 (Winter 1988): 44-51. Excerpt from novel.

                    Secondary Sources

A1117.4(S) Clark, VeVe. " 'I Have Made Peace with My Island': An Interview with Maryse Conde." <u>Callaloo</u> 12 (Winter 1989): 85.

A1117.5(S) Smith, Arlette M. "Maryse Conde's <u>Heremakhonon</u>: A Triangular Structure of Alienation." <u>CLA Journal</u> 32 (September 1988): 45.

A1118. CONNOR-BEY, BRENDA.

A1118.1 "Clarissa." <u>Obsidian II</u> 3 (Winter 1988): 126. Short fiction.

A1118.2 "Poems." <u>Obsidian II</u> 3 (Winter 1988): 104.

A1119. COPELAND, ANGELA MARIE.

A1119.1 "We Are Not Lost." <u>Essence</u> 19 (January 1989): 128.

A1120. CRAIG, CHRISTINE.

A1120.1 "Diary of a Disturbance." <u>Callaloo</u> 12 (Spring 1989): 288. Poem.

A1121. CURTIS, JEANNETTE.

A1121.1   "Friendship."   Essence 19 (February 1989): 129.
Poem.

A1121.2   "Native Sons."   Essence 19 (February 1989): 152.
Poem.

A1121.3   "Old Weary One."   Essence 19 (April 1989): 123.
Poem.

A1122.   DALTON, YVETTE C.

A1122.1   "Chocolate Milk and Corn Flakes."   Catalyst (Summer
1988): 40.

A1123.   DANIELS, LENORE.

A1123.1   "The Dress."   Catalyst (Fall 1989): 64.

A1124.   DASH, JULIE.

A1124.1   "Daughters of the Dust: A New Screenplay."   Catalyst
(Summer 1987): 27.

A1125.   DILLARD, LULA.

A1125.1   "To Lula with Love."   Ebony 43 (October 1988): 66.

A1126.   DIXON, CAROL.

A1126.1   "After the Beep."   Essence 20 (October 1989): 85.
Short fiction.

A1127.   DOBSON, NANNETTE.

A1127.1   "Nesting Girl."   Catalyst (Spring 1990): 21.

A1128.   EDWARDS, ELAINE MARIE.

A1128.1 "Marriage." _Shooting Star Review_ 2 (Autumn 1988):
13. Poem.

A1129. EMERY, DAWN.

A1129.1 "Lover." _Essence_ 19 (November 1988): 126. Poem.

A1130. FAIRBANKS, EVELYN.

A1130.1 _The Days of Rondo_. St. Paul, MN: Minnesota
Historical Society Press, 1990.

A1131. FERRELL, CAROLYN.

A1131.1 "Eating Confessions." _Callaloo_ 12 (Summer 1989):
32. Short fiction.

A1132. FORD, CASSANDRA.

A1132.1 "I Look in the Mirror." _Shooting Star Review_ 3
(Spring 1989): 15.

A1133. FOSTER, KIM ROUNDS.

A1133.1 "Woman Poem." _Shooting Star Review_ 2 (Autumn 1988):
33.

A1134. GILROY, BERYL.

A1134.1 "Boy Sandwich." _Callaloo_ 12 (Spring 1989): 282.
Short fiction excerpt.

A1135. GOODISON, LORNA.

A1135.1 "Della Makes Life." Callaloo 12 (Summer 1989): 482.
Short fiction.

A1136. GRABAR, MARY.

A1136.1 "The Old Woman." Catalyst (Spring 1990): 79.

A1137. GRAVLEY, ERNESTINE.

A1137.1 "Looking Out for Gramps." Catalyst (Spring 1990):
75.

A1138. GREEN, GWEN.

A1138.1 "Afro Wearin' Max Robinson." Catalyst (Fall 1989):
118.

A1138.2 "Closets." Catalyst (Fall 1989): 32.

A1139. GREENE, CHERYL Y.

A1139.1 "Woman Talk: A Conversation Between June Jordan and
Angela Davis." Essence 21 (May 1990): 92. Brown Marie,
joint ed.

A1139.2 "Words from a Sister in Exile." Essence 18
(February 1988): 60.

A1140. GREENE, RHONDA.

A1140.1 "Full Circle." Catalyst (Winter 1989): 10.

A1140.2 "Her Story." Catalyst (Spring 1990): 17.

A1140.3 "MEANS." Catalyst (Spring 1990): 54.

A1141. GRIFFIN, BETTYE.

A1141.1 "A.K.A. Lucy's Mom." <u>Shooting Star Review</u> 3 (Winter 1989/Spring 1990): 15. Short fiction.

A1142. GRISHAM, SHIRLEY (SAM).

A1142.1 "September Elegy." <u>Catalyst</u> (Winter 1989): 16.

A1143. HAILSTOCK, SHIRLEY.

A1143.1 "Oreo Cookies." <u>Shooting Star Review</u> 3 (Spring 1989): 36. Short fiction.

A1144. HALLIBURTON, KAREN.

A1144.1 "The Spirit of Malcolm." <u>Essence</u> 20 (November 1989): 107. Poem.

A1145. HARDY, DOROTHY C.

A1145.1 "Salutation." <u>Essence</u> 20 (September 1989): 147. Poem.

A1146. HARRIS, DORIS.

A1146.1 "The Afterbirth." <u>Essence</u> 19 (April 1989): 123. Poem.

A1147. HARRIS, KAREN E.

A1147.1 "maybe later." <u>Catalyst</u> (Winter 1989): 25.

A1148. HARRIS, MELANIE L.

A1148.1 "Bewitching." <u>Essence</u> 19 (November 1988): 143. Poem.

A1149. HARRIS, SHARON.

A1149.1 "Something is Fishy." _Essence_ 19 (February 1989):
160. Essay.

A1150. HASKINS, SONJA JANE.

A1150.1 "Dreadlocks." _Catalyst_ (Fall 1989): 97.

A1151. HAWKINS, GAIL N.

A1151.1 "The Night at Rosies." _Catalyst_ (Summer 1988): 78,
(Winter 1989): 88.

A1152. HEAD, BEVERLY V.

A1152.1 "even when." _Catalyst_ (Winter 1989): 78.

A1153. HENDERSON, SONYA.

A1153.1 "Three Strikes for You." _Essence_ 19 (March 1989):
136.

A1154. HERNDON, DAISY B.

A1154.1 "Parrr-tay!" _Catalyst_ (Spring 1990): 44.

A1155. HERRON, CAROLIVIA.

A1155.1 _Thereafter Johnnie_. New York: Random House, 1991.

A1155.2 "Thereafter Johnnie." _Callaloo_ 12 (Summer 1989):
465. Excerpt from the novel.

A1156.   HILL, DONNA.

A1156.1   <u>Indiscretions</u>.   New York: Odyssey Press, 1991.

A1157.   HOLCOMB, CLAIRE.

A1157.1   "Motherhood."   <u>Catalyst</u> (Spring 1990: 38.

Holmes, Safiya Henderson.   **SEE** 297 HENDERSON, SAFIYA.

A1158.   HUNT, CHERYL YVETTE.

A1158.1   "When She Danced."   <u>Essence</u> 19 (February 1989): 149.
Poem.

A1159.   HUNT, V.

A1159.1   "First Day for the Buggy."   <u>Catalyst</u> (Winter 1988):
87.

A1160.   ISMAC, ANNE.

A1160.1   "East Africa."   <u>Essence 19</u> (November 1988): 143.
Poem.

A1161.   JACKSON, CATHY M.

A1161.1   "Names Can Hurt."   <u>Essence</u> 19 (April 1989): 134.

A1162.   JACKSON, CINDY L.

A1162.1   "Winter Nights,"   <u>Shooting Star Review</u> 2 (Winter
1988): 9.

A1163.   JACKSON, KAI.

A1163.1 "I Grow Tall." <u>Catalyst</u> (Winter 1989): 38.

A1163.2   "The Sight of Ghosts." <u>Catalyst</u> (Winter 1989): 62.

A1164. JENNINGS, REGINA.

A1164.1 "Assata." <u>Essence</u> 20 (November 1989): 128. Poem.

A1164.2 "Aunt Helen." <u>Shooting Star Review</u> 2 (Autumn 1988):
2.

A1165. JOHNSON, AMRYL.

A1165.1 "Poems." <u>Black Scholar</u> 19 (July/August-
September/October 1988): 68.

A1166. JOHNSON, SHARON D.

A1166.1 "Destruction of a Nation." <u>Essence</u> 19 (April 1989):
128. Poem.

A1167. JOHNSON, JACQUELINE.

A1167.1 "Cleo's Bluers." <u>Catalyst</u> (Fall 1989): 84.

A1167.2 "Mosekas' Way." <u>Obsidian II</u> (Spring 1988): 66.
Poem.

A1167.3 "Pearls." <u>Obsidian II</u> (Winter 1988): 24. Poem.

A1168. JONES, KIM.

A1168.1 "Middle Passage." <u>Catalyst</u> (Summer 1988): 9.

A1169. JONES, MONA.

A1169.1 "Black Culture." <u>Essence</u> 19 (November 1988): 141.
Poem.

A1170. JORDAN, JENNIFER.

A1170.1 "The Wife." Essence 21 (July 1990): 66. Short
fiction.

A1171. JUDY, BETH.

A1171.1 "Sampler." Catalyst (Winter 1988): 18.

A1172. KARRIEM, JALEELAH.

A1172.1 "Just a Few Laughs Some Fun and Nothing Serious."
Catalyst (Winter 1989): 39.

A1172.2 "To the Boys W/ Love." Catalyst (Winter 1989): 88.

A1173. KAY, JACKIE.

A1173.1 "Train Journey I." Black Scholar 19 (July/August-
September/October 1988): 27. Poem.

A1174. KEYE, JADA.

A1174.1 "The Interim." Catalyst (Winter 1989): 52.

A1175. KILLIAN, DOROTHY JEAN.

A1175.1 "Appointment at 1:00 P.M." Obsidian II 3 (Summer
1988): 96. Poem.

A1176. KING, TABITHA.

A1176.1 Pearl. NY: New American Library, 1989.

A1177.   KNIGHT, JANICE M.

A1177.1   "Momma's Bible."   _American Visions_ 4 (April 1989):
22.   Short fiction.

A1178.   LAMBERT, ALFREDONIA THOMAS.

A1178.1   "What Will the Harvest Be?"   _Obsidian II_ 3 (Summer
1988): 70.

A1179.   LAMKIN, CATHERINE SANDERS.

A1179.1   "we have arrived."   _Catalyst_ (Fall 1989): 88.

A1180.   LAWRENCE, VALERIE.

A1180.1   "November Kiss."   _Shooting Star Review_ 2 (Winter
1988): 34.   Poem.

A1180.2   "Rites of Visit."   _Catalyst_ (Spring 1990): 18.

A1181.   LEAH-WHITE, SYBIL.

A1181.1   "Fool Crazy."   _Catalyst_ (Spring 1990): 45.

A1181.2   "The Remaining Shadow."   _Catalyst_ (Winter 1988): 18.

A1181.3   "The Wife (Mrs. So & So."   _Catalyst_ (Winter 1988):
84.

A1182.   LE FLORE, SHIRLEY BRADLEY.

A1182.1   "Dumas is Necessary."   _Black American Literature
Forum_ 22 (Summer 1988): 276.   Poem.

A1183.   LINDSEY, KAY.

A1183.1   "What Do I Call Home?"   _Catalyst_ (Spring 1990): 78.

A1184. LOCKE, SHARESE.

A1184.1 "And the Rain Came." Black American Literature
Forum 23 (Fall 1989): 460.

A1185. LORD, SHANNON.

A1185.1 "Shopping." Catalyst (Winter 1989): 60.

A1186. LOWE, JANICE.

A1186.1 "Between Acts." Callaloo 12 (Spring 1989): 292.

A1187. LYLES, LOIS.

A1187.1 "Chicago Blues Band." Catalyst (Fall 1989): 43.

A1187.2 "Last Christmas Gift." Catalyst (Winter 1989): 63.

A1187.3 "Teenage Son Looks at Mother." Catalyst (Spring
1990): 62.

A1187.4 "When Milton Laughs." Catalyst (Summer 1988): 14.

A1188. ENTRY OMITTED

A1189. McCAULEY, ROBBIE.

A1189.1 "My Father and the Wars: Excerpts from a Performance
Piece." Catalyst (Summer 1987): 41.

A1190. McCLOUD, DERILENE.

A1190.1 "The Beauty Myth." Catalyst (Winter 1989): 32.

A1191. McCONNELL, TONI.

A1191.1 "Few Men Like Daddy." Catalyst (Spring 1990): 34.

A1192. McCOURTIE, CHERYL.

A1192.1 "Where I Enter." <u>Essence</u> 19(April 1989): 83.

A1193. McLARIN, KIMBERLY J.

A1193.1 "Fried Pies." <u>Obsidian II</u> 2 (Summer 1988): 76.
Fiction

A1194. MACK, ROBIN REBECCA.

A1194.1 "The Music of Truth: The Work of Henry Dumas."
<u>Black American Literature Forum</u> 22 (Summer 1988): 287.

A1195. MALKERSON, HELEN V.

A1195.1 "Juneteenth." <u>Shooting Star Review</u> 2 (Summer 1988):
9. Short fiction.

A1196. MANCLE, MILDRED.

A1196.1 "The Third Thursday in August." <u>American Visions</u> 4
(April 1989): 18. Short fiction.

A1197. MARK, ELLEN.

A1197.1 "Her Eyes." <u>Shooting Star Review</u> 2 (Spring 1988):
15. Poem.

A1198. MASSEY, JUDY B.

A1198.1 "And What About Me." <u>Catalyst</u> (Winter 1989): 16.

A1198.2 "People Got Needs." <u>Catalyst</u> (Summer 1988): 94.

A1199. MAURER, ASTRID.

A1199.1 "My Father His Blood." Catalyst (Spring 1990): 19.

A1200. MAXWELL, MAGGI G.

A1200.1 "No Big Deal." Catalyst (Summer 1988): 65.

A1201. MILLER, PEGGY.

A1201.1 "I Remember Gagging on Turnips." Catalyst (Spring 1990): 23.

A1202. MITCHELL, CAROLYN A.

A1202.1 "Henry Dumas and Jean Toomer." Black American Literature Forum 22 (Summer1988): 297.

A1203. MITCHELL, VICKIE.

A1203.1 "Jabo." Catalyst (Fall 1989): 43.

A1204. MOORE, DOROTHEA M.

A1204.1 "Visions." Catalyst (Winter 1988):   91.

A1205. MOORE, JANICE TOWNLEY.

A1205.1 "The Agreement." Catalyst (Winter 1989): 72.

A1205.2 "Underwater Lady. Catalyst (Winter 1989): 70.

A1206. MOORE, NICOLE M.

A1206.1 "What I'm Not." Essence 19 (April 1989): 119. Poem.

A1207. MOOREHEAD, LISA.

A1207.1 "Listen Son." <u>Catalyst</u> (Fall 1989): 22.

A1208. MORDECAI, PAMELA.

A1208.1 "The House of Cards." <u>Callaloo</u> 12 (Spring 1989): 352. Poem.

Moreland, Jill Stacey   **See** NJERI, ITABARI.   A835

A1209. MUNI, KAI.

A1209.1 "Revelations." <u>Essence</u> 19 (July 1988): 136.

A1210. MURPHY, YVETTE.

A1210.1 "Men and Mothers." <u>Catalyst</u> (Fall 1989): 23.

A1210.2 "Minstrel Man." <u>Shooting Star Review</u> 2 (Summer 1988): 35. Poem.

A1210.3 "Play It Again." <u>Shooting Star Review</u> 2 (Winter 1988): 12.

A1210.4 "We." <u>Shooting Star Review</u> 3 (Spring 1989): 27. Poem.

A1211. NICHOLS, CHARLYNE.

A1211.1 "Henry Dumas: A Feminine Perspective." <u>Black American Literature Forum</u> 22 (Summer 1988): 316.

A1212. NIGHTENGALE, SHARON.

A1212.1 "Debra." <u>Catalyst</u> (Spring 1990): 47.

A1213. NJERI, ITABARI.

A1213.1 Every Good-bye Ain't Gone: Family Portraits and
Personal Escapades. New York: Times Books, 1990.

A1213.2 "A New Sexuality." Essence 19 (January 1989): 66.

A1213.3 "What's Love Got To With It?" Essence 20 (February
1990): 64. Excerpt from Every Good-bye Ain't Gone.

A1214. NORMAN, GEORGETTE M.

A1214.1 "Two Worlds." Catalyst (Winter 1989): 17.

A1215. OPITZ, MAY.

A1215.1 "Afro-German." Black Scholar 19 (July/August-
September/October 1988): 42. Poem.

A1216. PAGAN, MARGARET D.

A1216.1 "The Memory of a Mother's Face." American Visions 4
(April 1989): 22. Short fiction.

A1217. PERRY, ELAINE.

A1217.1 Another Present Era. New York: Farrar, 1990.

A1218. PERRY, ROZ.

A1218.1 "I Had a Mother Once." Catalyst (Spring 1990): 46.

A1219. PLUMMER, PAMELA QUARLES.

A1219.1 "Ayanna (Beautiful Flower)." Catalyst (Spring
1990): 104.

A1219.2 "Sanctuary." Catalyst (Spring 1990): 64.

A1220.   PORTER, CONNIE.

A1220.1   <u>All-Bright Court</u>.   Boston: Houghton Mifflin, 1991.

A1221.   PORTLOCK, ALICE.

A1221.1 "Reflections of Sunday Past."   <u>American Visions</u> 4
(April 1989): 20.

A1222.   PRATT, VICTORIA.

A1222.1   "Come Swiftly Sweet Morning."   <u>Callaloo</u> 12 (Summer
1989): 506.   Short fiction excerpt.

A1223.   QUNTA, CHRISTINE.

A1223.1   "The Truth."   <u>Essence</u> 20 (November 1989): 107.
Poem.

A1223.2   "We Need Poets."   <u>Essence</u> 20 (November 1989): 126.
Poem.

A1224.   RANDALL, MARGARET.

A1224.1   "Coatlicue."   <u>Catalyst</u> (Winter 1989): 20.

A1224.2   "Election Notes."   <u>Catalyst</u> (Summer 1988): 31.

A1225.   RAWLS, MELANIE.

A1225.1   "For Henry Dumas."   <u>Catalyst</u> (Fall 1989): 116.

A1225.2   "Little Girl."   <u>Catalyst</u> (Winter 1989): 23.

A1225.3   "My Little Boys."   <u>Catalyst</u> (Spring 1990): 63.

A1226.   REED, LORI ANN.

A1226.1 "Henry Dumas: A Selected Annotated Bibliography."
Black American Literature Forum 22 (Summer 1988): 339.

A1227. REYNOLDS, ALFRIEDA H.

A1227.1 "Herman." Essence 19 (February 1989): 144. Poem.

A1227.2 "Yesssss...I Am." Essence 19 (October 1988): 141.
Poem.

A1228. RHODES, JEWELL PARKER.

A1228.1 "The Accident." Shooting Star Review 3 (Winter
1989/Spring 1990): 8. Short fiction.

A1229. RICHARDSON, ABENA.

A1229.1 "Imprisoned Lovers," Essence 19 (April 1989): 122.
Poem.

A1230. RICHARDSON, MARIAH L.

A1230.1 "Raising Baby." Catalyst (Spring 1990): 56.

A1231. ROBINSON, DIANN W.

A1231.1 "judgment day rehearsal." Catalyst (Fall 1989): 86.

A1231.2 "Night Blossom." Catalyst (Fall 1989): 79.

A1231.3 "Sleeping Beauty's Children." Catalyst (Spring
1990): 52.

A1232. ROBOTHAM, ROSEMARIE.

A1232.1 "Jesse." Essence 21 (August 1990): 70. Short
fiction.

A1233. ROCHELLE, BELINDA.

A1233.1 "The Book of John." <u>Catalyst</u> (Fall 1989): 112.

A1233.2 "The Book of Leah." <u>Catalyst</u> (Spring 1990): 75.

A1233.3 "Dolls." <u>Catalyst</u> (Spring 1990): 35.

A1233.4 "The Mother Game." <u>Catalyst</u> (Spring 1990): 38.

A1233.5 "Poems." <u>Obsidian II</u> 3 (Winter 1988): 54.

A1234. ROEMER, ASTRID.

A1234.1 "About the Madness of a Woman." <u>Callaloo</u> 12 (Spring 1989): 412. Short fiction excerpt.

A1235. ROGERS, GLOREE.

A1235.1 "Love, or a Reasonable Facsimile." <u>Obsidian II</u> 3 (Summer 1988): 54. Fiction.

A1236. ROUSE, NANCY FROST.

A1236.1 "Echoes." <u>Catalyst</u> (Summer 1988): 27.

A1237. ROY, DARLENE.

A1237.1 "Henry Dumas -- Master Storyteller." <u>Black American Literature Forum</u> 22 (Summer 1988): 343.

A1238. ROY, LUCINDA.

A1238.1 "Poems." <u>Callaloo</u> 11 (Summer 1988): 547.

A1239. RUDDER, SONJA M.

A1239.1 "City Block Summer." <u>Black American Literature Forum</u> 23 (Fall 1989): 490. Poem.

A1240. RUSHIN, KATE.

A1240.1 "Comparative History." <u>Callaloo</u> 12 (Spring 1989): 290. Poem.

A1241. RUSSELL, BEVERLY A.

A1241.1 "Mine/All Mine." <u>Essence</u> 19 (February 1989): 152. Poem.

A1242. SANDERS, DORI.

A1242.1 <u>Clover</u>. Chapel Hill, NC: Algonquin Books, 1990.

A1243. SCOTT, SUSANNAH E.

A1243.1 "Ode to My Father." <u>Catalyst</u> (Spring 1990): 20.

A1244. SENIOR, OLIVE.

A1244.1 "Arrival of the Snake Woman." <u>Callaloo</u> 11 (Summer 1988): 491. Short fiction.

A1244.2 "Poems." <u>Callaloo</u> 11 (Summer 1988): 519.

A1244.3 "See the Tiki Tiki Scatter." <u>Callaloo</u> 11 (Summer 1988): 535. Short fiction.

Secondary Sources

A1244.4(S) Pollard, Velma. "An Introduction to the Poetry and Fiction of Olive Senior. <u>Callaloo</u> 11 *Summer 1988): 540.

A1244.5(S) Pollard, Velma. "Olive Senior: Journalist, Researcher, Poet, Fiction Writer." <u>Callaloo</u> 11 (Summer 1988): 479.

A1244.6(S) Rowell, Charles H. "An Interview with Olive
Senior." <u>Callaloo</u> 11 (Summer 1988): 480.

A1245. SEXTON, RUBY LEE.

A1245.1 "Moon Dreams." <u>Shooting Star Review</u> 3 (Winter
1989/Spring 1990): 19. Poem.

A1246. SHERMAN, CHARLOTTE WATSON.

A1246.1 "Somewhere a Woman is Dreading." <u>Catalyst</u> (Fall
1989): 96.

A1247. SILLIMAN, ANNA LISA.

A1247.1 "Become." <u>Catalyst</u> (Spring 1990): 65.

A1248. SLOAN, BEVERLY.

A1248.1 "Comings and Goings." <u>Catalyst</u> (Winter 1989): 73.

A1248.2 "Sundays." <u>Catalyst</u> (Summer 1987): 76.

A1249. SLOAN, PHYLLIS J.

A1249.1 "It is Well." <u>Essence</u> 19 (October 1988): 147,
(November 1988): 144. Poem.

A1250. SMITH, JENNIFER E.

A1250.1 "Poems." <u>Obsidian II</u> 3 (Spring 1988): 49.

A1251. SPRINGER, CHRISTINA.

A1251.1 "Poems." <u>Shooting Star Review</u> 2 (Winter 1988): 19.

A1252.   STONE, NAIMA.

A1252.1 "Sorrow Floats." <u>Catalyst</u> (Spring 1990): 53.

A1253.   SUMMERS, BARBARA.

A1253.1 "Solidarity." <u>Catalyst</u> (Summer 1988): 74.

A1254.   TEASLEY, LISA.

A1254.1 "Between Women." <u>Catalyst</u> (Winter 1989): 13.

A1254.2 "Ice and Oil." <u>Catalyst</u> (Summer 1988): 86.

A1254.3 "Sides of a Straight Line." <u>Catalyst</u> (Fall 1989):
59.

A1255.   TERENCE, SUSAN.

A1255.1 "Deer." <u>Catalyst</u> (Spring 1990): 39.

A1256.   THOM, LISBETH J.

A1256.1 "Downhill." <u>Catalyst</u> (Summer 1988): 81.

A1256.2 "Dress Me in Black'" <u>Catalyst</u> (Winter 1989): 58.

A1256.3 "Life." <u>Catalyst</u> (Winter 1989): 46.

A1256.4 "A Mother and a Daughter." <u>Catalyst</u> (Winter 1989):
59.

A1256.5 "No Siren Please." <u>Catalyst</u> (Winter 1989): 58.

A1256.6 "Twelve to Sixteen." <u>Catalyst</u> (Spring 1990): 101.

A1257.   THOMAS, CRISTAL.

A1257.1 "Ballad of a Pregnant Teen." Catalyst (Spring 1990): 46.

A1258. THOMPSON, DOROTHY PERRY.

A1258.1 "Fever Scan." Catalyst (Fall 1989): 59.

A1258.2 "My Fancy Tea Room." Black American Literature Forum 23 (Fall 1989): 498. Poem.

A1259. TISDALE, BRENDA.

A1259.1 "Improvisation." Essence 19 (November 1988): 142. Poem.

A1260. TOWNS, JEANNE R.

A1260.1 "All in the Name of Love." Catalyst (Fall 1989): 87.

A1260.2 "Daybreak." Catalyst (Winter 1989): 21.

A1260.3 "Sound of Terror." Catalyst (Fall 1989): 85.

A1261. TRAVIS, NANCY.

A1261.1 "Pure Purpose." Catalyst (Winter 1988): 52.

A1261.2 "Sophomore Year: Uprising." Catalyst (Winter 1989): 24.

A1262. TRAYLOR, ELEANOR W.

A1262.1 "Henry Dumas and the Discourse of Memory." Black American Literature Forum 22 (Summer 1988): 365-378.

A1263. TRUEITT, CYNTHIA BURTON.

A1263.1 "When I Die." Catalyst (Summer 1988): 9.

A1264. TYLER, VALERIE R.

A1264.1 "Brother." Black American Literature Forum 23 (Fall 1989): 469. Poem

A1265. VAIL, SANDRA.

A1265.1 "The Water Strider." Catalyst (Summer 1988): 42.

A1266. WALKER, PAMELA GARLAND.

A1266.1 "The Passage." Catalyst (Fall 1989): 33.

A1267. WALLACE, HARRIET.

A1267.1 "The Borrowed Bed." Catalyst (Spring 1990): 65.

A1268. WEBSTER, KATHRYN L.

A1268.1 "Victims." Shooting Star Review 2 (Autumn 1988): 26. Short fiction.

A1269. WEEMS, RENITA J., 1954-

A1269.1 "Amen, Sister." Essence 19 (September 1988): 63.

A1269.2 Just a Sister Away: A Womanist Vision of Women's Relationships in the Bible. San Diego, CA: LuraMedia, 1989.

A1269.3 "Just Friends." Essence 20 (May 1989): 60.

A1269.4 "When Love Hurts." Essence 19 (October 1988): 81.

A1270. WHITAKER, GINGER.

A1270.1 "Miss Rita." Obsidian II 3 (Winter 1988): 109. Short fiction.

A1271. WHITE, ROBIN ALISA.

A1271.1 "Freedom in My Twenties." <u>Shooting Star Review</u> 2
(Summer 1988): 12. Poem.

A1272. WILKINS, GLENDA S.

A1272.1 "Unwinding." <u>Catalyst</u> (Summer 1988): 65.

A1273. WILLIAMS, JILO.

A1273.1 "The Dance." <u>Catalyst</u> (Winter 1988): 76.

A1274. WILLIAMS, KRISTIN.

A1274.1 "The First Five Years." <u>Catalyst</u> (Winter 1988): 70.

A1275. WILLIAMS, NANCY ELLEN-WEBB.

A1275.1 "Cold Stove." <u>Catalyst</u> (Winter 1989): 50.
A1275.2 "Mary's Crownin Glory." <u>Catalyst</u> (Winter 1989): 24.

A1276. WILLIAMS-GARNER, DEBRA.

A1276.1 "Brown Babies." <u>Essence</u> 20 (September 1989): 135.
Poem.

A1277. WILLINGHAM, LOUISE.

A1277.1 "On Being 40." <u>Catalyst</u> (Fall 1989): 63.

A1278. WILSON, ROBERTA.

A1278.1 "Ladies' Night at Reid's." <u>Essence</u> 21 (March 1991):
76. Short fiction.

A1279. WINTERS, JOYCE M.

A1279.1 "Personal Politics." <u>Catalyst</u> (Winter 1989): 30.

A1280. YOUNG, PATRICIA.

A1280.1 "Look at Me." <u>Catalyst</u> (Fall 1989): 80.

Index of Authors

Primary authors are noted in upper case; secondary authors (including joint authors, editors, translators, and compilers) are given in upper and lower case. Items entered by title in the bibliography are so entered in the index. All references are to item numbers in the bibliography, not page numbers. Decimal numbers appear under whole numbers in the main section of the bibliography organized by writers to distinguish specific works of the writer and about the writer; the latter are designated by (S). Reference numbers followed by (AN) appear in the section on anthologies and collected works; those followed by (G) in the section on general works. A reference number with an A prefix indicates a work in a supplementary section with relevant writers or in the general supplement preceding this index.

A

Abajian, James de T., 628.4(S), 858(G)
Abdul, Raoul, 715(AN), 807(AN)
Abdullah, Omanii, 953(G)
Abel, Elizabeth, 477.17(S)
ABRAM, THERESA WILLIAMS, 001

ABRAMSON, DOLORES, 002
Abramson, Doris E., 097.2(S), 120.25(S), 285.31(S),359.21(S), 498.22(S), 858(G)
Abramson, Pam, 644.120(S)
ADA, 003, 271.4(S)
ADAMS, DAISIE HASSON, 004
ADAMS, DORIS B., 005

ADAMS, FRANKEYE MALIKA,
    A1093
ADAMS, JANUS, 006
ADAMS, JEANNETTE, 007
Adams, George R.,
    513.15(S)
Adams, Michael, 285.32(S)
Adams, Peter, 285.33(S)
Adams, Williams, 716(AN)
ADERO, MALAIKA, A1094
Adoff, Arnold, 717(AN),
    718(AN), 719(AN)
ADRINE-ROBINSON, KENYETTE,
    008
AFIF, FATIMAH, 009
Afro-American Voices,
    1770s-1970s, 720(AN)
Aguero, Kathleen, 779(AN)
AHMAD, DOROTHY, 010
AI, 011
Akers, Charles W.,
    672.17(S)
ALBA, NANINA, 012
ALDISA, OPAL PALMER, A1095
Aldridge, June E.,
    162.14(S), 162.15(S)
ALEXANDER, ADELE LOGAN,
    013
ALEXANDER, ELIZABETH, 014
Alexander, Harriet S.,
    A477.96(S)
ALEXANDER, MARGARET
WALKER. SEE WALKER,
    MARGARET, 645
Alhamisi, Ahmed, 721(AN)
ALLEGRA, DONNA, 015
Allen, Bonnie, 568.38(S)
ALLEN, SARAH A. SEE
    HOPKINS, PAULINE
    ELIZABETH, 309
Allen, William G.,
    672.18(S)
ALLISON, MARGARET M., 016
ALLMAN, REVA WHITE, 017
Ambrose, Amanda, 722(AN)
The American Negro Writer
    and His Roots, 859(G)
AMINI, JOHARI, 018   SEE
    ALSO LATIMORE,
    JEWELL, 400
AMIS, LOLA ELIZABETH
    JONES,   019
Ammons, Elizabeth,
    212.30(S)
ANDERSON, ANITA TURPEAU,
    020
ANDERSON, EDNA L., 021

ANDERSON, GLORIA EDWARDS,
    022
Anderson, Jervis, 860(G)
ANDERSON, KATHY ELAINE,
    023
ANDERSON, MIGNON HOLLAND,
    024
ANDERSON, SUSAN, A1096
Andrews, Larry, 081.63(S),
    A486.10(S)
Andrews, William L.,
    199.2(S), A378.8(S),
    406.2(S)
Anello, Ray, 644.121(S)
ANGELOU, MAYA, 025
Angola, Bibi, 566.3(S)
ANSA, TINA McELROY, A1097
ANTHONY, FLORENCE. SEE
    AI, 11
Apseloff, Marilyn,
    283.27(S), 283.28(S)
Arata, Esther Spring,
    861(G), 1033(G)
Arensberg, Liliane K.,
    025.37(S)
ARKHURST, JOYCE COOPER,
    026
ARMSTRONG, DENISE
    CARREATHERS, 027
ARMSTRONG, NAOMI YOUNG,
    028
Arnez, Nancy L., 480.7
ARNOLD, ETHEL NISHUA, 029
ARTHUR, BARBARA, 030
ASANTE, KARIAMU WELSH, SEE
    WELSH, KARIAMU, 668
Ascher, Carol, 862(G)
ATHENS, IDA GERDING, 031
Atlas, Marilyn J.,
    477.18(S), 477.19(S)
AUNT SALLY, 032
AUSTIN, DORIS JEAN, 033
Austin, Gayle, 120.24(S)
Avi-ram, Amitai F.,
    419.62(S)
Awkward, Michael, A1087(G)
AYERS, VIVIAN, 034

B

Babb, Valerie, 644.122(S)
BACON, MARY ALBERTA, 035
BAGBY, JEANNE S., 036
BAGLEY, JOYCE M., 037
BAILEY, GERTRUDE
    BLACKWELL, 038

Loff, John, 081.95(S)
Loff, Jon N., 081.96(S)
LOFTIN, ELOUISE, 417
Logan, Rayford W., 989(G)
LOGAN, ROSIE LEE. SEE
    JONES, ROSIE LEE
    LOGAN, 374
Loggins, Vernon,
    226.11(S),
    516.3(S), 672.44(S)
Lomax, Alan, 807(AN),
    323.52(S)
Lomax, Michael, 990(G)
LOMAX, PEARL CLEAGE, 418
LONG, NAOMI CORNELIA SEE
    MADGETT, NAOMI LONG,
    438
Long, Richard A., 808(AN)
LORD, SHANNON, A1185
LORDE, AUDRE, 419
LOUISE, ESTHER, 420
LOUISE, FANNIE, 421
Lounsberry, Barbara,
    477.45(S), 477.56(S)
LOVE, ROSE LEARY, 422
Love, Theresa R.,
    323.53(S)
LOWE, JANICE, A1186
Lupton, Mary Jane,
    212.40(S), 323.54(S),
    323.55(S), 477.57(S),
    644.169(S),
    A025.59(S)
LYLES, LOIS, A1187
LYN, 423
LYNN, EVE [pseud. of
    Evelyn   Crawford
    Reynolds], 424

M

MacCann, Donnarae,
    A493.32(S)
MACK, DONNA, 437
MACK. ROBIN REBECCA, A1194
McBAIN, BARBARA MAHONE.
    SEE   MAHONE.
    BARBARA, 440
McBROWN, GERTRUDE
    PARTHENIA, 425
McCALL, VALAIDA POTTER,
    426
McCALL, W.J.   SEE
    McCALL, VALAIDA
    POTTER, 426
McCAULEY, ROBBIE, A1189
McCLAUREN, IRMA,
    081.97(S), 427

McClauren-Allen, Irma,
    419.67(S)
McCLOUD, DERILENE, A1190
McCluskey, John,
    081.98(S), 445.37(S)
McCONNELL, TONI, A1191
McCOURTIE, CHERYL, A1192
McCRAY, CHIRLANE, 428
McCRAY, NETTIE [SALIMU],
    429
McCredie, Wendy J.,
    323.56(S)
McDowell, Deborah E.,
    212.41(S), 991(G),
    644.170(S),992(G)
McDowell, Margaret,
    513.22(S)
McDowell, Robert,
    186.60(S)
McELROY, COLLEEN, 430
McGHEE, MAUDE, 431
McGINNIS, JULIETTE, 432
McGowan, Martha J.,
    644.171(S)
McHenry, Susan, 118.8(S)
McKANE, ALICE WOODBY, 433
McKay, Nellie, 477.58(S),
    A477.106(S), 482.9(S)
McKinney, Rhoda E.,
    186.61(S)
McLARIN, KIMBERLY J.,
    A1193
McLaughlin, Andree Nicola,
    A1087(G)
McLEARY, EDNA TUBBS, 434
McMahon, Jean, 406.4(S)
McMICHAEL, MICHELLE SEE
    ZIMEME-KEITA, NZADI,
    713
McMILLAN, TERRY, 435
McMurry, Myra K.,
    025.47(S)
McNEIL, DEE DEE, 436
McPherson, Dolly A.,
    A025.60(S)
McPherson, James M.,
    614.3(S)
McTaggart, Mary, 475.5,
    475.6, 814(AN),
    815(AN)
MADGETT, NAOMI LONG, 438
Madhubuti, Haki,
    081.99(S),
    081.100(S),
    130.48(S),
    993(G)
Madhubuti, Safisha N.,
    081.101(S)

About the Compiler

CASPER LEROY JORDAN, a librarian, educator, and scholar of black studies, retired as Deputy Director of the Atlanta-Fulton Public Library and was formerly Associate Professor in the Atlanta University School of Library and Information Studies. Many of his publications focus on black librarianship, the black experience in America, and black achievements in the arts. He was a contributor to *The Encyclopedia of Library Information Science*, the *Dictionary of American Librarians*, the *Handbook of Black Librarianship*, *Ethnic Genealogy*, *Notable Black American Women*, and *Famous Black Firsts*.